The
INVISIBLE
SHINING

The INVISIBLE SHINING

The Cult of Mátyás Rákosi in Stalinist Hungary, 1945–1956

BALÁZS APOR

Central European University Press
Budapest–New York

Copyright © by Balázs Apor 2017
Published in 2017 by
Central European University Press

An imprint of the
Central European University Limited Liability Company
Nádor utca 11, H-1051 Budapest, Hungary
Tel: +36-1-327-3138 or 327-3000
Fax: +36-1-327-3183
E-mail: ceupress@press.ceu.edu
Website: www.ceupress.com

224 West 57th Street, New York NY 10019, USA
Tel: +1-732-763-8816 E-mail: meszarosa@press.ceu.edu

All rights reserved. No part of this publication may be reproduced, stored in a retrieval system, or transmitted, in any form or by any means, without the permission of the Publisher.

ISBN 978-963-386-192-9

Library of Congress Cataloging-in-Publication Data

Names: Apor, Balázs, author.

Title: The invisible shining : the cult of Mátyás Rákosi in Stalinist Hungary, 1945-1956 / Balázs Apor.

Description: Budapest ; New York : Central European University Press, 2017. | Includes bibliographical references and index.

Identifiers: LCCN 2017008775 (print) | LCCN 2017010563 (ebook) | ISBN 9789633861936 (pdf) | ISBN 9789633861929 (hardcover : alkaline paper)

Subjects: LCSH: Rákosi, Mátyás, 1892-1971--Public opinion. | Rákosi, Mátyás, 1892-1971--Influence. | Cults--Political aspects--Hungary--History--20th century. | Public opinion--Hungary--History--20th century. | Communism--Hungary--History--20th century. | Nationalism--Hungary--History--20th century. | Hungary--Politics and government--1945-1989.

Classification: LCC DB956.6.R34 (ebook) | LCC DB956.6.R34 A66 2017 (print) | DDC 943.905/2092--dc23

LC record available at https://lccn.loc.gov/2017008775

Printed in Hungary by
Prime Rate Kft., Budapest

Table of Contents

Abbreviations IX

Acknowledgments XI

Introduction 1
    The Stalinist Leader Cult: Origins, Interpretations and Functions 1
    The Stalinist Leader Cult in Postwar Eastern Europe 15
    The Stalinist Leader Cult in Hungary 24
    A Note on Terminology 27

I THE CONSTRUCTION OF THE CULT 31

1 The Chronology of Cult Construction (1925–1953) 33
    Rákosi and the Hungarian Communists: The Road to Power 33
    Cultic Traditions and Modern Personality Cults in Hungary 39
    The "Hero of the Comintern": The Origins of the Rákosi Cult 45
    The Cult in the Party (1945–1947) 51
    The Legitimization Offensive (1948–1949) 64
    The Full-Blown Cult (1949–1953) 68

2 The Institutions and Agents of Cult Construction 79
    Institutions of Cult-Building 80
    The Agents of the Cult 83
    Rákosi and the Rákosi Cult 86

3 "The Biography is a Very Serious Issue":
The Role of Biographies in Constructing the Rákosi Cult 95
    Biographies and Stalinist Political Culture 95
    The Biographies of Rákosi 101
    The Official Biography 106
    The Biographical Narrative 111
    Behind the Constructed Façade 120

4 "He Was Created by a Thousand Years":
  Nationalism and the Leader Cult ... 127
    Nationalism and Communism ... 128
    Stalin, the Mini-Stalins, and National Traditions ... 131
    Rákosi, the Ultimate Freedom Fighter ... 135

5 "Comrade Rákosi Lives with Us": The Visual and the Spatial Aspects
  of the Rákosi Cult ... 147
    Rákosi, the "Sacred Center" ... 150
    Visualizing the Leader ... 155
    The Spatial Allocation of Rákosi's Images ... 161
    Signposts of Progress: Renamings ... 167

II RESPONSES TO THE CULT'S EXPANSION ... 175

6 "Love for Comrade Rákosi Has Become Deeper":
  The Communicative Influence of the Cult ... 177
    Popular Opinion and the Stalinist "Source Lens" ... 177
    The Popularity of the Leader ... 185
    The Elections of 1949 ... 189
    The "Rákosi Constitution" ... 191
    "For Rákosi, thanks; for Rajk, the gallows!" ... 194
    "Even the Air Changes": Narratives of Rákosi's Words ... 195
    "Comrade Rákosi, Listen to My Problems as If You Were My Father":
    Letters to the Leader ... 199

7 "Death to Uncle Rákosi!" Negative Perceptions of the Cult ... 209
    Critiques and Iconoclasts ... 212
    Jokes and Political Rumors ... 219

8 Ignorance is Bliss: Popular Indifference and the Shortcomings
  of Communist Propaganda ... 231
    The Cult's Audience ... 234
    The Cult's Agents ... 239
    The Rákosi Cult: Circulation and Responses ... 255

III THE DISMANTLING OF THE CULT ... 261

9 The "New Course" and the Decay of the Rákosi Cult, 1953–1956 ... 263
The Death of Stalin and the Rákosi Cult ... 266
Cult Criticism in 1953–1956 ... 271

10 The Collapse of the Rákosi Cult ... 299
The Twentieth Congress and the "Secret Speech" ... 299
"We Were Surprised by the Twentieth Congress":
The Effects of the "Secret Speech" on the Rákosi Cult ... 302
"It Hurts to See Comrade Rákosi Leave Like This":
Rákosi's Abdication and the Uprising of 1956 ... 315
"We Should Not Let Even the Illusion of the Personality Cult Appear":
Denouncing the Cult in the Kádár Era ... 319
From Politics to History ... 325
The "Withering Away" of the Rákosi Cult ... 327

Conclusion ... 335
Bibliography ... 345
Index ... 377

Abbreviations

ÁBTL – Állambiztonsági Szolgálatok Történeti Levéltára
(Historical Archives of the Security Services)

APO – Agitációs- és Propagandaosztály (Department of Agitation and Propaganda)

ÁVH – Államvédelmi Hatóság (State Defense Authority)

ÁVO – Államvédelmi Osztály (State Defense Department)

CPSU – Communist Party of the Soviet Union

DISZ – Dolgozó Ifjúság Szövetsége (Alliance of Working Youth)

FKgP – Független Kisgazda Földmunkás és Polgári Párt (Smallholders' Party)

IIB – Ideiglenes Intéző Bizottság (Provisional Executive Committee)

KEB – Központi Ellenőrző Bizottság (Central Control Committee)

KMP – Kommunisták Magyarországi Pártja (Hungarian Party of Communists)

MDP – Magyar Dolgozók Pártja (Hungarian Workers' Party)

MEFESZ – Magyar Egyetemi és Főiskolai Egyesületek Szövetsége
(Alliance of Hungarian University and College Associations)

MKP – Magyar Kommunista Párt (Hungarian Communist Party)

MNDSZ – Magyar Nők Demokratikus Szövetsége
(Democratic Alliance of Hungarian Women)

MOL – Magyar Országos Levéltár (Hungarian National Archives)

MSZDP – Magyarországi Szociáldemokrata Párt
(Hungarian Social Democratic Party)

MSZMP – Magyar Szocialista Munkáspárt (Hungarian Socialist Workers' Party)

OPO – Országos Propaganda (Agitációs) Osztály
(Propaganda [Agitation] Department)

OSA – Open Society Archives

OSZK GP – Országos Széchényi Könyvtár Grafikai Plakáttár
(Poster Archives of the National Széchényi Library)

PIL – Politikatörténeti Intézet Levéltára (Archives of the Political History Institute)

Acknowledgments

This book has been a long time in the making. The reasons for the delay in getting the manuscript ready for publication partly had to do with the rapid—and somewhat unexpected—expansion of my family, and the fact that I moved to new countries (and jobs) twice in the last ten years or so. But quite frankly, I grew weary of the topic of leader cults and of the main protagonist of this book, Mátyás Rákosi, and I was ready to move on to explore new fields of research. At the same time, certain parts of the manuscript have been published as standalone book chapters and journal articles, and for a time I considered my affair with the cult of communist leaders to be over. But the cult slowly crept back into my life: new historical monographs were published on the subject, and exciting opportunities arose in recent years to collaborate with colleagues. However, it was the rise of new authoritarian leaders in the wake of the financial crisis that eventually made me reconsider my views and attitude towards the subject. The spread of populism across the globe and the return of the "strong leader" to center stage provoked the revival of cultic representations of political figures. The rising tide of anti-democratism and anti-intellectualism paved the way for the rise of magnetic individuals who claim to possess the ultimate cure to society's problems, preach radical change, and appeal to emotions instead of reason. Even certain aspects of the Stalin cult have returned in post-Soviet Russia, and manifest themselves in increasingly positive representations of the former dictator's historical role. Without doubt, the specter of the leader cult continues to haunt the European continent. It is the resilience of this specter that eventually persuaded me to re-conceptualize and rewrite the entire manuscript, but also to revise the overall argument. Although the main protagonist of the book is still the Hungarian Stalinist leader, Rákosi, the narrative draws upon national and international comparisons, and interprets the phenomenon in the context of the Sovietization of Central and Eastern Europe. I believe that the book goes beyond the framework of a mere case study and it highlights some of the more generic features of political cults, while it brings some of the universal strategies of cult construction into the spotlight as well. If this book enhances in any meaningful way our understanding of how magnetic leaders operate, then its publication was not in vain.

Over the long years I have spent studying the cult of the Communist leader I benefited from the guidance, advice, and feedback of a long list of people; academics, students, friends, and family members alike. I am grateful to them all, but since it would be impossible to thank them here individually, I would only mention those whose opinions directly contributed to the formation of the current manuscript. First and foremost, I would like to thank my academic mentors, Arfon Rees and Lajos Tímár, for their support and academic guidance during my career as a PhD student in the early 2000s. I am also indebted to my fellow-travelers in cult studies Jan C. Behrends and Polly Jones, with whom I organized the memorable workshop "Stalin and the Lesser Gods: The Leader Cult in Communist Dictatorships in Comparative Perspective (1928–61)" on May 15–16, 2003, at the European University Institute in Florence. The vibrant discussions with the participants in the conference room, at the dinner table, or over a beer, shaped my views on the cult significantly. I would also like to express my gratitude to the people who took the time to read and comment on my PhD dissertation or excerpts from it. The list includes David Brandenberger, Sarah Davies, Gábor Gyáni, György Gyarmati, Peter Kenez, József Ö. Kovács, Éva Standeisky, and Tibor Valuch, but also members of the PhD defense panel in Florence, László Bruszt, Árpád von Klimo, and Robert Service. Their comments were incredibly useful, and I have learned a lot from them. I am thankful to Judith Devlin for keeping my interest in the cult alive during our casual as well as our more formal discussions about the topic in Dublin. Special thanks to Kevin Morgan for the various initiatives—conference panels, journal issue, workshop, documentary—to work together, and for his invaluable insights during our conversations on the subject. The detailed comments and observations of the two anonymous reviewers who reviewed this manuscript were extremely helpful, as well, and I am grateful for them. In addition, I remain indebted to my copy-editors, Aoife O'Gorman, and the anonymous editor at CEU Press for ruthlessly eliminating the linguistic and stylistic shortcomings of the text.

Several people and institutions helped me along the way through providing guidance, resources, or financial support for the project. The late Árpád Pünkösti, the author of Rákosi's biographies, was always ready to respond to my queries and direct me towards relevant primary sources whenever I got stuck with my research. I am grateful to my grandfather who gave me his copy of the literary anthology published on the occasion of Rákosi's sixtieth birthday, instead of throwing it into the bin. Péter Németh should also be thanked for lending me a copy of the book on the Rákosi trials (which is still sitting on my shelf) many years ago. I would also like to acknowledge the support of two Hungarian research institutes, the Political History Institute and the Twentieth Century Institute for their financial support at the early stages of this project.

Most of the ideas in this book were conceived in the intellectually nurturing environment at the European University Institute. I would like to thank all my friends for making those years unforgettable. While it would be impossible to list them all here due to spatial limitations, John Cronin, Evelyn Flanagan, and Euan MacDonald deserve special mention. In addition, Euan deserves special credit for his constant meta-conceptual observations. Last but not least, I am extremely grateful to my family for tolerating my ongoing interest in the absurd representations of dubious political figures. I do hope that my children will not have to live in times in which such representations define social relationships and political cultures. There is still hope.

Some of the chapters in this book are based on previously published articles, and some recycled smaller parts of earlier publications. I would hereby like to thank all the respective publishers for granting me permission to reuse the material for the purposes of this book. The details of previous publications are listed below or in the footnotes.

The Introduction is unpublished, but includes revised short excerpts from "Communist Leader Cults in Eastern Europe: Concepts and Recent Debates," in Anssi Halmesvirta, ed., *Cultic Revelations: Cult Personalities and Phenomena* (Tampere: Historietti Oy, 2011), 27–43, and "Sovietisation,

Imperial Rule and the Stalinist Leader Cult in Central and Eastern Europe," in Róisín Healy and Enrico Dal Lago, ed., *The Shadow of Colonialism on Europe's Modern Past* (Basingstoke: Palgrave, 2014), 228–244.

Chapter 3 has been published before, but has been revised for the purposes of this book from "Leader in the Making: The Role of Biographies in Constructing the Cult of Mátyás Rákosi," in Balázs Apor, Jan C. Behrends, Polly Jones and E.A. Rees, ed., *The Leader Cult in Communist Dictatorships: Stalin and the Eastern Bloc* (Basingstoke: Palgrave, 2004), 63–80.

Chapter 4 is a significantly reworked and extended version of "National Traditions and the Leader Cult in Communist Hungary in the Early Cold War Years," in "Communism and the Leader Cult," special issue, *Twentieth Century Communism: A Journal of International History* 1, no. 1 (2009): 50–71. (Published by Lawrence & Wishart.)

Chapter 5 grows out of my chapter "Spatial Aspects of the Communist Leader Cult: The Case of Mátyás Rákosi in Hungary," in Balázs Apor, Péter Apor and E.A. Rees, ed., *The Sovietization of Eastern Europe: New Perspectives on the Postwar Period* (Washington, DC: New Academia Publishing, 2008), 149–69. Chapter 5 also re-used some paragraphs from "Images of a Mini-Stalin: The Case of Mátyás Rákosi in Hungary," *Communisme*, no. 90 (2007): 91–103.

Chapter 8 is a revised and extended version of my chapter "'Ignorance is Bliss': Cult Reception and Popular Indifference in Communist Hungary (1947–1956)," in Benno Ennker and Heidi Hein-Kircher, ed., *Der Führer im Europa des 20. Jahrhunderts* (Marburg: Verlag Herder-Institut, 2010), 90–107.

Parts of Chapter 10 have been published as "The Secret Speech and its Effect on the 'Cult of Personality' in Hungary," *Critique: Journal of Socialist Theory* 35, no. 2 (2007): 229–247. The chapter is an extended and revised version of the original article. The website of the journal is: www.tandfonline.com.

Dublin, 23 November 2016.

Introduction

The oxymoron in the title of this book warrants an explanation. The phrase "invisible shining" was borrowed from an unknown Hungarian who expressed his gratitude for the enactment of the Stalinist constitution in 1949 to the general secretary of the Hungarian Workers' Party, Mátyás Rákosi. In a letter to the official newspaper *Szabad Nép*, he praised the leader for helping draft the country's new fundamental laws: "next to the name of Stalin, the name of Rákosi radiates invisibly between the lines of the constitution."[1] Oxymoron or not, the expression epitomizes the Stalinist leader cult in Hungary. Rákosi, as one of the most diligent disciples of Stalin in the Soviet bloc, certainly had his "shining" moments. The orchestrated worship of his persona was ubiquitous, and it even outclassed—or outshone—the institutionalized veneration of most of his colleagues in the region. At the same time, his cult inspired little popular support and remained almost "invisible," and its remnants disappeared swiftly from the nation's collective memory after 1956. This book is a history of Rákosi's "invisible shining" and the Communist regime's attempt to implement the Stalinist leader cult in postwar Hungary.

The Stalinist Leader Cult: Origins, Interpretations and Functions

The cult of Rákosi was the product of the Sovietization of Hungary after World War II. It emerged as part of the imperial project to strengthen Moscow's grip over the new borderlands of Soviet civilization. Its

---
[1] MOL, 276. fond 108/17.

ascension was thus determined by Bolshevik ideology, the myths and ritual practices of the working-class movement, and Soviet geopolitical strategies in Central and Eastern Europe. The following sections will provide a brief overview of the origins of the leader cult in Stalinist political culture and the role of the phenomenon in advancing the Sovietization of postwar Eastern Europe.

The extraordinary veneration of Party leaders was arguably one of the most pervasive attributes of Stalinist political culture. The cult of prominent politicians evolved in a political system that was anti-clerical—even atheist—and was allegedly inspired by the scientific principles of Marxism. The elevation of sometimes uncharismatic and colorless individuals to the position of demi-gods and the astonishing reverence that they received, therefore, was one of the many paradoxes of the history of Communism. The worship of leaders was not invented by the Communists, however. Cultic images and practices have accompanied official representations of leadership since time immemorial. The cults of ancient emperors, Christian saints, or medieval rulers are among the most obvious examples of reverence of a particular person. The onset of modernity—the revolutionary movements of the nineteenth century in particular—triggered the transformation of symbolic systems, yet the tradition of representing remarkable individuals—monarchs, dictators, revolutionary figures, national heroes, celebrities, and so on—in cultic terms survived.[2] The authoritarian regimes of the twentieth century continued to rely heavily on the symbolic capital invested in the leader. Military figures such as Marshal Piłsudski in Poland, Carl Gustaf von Mannerheim in Finland, and Kemal Atatürk in Turkey were all portrayed in charismatic terms, while the cultic veneration of Hitler, Mussolini, and Stalin became a fundamental part of the "totalitarian" experience.[3]

---

[2] Two of the most emblematic examples of romantic hero worship in the nineteenth century are the cults around Napoleon Bonaparte and Garibaldi. See Sudhir Hazareesingh, *The Legend of Napoleon* (London: Granta Books, 2004); and Lucy Riall, *Garibaldi: Invention of a Hero* (New Haven, CT: Yale University Press, 2008).

[3] For the Hitler cult, see Ian Kershaw, *The "Hitler Myth": Image and Reality in the Third Reich* (Oxford: Oxford University Press, 1987). For the worship of Mussolini, see Simonetta Falasca-Zamponi, *Fascist Spectacle: The Aesthetics of Power in Mussolini's Italy* (Berkeley: University of California Press, 1997); Piero Melograni, "The Cult of the Duce in Mussolini's Italy," in "Theories of Fascism," special issue, *Journal of Contemporary History* 11, no. 4 (1976): 221–37;

The cults of twentieth-century dictators, including the cult of Stalin, have traditionally been analyzed with the help of Max Weber's concept of charisma.[4] Weber's definition has been criticized, supplemented, and even discarded by scholars, yet the term has displayed an enduring relevance, and it continues to feature in academic debates on the nature of modern dictatorships.[5] While the overall analytical value of the concept will not be discussed at length in this book, it should be noted that Weber's theory strengthened the focus of scholarly inquiries on individual leaders and on the origins of their charismatic appeal. In the case of Communist leader cults, this trend was manifested in discussions that linked the "cult of personality" to Stalin's achievement of dictatorial power.[6] The individual (Stalin) and the cult's genesis remained the focus of attention: the

---

and Luisa Passerini, *Mussolini immaginario. Storia di una biografia, 1915–1939* (Bari, Laterza 1991). For a comparative discussion, see Martin Loiperdinger, ed., *Führerbilder: Hitler, Mussolini, Roosevelt, Stalin in Fotografie und Film* (Munich: Piper, 1995). For case studies on the cult of military leaders in interwar Europe, see Heidi Hein-Kircher, *Der Piłsudski-Kult und seine Bedeutung für den polnischen Staat 1926–1939* (Marburg: Herder Institut, 2002); Anssi Halmesvirta, "A Foreign Benefactor and a Domestic Liberator: The Cults of Lenin and Mannerheim in Finland," *Scandinavian Journal of History* 34, no. 9 (2009): 414–32; and Yael Navaro-Yashin, *Faces of the State: Secularism and Public Life in Turkey* (Princeton: Princeton University Press, 2002).

[4] Max Weber, "The Types of Legitimate Domination," in Max Weber, *Economy and Society: An Outline of Interpretive Sociology*, vol. 1 (Berkeley and Los Angeles: University of California Press, 1978), 212–301; and Max Weber, "Charisma and Its Transformation," ibid., vol. 2, 1111–57.

[5] See, for example, Luciano Cavalli, *Charisma, Dictatorship and Plebiscitary Democracy* (Florence: Università degli studi di Firenze, 1984); E. A. Rees, "Leader Cults: Varieties, Preconditions and Functions," in Balázs Apor, Jan C. Behrends, Polly Jones, and E. A. Rees, *The Leader Cult in Communist Dictatorships: Stalin and the Eastern Bloc* (Basingstoke: Palgrave, 2004), 3–26, here 3–5; and Aristotle A. Kallis, "Fascism, 'Charisma,' and 'Charismatisation': Weber's Model of 'Charismatic Domination' and Interwar European Fascism," *Totalitarian Movements and Political Religions* 7, no. 1 (2006): 25–43. See also the special issue of *Totalitarian Movements and Political Religions* 7, no. 2 (2006).

[6] Graeme Gill, "Personality Cult, Political Culture and Party Structure," *Studies in Comparative Communism* 17, no. 2 (1984): 111–21; Graeme Gill, "Political Myth and Stalin's Quest for Authority in the Party," in *Authority, Power and Policy in the USSR: Essays Dedicated to Leonard Schapiro*, ed. T. H. Rigby, Archie Brown, and Peter Reddaway (London: Macmillan, 1983), 98–117; Graeme Gill, "Personal Dominance and the Collective Principle: Individual Legitimacy in Marxist-Leninist Systems," in *Political Legitimation in Communist States*, ed. T. H. Rigby and Ferenc Fehér (London: Macmillan, 1982), 94–110; Jeremy T. Paltiel, "The Cult of Personality: Some Comparative Reflections on Political Culture in Leninist Regimes," *Studies in Comparative Communism* 16, nos. 1–2 (1983): 49–64; and Robert J. Thompson, "Reassessing Personality Cults: The Case of Stalin and Mao," *Studies in Comparative Communism* 21, no. 1 (1988): 99–128.

cult was equated with one-man rule and was often believed to stem from the Soviet leader's psychological predisposition to encourage eulogies of his persona.[7] Such approaches, however, generally failed to account for the hierarchical nature of leader worship and its spread in the peripheries of the Soviet sphere of influence. In addition, the early historiography of the cult paid little attention to the ritual aspects of the phenomenon and the role of institutions and individuals (other than Stalin) in constructing the leader's mythical persona.

While Weber's ideas were generally used to endorse interpretations that focused on ruptures—extraordinary situations—rather than continuities, and on individuals rather than cultic systems, many of his observations remain valid.[8] His notion of "manufactured charisma"; his discussion of the routinization of charisma and "hereditary charisma"; the concept of the highly impersonal "office charisma"; and the idea that exceptional qualities are not inherent in the person but are attributed to him/her by his/her following could certainly be deployed in the analysis of Communist leader cults. "Stalinist charisma" was undoubtedly constructed. The examples of Stalin and his "best disciples" in Eastern Europe show the desperate attempt of Communist propaganda to confer an aura of exceptionality upon the regime's leaders. Manufactured charisma, however, was not applied only to individuals. Soviet-type systems obsessively attributed charismatic qualities to institutions, organizations (the Party), political positions (the Party secretary), and even on certain political measures (the Five-Year Plan) or historical events (the revolution).[9] It was the entire regime, and not a single individual, that was portrayed in charismatic

---

[7] See, for example, Robert C. Tucker, *Stalin in Power: The Revolution from Above, 1928–1941* (New York: Norton, 1990).

[8] For the relevance of the notion in the Communist context, see Robert C. Tucker, "The Theory of Charismatic Leadership," in "Philosophers and Kings: Studies in Leadership," special issue, *Daedalus* 97, no. 3 (1968): 731–56; Carol Strong and Matt Killingsworth, "Stalin the Charismatic Leader? Explaining the 'Cult of Personality' as a Legitimation Technique," *Politics, Religion and Ideology* 12, no. 4 (2011): 391–411; Jan Plamper, "Introduction: Modern Personality Cults," in *Personality Cults in Stalinism / Personenkulte im Stalinismus*, ed. Klaus Heller and Jan Plamper (Göttingen: V & R Unipress, 2004), 13–42; and Balázs Apor, "Communist Leader Cults in Eastern Europe: Concepts and Recent Debates," in Anssi Halmesvirta, ed., *Cultic Revelations: Studies in Modern Historical Cult Personalities and Phenomena*, Spectrum Hungarologicum (Jyväskylä-Pécs: University of Jyväskylä, 2010), vol. 4, 2010: 37–62.

[9] Rees, "Leader Cults," 22.

terms. Communist propaganda in the Stalinist period, therefore, could be viewed as a monumental attempt to manufacture an impersonal, collective charisma for the whole establishment.

Problems with the notion of charisma notwithstanding, scholarly attention to the genesis of the cult has enhanced our general understanding of its origins. Historians normally identify the roots of the leader cult in the Marxist tradition that appraised the role of great individuals in the transformation of society (Georgi Plekhanov), the pervasiveness of millenarian thought around the turn of the nineteenth and twentieth centuries that manifested itself in the emergence of cultic representations in the working-class movement, and the popular yearning for the advent of extraordinary personalities in European societies after World War I. Special attention has been paid to Russian intellectual traditions, the role of patronage networks and *blat* relations in the shaping of the cult, and to the militant, conspiratorial nature of the pre-revolutionary Communist movement that produced a series of authority figures.[10] The Lenin cult of the early 1920s was mostly the product of a combination of these factors.[11] The Lenin myth was later exploited by Stalin to justify his own position in the Party. Stalin's cult was initially based on the Lenin-Stalin connection, which was portrayed as a master-apprentice relationship and symbolized the succession of power.[12] By the mid-1930s the worship of Stalin had surpassed that of Lenin, and the export of Stalin's cult to Central and Eastern Europe triggered the reinterpretation of the symbolic link between the

---

[10] For Russian intellectual traditions, see Barbara Walker, "Iosif Stalin, 'Our Teacher Dear': Mentorship, Social Transformation, and the Russian Intelligentsia Personality Cult," in Heller and Plamper, *Personality Cults in Stalinism*, 45–59; Irene Masing-Delic, "Purges and Patronage: Gor'kii's Promotion of Socialist Culture," in Ibid., 443–68; Sheila Fitzpatrick, "Patronage and the Intelligentsia in Stalin's Russia," in *Challenging Traditional Views of Russian History*, ed. Stephen G. Wheatcroft (Basingstoke: Palgrave, 2002), 92–111. See also Jan Plamper's introduction to his book *The Stalin Cult: A Study in the Alchemy of Power* (New Haven, CT: Yale University Press, 2012).

[11] On the Lenin cult, see Benno Ennker, *Die Anfänge des Leninkults in der Sowjetunion* (Cologne: Böhlau, 1997); Nina Tumarkin, *Lenin Lives! The Lenin Cult in Soviet Russia* (Cambridge, MA: Harvard University Press, 1997); Olga Velikanova, *Making of an Idol: On Uses of Lenin* (Göttingen: Muster-Schmidt, 1996).

[12] On the role of the Lenin link in Stalin's cult, see Graeme Gill, "The Soviet Leader Cult: Reflections on the Structure of Leadership in the Soviet Union," *British Journal of Political Science* 10, no. 2 (1980): 167–86.

two leaders.¹³ The foundation myth of the Stalin cult after the war was represented in Communist propaganda in terms of a prophet-messiah relationship, which relegated Lenin's role to preparing the way for the coming of Stalin.

The cradle of the Stalinist leader cult was Bolshevik mythology. The attempt to realize socialist utopia on Earth was manifested in the creation of new myths, symbols, and ritual practices and the formulation of a master narrative, which permeated novels, political biographies, historical works, and newspaper articles.¹⁴ The core Soviet myths included the myth of the Party, the myth of the revolution, and—after 1945—the myth of the "Great Patriotic War." The Soviet system of myths had its own heroes. The apogee of heroic culture was undoubtedly the Stalin period, which elevated to hero status "revolutionary heroes," Stakhanovites, aviators, border guards, partisans, and even those who denounced their relatives.¹⁵ The proliferation of everyday supermen was complemented with the cult of martyrs and the heroic dead. The Party secretary was an integral component of the new Bolshevik pantheon. In fact, he was the super-hero of the heroic age and the super-symbol that absorbed all symbols of Soviet power. The myth of the leader was summarized in his biographies that cemented his fictional persona to the master narrative promoted by the regime. Stalin's figure, for example, was tied to the founding myths of the Soviet state: the revolution, Lenin, and later on, World War II.

The leader cult, with its routinized practices—letter-writing, expressions of gratitude, rhythmic applause, the making of pledges, and so

---

[13] The most important monographic discussions of the Stalin cult include Jeffrey Brooks, *Thank You, Comrade Stalin! Soviet Public Culture from Revolution to Cold War* (Princeton: Princeton University Press, 2001); Graeme Gill, *Symbols and Legitimacy in Soviet Politics* (Cambridge: Cambridge University Press, 2011); James L. Heizer, "The Cult of Stalin, 1929–1939" (PhD dissertation, University of Kentucky, 1977); and Plamper, *The Stalin Cult*. See also the relevant chapters in David Brandenberger, *Propaganda State in Crisis: Soviet Ideology, Indoctrination, and Terror under Stalin, 1927–1941* (New Haven, CT: Yale University Press, 2011).

[14] On the construction of the Bolshevik metanarrative, see Gill, *Symbols and Legitimacy*.

[15] On the myth of the proletariat and its relationship to the cult of leaders, see Claude Pennetier and Bernard Pudal, "Stalinism: Workers' Cult and Cult of Leaders," in "Communism and the Leader Cult," special issue, *Twentieth Century Communism* 1, no. 1 (2009): 20–29. For a comparative assessment of socialist heroes, see Silke Satjukow and Rainer Gries, eds., *Sozialistische Helden. Eine Kulturgeschichte von Propagandafiguren in Osteuropa und der DDR* (Berlin: Links, 2002). For the cult of Pavlik Morozov, see Catriona Kelly, *Comrade Pavlik: The Rise and Fall of a Soviet Boy Hero* (London: Granta, 2004).

on—should also be viewed and interpreted in the context of the complex system of Bolshevik rituals. Stalinist political culture in particular featured a high degree of ritualization of state-societal relations.[16] Denunciation, criticism, self-criticism, and other means of public confession spread through Soviet society from top to bottom, involving prominent Party dignitaries and politically disenfranchised individuals alike. The routinization of such practices led to the ritualization of the use of language, resulting in the semantic emptiness of certain concepts and expressions. The regime also promoted a set of public rituals to celebrate itself and to re-enact—and thereby re-affirm—authority relations in society. Mass demonstrations and Party meetings at various levels of the Soviet institutional hierarchy gradually adopted a standardized format and became routine activities. While the leader cult had its own distinct set of rites, the Party secretary was also the focal point of the regime's public rituals. During demonstrations, public holidays, and festivities, the leader (or an image of him) generally occupied the center of all activities. In the case of denunciations or self-criticism, his name was frequently invoked in the hope of providing absolute credibility to the act of confession. Stalinist rituals thus provided a routinized remodeling of the practice of "working towards the *vozhd'*."[17]

The excessive ritualization of the cult prompts the question: was the Stalinist leader cult merely the resurrection of pre-modern, Byzantine symbolic practices, or was it also shaped by the trends of European modernity? Undoubtedly, the systematic exaltation of Communist notables

---

[16] On the emergence of Soviet ritual culture, see James von Geldern, *Bolshevik Festivals, 1917–1920* (Berkeley: University of California Press, 1993); J. Arch Getty, "*Samokritika* Rituals in the Stalinist Central Committee, 1933–38," *Russian Review* 58, no. 1 (1999): 49–70; Alexei Kojevnikov, "Rituals of Stalinist Culture at Work: Science and the Games of Intraparty Democracy circa 1948," *Russian Review* 57, no. 1 (1998): 25–52; Christel Lane, *The Rites of Rulers: Ritual in Industrial Society; The Soviet Case* (Cambridge: Cambridge University Press, 1981); Karen Petrone, *Life Has Become More Joyous, Comrades: Celebrations in the Time of Stalin* (Bloomington: University of Indiana Press, 2000); and Malte Rolf, *Soviet Mass Festivals, 1917–1991* (Pittsburgh: University of Pittsburgh Press, 2013).

[17] The expression "working towards the Führer" was coined by Ian Kershaw in his article "'Working towards the Führer': Reflections on the Nature of the Hitler Dictatorship," *Contemporary European History* 2, no. 2 (1993): 103–118. The phrase has been adopted to the Soviet context by several authors, including Benno Ennker, "The Stalin Cult, Bolshevik Rule and Kremlin Interaction in the 1930s," in Apor et al., *The Leader Cult*, 83–101; and Malte Rolf, "Working towards the Centre: Leader Cults and Spatial Politics in Pre-War Stalinism," in Ibid., 141–57.

significantly resembled religious rituals and the cults of traditional monarchs and emperors. The Stalin cult's debt to the worship of tsars has often been acknowledged, but the predominantly iconographic and hagiographic representations of the regime's leaders, the rigidity of the cult's rituals, and the tendency to portray prominent politicians as omnipotent and omnipresent rulers also highlight the importance of tradition (and continuity) in the veneration of Stalinist leaders. The archetypal imagery (father, teacher, and leader) of Communist politicians and the paternalistic perception of the community ("the Great Family of Stalinism") the first secretary was supposed to personify sheds additional light on the pre-modern qualities of the leader cult.[18] Such patriarchal representations of society infantilized most of the population.[19] It was the task of Party leaders—represented as father and teacher figures—to raise society from its childlike state to intellectual and political maturity (or adulthood).[20]

The archaic appeal—but not the archaic nature—of Bolshevism is further supported by interpretations that define Communism as a political religion.[21] The centrality of dogma (Marxism-Leninism); the universal

---

[18] Katerina Clark has extensively analyzed primordial representations of Soviet society in Soviet novels. She has argued that such an archaic image of the community constituted a "new utopian kinship model." Katerina Clark, *The Soviet Novel: History as Ritual* (Bloomington: University of Indiana Press, 2000), 129.

[19] Hans Günther, "The Heroic Myth in Socialist Realism," in *Traumfabrik Kommunismus/Dream Factory Communism*, ed. Boris Groys and Max Hollein (Ostfildern: Hatje Cantz, 2003), 106–24; Peter Kenez, *The Birth of the Propaganda State: Soviet Methods of Mass Mobilization, 1917–1929* (Cambridge: Cambridge University Press, 1985), 7–8. Since the Soviet community remained predominantly paternalistic, there was little room in the core mythology for the female element. Although the concept of the Soviet motherland had a significant role in the system of cults, the dominance of the male leader cult (the father) was apparent throughout the Stalinist period. It was only the Ceaușescu era in Romania that realized a certain gender balance in the area of leader worship, with the placement of Elena Ceaușescu, the wife of the dictator, in the spotlight.

[20] The efforts of the Soviet regime to remold society were labeled by scholars as "total" or "permanent education" and the Soviet state as a "permanent classroom." Péter György, "A mindennapok tükre, avagy a korstílus akarása," in *A művészet katonái: Sztálinizmus és kultúra*, ed. Péter György and Hedvig Turai (Budapest: Corvina, 1992), 14; Rees, "Leader Cults," 19. On the origins of the idea of "permanent education" in Lenin's thought, see Richard Stites, "The Origins of Soviet Ritual Style: Symbol and Festival in the Russian Revolution," in *Symbols of Power: The Esthetics of Political Legitimation in the Soviet Union and Eastern Europe*, ed. Claes Arvidsson and Lars Erik Blomqvist (Stockholm: Almqvist & Wiksell International, 1987), 33–36.

[21] Theoreticians of "political religion" link the sacralization of politics to the rise of modernity. The process may be uniquely modern, but the themes it evoked were ancient. The subject of political religion has a substantial literature. See, most importantly, Emilio Gentile, *Politics*

claims of the doctrine; the monumental attempt to create a new type of man; the teleological, Manichean view of historical progress; the importance of public confessions (self-criticism) and procession-like mass demonstrations; the significance of holy places (Red Corners or the Lenin Mausoleum) and relics; and the tendency to stigmatize dissidents as apostates all highlight the resemblance of Soviet-type regimes to religious belief systems. The cult of Party leaders also had religious parallels (and origins).[22] The leader's biography could be interpreted as the story of the nation's redemption, while his god-like omnipresence was promoted through the dissemination of his portraits, which often functioned as icons.[23] The cult's rituals were similar to religious practices. The occasional empty seat reserved for him at Party meetings, the rhythmic applause and chanting, and the writing of letters of gratitude and poetic appraisals of his mythical persona all had their equivalents in traditional religions.[24] Like Orthodox rituals, such practices aimed at realizing a certain spiritual unity

---

  as Religion (Princeton: Princeton University Press, 2006). See also Philippe Burrin, "Political Religion: The Relevance of a Concept," History and Memory 9, nos. 1–2 (1997): 321–49; Richard Faber, ed., Politische Religion – religiöse Politik (Würzburg: Königshausen & Neumann, 1997); Marcin Kula, "Communism as Religion," Totalitarian Movements and Political Religions 6, no. 3 (2005): 371–81; Hans Maier, ed., "Totalitarismus" und "Politische Religionen": Konzepte des Diktaturvergleichs (Paderborn: Schöningh, 1996); Stanley G. Payne, "On the Heuristic Value of the Concept of Political Religion and Its Application," Totalitarian Movements and Political Religions 6, no. 2 (2005): 163–74.

[22] Red Corners were places in schools, offices, Party and governmental institutions, and so on where Communist propaganda material—pictures, posters, wall newspapers, texts—was on display. On the religious roots of the Lenin cult, see Nina Tumarkin, "Religion, Bolshevism and the Origins of the Lenin Cult," Russian Review 40, no. 1 (1981): 35–46; George Louis Kline, "The 'God-Builders': Gorky and Lunacharsky," in George Louis Kline, Religious and Anti-Religious Thought in Russia (Chicago: University of Chicago Press, 1968), 103–26. On the religious origins of Communism in Russia, see Nikolai Berdyaev, The Origin of Russian Communism (London: Geoffrey Bles, 1948).

[23] On the role of the leader in Soviet iconography, see Victoria E. Bonnell, Iconography of Power: Soviet Political Posters under Lenin and Stalin (Berkeley: University of California Press, 1997).

[24] The notion of "political religion" is not without problems, and it has triggered substantial legitimate criticism. One problem critics have reflected on is the tendency of scholars operating in this particular conceptual framework to focus on political and ideological intentions, rather than the social dynamics and popular reception of modern dictatorships. Another problem is such scholars' propensity to emphasize systemic similarities rather than historical specificities between various regimes. A third problem is the overall inflation of the term to incorporate a wide range of political beliefs (ranging from Nazism to political correctness). Finally, there is the problem that such scholars tend to marginalize the importance of historical continuities in sacral perceptions of politics. See, for example, David R. Roberts, "'Political Religion' and the Totalitarian Departures of Inter-War Europe: On the Uses and Disadvantages of an Analytical Category," Contemporary European History 18, no. 4 (2009): 381–414.

between the leader and the led.²⁵ In general, the centrality of the Party secretary in the regime's ritual activities conferred a degree of sacrality upon him and bolstered divine representations of his character.²⁶

The survival of pre-revolutionary political attitudes and social practices also greatly strengthened the traditional, primordial elements of Stalinist rituals. Political scientists analyzing the notion of "political culture" in the 1970s and 1980s have claimed, for example, that the relative stability of Stalin's cult was—to a certain degree—enhanced by continuities in Russian political culture.²⁷ The preference for a paternalistic state in traditional peasant societies, the tendency to personalize politics, the affective attachment to rulers, and the survival of "naive monarchism" all contributed to the revival of cultic figures in allegedly secular polities. More recently, J. Arch Getty has argued that the cult of leaders belonged to the age-old tradition of patrimonialism and clientelism in Russian society.²⁸ Its reappearance in the Stalinist Soviet Union was not the result

---

[25] Lars Erik Blomqvist, "Introduction," in Arvidsson and Blomqvist, *Symbols of Power*, 14.

[26] On the relationship between sacrality and centrality, see Clifford Geertz, "Centers, Kings, and Charisma: Reflections on the Symbolics of Power," in *Rites of Power: Symbolism, Ritual, and Politics since the Middle Ages*, ed. Sean Wilentz (Philadelphia: University of Pennsylvania Press, 1985), 13–38. For the role symbolic centers played in Soviet political culture, see Jan Plamper, "'The Hitlers Come and Go…' The Führer Stays: Stalin's Cult in East Germany," in Heller and Plamper, *Personality Cults in Stalinism*, 301–29; Rolf, "Working towards the Centre"; Ferenc Tallár, "Sztálinizmus és reszakralizáció," *Valóság* 32, no. 2 (1989): 32–51. The religious character of the Communist leader cult has been compared to the mysticism of the worship of medieval kings. Ernst Kantorowicz's famous theory of the king's two bodies has inspired scholars to make a distinction between the Communist leader's mystical (immortal) body and his physical body. In Soviet civilization, however, the idea of immortality was conveyed not so much by the person but by the Party. It was the Party that was represented as a collective immortal body that constantly reproduced itself through the physical bodies of its members. See Ernst Kantorowicz, *The King's Two Bodies: A Study in Mediaeval Political Theology* (Princeton: Princeton University Press, 1957). For the use of the theory in the Soviet context, see Bonnell, *Iconography of Power*; Katalin Sinkó, "A politika rítusai: emlékműállítás, szobordöntés," in György and Turai, *A művészet katonái*, 67–79; and Malte Rolf, "The Leader's Many Bodies: Leader Cults and Mass Festivals in Voronezh, Novosibirsk, and Kemerovo in the 1930s," in Heller and Plamper, *Personality Cults in Stalinism*, 197–206.

[27] On the notion of "political culture," see Archie Brown and Jack Gray, eds., *Political Culture and Political Change in Communist States* (New York: Holmes & Meier Publishers, 1979); Stephen R. Burant, "The Influence of Russian Tradition on the Political Style of the Soviet Elite," *Political Science Quarterly* 102, no. 2 (1987): 273–93; George Schöpflin, *Politics in Eastern Europe 1945–1992* (Oxford: Blackwell, 1993); Stephen White, *Political Culture and Soviet Politics* (Basingstoke: Macmillan, 1979).

[28] J. Arch Getty, *Practicing Stalinism: Bolsheviks, Boyars and the Persistence of Tradition* (New Haven, CT: Yale University Press, 2013).

of a conscious choice; it was, in fact, rather instinctive. The Bolsheviks—being the products of social and cultural traditions themselves—relied on conventions and customs that seemed natural to them and continued to exercise power with the help of patrimonial and cultic practices. For them, no alternative models existed.[29] The appeal of the cult to traditional social values might suggest that Soviet rituals of power were to some extent in accordance with society's expectations. The surprising endurance of cultic practices in Eastern Europe in the post-Stalin period, and the return of the "charismatic" leader to politics—most notably Vladimir Putin—after the collapse of Communist regimes, indicate the persistence of a certain cultural predisposition for the exaltation of authority figures. Nonetheless, despite the similarities between the political cultures of the countries of the Soviet bloc, the worship of the Party secretary outside the Soviet Union generally failed to inspire strong support. It was instead considered a foreign import that was alien to national traditions.

While the worship of Stalinist leaders reflected the continuity of tradition, it was also entangled with the processes of modernity. The cult was adjusted to suit the needs of modern mass politics, and it was deployed by the Bolsheviks as a means of mobilizing the population for the goals of their modernizing revolution. Stalin became the symbol of Soviet technological achievements, and he personified the overall attempt to catch up with, and overtake, the modern industrial economies of the West. The cult was an important component of the industrialization campaign—pledges to increase production were made to the leader—and the manufactured persona of the Party secretary also epitomized the core values of the Soviet civilizing mission.[30] He, in fact, became the personification of the New Soviet Man—the ideal-typical product of Soviet modernity. In addition, the construction of the leader myth fully exploited the means of modern mass media. Images of Communist politicians were transmitted by journals and newspapers, the leader's speeches were broadcast on

---

[29] "When they or some among them had doubts about what seemed natural, about contradicting the scientific rationalism they claimed, they went ahead and did the natural thing, the intuitive thing, the thing that combined science and superstition, while at the same time denying—even to themselves—they were doing it. Somewhere in the back of their minds, Lenin was a saint." Getty, *Practicing Stalinism*, 73. See also 95.

[30] On the Soviet civilizing mission, see Vadim Volkov, "The Concept of Kul'turnost': Notes on the Stalinist Civilizing Process," in *Stalinism: New Directions*, ed. Sheila Fitzpatrick (London: Routlegde, 2000), 210–30.

the radio, and he appeared on cinema screens and, in the second half of the twentieth century, on television. As a result, the worship of Stalinist leaders turned into an institutionalized, highly centralized, and controlled mechanism and reached unprecedented levels in the respective societies. The post-Stalin period witnessed the further "modernization" of the leader's myth and the gradual replacement of archetypal images with more modern representations. The technocratic and managerial skills of the first secretaries came to be highlighted instead of their mystical qualities, and they were more often portrayed as good managers or talented presidents than all-powerful demi-gods.[31] To some extent, the modernization of Soviet-type leader cults resulted in the gradual blurring of distinctions between the representations of Communist notables and the images of non-Communist political figures in the West. Like politicians such as Charles de Gaulle, Konrad Adenauer, or John F. Kennedy, Communist Party secretaries of the late Socialist period were all represented as charismatic individuals and as talented statesmen with formidable foresight.[32]

It appears that the Stalinist leader cult—like all complex historical phenomena—was the product of both continuities and discontinuities. It reflected both the uninterrupted flow of tradition and the impact of modernity. Undoubtedly, the Bolsheviks' intention was to propel their country into modernity, and the dream of creating an alternate civilization, based on the values associated with Enlightenment rationality, continued to shape their policies until the collapse of the Soviet Union. At the same time, they remained captive to tradition and resorted to age-old political practices to achieve their goals. The cult, therefore, could be interpreted in the framework of Stalinist neo-traditionalism: it was supposed to advance the Party's modernist agenda, yet it ultimately contributed to the survival of traditional institutions and methods of exercising power.[33]

---

[31] The change in the imagery of Polish Party secretaries has been analyzed by Marcin Zaremba, "The Second Step of a Ladder: The Cult of the First Secretaries in Poland," in Apor et al., *The Leader Cult*, 261–77.

[32] On the myth of de Gaulle, see Sudhir Hazareesingh, *The Shadow of the General: Modern France and the Myth of de Gaulle* (Oxford: Oxford University Press, 2012). For a recent assessment of charismatic individuals in modern politics, see Berit Bliesemann de Guevara and Tatjana Reiber, eds., *Charisma und Herrschaft: Führung und Verführung in der Politik* (Frankfurt am Main: Campus Verlag, 2011).

[33] On the notion of neo-traditionalism, see Terry Martin, "Modernization or Neo-Traditionalism? Ascribed Nationality and Soviet Primordialism," in *Russian Modernity: Politics, Knowledge and Practices, 1800–1950*, ed. David L. Hoffmann and Yanni Kotsonis (Houndmills,

The interplay of modernity and tradition was mirrored in the multiplicity of functions the cult played in Soviet-type societies. Traditional images of power were recycled with the aim of pursuing modern mass mobilization campaigns (domestic and international) in societies that were largely unfamiliar with Marxist theory and tended to perceive politics in personalized terms.[34] Whereas popular perceptions normally regard the worship of the leader as an excessive (primeval) feature of Stalinist rule that was promoted by a paranoid, megalomaniac dictator, the function of Communist political rituals was more complex. The leader cult, in fact, was an intricate system of myths and rituals that was meant to bolster symbolic and affective attachment to the regime and thereby to widen the social base of Communist rule and to keep society in a state of permanent mobilization. The cult included both representations (texts and images) and practices (rites), and it was not merely a side effect of the establishment of dictatorial regimes: it was an inherent component of the Communist system of rule, with a range of political, social, cultural, and even economic functions. The archaic, mystical, superhuman traits of the Party secretary's constructed persona—images of the omnipotent, omnipresent, and infallible leader—were to strengthen the regime's legitimacy through the forging of emotional ties between the leader and society.[35] He was depicted as the representative of the cause, a symbol of unity, and an embodiment of the professed ideology and system of values. Archetypal representations of the leader that posited him as a father figure were sought to enhance a sense of (emotional) community, which was usually portrayed with the metaphor of the family. Next to a range of traditional symbolic functions,

---

Basingstoke: Macmillan, 2000), 161–83. This is not to discredit the modernist interpretation of the Stalinist Soviet Union, of course. As David L. Hoffmann has pointed out, for example, the modernist and neo-traditionalist paradigms are not mutually exclusive. The cult, in fact, could be interpreted from both perspectives. David L. Hoffmann, *Stalinist Values: The Cultural Norms of Soviet Modernity, 1917–1941* (Ithaca: Cornell University Press, 2003), 194. For the modernist interpretation of Stalinism, see also David L. Hoffmann, *Cultivating the Masses: Modern State Practices and Soviet Socialism, 1914–1939* (Ithaca: Cornell University Press, 2011); and Stephen Kotkin, *Magnetic Mountain: Stalinism as a Civilization* (Berkeley: University of California Press, 1995).

[34] David Brandenberger, "Stalin as Symbol: A Case Study of the Personality Cult and Its Construction," in *Stalin: A New History*, ed. Sarah Davies and James Harris (Cambridge: Cambridge University Press, 2006), 249–70.

[35] On the role of affective ties toward the leader, see Erik van Ree, *The Political Thought of Joseph Stalin: A Study in Twentieth-Century Revolutionary Patriotism* (London, New York: RoutledgeCurzon, 2002), 155–68.

the cult also served more rational, pragmatic purposes. It was exploited by the leader to maintain control over the Party elite and was promoted to advance the Soviet civilizing process, by creating an identity model for society to emulate.[36] The cult was also deployed as the prime symbolic incentive to mobilize the population for the achievements of the regime's economic targets. In the Soviet "moral economy," society was expected to intensify work efforts in order to express its gratitude to the leader for his "gift": the Party's supposed achievements, and the socialist utopia, which would only materialize in the distant future.[37]

The expansion of the Soviet sphere of influence after World War II amplified the supranational aspects (and functions) of the cult. Stalin emerged as "the father of peoples" who represented unity among the ethnically and culturally diverse territories that fell under Soviet rule.[38] The promotion of mythical images of the Soviet leader thus became instrumental in the expansion of the Soviet borderlands. The primary function of the Stalin cult after World War II was to advance the integration of the satellite countries to the Soviet imperial core through ritual means. The seventieth birthday of the Soviet leader in December 1949, therefore, was a significant attempt at creating a transnational cult community, and it marked the final ritual act of Sovietization in the Soviet sphere of influence.[39]

The cult was adjusted to address different audiences, and it showed a different face to different social groups. To the army the Party secretary was shown as a genius military strategist. To children he was shown as a "friend" and role model. To the intelligentsia he was shown as a patron of arts and the "coryphaeus of sciences." To functionaries he was shown as a symbol of cohesion. To ordinary Party members he was shown as the

---

[36] On the role of the cult in ensuring the obedience of Stalin's inner circle, see Ennker, "The Stalin Cult."

[37] On the intimate link between production campaigns and the leader cult, and the role of the cult in the Soviet moral economy, see Brooks, *Thank You, Comrade Stalin!*

[38] Jan Plamper, "Georgian Koba or Soviet 'Father of Peoples'? The Stalin Cult and Ethnicity," in Apor et al., *The Leader Cult*, 123–40.

[39] The notion of the "cult community" is analyzed in detail in Alexey Tikhomirov, "The Stalin Cult between Center and Periphery: The Structures of the Cult Community in the Empire of Socialism, 1949–1956; The Case of GDR," in *Der Führer im Europa des 20. Jahrhunders*, ed. Benno Ennker and Heidi Hein-Kircher (Marburg: Herder Institut, 2010), 297–321.

embodiment of the Party's authority. To workers he was shown as the personification of proletarian rule.[40] The differentiation between the three dominant aspects of Stalin's imagery—leader, teacher, and friend—indicates an attempt by Communist propaganda to mold a different leader-image for different social groups.

The Stalinist Leader Cult in Postwar Eastern Europe

The Sovietization of Central and Eastern Europe after World War II entailed the importation of the Stalin cult from the Soviet Union and the adaptation of leader worship to local Party secretaries. Inspired by the Soviet model, the manufacturing of "mini-Stalins"—including Bolesław Bierut, Gheorghe Gheorghiu-Dej, Klement Gottwald, Georgi Dimitrov, and Mátyás Rákosi—became the dominant act in the political theater of the respective countries in the late 1940s and early 1950s. The transplantation of the cult to Eastern Europe, however, was not a uniform process. The system of myths and rituals that surrounded prominent Communist politicians was adjusted to local social and cultural contexts and was shaped by national traditions of state-building. At the same time, the development of cultic practices in the new Soviet borderlands was fairly uneven. In most cases, the implementation of the Soviet-type leader cult faced significant obstacles; there were only a few countries where the cult developed relatively smoothly. One of the most obvious general reasons for the lack of popularity of the new leaders was the overall lack of support for Communist parties in the region, but there were country-specific reasons, too. In Poland, for example, traditional anti-Russian sentiments—aggravated by Soviet occupation during the war—and the strong position of the Catholic Church seriously undermined the symbolic policies of the regime. In East Germany, the traumatic memories of German expellees from Eastern Europe, Red Army violence in the last phase of the war, and the looming shadow of the Hitler cult were all responsible for the

---

[40] On the "coryphaeus of science" imagery, see Ethan Pollock, "Stalin as the Coryphaeus of Science: Ideology and Knowledge in the Post-War Years," in Davies and Harris, *Stalin: A New History*, 271–88.

sluggish development of Stalinist leader cults in the country.[41] Yugoslavia and Albania were at the other end of the spectrum. There, Soviet-type leader cults emerged almost spontaneously, independently of the Soviet military presence in the rest of Eastern Europe. The cults of Josip Broz Tito in Yugoslavia and Enver Hoxha in Albania combined the myth of a successful war leader with the heroic imagery of a Communist Party secretary, and they both managed to acquire genuine popular support—in the beginning at least—without the excessive use of Soviet techniques of mass persuasion. In the countries of the Western Balkans, the inception of the Soviet-type leader cult seems to have preceded the Sovietization of political and cultural institutions.[42] While the leaders' initial popularity—or the lack thereof—shaped the way the cult was perceived by society, it was not necessarily a precondition of successful cult-building. The Communist regimes of Central and Eastern Europe gradually assumed complete control over the public sphere and acquired the means to ensure participation in political rituals. The cult, therefore, grew continuously, irrespective of the level of popular support for the Party's leader. Whether the cult's codes and messages were welcomed and internalized by society is a different question.

There is a tendency among historians to treat the ritual aspects of Sovietization as a somewhat marginal phenomenon. This is clearly demonstrated by the limited scholarly attention the cult has received in the historiography of the Soviet bloc. Even after the modest "boom" in cult studies since 2004 and the subsequent reassessment of the role of organized leader worship in the establishment of Communist regimes, the ritual dimensions of cult-building remain relatively unexplored.[43] The emphasis tends to be on the representations—textual and visual—of Party leaders and on the narrative aspects of myth-building, and not so much on the

---

[41] Jan C. Behrends, "Exporting the Leader: The Stalin Cult in Poland and East Germany (1944/45–56)," in Apor et al., *The Leader Cult*, 161–78; Plamper, "The Hitlers Come and Go…"; Dieter Vorsteher, ed., *Parteiauftrag: Ein neues Deutschland. Bilder, Rituale und Symbole der frühen DDR* (Munich and Berlin: Koehler & Amelang, 1997).

[42] Stanislav Sretenovic and Artan Puto, "Leader Cults in the Western Balkans (1945–1990): Josip Broz Tito and Enver Hoxha," in Apor et al., *The Leader Cult*, 208–25.

[43] The most important publications since 2004 include Apor et al., *The Leader Cult*; Heller and Plamper, *Personality Cults in Stalinism*; Plamper, *The Stalin Cult*; Ennker and Hein-Kircher, *Der Führer im Europa*, and "Communism and the Leader Cult."

ritual practices that endorsed the cultic imagery of Communist notables. In addition, cults are often treated as singular phenomena by historians. They are normally analyzed in relation to a single leader, dictator, monarch, or emperor and are interpreted—in modern times at least—as the irrational side of personalized executive power. This preoccupation with a single leader is also reflected in the way the phenomenon was conceptualized in Bolshevik political rhetoric: the "cult of personality."[44] The term originated in the language of the Communist movement, and it entered popular parlance after Khrushchev's famous revelations about Stalin at the Twentieth Congress of the CPSU in February 1956. It was also used extensively in postwar Kremlinology to highlight the nature of the Soviet leader's rule.[45] The analytical value of the notion has recently been criticized by a number of historians, although some of the alternative concepts suggested ("the cult of the number one") seem equally imprecise, as they retain the focus on the individual leader.[46] One of the main problems with the term—leaving aside the fact that very little was personal about the "cult of personality"—is that it has, for a long time, obscured important aspects of the phenomenon. Stalinist leader cults were not isolated phenomena; they formed an integrated, hierarchical system. Moreover, the systemic dimension of leader worship was not an accidental development: the cult was constructed as a system from the beginning. The worship of Stalin emerged in the framework of the twin cults of Lenin and Stalin, and while Stalin's veneration overshadowed that of Lenin by the late 1930s, a number of lesser cults had developed by that time around members of Stalin's inner circle.[47] The Sovietization of Eastern Europe triggered the further extension of the Soviet ritual system to the countries under Communist rule.

---

[44] The term "Bonapartism" was also used occasionally. Both concepts emerged from the language of the working-class movement.

[45] For a brief history of the term, see Plamper, "Introduction"; Apor, "Communist Leader Cults"; and Apor, "Kommunikáció és rítusnyelv: 'személyi kultusz' és kommunista nyelvhasználat," *Korunk* 3, no. 3 (2010): 69–75.

[46] The concept is borrowed from Arthur Koestler's novel *Darkness at Noon*, and its use was advocated most recently by Yves Cohen. See Yves Cohen, "The Cult of Number One in an Age of Leaders," *Kritika: Explorations in Russian and Eurasian History* 8, no. 3 (2007): 597–634.

[47] On the spreading of the cult in the peripheries, see Chapter 2 in Getty, *Practicing Stalinism*; Rolf, "Working towards the Centre"; and Rolf, "The Leader's Many Bodies." See also Ennker, "The Stalin Cult."

The highest echelons of the international system of Stalinist leader cults were occupied by the spiritual forefathers of Communism (Marx and Engels), the actual founding father of the Soviet Union (Lenin), and "the Lenin of today" (Stalin). Their position in the symbolic hierarchy of the Stalinist pantheon remained incontestable. The second rung of the "ladder of cults"—as Władysław Gomułka once labeled the system—was occupied by Stalin's entourage and the leaders of international Communist parties.[48] Their status depended essentially on their place in Stalin's favor, and—more generally—on their relationship with the Soviet leadership. The most prominent representatives of the satellite countries were constantly compared to Stalin's genius in cultic texts, which reaffirmed their subordinate role in the Soviet hierarchy of heroes. The image of the Soviet leader as a larger-than-life figure who triumphed over Nazi Germany functioned as the most palpable reminder of local Party leaders' inferior position in the symbolic system. Apart from the international hierarchy of cults headed by Stalin, a similar hierarchy existed in every country of the bloc. The representations of military figures assumed cultic proportions in the case of Konstantin Rokossovsky in Poland or Mihály Farkas in Hungary, but certain prominent members of the national leaderships were also treated as exalted figures (such as Ana Pauker in Romania).[49]

While heroic images of some of the lesser figures in the Party leadership were promoted, the domestic boundaries of the Stalinist ritual system remained unclear: some cults were tolerated, while others were suppressed. The regime, despite its monumental investment in the construction of new idols, actually remained uneasy about the unintended consequences of cult-building and the spontaneous, uncontrolled spread of cultic discourse. But the cult spread fast: the Stalin cult was a powerful example that was emulated in a micro-environment, resulting in the tendency to reproduce cultic practices at the lower levels of the institutional hierarchy. The practice was dubbed "leaderism" in Party-speak and was

---

[48] Zbigniew Brzezinski, *The Soviet Bloc: Unity and Conflict* (Cambridge, MA: Harvard University Press, 1967), 65.

[49] On the cult of Rokossovsky, see Jan C. Behrends, "Rokossowski Coming Home: The Making and Breaking of an (Inter-)national Hero in Stalinist Poland, 1949–1956," *Hungarian Historical Review* 5, no. 4 (2016): 767–89.

viewed with suspicion at the top.⁵⁰ "Leaderism," however, was apparent at all levels of the Soviet administration.⁵¹ The promotion of lesser leaders was usually connected to abuses of power and to a pragmatic, materialistic agenda to gain access to rare resources. Thus the appearance of self-acclaimed idols in local Party committees, factory managements, or collective farms was not endorsed by the Party. Since producing too many heroic figures could potentially devalue the mythical persona of Party leaders, the regime sought to curb such phenomena: unsanctioned cults at the lower end of the Party bureaucracy were not meant to become part of the ritual system. Therefore, the Stalinist period was not only an era of excessive myth construction; it also witnessed a constant struggle against potentially subversive cultic practices. Paradoxically, cult-building and the suppression of cultic phenomena both featured the political theater of Communist regimes.

The tendency among historians to focus on the representations of leaders endorsed the perception that the constructed personae of the mini-Stalins in the Soviet bloc were merely clones of Stalin's mythical image. An analysis of the textual or visual depictions of Communist politicians might support this interpretation. However, if one takes into consideration the specific national features of leader worship, the picture becomes considerably more complex. While the Stalin myth remained the prime example to follow, the cults of lesser Party leaders were somewhat dissimilar. Sovietization brought about the introduction of an integrated, international system of myths and cults, but cultic practices and the cultic language emerged with varying intensity in the countries of the Soviet bloc. In some cases the conditions were more favorable to the leader's veneration than in others. There were Party secretaries who promoted the exaltation of their own personality enthusiastically, while others remained relatively modest. The veneration of Bierut and Gheorghiu-Dej, for example, was less intense than the cults of Rákosi and Gottwald, which assumed

---

⁵⁰ "Leaderism" *(vozhdism)* was a general term to depict abuses of power, but its field of reference could also include the sycophantic adulation of lower-level Party functionaries, directors of collective farms or industrial units, etc.

⁵¹ Sheila Fitzpatrick, *Everyday Stalinism: Ordinary Life in Extraordinary Times; Soviet Russia in the 1930s* (Oxford: Oxford University Press, 1999), 28–35; Sheila Fitzpatrick, *Stalin's Peasants: Resistance and Survival in the Russian Village after Collectivization* (New York: Oxford University Press 1994), 174–204.

monumental proportions.⁵² As Arfon Rees has noted, the cult functioned, to an extent, as a barometer of Sovietization, indicating the commitment of the local Party elite to the introduction of Stalinist institutions and political practices.⁵³

Despite the fact that the cults of satellite leaders were modeled primarily on the Stalin cult, they were each, to some degree, distinctive. The problem of adoption versus innovation—or the extent to which such cults were based on the mechanical copying of the Soviet model, and the extent to which they were rooted in specific local traditions—is, in fact, one of the most intriguing aspects of the worship of the "mini-Stalins." While the importance of the Soviet example in the development of cultic practices in the Soviet bloc remains unquestionable, the satellite cults were also shaped significantly by local, national traditions. Communist leaders were compared to historical figures and national heroes, and themes from national mythology were integrated into the imported, Soviet-type leader cult. The adding of national tropes to the Soviet model of leader worship created a certain leeway for the development of each local leader cult. Nonetheless, they all operated under the aegis of the worship of Stalin and remained constrained by it.

One of the most significant differences between the cult of Stalin and the cults of satellite leaders was that Stalin's symbolic authority and his claim to leadership was buttressed by a connection to Lenin. Such a connection never became a central component of the cults of the "lesser gods." This absence partly had to do with the low symbolic capital Lenin's name carried in postwar Central and Eastern Europe. There the local Communist parties attempted to legitimize their status through appeals to national traditions and by forging continuities between the nation's past and the political aspirations of the Party. Moreover, the symbolic authority of local leaders was derived from Stalin—they were all his "best disciples"—and not from Lenin, while their myths were linked more closely to national traditions than to the Bolshevik Revolution of 1917.

---

⁵² Izabella Main, "President of Poland or 'Stalin's Most Faithful Pupil'? The Cult of Bolesław Bierut in Stalinist Poland," in Apor et al., *The Leader Cult*, 179–93; and Alice Mocanescu, "Surviving 1956: Gheorghe Gheorghiu-Dej and the 'Cult of Personality' in Romania," in Ibid., 246–60.

⁵³ Rees, "Leader Cults," 8.

Apart from the marginality of the Lenin connection and the emphatic appeal to national traditions, the cults of the "mini-Stalins" differed from the worship of the Soviet generalissimo mostly in terms of intensity. The sub-cults of satellite leaders never reached the magnitude of the Stalin cult. Cult construction, in general, was less efficient and more contingent than in the realm of Big Brother, and time-consuming projects, such as feature films or monumental statues that portrayed the leader, were rarely undertaken. The cults of local Party secretaries remained primarily on a textual level, and their rites were less integrated into everyday social practices than in the Soviet Union. The relative modesty of the orchestrated veneration of the "lesser gods" correlates with the brevity of their rule and with the swiftness of Sovietization in the context of the Cold War. Due to the time pressure of implementing the Soviet model, the introduction of leader cults in the countries of the bloc was a rapid process and not a gradual evolution, as it had been in Stalin's Russia. In the Soviet Union, the Stalin myth had a stabilizing function, and its promotion tended to be more intense in periods of consolidation than during times of social upheaval (the first Five-Year Plan, the Great Terror, the first phase of World War II). By contrast, in postwar Eastern Europe, cult-building was entangled with other—equally emphatic—political campaigns: industrialization, collectivization, the terror, the Sovietization of culture, and so on. There, the ingredients of the Stalinist political package were implemented all at once, resulting in a congestion of symbolic political practices. The cult, therefore, contributed to the destabilization of the regime and the escalation of systemic crisis in the long run, and it provoked social antagonism rather than popular consent.[54]

The Sovietization of Eastern Europe did not merely entail the sculpting of god-like figures out of ordinary Party functionaries; it altered the

---

[54] System paralysis is a key theme in Gyarmati's recent analysis of the Rákosi era, although he does not assign much significance to the cult in the escalation of the crisis. See György Gyarmati, *A Rákosi-korszak: Rendszerváltó fordulatok évtizede Magyarországon, 1945–1956* (Budapest: ÁBTL-Rubicon, 2011). David Brandenberger's book on Stalinist propaganda—published in the same year—also revolves around the notion of a chaotically managed state on the verge of paralysis. Brandenberger, *Propaganda State in Crisis*. There were remarkable exceptions to this trend, of course. Where the Stalinist practice of exaltation met with genuine popularity and was harmonious with national traditions, the cult became instrumental in ensuring social support. The cults of Tito and Enver Hoxha, for example, successfully challenged the symbolic authority of Stalin and stabilized their respective regimes.

veneration of Stalin too. The cult of the Soviet leader was adjusted to different political cultures and national traditions, and it was also transformed in the process. The local variations of the Stalin myth and the differences in the veneration of his "best disciples" offer a revealing indicator of the willingness of Soviet bloc countries to proceed with the Sovietization project. Gomułka claimed retrospectively (in 1956) that the national Party elites were, in fact, rather reluctant to implement the leader cult but were forced to do so.[55] Such a claim, however, is hard to support with archival sources. Therefore, the extent to which the formulation of cultic figures from the local Party secretaries were influenced by Soviet orders remains unclear. It seems more plausible that the satellite cults emerged partly as a result of self-Sovietization and were to a lesser extent shaped by Soviet directives. The majority of Eastern European Communist leaders had received their ideological training in Moscow, and they were also exposed to the Stalin cult from the 1930s on. Therefore, they subscribed to the veneration of the Soviet leader after World War II without much hesitation. While the lesser cults were created—at least partly—on the initiative of local Party elites, the construction of the Stalin cult in the Soviet imperial borderlands was monitored from the center, Moscow. Thus the Soviet-type leader cult emerged in the satellite states as a combined result of imposed Sovietization and self-Sovietization.

Despite the hierarchical nature of the Soviet symbolic system, the relationship between the Stalin cult and local sub-cults was not just a top-down one. Although the key features of the representation of satellite leaders were determined by the Soviet model, the exportation of the Stalin myth to Central and Eastern Europe gave new life to the Soviet dictator's own cult. There was a degree of competition among the national Party secretaries for Stalin's favor and for the position of "Stalin's best apprentice" in the bloc, which shaped the development of cultic practices in the Soviet borderlands. "Working towards Stalin" thus had an international dimension: national Party elites tried to outdo each other in the veneration of Stalin—exemplified by the celebration of Stalin's seventieth birthday in the region—to demonstrate their unconditional loyalty toward the Soviet Union and its leader. Besides contributing to the further expansion of

---

[55] Brzezinski, *The Soviet Bloc*, 65.

the Stalin cult, the cults in the peripheries also complemented each other. When the secretary of a national Communist Party traveled to "fraternal" countries, for example, he would receive the same enthusiastic veneration as he received at home. Instances of mutual renamings (factories, collective farms, hospitals) demonstrate the international dynamics of the cultic system. By providing symbolic support to a national leader on the international plane, the countries of the Eastern bloc contributed to the maintenance of the phenomenon in local environments.

Hierarchical relations notwithstanding, the Stalinist leader cult was not limited to the countries of the Soviet bloc. The interwar period had already witnessed the emergence of Soviet-type hero worship in the Western European Communist movement, with the rise to power of a new generation of Stalinist leaders, most notably Maurice Thorez in France and Harry Pollitt in the United Kingdom.[56] After Stalin's triumph over Hitler in the "Great Patriotic War," rituals of leader veneration became even more prominent in the day-to-day practices of the respective Communist parties. Stalin remained the central figure in such rituals, but the symbolic authority of Thorez and Pollitt also grew somewhat, while their cults became—loosely—integrated into the Stalinist symbolic hierarchy. But it was not merely diligent self-Sovietization by Western Communist leaders that prompted the escalation of Stalin's cult beyond the boundaries of the Soviet bloc. Victory in the war had secured genuine popularity for the Soviet leader and elicited spontaneous expressions of reverence for him in several European countries (especially in Italy and France). Therefore, the Stalin cult had a remarkable influence on the development of symbolic politics on the European continent in the immediate postwar period.

---

[56] Norman LaPorte and Kevin Morgan, "'Kings among Their Subjects'? Ernst Thälmann, Harry Pollitt and the Leadership Cult as Stalinization," in *Bolshevism, Stalinism and the Comintern: Perspectives on Stalinization, 1917–53*, ed. Norman LaPorte, Kevin Morgan, and Matthew Worley (Basingstoke: Palgrave, 2008), 124–45.

The Stalinist Leader Cult in Hungary

The cult of Rákosi was arguably one of the most pervasive examples of orchestrated adulation in the Soviet bloc. While the cult never came close to reaching the magnitude of the veneration of Stalin, Rákosi's ambition to outshine the other "best disciples" and become the best of the best was clearly manifest in his diligence in promoting the Soviet-type leader cult in Hungary. Nonetheless, the Rákosi cult was integrated into the transnational ritual culture of Sovietized Eastern Europe, and its trajectory was significantly constrained by the hierarchical relations of the Stalinist symbolic system.

After Rákosi's fall, the stage-managed worship of him remained on the margins of Hungarian historiography for a long time. Under János Kádár's administration (1956–1989), historians mostly ignored the symbolic practices of Hungarian Stalinism, or the significance of political rituals was obscured by rigid ideological interpretations of the recent past.[57] It was not until the late 1980s and early 1990s that scholarly interest in the veneration of Communist politicians emerged in Hungary. Features of the cult were analyzed by art historians, literary scholars, sociologists, historians, and even by former propagandists, but book-length studies and systematic assessments of the phenomenon were not produced.[58] While analyses of the Rákosi cult have grown in number since 1989, many aspects of it remain largely unexamined by historians. Such aspects include the origins of cultic practices; the appeal of leader worship to national traditions; the hierarchical stratification of the cult; the connection of

---

[57] A typical example of such an approach is Mihály Korom, "A személyi kultusz néhány kérdése és az európai népi demokráciák," manuscript, MSZMP Politikai Főiskola (Budapest: MSZMP Politikai Főiskola, 1987).

[58] For the most important works that address the cult—apart from memoirs—in detail, see János Nemes, *Rákosi Mátyás születésnapja* (Budapest: Láng, 1988); György Szücs, "Rákosi Mátyás Művek (A szocialista vezető képi megjelenítésének kérdéséhez)," in *Az ostromtól a forradalomig. Adalékok Budapest múltjához 1945–1956*, ed. Zsuzsanna Bencsik and Gábor Kresalek (Budapest: Budapest Főváros Levéltára, 1990), 63–90; Ferenc Hammer, *Diktatúra és vezérkultusz: A magyarországi kommunista diktatúra létrejöttének tudásszociológiai előzményei* (Budapest: Oktatáskutató Intézet, 1992); Ágnes Horváth, "The Nature of the Trickster's Game: An Interpretative Understanding of Communism" (PhD dissertation, European University Institute, Florence, 2000); Gyarmati, *A Rákosi-korszak*, 296–327. See also the relevant chapters in Árpád Pünkösti, *Rákosi a hatalomért 1945–1948* (Budapest: Európa, 1992); and Árpád Pünkösti, *Rákosi a csúcson 1948–1953* (Budapest: Európa, 1996).

the hagiographic representation of the Party secretary with the Bolshevik historical meta-narrative; the spatial dimensions of the cult; and so on. This book is a modest attempt to fill some of these gaps.

The Rákosi myth, like the orchestrated veneration of his colleagues in neighboring countries, was constructed. The making of the cult—and not the textual or iconographic representations of the leader—is, in fact, the central theme of this volume.[59] The individuals and institutions responsible for creating and promoting godlike interpretations of the leader applied three main methods of cult-building. The most essential genre that was used to project mythical images of the Party secretary was the biography, which was heavily exploited in Communist propaganda to promote the Bolshevik version of (Party) history in an accessible—and highly hagiographic—way. The overall appeal of the leader's myth to national traditions was equally significant. Attempts to integrate Communist politicians into the pantheon of national heroes were supposed to broaden the reach of the cult and enhance its mobilizing potential. The ambition to infuse Soviet-type leader worship with elements of Hungarian nationalism went hand-in-hand with the endeavor to create the image of an omnipresent leader. This the regime sought to achieve not only through verbal means, describing him as an ever-present and omniscient figure, but also through visual means, which included the invasion and occupation of symbolic space and the decoration of the Soviet universe with likenesses of the leader. The cardinal significance of biographies, national traditions, and space in the building of the cult are explored in Part 1 of the book.

The formation of the leader's mythical persona was closely supervised, and its public reception was constantly monitored. The regime was anxious to control every aspect of cult construction, and it was curious to know how people perceived and responded to Rákosi's divine imagery. Ultimately, both ambitions failed. Despite every effort to centralize and standardize the manufacturing of cultic products, the cult developed in

---

[59] Historians of the Communist leader cult tend to concur that the cult was made. In his monograph on the Stalin cult, for example, Jan Plamper has analyzed in detail the role of individuals (including Stalin), state institutions, and informal patronage networks in the construction of Stalin portraits. However, he has paid little attention to other cult products and the function of propaganda organs and related Party departments in the coordination of the process of myth-making. Plamper, *The Stalin Cult*, 165–202.

a somewhat spontaneous and uncontrolled way. At the same time, the attempt to capture an accurate picture of societal reactions to the cult yielded less-than-reliable results. Nonetheless, the mechanisms of construction and supervision remained closely tied, linking the spheres of cult production and cult reception. Part 2 of the book investigates this relationship further by analyzing popular responses to the choreographed worship of the Hungarian Party secretary.

Construction was intimately linked to deconstruction as well. The fall or death of prominent Communists was often followed by the elimination of their mythical images, but the struggle against the "cult of personality"—the suppression of "leaderism," in other words—remained an integral part of cult-building in the Stalinist period and was concurrent with the expansion of officially sanctioned ritual practices. Part 3 focuses on the Party's feeble policies to dismantle the Rákosi cult in Hungary after the death of Stalin. The changing power relations in Moscow and in Budapest, the hesitation of the Party bureaucracy to de-sanctify the leader, and Rákosi's reluctance to take the blame for promoting godlike representations of his persona all contributed to the spontaneous and inconsistent way the cult was eliminated.

The Rákosi years in Hungary may seem like a footnote in the global history of Stalinism. However, the organized veneration of the Hungarian dictator offers an important glimpse into the functioning of the Stalinist cultic system at the peripheries of the Soviet sphere of influence and highlights the significance of ritual practices in the process of Sovietization. Moreover, the history of the Rákosi cult points up some of the more generic features of cult-building. Since the discrepancy between the person's actual qualities and his mythical persona could not have been any greater, the orchestrated worship of Rákosi demonstrates the importance of agency and construction in the emergence of cultic phenomena. While spontaneity, personal magnetism, and popularity often play their part in the rise of strong leaders, cults that are deployed with the aim of consolidating power are almost always constructed. The creation of cultic figures involves the production of a set of canonized texts and the introduction of a range of standardized ritual practices, which requires time, planning, resources, institutions, and staff. Since the centralized institutional framework and the degree of political commitment needed to realize such symbolic projects are more likely to emerge in authoritarian regimes than in democratic systems, full-blown cults normally materialize in closed societies and in dictatorial environments.[60] For this reason, parallels with cultic phenomena in democratic contexts will only be considered to a limited extent, although their relevance is acknowledged.

The structure of this book reflects its argument that leader cults are of a constructed nature. The main strategies of building a cultic persona for Rákosi will assume center stage in the discussion; therefore, the chapters will follow a thematic rather than a chronological order. While the three key strategies of cult construction analyzed in this book were key to the apotheosis of the Hungarian Party leader, they were not specific to the Hungarian context. Such strategies, in fact, seem to constitute the core set of the universal toolkit of cult construction. Most cults rely on mythical biographies that justify the leader's bid for power and depict him as the embodiment of the respective political community (nation, party, class, and so on). At the same time, most cults buttress the image of the ever-present and all-seeing ruler with the mass circulation of portraits. The Rákosi cult, therefore, has broader implications: while it demonstrates the importance of myths and rituals in the Sovietization of postwar Hungary, it also sheds light on some of the more universal features of cult-building in modern history.

A Note on Terminology

The book has adopted the term "leader cult" instead of the controversial phrase "cult of personality" to depict the organized veneration of Party leaders. The decision to avoid employing the phrase "cult of personality" as an analytical concept is a conscious one. As a number of scholars have pointed out, the notion is not without problems.[61] It carries immense political—mostly negative—connotations, and it was almost never used

---

[60] As also argued in Daniel Leese, "The Cult of Personality and Symbolic Politics," in *The Oxford Handbook of the History of Communism*, ed. Stephen A. Smith (Oxford: Oxford University Press, 2014), 342.

[61] Plamper, "Introduction"; Cohen, "The Cult of Number One"; and Apor, "Communist Leader Cults."

to refer to the cults of Party leaders at the time when such phenomena actually flourished. Therefore, the construction of one of the most pervasive cults in modern history—the Stalin cult—was never defined as a cult while it was being built. It was due to the impact of Nikita Khrushchev's "secret speech" at the Twentieth Congress of the CPSU that the systematic veneration of Stalin became synonymous with the phrase.[62] However, Khrushchev defined Stalin's "cult of personality" in rather vague terms and used the notion as a cover term. The semantic field of the concept thus included the deification of Party leaders, the abuse of power by a small clique, the purges and the show trials, forced industrialization, and so on. Communist historians, as well as many historians after 1989/1991, continued to define "personality cult" in a remarkably similar way. The concept is described in historical works in a fairly broad and somewhat imprecise way, and it is usually applied as a metaphor to depict the entire Stalinist era.

Those few historians who have reflected critically on the dubious semantic qualities of the term in the past have made valuable attempts to reconstruct the shifts in the meaning of the concept on the basis of ideological/philosophical texts.[63] They have, however, generally overlooked the impact of "Party-speak" on the history of the notion. Therefore, like most Sovietologists, they continued linking the rise of the term to Khrushchev's denunciation of Stalin's sins. The concept, however, had been an essential component of Party language long before 1956 and functioned as a general term of condemnation within the Communist movement.

---

[62] The fact that cult construction involved the denial of the "cult of personality" was not necessarily a sign of the regime's hypocrisy (even if hypocrisy, in general, was part of the way the system functioned). Since its inception, the working-class movement had struggled with the negative connotations the concept conjured up. For example, Hungarian Social Democrats in the nineteenth century, as well as the Communist leaders of the 1919 Hungarian Republic of Soviets, were eager to construct their own pantheon of heroes and mythical forefathers while retaining a critical attitude toward the "cult of the individual." For more details, see Boldizsár Vörös, *"A múltat végképp eltörölni"? Történelmi személyiségek a magyarországi szociáldemokrata és kommunista propagandában 1890–1919* (Budapest: MTA Történettudományi Intézet, 2004).

[63] Jan Plamper, for example, has sketched an outline of the history of the concept in Marxist tradition, focusing on philosophical assessments of the role of great individuals in history, from Karl Kautsky onwards, to Plekhanov, Lenin, Stalin, and finally Khrushchev: Plamper, "Introduction." For a similar approach, see Cohen, "The Cult of Number One," and Pennetier and Pudal, "Stalinism." An attempt to outline the perception of the role of great individuals in Marxist tradition is provided by van Ree, *The Political Thought of Joseph Stalin*.

The accusation of cultivating a "cult of personality," in fact, was a standard way of stigmatizing a political rival in Soviet political culture. The charge could either precede his/her removal or follow the fall (or death) of the Party's leader, when the denunciation of the predecessor was exploited to confer legitimacy on the successors. Moreover, the term "cult of personality" remained part of the vocabulary of "ordinary" denunciation rituals that targeted less prominent representatives of the establishment (local Party dignitaries, factory managers, directors of collective farms, etc.). While the concept continued to feature the symbolic practices of Party life throughout the Stalinist period, its theoretical and ideological importance faded away. Therefore, a closer study of the everyday use of the term in the language variant spoken by Party members—rather than an analysis of ideological treatises—would arguably bring us closer to understanding the function of the term in Bolshevik political culture.[64]

The ritualized usage of the term contributed to the blurring of its meaning. The obscure nature of the concept "personality cult," however, was merely one example of the general semantic vagueness of the language variant spoken by the Party elite and the Party bureaucracy.[65] Nevertheless, using the notion in an unclear, ambiguous way had its advantages. The hollowness of the phrase could be exploited during rituals of criticism/self-criticism, for example, because it enabled the speaker to formulate a vague—and ultimately harmless—critique. The concept's relative frequency in the context of such rituals is partly responsible for the obscure character of the notion.

---

[64] For a more detailed discussion of the use of the term in Party-speak, see Apor, "Communist Leader Cults," 29–36.

[65] Critiques of "Party-speak" have argued that the proliferation of semantic ambiguities resulted in the Party's overall failure to communicate its messages effectively. The regime generally remained incapable of presenting the complex theoretical notions of Marxism to the population, which led to frequent misperceptions of concepts that were fundamental to Bolshevik ideology. For contemporaneous linguistic assessments of the language of the Party, see Iván Fónagy and Katalin Soltész, *A mozgalmi nyelvről* (Budapest: Művelt nép, 1954); and Lajos Lőrincze, "Mozgalmi nyelvünk kérdései és a jó magyar nyelv," in Lajos Lőrincze, *Nyelv és élet* (Budapest: Művelt nép, 1953), 79–99. The semantic emptiness of some of the key concepts of Bolshevik ideology was analyzed in Lóránt Czigány, "Államosított szavaink átvilágítása, avagy szótáríróink diszkrét bája," *Kortárs* 44, no. 7 (1999): 1–32. For a comprehensive discussion of "Soviet imperial language," see Szergej Tóth, "A szovjet birodalmi nyelv, avagy a totalitarizmus grammatikája," *Aetas* 6, no. 1 (1991): 5–39; and Michael Waller, *The Language of Communism: A Commentary* (London: Bodley Head, 1972).

The semantic emptiness and the ritualized use of the phrase "cult of personality" in Party-speak suggest that caution must be exercised when using the term as an analytic category. In fact, the term "leader cult" seems more fitting—and less burdened with political connotations—to describe the orchestrated veneration of prominent political figures in the Soviet context. Since the word "leader" could refer to high-ranking Party officials as well as to local Party notables, the phrase "leader cult" enables us to interpret the worship of the individual Party leader and the hierarchal dimensions of the cultic system under a single conceptual umbrella. Nonetheless, the limitations of the term also have to be acknowledged. "Leader cult" denotes a system of cultic representations and practices that is promoted by a range of institutions with the aim of supporting a certain political agenda through symbolic means. Thus the term fails to encompass general cultic behavior—such as certain religious practices or the exaltation of modern celebrities—outside the political sphere.

PART I

THE CONSTRUCTION OF THE CULT

Chapter 1
The Chronology of Cult Construction (1925–1953)

> "Rákosi's word is the word of history. A milestone, a lighthouse, the hundred-million-horsepower engine of progress."[1]
>
> BÉLA ILLÉS

Rákosi and the Hungarian Communists: The Road to Power

The protagonist of this book, Mátyás Rákosi, was born in 1892 in the Bácska region, in the southern borderlands of the Austro-Hungarian Empire.[2] He was the fourth child of a Jewish merchant who put his family on the path of assimilation. Religion did not play a significant part in the children's upbringing, and the family, originally named Rosenfeld, changed its name to Rákosi in 1904. Despite the father's unsteady financial circumstances, Mátyás received a decent education, and after graduating from secondary school, he continued his studies in Budapest at the Eastern Academy of Commerce. When he arrived at the Academy in 1910, he was already a member of the Hungarian Social Democratic Party, and in the following year, he joined the Galilei Circle, the main debating club of radical intellectuals in early-twentieth-century Budapest. The Budapest years were the formative years for the young Rákosi: he left the capital in 1912 a committed and theoretically trained socialist.[3] His transition from socialism to Communism was triggered by the Great War—most of which he spent in captivity in faraway Siberia—and the Russian Revolution of 1917. When he finally escaped from the prisoner-of-war camp in early 1918, he was already a Bolshevik sympathizer. Nonetheless, according to Rákosi himself, it was

---

[1] *Irodalmi Újság*, December 4, 1951.
[2] For historical assessments of Rákosi's life, see Tibor Hajdu, "Kérdőjelek Rákosi Mátyás hiányzó portréjához," In *Vélemények/Viták A felszabadulás utáni történetünkről*, ed. Sándor Balogh, vol. 1 (Budapest: Kossuth, 1987), 312–18; Nemes, *Rákosi Mátyás születésnapja*; Pünkösti, *Rákosi a csúcson*; Pünkösti, *Rákosi a hatalomért*; Árpád Pünkösti, *Rákosi bukása, száműzetése és halála 1953–1971* (Budapest: Európa, 2001); and István Feitl and Levente Sipos, "Előszó," in Mátyás Rákosi, *Visszaemlékezések 1892–1925*, vol. 1 (Budapest: Napvilág, 2002), vii–lxiii.
[3] Rákosi, *Visszaemlékezések 1892–1925*, vol. 1, 102.

the collapse of the Austro-Hungarian Empire and the bourgeois-democratic revolution in October (called the Aster Revolution) that turned him into a dedicated Communist.[4] He was among the first to join the newly founded Hungarian Party of Communists (KMP) at the end of November 1918, and he participated in the first (failed) Communist experiment in Hungary in 1919. As a competent and enthusiastic organizer, he was entrusted with important tasks during the Hungarian Republic of Soviets (March–August 1919)—his positions included people's commissar of social production—but he never became part of the inner sanctum of the revolutionary government.[5]

After the collapse of the Hungarian Republic of Soviets, Rákosi followed the government to exile in Vienna, where he gained the trust of the leader of the Hungarian Communists, Béla Kun. It was Kun who nominated him to travel to the Soviet Union and report to Lenin about Hungary's experience with the Soviet model. The trip to Moscow was the main catalyst of Rákosi's career in the international Communist movement. As emissary of the Comintern, he was sent on various missions abroad until he was eventually arrested in Budapest in 1925. His trials, discussed in detail in this chapter, brought him fame and earned him the title "the Hungarian Dimitrov." Fame came at a price, though. Rákosi remained in prison for the next fifteen years and was released only in 1940 to the Soviet Union, in exchange for a number of flags that Tsarist Russia captured during the 1848–1849 Hungarian War of Independence. He returned to Moscow as the uncontested leader of the Hungarian Communists, but the new position also meant new challenges. The Stalinist purges of 1936–1938 had decimated the Hungarian Communist community in the Soviet Union—killing Kun as well—and it was Rákosi's job to reorganize what was left of the Party.

The wartime years in exile brought together the future Communist leaders of Hungary—Ernő Gerő, Mihály Farkas, and József Révai—under Rákosi's command. None of them had played a significant role in the events of 1919, and they all assumed prominence after the Party's "elders"

---

[4] Ibid., 281.
[5] His positions during the Hungarian Republic of Soviets included the following: March 21–April 3: deputy people's commissar of commerce; April 3–July 17: people's commissar of social production; July 17–August 1, commander of the Red Guard.

had been eliminated in the Stalinist terror. Gerő was the most experienced member of the group, and he was also well integrated into the Stalinist regime as an NKVD officer. Both Gerő and Farkas were veterans of the Spanish Civil War, whereas Révai had earned his reputation in the Hungarian Communist movement as a journalist and theoretician. They all accepted Rákosi's leadership without much hesitation and contributed to the Soviet war effort against Nazi Germany under his guidance, mostly as propagandists. (Révai, for example, was in charge of the Moscow-based Hungarian-language radio station Radio Kossuth.) The three politicians returned home in late 1944 to rebuild the Party in Hungary and prepare for the return of its leader. When Rákosi arrived in Hungary in late January 1945, very few Party members questioned his claim to leadership.

The Hungarian Communist Party may have gained a new leader in 1945, but it still lacked popular support. The general public's lukewarm reaction to the Party partly had to do with the movement's troubled past in Hungary.[6] The KMP existed for only a few months in 1918–1919 before it was buried under the rubble of the Hungarian Republic of Soviets. Although it was re-founded in 1922 in Vienna, it remained ridden with factionalism. While the Communist émigrés—mostly Kun and Jenő Landler—bickered with one another, the activists who returned to Hungary had difficulties reviving underground Party cells. They failed to transform the short-lived Socialist Workers' Party of Hungary into a legal cover party for the illegal Communist movement in 1925, and they also failed to prevent the infiltration of their ranks by police agents. The Stalinist terror eventually put a brutal end to factionalism, but the Party never managed to garner mass support in Hungary. (Industrial workers seem to have remained loyal to social democracy.) During the war, Party membership plummeted due to mass arrests, and the local leadership, isolated from Moscow, eventually decided to dissolve the KMP in 1943, after the disbandment of the Comintern in the Soviet Union. A new party (the Peace Party) was formed soon thereafter that promoted pacifism and followed the popular-front

---

[6] On the activity of the illegal Communist movement in Hungary in the interwar period, see Bennett Kovrig, *Communism in Hungary: From Kun to Kádár* (Stanford: Hoover Institution Press, 1979), 69–150; Péter Sipos, *Legális és illegális munkásmozgalom Magyarországon 1919–1944* (Budapest: Gondolat, 1988); and Ágnes Szabó, *A Kommunisták Magyarországi Pártja újjászervezése 1919–1925* (Budapest: Kosuth, 1971).

strategy. However, it was not until the arrival of the Red Army and the return of Gerő and Révai in late 1944 that a disciplined, Soviet-type organization, the Hungarian Communist Party (MKP), was established.

The feeble support for the Communist movement in Hungary was closely linked to the rise of anti-Semitism in interwar Hungary and the popular perception of the Communist Party as a Jewish organization.[7] The high proportion of Jewish intellectuals in the Hungarian working-class movement before 1945, their involvement in the events of 1919, and the fact that the postwar leaders of the MKP—Rákosi, Gerő, Farkas, Révai—all came from Jewish, petty-bourgeois backgrounds reaffirmed the image of Communism as a "Jewish conspiracy" in the eyes of many.[8] The Party leadership was very much aware of the persistence of anti-Semitism in Hungarian society. Therefore, postwar Communist propaganda carefully avoided mentioning the Jewish background of the movement's most prominent representatives, and it tried to emphasize the Party's links to Hungarian national traditions instead.

Despite the persistence of popular stereotypes concerning the Communists, the first few months of 1945 witnessed a remarkable increase in the MKP's popularity. Membership skyrocketed: the organization had only a few thousand members in January, but by October, Party membership had reached half a million.[9] The sudden improvement of the Party's perception in Hungarian society was the result of the traumatic experience of the war and the spectacular collapse in late 1944 of the authoritarian establishment headed by Miklós Horthy. The conflict left behind a fragmented society and a country in ruins. Hungary turned into a battlefront in the last phase of the war, resulting in the destruction of factories, homes, livestock, and human life. Over one million Hungarian citizens were killed in World War II—including around 600,000 Jews who perished in the Holocaust—and over 40 percent of the country's national wealth was lost.[10] The

---

[7] Anikó Prepuk, *A zsidóság Közép- és Kelet Európában a 19–20. században* (Debrecen: Csokonai, 1997).

[8] Róbert Szabó, *A kommunista párt és a zsidóság Magyarországon 1945–1956* (Budapest: Windsor, 1997); and Éva Standeisky, *Antiszemitizmusok* (Budapest: Argumentum, 2008).

[9] Ferenc Pölöskei, Jenő Gergely, and Lajos Izsák, eds., *Magyarország története 1918–1990* (Budapest: Korona, 1995), 181.

[10] László Kontler, *A History of Hungary: Millennium in Central Europe* (Basingstoke: Palgrave Macmillan, 2002), 387–88.

plundering of the Wehrmacht and the Red Army provoked the collapse of the economy, which culminated in one of the largest hyperinflations in world history. In this particular historical context, the Communists' call for the country's reconstruction fell on fertile ground. Their slogans advocating equality, land reform, and the punishment of war criminals had a significant appeal, whereas their attempt to include formerly disenfranchised social groups in political affairs brought them genuine popularity. However, it needs to be highlighted that pragmatism—and even opportunism—was also a factor in the unexpected rise of the party's popularity. While the future seemed uncertain in 1945, it was clear to most Hungarians that the Communists would play a significant role in shaping the country's political landscape.

The unexpected success of the Party's mobilization campaign convinced the leadership—including Rákosi—that the first postwar elections in November 1945 would result in a landslide victory for the MKP. To the Communists' great disappointment, the Smallholders' Party (FKgP) won the elections, gaining 57 percent of the votes, while the MKP received a mere 17 percent.[11] For Rákosi this was a bitter pill: in joining the coalition government, his primary ambition was to discredit and eliminate the Party's main political opponent. With the help of the Red Army and Marshal Voroshilov, head of the Allied Control Commission in Hungary, the Communists obtained key positions—including the Ministry of Internal Affairs—in the new government, and they also gained control over the political (secret) police. With such powerful allies supporting the Party's bid for power, Rákosi's "salami tactics" (as he called them) against the Smallholders were bound to succeed. Using a trumped-up case—the so-called "anti-republican conspiracy"—as a pretext, the MKP managed to dissolve the FKgP in 1947, and it expelled the remaining opposition parties from the political arena the following year.

The year 1948 witnessed further dramatic changes. Termed the "Year of the Turn" by Rákosi himself, 1948 was the year that full-blown Sovietization was launched in Hungary.[12] The merger of the MKP and the MSZDP in June of that year effectively eliminated the Social Democrats,

---

[11] Ignác Romsics, *Magyarország története a XX. században* (Budapest: Osiris, 2000), 284.
[12] Mátyás Rákosi, *A fordulat éve* (Budapest: Szikra, 1948).

and it resulted in the creation of a Soviet-type monolithic party, the Hungarian Workers' Party (MDP). The establishment of the new Party accelerated the construction of the Stalinist dictatorship and the obliteration of remaining opposition to Communist rule. The Catholic Church, for example, suffered a severe blow with the nationalization of schools in June 1948 and with the arrest—on Christmas Day—of one of the country's most popular and most ardently anti-Communist public figures, Cardinal József Mindszenty. The Party's political dominance was confirmed by the elections of 1949, which, together with the enactment of the new constitution in August 1949 and the introduction of the Soviet-type system of councils in 1950, constituted the final phase of the Communist takeover in Hungary. The Stalinist economic model—involving central planning, forced industrialization, and the collectivization of agriculture—was also adopted in 1950, with the launching of the First Five-Year Plan. Ultimately, the conclusion of Sovietization cemented Communist rule in Hungary and consolidated Rákosi's position at the apex of the Party.

The cultic biographies of Rákosi published in the 1950s portrayed the Communist politician's path to power as a straightforward, almost organic, process: the rise of a man who was predestined to lead his nation. Rákosi's ascent to prominence, however, owed much to historical contingency. He spent most of the Great War in a prisoner-of-war camp, and he was locked away for most of the interwar period in a Hungarian prison cell. Horthy's prison might have saved Rákosi's life: while his Hungarian comrades were being eliminated in the Stalinist purges of 1936–1938, he was celebrated as a hero of the international Communist movement. When he was finally released from prison, very few potential rivals were left in the Hungarian Communist movement who could challenge his claim to leadership. Chance, therefore, seems to have played a part in Rákosi's political career. But it was not only happenstance and prison bars that led to his rise in the Party. Rákosi was a diligent, committed, and incredibly ambitious Communist. His dedication to the cause, his meticulousness, and his lust for power, therefore, all contributed to his advancement to the position of Hungary's Stalinist dictator.

Cultic Traditions and Modern Personality Cults in Hungary

The cult of the Hungarian Party secretary was introduced in a country that possessed a wide variety of cultic traditions. Hungary had assembled a fairly impressive heroes' pantheon by the time of the Communist takeover in 1948–1949—a pantheon that consisted of a multiplicity of remarkable historical figures. The first Hungarian royal family, the House of Árpád (1000–1301), for example, provided the country with five saints during the centuries, including the founder of the state, Saint Stephen (1000/1001–1038).[13] Besides accumulating a rich collection of legendary rulers and maintaining a vivid tradition of dynastic saint cults, Hungary also displayed a notable tendency to elevate freedom fighters into its heroes' pantheon. The frequency of anti-Ottoman and anti-Habsburg insurrections, uprisings, and rebellions in the early modern era packed Hungarian history with rebels, revolutionaries, and freedom fighters. The traditional admiration of the anti-Habsburg rebel-hero (the *kuruc*) of the seventeenth century culminated in the cult of Prince Ferenc Rákóczi II, leader of the War of Independence against Austria in 1703–1711.[14]

The rise of Hungarian nationalism in the early nineteenth century, and especially the cathartic events of 1848–1849, contributed to the emergence of modern national mythology. The new myths, beliefs, and rituals that came with nationalism extended the heroes' pantheon, and they modified the perception and the imagery of previously canonized historical figures. The re-folklorization of historical personalities (such as Rákóczi) in the nineteenth century, and the proliferation of heroes in the period, were predominantly facilitated by the Revolution and War of Independence of 1848–1849. The struggle—especially its tragic ending—contributed to the emergence of myths, tales, and legends about the individuals involved,

---

[13] The cults of medieval Hungarian monarchs and their use for propaganda purposes has been analyzed in detail by Gábor Klaniczay, *Holy Rulers and Blessed Princesses: Dynastic Cults in Medieval Central Europe* (Cambridge: Cambridge University Press, 2002).

[14] The Rákóczi myth has a substantial literature. See, for example, Kálmán Benda, "A Rákóczi-hagyomány," *Confessio* 9, no. 3 (1985): 54–58; Katalin Mária Kincses, *Kultusz és hagyomány: Tanulmányok a Rákóczi-szabadságharc 300. évfordulójára* (Budapest: Argumentum, 2003); Béla Köpeczi and Ágnes R. Várkonyi, *II. Rákóczi Ferenc* (Budapest: Akadémiai kiadó, 2004), 552–62; and Zoltán Magyar, *Rákóczi a néphagyományban* (Budapest: Osiris, 2000).

and it instantly gave rise to the "cult of 1848."[15] The day of the revolution, March 15, assumed a focal position in the nation's memory, and it spontaneously turned into a national holiday.[16]

The upheaval of 1848–1849 gave the nation a father figure (Lajos Kossuth), military heroes (like the Polish general József Bem), a poet/hero (Sándor Petőfi), and a number of martyr/heroes, such as Count Lajos Batthyány and the thirteen Hungarian generals executed in Arad in October 1849. Popular reverence for Kossuth emerged as the most prominent hero-worship of the time, and it became the most pervasive cult in modern Hungarian history.[17] Kossuth was called "Moses of the Hungarians," "Our Father," "God's Second Son," "the Champion of the Pulpit," "the Messiah of the Nation," "the Hermit of Turin," or "the Holy Elder." On occasion, he was compared to historical personalities such as Genghis Khan and George Washington.[18] He became the symbol, the physical embodiment, of all the endeavors and aims of 1848 and was generally seen as epitomizing the revolution. In the decades following his death, countless memorials and busts to him were erected in public spaces, and hundreds of places across the country were renamed for the deceased leader, reinforcing Kossuth's position as the focal point of Hungarian symbolic space. The cult of Kossuth remained pervasive after the fall of the Dual Monarchy, although it never assumed the status of an official cult promoted by state institutions. It was essentially a cult of resistance and anti-Habsburg sentiments, and it was not incorporated into state-building efforts before 1945. As a symbol of opposition, Kossuth was also a suitable figure for the

---

[15] Mária G. Merva, ed., '48 kultusza. Tanulmányok (Gödöllő: Gödöllői Városi Múzeum, 1999).

[16] On the history of the commemorations of March 15 in Hungary, see András Gerő, "March the Fifteenth," in András Gerő, *Modern Hungarian Society in the Making: The Unfinished Experience* (Budapest-New York: CEU Press, 1995), 238–49. See also András Gerő, *Képzelt történelem. Fejezetek a magyar szimbolikus politika XIX-XX. századi történetéből* (Budapest: Eötvös Kiadó, PolgART, 2004), 163–80; and György Gyarmati, *Március hatalma – a hatalom márciusa: fejezetek március 15. ünneplésének történetéből* (Budapest: Paginarium, 1998).

[17] On Kossuth and his myth, see especially Gerő, *Képzelt történelem*, 53–78. See also Róbert Hermann, "A Kossuth-kultusz," in *"...Leborulok a nemzet nagysága előtt." A Kossuth-hagyaték* (Budapest: Magyar Nemzeti Múzeum, 1995), 155–59; and Gyula Ortutay, *A nép művészete* (Budapest: Gondolat, 1981), 131–43. See also the relevant chapters in István Deák, *The Lawful Revolution: Louis Kossuth and the Hungarians, 1848-1849* (London: Phoenix, 2001); and Róbert Hermann, *Kossuth Lajos élete és kora* (Budapest: Pannonica, 2002).

[18] Gerő, *Képzelt történelem*, 56.

illegal Communist Party. The Party accepted him as an essential part of the national canon and even named the radio station that broadcast from the Soviet Union during World War II "Radio Kossuth." The MKP also actively promoted the Kossuth cult after the war. His name became the country's most frequently chosen street name, but it was also attached to collective farms and Pioneer squads and even became a cigarette brand.

The Kossuth cult was partly a "cult from below," and it functioned as a powerful counter-cult to the officially promoted cultic images of heads of state in Hungary between 1867 and 1945. The official cults of Franz Joseph I and Admiral Miklós Horthy, on the other hand, were both integrated into the nation- and state-building efforts of the respective regimes at the time. The organized reverence for the Habsburg monarch, for example, appealed to sentiments of naive monarchism in Hungarian society, as it tried to instill a widely accepted worship of the ruler.[19] The modernized version of dynastic cult traditions, however, remained largely unsuccessful. The cult of Franz Joseph I was unable to undermine Kossuth's symbolic authority and weaken his image as the father of the nation. It was not the Habsburg emperor whom Hungarian society venerated but the leader of the anti-Habsburg War of Independence.

The Horthy cult was far more successful than the orchestrated worship of Franz Joseph.[20] This had to do with the symbiotic relationship between Horthy's persona and the cult of irredentism it became associated with in the interwar period. The shock of the Trianon Peace Treaty and the breakup of historic Hungary triggered the powerful revival of political symbolism and led to the emergence of a revisionist ideological

---

[19] On Franz Joseph I and his perception in Hungarian society, see Lóránt Czigány, "'Neved ki diccsel ejtené…' Személyi kultusz Ferenc József és Rákosi Mátyás korában," in Lóránt Czigány, *Nézz vissza haraggal!* (Budapest: Gondolat, 1990), 70–98; András Gerő, *Emperor Francis Joseph, King of the Hungarians* (Wayne, NJ: Center for Hungarian Studies and Publications, 2001); and Gerő, *Képzelt történelem*, 83–109. For myths of the good ruler and naive monarchism in the Russian-Soviet context, see Michael Cherniavsky, *Tsar and People: Studies in Russian Myths* (New Haven, CT: Yale University Press, 1961); and White, *Political Culture*, 22–63.

[20] On the Horthy cult, see Dávid Turbucz, *A Horthy-kultusz* (Budapest: MTA Bölcsészettudományi Kutatóközpont, 2016); Dávid Turbucz, "A Horthy-kultusz," in *A magyar jobboldali hagyomány*, ed. Ignác Romsics (Budapest: Osiris, 2009), 138–66; Dávid Turbucz, "A Horthy-kultusz kezdetei," *Múltunk* 54, no. 4 (2009): 156–99; Dávid Turbucz, "Az 'országépítő' kormányzó képének megjelenése az 1920-as évek második felében," *Kommentár*, no. 3 (2011): 32–44; and Tibor Dömötörfi, "A Horthy-kultusz elemei," *História* 12, no. 12 (1990): 23–26.

paradigm with new myths and rituals.[21] Horthy came to personify the idea of revisionism, and he was portrayed as the safeguard of the nation's resurrection. His cult played on existing authoritarian political traditions in Hungarian society and was promoted through the exaltation of his persona in the press, demonstrations of emotional attachment to the leader, acts of renaming, and so on. Although Horthy remained popular among certain social groups, the traumatic experience of World War II largely discredited his mythical representations and led to the disappearance of the regent from Hungarian symbolic space after 1945.[22] Nevertheless, the Communists could not simply ignore the symbolic capital once possessed by his persona, and his cult affected the way Rákosi was represented in the postwar context. The Communists acknowledged the need for a strong leader figure, and they borrowed some patterns of portraying such individuals from the prewar period. At the same time, vestiges of the Horthy cult continued to haunt the Party as fragments of the admiral's cultic image resurfaced in certain parts of Hungarian society in the 1950s, posing a lasting challenge to the Rákosi myth.

The idea of revisionism, the cult of irredentism, and the cult of Horthy constituted a complex self-referential cultic system that was flexible enough to provide space for the emergence of various sub-cults. The glorification of Horthy became the primary model for such practices, and the imagery and vocabulary of his cult were recycled in the cultic representations of lesser leaders. The mid-1930s in particular saw an intensification of cult-building tendencies. Gyula Gömbös's appointment as prime minister in 1932 was followed by the emergence of a short-lived leader cult around him that assumed monumental proportions during and after the elections of 1935.[23] The militant Mussolini fan and former leader of

---

[21] On the cult of irredentism, see Miklós Zeidler, *A magyar irredenta kultusz a két világháború között* (Budapest: Teleki László Alapítvány, 2002). On the ideological significance of revisionism, see Miklós Zeidler, *A revíziós gondolat* (Budapest: Osiris, 2001). On the general ideological framework of interwar Hungary, see Paul A. Hanebrink, *In Defense of Christian Hungary: Religion, Nationalism and Antisemitism, 1890–1944* (Ithaca and London: Cornell University Press, 2006).

[22] However, it has recently gone through a remarkable revival. See Turbucz's blog on the subject: http://horthy-mitosz.blog.hu/ (accessed April 2, 2012).

[23] Jenő Gergely, *Gömbös Gyula. Politikai pályakép* (Budapest: Vince, 2001), 262–66 and 309–15; József Vonyó, "Diktatúra – olasz mintára. A Gömbös-csoport az államról a harmincas évek első felében," in József Vonyó, *Gömbös Gyula és a jobboldali radikalizmus. Tanulmányok* (Budapest: Pannónia, 2001), 52–65.

the Race-Protecting Party was routinely called the *"vezér"* (leader), and he was also occasionally likened to Kossuth. His premature death in 1936 further boosted his cult. Gömbös was called a "prophet" and the "last shaman of his people" by one of his followers in 1942. He was depicted in paintings, and a statue was erected in his honor in Budapest.[24] The exaltation of Gömbös was, however, rapidly swept away by World War II and the subsequent postwar turmoil.

Although there are obvious similarities between the cults of Horthy, Gömbös, and Rákosi—as there would be between any modern leader cults—there were actual continuities in the representation of political leaders in the interwar and the postwar eras. Such continuities were partly responsible for the similar way political figures were portrayed in the media. Thus the Communist leader cult—which was essentially a Soviet import—relied significantly on state- and nation-building practices of the interwar period. One could even claim that the Communist leader cult was—to some extent—a continuation of traditional state- and nation-building strategies in Hungary. The personalization of politics, including the practice of representing political leaders in quasi-mythical terms, had been a prominent feature of modern Hungarian politics before World War II and remained so until 1956. At that point the restored Communist regime under János Kádár deliberately broke with the infamous "cult of personality," and Kádár, despite his growing popularity, never became the subject of an institutionalized cult. Thus one might find more similarities in the representation of political figures between the Horthy and the Rákosi eras than between the Rákosi and Kádár eras.[25]

The 1930s featured a fairly coherent cultic discourse whose codes, linguistic components, and metaphors survived the cataclysm of the war. Representations of Gömbös, for example, closely resemble propagandistic depictions of Rákosi. Gömbös's cultic persona during the 1935 election campaign was tied to the utopian vision of creating a "New World" and a society of the "New Hungarian Man."[26] The central component of this

---

[24] Gergely, *Gömbös*, 309.
[25] One historian even called Kádár a "cult-less" man. János M. Rainer, "Kádár János: A kultusz nélküli ember," *Rubicon* 18, no. 9 (2007): 42–49. The transformation of Communist leader cults will be explored further in the last chapter of the book.
[26] The following section is based on an analysis of two Gömbös papers, *Új Magyarság* and *Függetlenség*, in the election campaign period between March 5 and April 9, 1935.

"New World" was an organic and patriarchal image of the nation, which was often described as a family, a mystical community consisting of citizens united by a unified worldview (nationalism), characterized by collective consciousness, and demonstrating dynamism and power. Gömbös's "New Man" was a young, dynamic, militant, and essentially masculine figure whose identity was to be defined by the idea of national solidarity and the national "community of fate."

The choreography of Gömbös's meetings with the electorate was also portrayed in terms strikingly similar to Rákosi's visits to the countryside a decade later. The prime minister's tours were usually portrayed as joyful celebrations.[27] Gömbös and his close associates were supposedly welcomed with "unprecedented enthusiasm" and "love and understanding" wherever they went. Their arrivals in electoral districts were portrayed as victory marches: they often marched through makeshift triumphal arches decorated with flowers amid a "roaring ovation."[28] Their speeches were followed by long applause, which was meant to illustrate the harmony between the orator and his audience. The press reports describing ceaseless enthusiasm among the population were meant to endorse the idea that the "Hungarian millions" were united under the banner of Gömbös's political program. Such descriptions contributed to the crystallization of the idea that he was the chosen man to lead his nation toward a brighter future. He was portrayed as a statesman who "draws his powers from the thousand-year-old ancestral soil of the Hungarian people," someone who "is nourished by ancient Hungarian spiritual sources," and a man who was linked to the nation through ties of blood.[29] His persona thus assumed a timeless and highly abstract entity: that of the nation's collective consciousness.

The culture of cultic representations in the interwar period did not disappear with the collapse of the Horthy regime in late 1944, and some of its tropes and components were recycled in the postwar era.[30] Therefore,

---

[27] See, for example, *Új Magyarság*, March 27, 1935.

[28] See, for example, *Új Magyarság*, March 19, 1935.

[29] *Függetlenség*, March 10, 1935; and *Függetlenség*, March 27, 1935.

[30] Although the culture of laudatory representations of political leaders did not vanish after the war, the cultic dimensions of leader images were scaled down during the coalition years in 1945–1947.

it seems reasonable to claim that although the Stalinist leader cult originated in the Soviet Union, the language employed to deify the leaders of the Hungarian Communist Party did not originate there. The vocabulary of the Communist leader cult, the verbal techniques of representing leaders, and some of the metaphors used to illustrate the extraordinary qualities of Communist politicians were strikingly similar to the verbal repository of interwar cultic representations. The reliance on apocalyptic and militant imagery, the portrayal of the national community as a family in need of a father figure, and the emphasis on monumental utopian ambitions to create a New World and a New Man must have sounded awfully familiar to postwar Hungarian society. It seems that even as radically different political regimes came and went, the language of cult construction remained relatively unchanged. This indicates that the possibility of creating alternative discourses of cult construction tends to be rather limited. The reason for that has to do partly with the overlap between the languages of religious and political cults. The language of religious veneration continued to define the core vocabulary of modern secular leader cults, and religious (often biblical and apocalyptic) images constituted the foundation of modern cultic representations of political leaders.

The "Hero of the Comintern": The Origins of the Rákosi Cult

Rákosi was probably the first person to have actually used the phrase "Rákosi cult." In a letter written in the Szeged prison on March 26, 1936, he warned his brother, Zoltán Bíró, not to send him letters with too much information on the "Rákosi cult," because the censors would not forward those.[31] Whether Rákosi foresaw the future, with his persona dominating the Hungarian public sphere, is unlikely. Nevertheless, he placed himself in the position of a prophet. "Come what may, the future is ours" were

---

[31] PIL, 720. fond 4. Rákosi had two brothers in the Communist movement, Zoltán and Ferenc. Both had remarkable careers in the Party after 1945, but they changed their name from Rákosi to Bíró. The idea for the change most likely came from Rákosi himself, who seems to have been concerned with the symbolic value of his own name. On the fate of Rákosi's family, see Tibor Molnár, "A Rákosi-család kapcsolata Bácskával," *Archivnet* 14, no. 3 (2014), http://www.archivnet.hu/hetkoznapok/a_rakosicsalad_kapcsolata_bacskaval.html?oldal=1 (accessed April 4, 2016).

among his last words in front of the court that sentenced him to life imprisonment in 1935.[32] Prophet or not, it is no exaggeration to claim that the foundations of the Rákosi cult were already laid down in the interwar period. However, the first attempts to promote the adulation of him originated not in Hungary but in the Soviet Union. The Rákosi trials of 1925–1926 and 1934–1935 were accompanied by intense international propaganda campaigns for his release.[33] The Comintern and the Soviet leaders were hoping to exploit the propaganda value of the trials; thus they looked forward to both procedures with high expectations.[34] The popularization of the "hero of the Comintern" at the time of his trials entailed the organization of countless mass meetings and demonstrations from the Soviet Union to the United States that all expressed solidarity with the Communist leader. Rákosi's release was demanded in thousands of letters addressed to the court in Hungary[35] and by numerous articles in European and Soviet newspapers.[36] Leftist intellectuals of international reputation, such as Romain Rolland, Martin Andersen Nexö, Klara Zetkin, and Henri Barbusse demanded the release of the Hungarian Communist politician. In Moscow, an embellished biography of Rákosi was published—in both Russian and Hungarian—that created grounds for his further exaltation.[37]

The campaign for the popularization of Rákosi was coordinated by Béla Kun and the Comintern, which elected the imprisoned leader to its Executive Committee in 1935.[38] Rákosi received Moscow's directives via his

---

[32] PIL, 720. fond 3. V. kötet.

[33] A collection of documents that attempted to buttress the Rákosi myth was published in the 1950s. Sándor Győrffy, ed., *A Rákosi-per* (Budapest: Szikra 1950).

[34] Pünkösti, *Rákosi a hatalomért*, 18–19.

[35] PIL, 720. fond 3. IV. kötet, VI. kötet.

[36] These included *Populaire* and *Humanite* in France, the *Manchester Guardian* in England, and *Völkischer Kurir* and *Rote Fahne* in Germany. The dramatic tone was essential in such articles. The *Manchester Guardian*, for example, reported on Rákosi's conditions in prison in the following way: "His cries of pain often resound through the whole prison, and it may happen that he receives serious injury by the intolerable strain on muscles or sinews." *Manchester Guardian*, February 1, 1929.

[37] E. Téglás, *Mátyás Rákosi* (Moscow, 1937). A similar propagandistic biography was published about Dimitrov after the Leipzig trial: Stella Dimitrova Blagoeva, *Dimitrov: A Biography* (New York: International Publishers, 1934).

[38] Pünkösti, *Rákosi a csúcson*, 64.

defense lawyers, who forwarded instructions concerning his behavior in front of the court.[39] The workers' meetings in Germany, Belgium, France, and the United States and the letters of solidarity drafted at such meetings were encouraged by the local agents of the Comintern, but the Soviet state also took part in constructing the cultic image of the Hungarian politician. The Soviet Union, in fact, became the center of activities expressing solidarity with Rákosi: articles in *Pravda* and *Izvestia* promoted his persona, and mass meetings demanding his release were organized in Stalin's Russia.[40] The emerging reverence for the Hungarian leader triggered some renaming, including that of a Hungarian brigade that fought in the Spanish Civil War. In the Soviet Union, the Krasanov family, whose daughter was born on the day Rákosi was convicted (February 8, 1935), named her after him.[41] In addition, some cult artifacts appeared while the leader was still in prison. One of Rákosi's fellow inmates in jail, Imre Horváth, allegedly sold some of the Communist leader's prison relics, including his tub and his tableware.[42]

The illegal Communist Party in Hungary (KMP) also tried to exploit the Rákosi trial for propaganda purposes. One of the KMP's leaflets claimed that "the Rákosi trial should be utilized in the class war, and the memory and goal of the [Hungarian] Republic of Soviets [of 1919] should be linked with everyday struggles in a graphic way."[43] The propaganda of the time often referred to the "thousand-year-long struggle" between progress and reaction that continued with the Rákosi trial. Such materials frequently compared Rákosi to Dimitrov[44] and described Rákosi as the real accuser, and not as a convict.

During Rákosi's trials and the fifteen years he spent in prison, Soviet newspapers, as well as leftist European dailies, called him the "leader of

---

[39] Pünkösti, *Rákosi a hatalomért*, 18–19. One of the legal consultants in the trial of 1935 was David Levinson, who was a defense lawyer in the Sacco-Vanzetti trial in the United States but also participated in the Dimitrov trial in Germany.

[40] See Győrffy, *A Rákosi-per*, for more details.

[41] Pünkösti, *Rákosi a hatalomért*, 22–23.

[42] Ibid., 45.

[43] PIL, 677. fond 1/119.

[44] "Hungary has her own Dimitrovs: the Rákosis," PIL, 677. fond 1/120.

workers,"⁴⁵ the well-known or prominent leader of the Hungarian working-class movement,⁴⁶ or "the dauntless and self-sacrificing leader of the Hungarian workers."⁴⁷ Rákosi's behavior before the court, where his words "fell like a sledgehammer" and he "turned the judges' bench into the convict's bench," and his endurance in prison turned him into a hero and the living legend of the Hungarian Communist movement. As Ernő Gerő remarked in 1940 upon Rákosi's release from prison: "His name became the symbol of the brave, self-sacrificing theoretical struggle of the Communist soldier, and his behavior in front of the bourgeois court the example of Bolshevik courage."⁴⁸

As a result of the international propaganda campaign for the release of Rákosi, he emerged with a significant reputation. He became the "Hero of the Comintern" who served as a model of Communist behavior and courage in front of the court. His fortitude turned him into the Horthy regime's accuser, articulating the Communist movement's charges against the reactionary government in public. During his second trial, in 1934–1935, when he had to face the court for his role in the Hungarian Republic of Soviets, he became the personification of the principles and ideas of 1919. The Gömbös government attempted to stigmatize 1919 and Communist ideology in general and turned the Rákosi trial into a media event eagerly followed by the press. Rákosi's defense lawyer aptly remarked that the court's goal was less about passing judgment on the defendant's activity *per se* than about criminalizing and condemning an entire historical event: the Hungarian Republic of Soviets of 1919.⁴⁹ By raising legal charges against a historical narrative embodied by the Communist politician, the Horthy regime contributed—paradoxically—to the emergence of the postwar Rákosi myth in which the leader personified the successes of 1919. Therefore, the image of Rákosi as the leader of the 1919 Hungarian Republic of Soviets did not first appear in Communist propaganda—Kun, the actual leader, had not yet been purged in the Soviet Union—but was

---

[45] "Dimitrov Rákosi Mátyásért," in Győrffy, *A Rákosi-per*, 228.
[46] *Pravda*, November 5 and 7, 1940, in Győrffy, *A Rákosi-per*, 560, 562.
[47] "Szabadítsátok ki Rákosi Mátyást!" *Sarló és Kalapács*, November 15, 1935, in Győrffy, *A Rákosi-per*, 468–69.
[48] Ernő Gerő, "Rákosi Mátyás kiszabadult," *Új Hang*, December 1940, in Győrffy, *A Rákosi-per*, 564.
[49] PIL, 720. fond 3. III. kötet.

suggested unintentionally by the propaganda of the enemy: the Horthy regime.[50]

Rákosi's image as the hero of the international working-class movement emerged in parallel with similar cults around Dimitrov, Dolores Ibarruri, Ernst Thälmann, Antonio Gramsci, and others. International Communist leaders who were not in power were treated as exceptional figures in the respective movements, similarly to how Bolshevik leaders were portrayed by Soviet propaganda. Entry to the international pantheon of Communist heroes in the Stalinist period was most often linked to a trial in front of a "reactionary" tribunal. The example was set by the 1933 Dimitrov trial in Leipzig, and the representations of subsequent trials against Communist politicians followed the same model. Rákosi was compared to Dimitrov during his second trial; the Finnish Communist Toivo Antikainen earned the title "Dimitrov of the Nordic countries" when he was sentenced to life imprisonment in 1934; and even Luis Carlos Prestes in distant Brazil considered it vital to follow the example of the Bulgarian Communist.[51] Arrests and trials thus became essential components of the cults of Comintern heroes in the interwar period, which also explains why such events were central to the hagiographies of Stalinist leaders after 1945. Trials were not indispensable in the creation of cults, however. The most notable example of a hero myth without an actual show trial was the cult around the German Communist Ernst Thälmann (the Nazis could not risk another humiliation after the Dimitrov affair); other examples include Otto Kuusinen in Finland and Tom Mann in Britain.[52]

---

[50] A collection of documents on Stalinist purges in the Comintern, including the Kun case: William J. Chase, *Enemies within the Gates? The Comintern and the Stalinist Repression, 1934–1939* (New Haven, CT: Yale University Press, 2001).

[51] Tauno Saarela, "Dead Martyrs and Living Leaders: The Cult of the Individual within Finnish Communism," in "Communism and the Leader Cult," 35; and Marco Aurélio Santana, "Re-Imagining the Cavalier of Hope: The Brazilian Communist Party and the Images of Luis Carlos Prestes," in "Communism and the Leader Cult," 110–28.

[52] On the Thälmann cult, see René Börrnert, *Wie Ernst Thälmann treu und kühn! Das Thälmann-Bild der SED in Erziehungsalltag der DDR* (Bad Heilbrunn: J. Klinkhardt 2004); and Anette Leo, "'Deutschlands unsterblicher Sohn...' Der Held des Widerstands Ernst Thälmann," in Satjukow and Gries, *Sozialistische Helden*, 101–14. See also the relevant chapters of Alan L. Nothnagle, *Building the East German Myth: Historical Mythology and Youth Propaganda in the German Democratic Republic, 1945–1989* (Ann Arbor: University of Michigan Press, 1999). For the cult of Tom Mann in the Communist Party of Great Britain, see Antony Howe, "'Our

The Comintern's role in encouraging the founding of Communist hero cults across Europe seems to have been instrumental, although research on the mechanisms and the dynamics of the process is scarce. Some historians claim that Moscow had a significant impact on the shaping of the cults of Pollitt and Mann in Britain and that Comintern agents played an important role in crafting the personae of Thorez in France, Prestes in Brazil, and Edgar Lalmand in Belgium.[53] However, Moscow's exact role in the creation of such cults and the function of the Comintern or the International Red Aid as mediators of cult-building between the Soviet Union and local Communist parties needs to be explored further, primarily on the basis of Soviet archives. While the Comintern's contribution to the proliferation of Communist heroes requires further clarification, one could claim that the transference of Stalinist heroic culture to non-Soviet countries had begun well before World War II. In addition, the glorification of non-Soviet Communist leader figures emerged in countries that witnessed a flourishing cult of authoritarian leader personalities: Franco in Spain, Hitler in Germany, Mussolini in Italy, Piłsudski in Poland, or Horthy in Hungary. In a sense, the cults of Comintern heroes functioned as counter-cults in a wider European context—they were supposed to challenge the symbolic authority of "reactionary" regimes and their leaders. Jan Plamper is right in pointing out that leader cults in the interwar period were relational (i.e., Stalin vs. Hitler or Churchill), but it also needs to be highlighted that not just individual leaders but entire cultic systems were competing with each other at the time.[54] The international system

---

Only Ornament': Tom Mann and British Communist 'Hagiography,'" in "Communism and the Leader Cult," 91–109.

[53] On Mann, see Howe, "Our Only Ornament." For the cult of Pollitt, see LaPorte and Morgan, "Kings among Their Subjects." For Lalmand, see José Gotovitch, "Construction and Deconstruction of a Cult: Edgar Lalmand and the Communist Party of Belgium," in "Communism and the Leader Cult," 128–52. The author claims that Comintern agent Andor Berei effectively created the cult around Lalmand, and that in France, Eugéne Fried "installed the charismatic Thorez as leader, and promoted the growth of his personality cult." Gotovich, "Construction and Deconstruction of a Cult," 135.

[54] Plamper, *The Stalin Cult*, 14–15. Cults, in fact, are always relational. Cult figures are normally contrasted with a "negative Other," a villain who represents the antithesis of all the positive values the leader stands for. In Stalinist political culture Trotsky emerged as Stalin's nemesis, but he was replaced by Tito in Soviet propaganda after 1948. In Communist Hungary, László Rajk, Mindszenty, and Horthy emerged as Rákosi's arch-villains in official communications. The parallel cults of Franz Joseph and Lajos Kossuth in late-nineteenth-century Hungary offer further insights into the dynamic relationship between cults and counter-cults.

of Communist cults was an expansion of Stalinist heroic culture, and it formed a more coherent and unified system than its right-wing authoritarian counterpart. The latter was more focused on the leader figure in a national context, and its international dimensions were less remarkable. The cults of Communist leaders also differed from the cults of Nazi or fascist leaders in some other respects. Nazi and fascist rituals and cultic practices made a strong appeal to emotions and the irrational. The public appearances of leaders were carefully staged, the speeches were dramatic, and the postures were cinematic.[55] While Communist leader cults also had a remarkable affective dimension—Stalin's image as a father, for example—they made a strong appeal to reason (science and planning) and—unlike the pompous Nazi and fascist cults—to modesty and puritanism.[56] In addition, peace and calm emerged as the dominant attributes of Communist leaders, as opposed to the violence and masculine virility in the representations of fascist politicians. The Rákosi myth, as it crystallized in the mid-1930s, became part of the international system of Communist hero cults, and as such, it contributed to the Stalinist offensive to challenge the growing dominance of right-wing authoritarian regimes on the symbolic battlefield.

The Cult in the Party (1945–1947)

The Rákosi myth that emerged in the interwar period became a central component of postwar Communist propaganda—although in a somewhat modified form. The cult of the Comintern hero, which was crafted in the Soviet Union for an international audience and was used in the universal symbolic warfare against fascism, was gradually transformed into a cult of a Soviet-type Party leader. As such, it was based primarily on the model created by Stalin worship, and although it remained a part of the transnational system of Communist cults, it was now redesigned for a more limited, national audience. Thus Hungarian national and cultic traditions became more systematically integrated into the imagery of Rákosi after 1945.

---

[55] Simonetta Falasca-Zamponi, "The 'Culture' of Personality: Mussolini and the Cinematic Imagination," in Heller and Plamper, *Personality Cults in Stalinism*, 83–108.
[56] Rees, "Leader Cults," 16–17.

The year 1945 is usually perceived as a watershed in Hungarian history. However, the endurance of cultic patterns of leader representations in the creation of political identities and in the process of state-building seems to indicate that 1945 was, ultimately, not such a radical break. Moreover, cultic representations of Rákosi featured prominently in Communist newspapers during the coalition years of 1945–1947; thus the foundations of his orchestrated worship had been laid down well before the solidification of the Party-state in 1948–1949.[57] One could certainly identify a cult within the Communist Party in the immediate postwar period, but the cultic image of the leader was also meant to appeal to a more general audience through national leverage. The cult phenomenon, however, was not restricted to Rákosi alone: although he was portrayed as the indisputable leader of the Party and was already described in this period as the "leader" (*vezér*), "our father" (*édesapánk*), and "teacher" (*tanító*), other Communist leaders were also presented in laudatory terms in Communist newspapers. Cult-building in the period was not yet institutionalized either. The most important medium to transmit the embellished images of the leader was the Communist newspapers, primarily *Szabad Nép*. Communist propaganda at the time was not yet dominated by the leader's persona; its primary goal was to increase support for the Party by exploiting the popular enthusiasm of the postwar reconstruction.

The term "manufactured charisma" seems fitting to describe the construction of the Rákosi myth. Rákosi was far from being a physically attractive person; therefore creating a positive image for him required remarkable efforts. Thus the fact that his cult reached such magnitude should be considered a notable achievement of Communist propaganda. The Hungarian Party leader's physical appearance initially disappointed society. He was a small man (around 155–157 cm tall), fairly bulky, with long arms, a short neck, and a sizeable, totally bald, head.[58] Contemporaries remembered him, for instance, as an egghead, bald as a billiard ball, and an "obese Napoleon."[59] His oratorical skills were not particularly

---

[57] Commentators in the media usually claim—wrongly—that the cult only kicked off in 1948–1949. Such opinions were articulated most recently in the television program Ősök tere: http://mno.hu/kereses/?search_txt=R%C3%A1kosi&ujkeres=1&mire=video&to_y=2012&to_m=09&to_d=20&from_y=2011&from_m=09&from_d=20 (accessed September 20, 2012).

[58] Pünkösti, *Rákosi a hatalomért*, 36.

[59] Ibid., 37.

remarkable either: he spoke in a rather nasal voice and with an unusual accent. Although Rákosi's image seems to have lacked any aesthetic appeal, his personality had a certain magnetism, as many contemporaries often noted. He was known for his exceptional memory, his education, and for a certain intellectual charm that captivated even some of his political opponents. During a Hungarian diplomatic delegation's 1946 tour of Europe and the United States, for example, the local media often described Rákosi in a positive light.[60]

Although the exaltation of Rákosi before World War II had a different function than after the Communist takeover in Hungary, the discursive base of his persona had nevertheless been created in the interwar period. Before 1945 he was usually portrayed as a typical hero figure, a professional revolutionary willing to sacrifice his life for the labor movement. After 1945, Rákosi was assigned a new role: that of a Soviet-type leader and a father figure of the Stalinist "great family." Due to the prewar origins of the Rákosi myth, the change of imagery was not so drastic. The myth of the Rákosi trials, in fact, remained the cornerstone of the transforming cult. The aura of symbolic authority that Rákosi had gained during his trials made him the incontestable leader of the Hungarian Communist movement and continued to fuel the engine of cult construction.[61] The myth of the trials was sustained after 1945 by one of the most important cult relics of the time, Zoltán Vas's prison diary *Tizenhat év fegyházban* (Sixteen Years in Prison).[62] The diary was first published in the Soviet Union in 1940 and was published again in Hungary as early as 1945. The book, republished almost every year between 1945 and 1953, provides a dramatic account of the first Rákosi trial (1925) and the years Rákosi and Vas spent together as prisoners in Vác. Because it was the first cult product produced in Hungary after 1945, Vas's diary became the prime inspiration of cultic representations of the Communist leader.

---

[60] Ibid., 195–98; Mátyás Rákosi, *Visszaemlékezések 1940–1956*, vol. 1 (Budapest: Napvilág, 1997), 278–90.

[61] The Hungarian Communist émigrés who survived the purges looked forward to Rákosi's arrival in the Soviet Union in 1940 with high expectations and regarded him as the potential figure who could reorganize the shattered Party. Katalin Petrák, *Magyarok a Szovjetunióban 1922–1945* (Budapest: Napvilág, 2000), 335–41.

[62] Zoltán Vas, *Tizenhat év fegyházban* (Budapest: Szikra, 1951).

The implementation of the Soviet leader cult discourse after the war was also eased by the fact that the majority of the Communist political elite—having been trained in Moscow—was already accustomed to using the vocabulary of the cult and was willing to contribute to its adoption in the Hungarian context. The second-in-command of the Party, Ernő Gerő, began to call Rákosi "the leader" from early 1945 on, and if we can believe the reminiscences of Márton Vas—the son of Zoltán Vas—the Politburo decided after the first postwar May 1 demonstrations to launch the cult of Rákosi onto the public sphere. At an informal meeting, the Politburo members discussed the pragmatic aspects of creating a leader figure for the Party, someone who could mobilize the population to advance the MKP's goals.

> We have just decided that in the future it would only be possible to hail the Party and Rákosi. The Party is Rákosi, Rákosi is the Party. He is the leader of the people. The Politburo declared that there is a need for a leader like Horthy, Lenin, Stalin, whom the people could follow.[63]

Although other sources do not indicate such a blatantly pragmatic attitude to cult-building in the Party leadership, the Rákosi myth was exploited to strengthen Party unity from very early on. One regional Party secretary, for example, already compared Rákosi to the Messiah in 1945.[64] Another one called him "the great leader of the Hungarian proletariat" in February 1945, barely a month after Rákosi had returned to Hungary.[65]

The core myth of the Rákosi cult that emerged in the interwar period was gradually expanded in the postwar years to include the achievements of reconstruction, which Communist propaganda systematically accredited to Rákosi. One of the primary methods of popularizing the leader of the Party, in fact, was the association of achievements with his name. Following the example of the Stalin cult, Rákosi and other leaders were systematically—and often undeservedly—credited for realizing certain political and economic goals that were achieved through collective effort.[66]

---

[63] Pünkösti, *Rákosi a hatalomért*, 112–13.
[64] Ibid., 83.
[65] *Szabad Magyarország*, February 28, 1945.
[66] On the technique of "success attribution" in the Soviet context, see Gill, "The Soviet Leader Cult."

Ernő Gerő, for example, was frequently called "*a hídverő*" (the bridge constructor) for directing the rebuilding of the bridges over the Danube that the retreating German army had blown up in 1945. Rákosi's name was also linked to the accomplishments of reconstruction.[67] As early as March 1945, he was described by *Szabad Magyarország* as "the watchful director of the struggle for the country's democratic reconstruction."[68] Communist propaganda ascribed the land distribution reform of 1945 to the MKP leader (as well as minister of agriculture Imre Nagy, who would become in 1953 the greatest political rival of Rákosi), and he was hailed as the "father of the forint" after the introduction of the new currency in August 1946.[69] With the intensification of leader-centered propaganda in 1947, the practice of attributing political achievements to Rákosi became routine. The Party secretary was praised for uncovering the "anti-republican conspiracy" in 1947, for the return of the prisoners of war from the Soviet Union (in that case with good reason), and for the settlement of Hungarian refugees expelled from Czechoslovakia.[70]

The land distribution reform, though it was directed by Imre Nagy and was also supported by the National Peasant Party and the Smallholders' Party, became the first political achievement after 1945 that Communist propaganda gradually attributed to Rákosi. "Blessed should be the name of he who has granted us land," a delegation of farmers from Szolnok County told Rákosi in early March, according to *Szabad Nép*.[71] The land reform also provided an exceptional opportunity to indicate Rákosi's prophetic qualities, since he had claimed in front of the court in 1926 that "land will only be distributed in Hungary by the Communists!"[72]

---

[67] On the history of Party conflicts in the coalition era, see Lajos Izsák, *A koalíció évei Magyarországon 1944–1948* (Budapest: Kozmosz könyvek, 1986); Mária Palasik, *Chess Game for Democracy: Hungary between East and West, 1944–1947* (Montréal: McGill-Queen's University Press, 2011); János M. Rainer and Éva Standeisky, eds., *A demokrácia reménye: Magyarország, 1945* (Budapest: 1956-os Intézet, 2005); and István Vida, *Koalíció és pártharcok 1945–1948* (Budapest: Magvető, 1986).

[68] *Szabad Magyarország*, March 4, 1945.

[69] For the stabilization of the currency, see Sándor Ausch, *Az 1945–1946. évi infláció és stabilizáció* (Budapest: Kossuth, 1958).

[70] On postwar migration in Hungary, see Ágnes Tóth, *Telepítések Magyarországon 1945–1948 között. A németek kitelepítése, a belső népmozgások és a szlovák-magyar lakosságcsere összefüggései* (Kecskemét: Bács-Kiskun Megyei Önkormányzat Levéltára, 1993).

[71] *Szabad Nép*, March 9, 1945.

[72] Győrffy, *A Rákosi-per*, 129.

The sentence became one of Rákosi's most frequently cited statements, and it later reappeared in newspaper articles and literary eulogies and was quoted at mass meetings and demonstrations. The first publication to collect Rákosi's writings and speeches (from the interwar period) also underlined the leader's image as a prophet. The reviews of the book, *A magyar jövőért* (For the Hungarian Future, 1945), portrayed Rákosi as an all-knowing seer. One reviewer in *Szabad Nép* remarked: "those who read Rákosi's book carefully would realize that what the Communist Party predicted years ago has now been accomplished." Consequently, the book "highlights the way to the future."[73]

Aside from Rákosi's involvement in the land reform, Communist propaganda also exploited his role in the return of Hungarian prisoners of war from the Soviet Union. Rákosi's correspondence with Stalin on the matter was made public to accentuate his role,[74] and press reports on the homecoming of former prisoners emphasized the outbursts of gratitude toward the MKP leader. (The theme was also portrayed frequently by political posters at the time.) In one such report, an old lady thanked the Party secretary for the return of her sons from captivity:

> An eighty-year-old, gray-haired matron whose two sons had returned from captivity the day before handed over a beautiful milk loaf: "Please accept it," she wept into the microphone. "I woke up at dawn, I kneaded it myself, I baked it, and I have come here on foot, just to thank you for my sons. God bless you for that . . ." Thousands and thousands of women were crying together with the happy peasant granny.[75]

On another occasion, in the village of Bácsalmás, where Rákosi was greeted with gifts—sheep, pigs, ducks, and so on—an old lady cried out: "Long live Mátyás, liberator of the captives!" which was followed by "enormous cheering and applause."[76]

The merging of Rákosi's name with political achievements promoted the image of an all-knowing, omnipotent leader. The idea that the leader was aware of and cared for even the smallest problems of the people was

---

[73] *Szabad Nép*, June 10, 1945.
[74] Rákosi, *Visszaemlékezések 1940–1956*, vol. 1, 212–13.
[75] *Szabad Nép*, August 12, 1947.
[76] *Szabad Nép*, July 1, 1947.

the logical conclusion of crediting all positive achievements to the Party secretary. This image was strengthened by the publication of letters to Rákosi that usually requested the leader's help in various matters. The press also published Rákosi's responses to such petitions. Although such letters—or at least some of them—might have been the fabrications of zealous journalists and propagandists, a substantial number of the published requests were undoubtedly authentic. On one occasion, a small girl, Ida Csombor from Jászjákóhalma, asked "Uncle Rákosi" to provide her with school textbooks, because her family was poor: "I turn to you because I know that you help every child of the proletariat."[77] Rákosi allocated 100 forints to the girl's family to purchase the necessary books. In another case, as reported in *Szabad Nép*, the parish priest of Tápiószentmárton asked for the leader's help in replacing the lost bell of the local church.

> "We have heard that Mr. Vice-Prime Minister has retrieved the bells of so many villages before. Ours has gone missing too." "The bell will be recovered," promised Rákosi.[78]

Many letters to the leader reflected on the political events of the coalition period. Such letters, besides cursing "reactionaries," expressed the authors' gratitude to the leader for making the right political decisions. The letters published in the first few months of 1947, for example, constantly demanded the execution of those convicted of the "anti-republican conspiracy" and thanked Rákosi for uncovering the plot.[79] Indeed, by the late coalition period, the element of gratitude emerged as a major trope in letters to the leader. Moreover, in reports about popular reactions to his public appearances, gratitude—in the form of applause and chanting—also prevailed. Although the Rákosi cult was still confined to the Communist Party, the press already promoted behavioral norms and emotions that the population was supposed to emulate in the leader's proximity: gratitude and love.

---

[77] *Szabad Nép*, January 9, 1947.
[78] *Szabad Nép*, August 19, 1947.
[79] On the "conspiracy," see Mária Palasik, "A jogállam csapdái Magyarországon 1947 első felében. (A Magyar Közösség pere mint eszköz a kisgazdapárt hatalomból történő kiszorításához)," *Századok* 125, no. 6 (1995): 1305–35; István Vida, "A Magyar Közösség és a Kisgazdapárt," *Történelmi Szemle* 12, no. 1 (1970): 111–24.

Rákosi on Stage

In the coalition period, Rákosi's cult was constructed primarily on a textual level, but during the same era, the foundations of cult rituals were also laid. Apart from applying a wide range of textual techniques to promote Rákosi's image as an esteemed national politician, the staging of the leader also gained a prominent role in the creation of the cult. Rákosi's public appearances were carefully planned and were represented in the press through the use of cultic vocabulary. The meetings between Rákosi and the people gradually assumed a ritualized format, and the repetitive nature of reports about such events also paved the way for the ritualization of the relationship between the leader and the led.

The May 1 celebrations in Budapest, organized under the aegis of the coalition, became Rákosi's first noteworthy public appearance after his return to the country from the Soviet Union. *Szabad Nép* described the demonstration using Soviet-style rhetoric and called it a "single stream of fire." The newspaper emphasized that the monumental portraits of Lenin and Stalin dominated the spectacle and that pictures of Rákosi were also carried by the people among the photos of the leaders of the coalition parties. The audience and the atmosphere seemed to encourage an impressive debut. It was no wonder that *Szabad Nép* reported about Rákosi's entry in a sensationalized way:

> The leader of the Hungarian Communist Party, Mátyás Rákosi, stepped onto the tribune. He was welcomed with immense enthusiasm. "Long live Rákosi! Long live Rákosi!" resounded from the crowd, placed in the huge square, for minutes. "Freedom!" Comrade Rákosi began his speech and hundreds of thousands roared back from every corner of the square: "Freedom!"[80]

The newspaper published the leader's speech in full, along with the real or fictitious reactions of the audience. According to the journalists, the people responded to the speech with "applause," "thunderous acclaim," "Long live Rákosi!" "sustained cheering and applause," "endless hurrahs," and so on. Such phrases suggesting the spectators' great enthusiasm later became obligatory to intersperse in reports not just of Rákosi's speeches but also those of other Communist politicians.[81]

---

[80] *Szabad Nép*, May 3, 1945.

[81] Newspaper reports about applause during the Party leader's speeches have been analyzed by Zsolt Horváth, "Tá-tá tá-ti-tá, tá-ti-ti-tá!" *História* 9, nos. 5–6 (1987), 13–15.

The May 1 demonstration in front of the Parliament in Budapest and its representation in the Communist press was one of the first signs of Rákosi's veneration after the war. Despite the fact that the May 1 demonstration was held jointly by the coalition parties, *Szabad Nép* focused primarily—almost exclusively—on the figure of Rákosi. Later reports on Rákosi's speeches followed the same pattern, and they became important vehicles in the construction of the leader's persona. Whenever Rákosi delivered a speech in public, his words were cited extensively, often in full. The style and the vocabulary of accounts of the May 1 demonstration were gradually standardized in the coalition era and remained unchanged until June 1953, the beginning of the "New Course." The speeches of the *"vezér"* were generally preceded by prolonged ovations, cheering, and "lengthy applause," and there was an outburst of emotion after his address. Those present would normally stand up and express their fervor by enthusiastically clapping and chanting the leader's name. Reports in *Szabad Nép* such as the one about an audience "drunk with joy" that celebrated "the leader of our Party" with "prolonged rhythmic applause" became customary.[82]

As in the Horthy era, mass demonstrations, visits to factories, and tours in the countryside were heavily exploited in crafting a public image for the leader. Descriptions of Rákosi's visits were idealized representations of the meeting of ordinary people and their benevolent leader, and they were supposed to demonstrate his accessibility. Happiness and gratitude were recurring motifs in such accounts, and scenes of little children handing gifts to the leader were common ways to illustrate these emotions at work. The Party secretary was portrayed as a man of the people and an accessible, everyday person in detailed accounts of his encounters with the locals: he would take a walk around the given location (village, factory, etc.), chat with the people about their problems, and sometimes even share their meal with them. His visits, especially those in the countryside, often lasted until sunset.

The standardization of the representations of Rákosi's visits is exemplified by *Szabad Nép*'s account of his trip to two villages, Harta and Hajós. A group of Hungarian refugees expelled from Czechoslovakia had been settled in those villages; thus the visit had a symbolic significance, and

---

[82] *Szabad Nép*, May 23, 1945; *Szabad Nép*, May 9, 1945.

it provided a good opportunity for Communist propaganda to promote the Party leader as a representative of national interests. *Szabad Nép*'s report started with the image of Rákosi as a caring farmer—he was visiting the countryside after all—carefully observing the state of the soil on the way to his destination: "The worries of the good farmer are troubling the mind of Mátyás Rákosi."[83] In Harta a triumphal arch of boughs greeted the "leader of the workers."[84] In his speech Rákosi claimed that the reason for his visit was to observe the situation of the refugees in person "and not just read about it in the reports." He behaved accordingly: he walked around the village, inquired about the locals' everyday difficulties, and "consoled the dispirited." On his way to Hajós, he made an allegedly spontaneous stopover in Kalocsa, supposedly because the people would not let the unexpected visitor pass until they had heard his "improvised" speech. After arriving in Hajós, he had lunch with a new landholder who expressed his gratitude to the Communist leader for the land reform. "I became my own master, and for this I am primarily grateful to the Communists and to Mátyás Rákosi." The tireless leader even had time to pay a visit to a widowed lady who could not attend the meeting because she was lying in her sickbed. The MKP leader left the village at dusk, at the end of a long day.

Szabad Nép's report provided a fairly comprehensive overview of Rákosi's cultic images: he was portrayed as a politician pursuing policies of national significance (the resettlement of Hungarian refugees, land reform), and as a benevolent and accessible father figure who paid attention to the everyday problems (material, emotional, or health-related) of the "little people." At the same time, the newspaper also emphasized the emotional responses that the leader's presence was supposed to trigger: gratitude and happiness.

---

[83] The report is from *Szabad Nép*, April 21, 1947.

[84] Triumphal arches made out of boughs were also widely used during election campaigns in the interwar period.

The Elections of 1947

Accessibility and benevolence emerged as the most significant parts of the leader's persona by the elections of 1947.[85] These elections solidified the image of Rákosi as an approachable, down-to-earth politician and a "man of the people." During the propaganda campaign that preceded one of the most infamous elections in Hungarian history, Rákosi appeared in public often, and many more letters to the Party leader were published by Communist newspapers. In general, the rigged elections of 1947 consolidated the archetypal and paternal imagery of the MKP secretary. Although Rákosi had sporadically been labeled "teacher" in 1945,[86] not until the 1947 elections was the epithet cemented to the imagery of the leader. During the campaign, in August 1947, *Szabad Nép* frequently described the MKP secretary as the "Teacher of the Nation," whose words provided guidance to the Hungarian people and had an inspiring and enlightening effect on those who heard them.[87] Apart from the solidification of the teacher image, the frequency of depictions that portrayed Rákosi as a father figure also increased during the election campaign. An ex-prisoner of war, for example, called Rákosi "our father" and expressed his gratitude for the MKP leader's benevolence.[88] Nevertheless, it was not until 1949 that the epithet "father" was firmly attached to the persona of the Party leader.

As has been indicated, accessibility and benevolence were central themes in the portrayal of Rákosi and other Communist politicians at the time of the elections. Communist newspapers tried to emphasize the humane, personal side of the Party's leaders, for example by presenting their everyday habits or describing their favorite dish or book. Such

---

[85] The elections of 1947 have been analyzed by Károly Szerencsés, *A kékcédulás hadművelet (Választások Magyarországon 1947)* (Budapest: IKVA, 1992). See also Lajos Izsák, "A parlamentarizmus vesztett csatája – 1947," in *Parlamenti választások Magyarországon, 1920–1998*, ed. György Földes and László Hubai (Budapest: Napvilág, 1999), 235–58.

[86] For example: "Mátyás Rákosi appeared among the Hungarian people, who never needed a leader, a teacher, and a guide more desperately than in these times." *Szabad Magyarország*, July 15, 1945.

[87] "The teacher of the nation—one can feel from his words. His words reassure, uplift, and guide, and those who hear them will go home a little cleverer afterwards." *Szabad Nép*, August 22, 1947.

[88] "Together with many of my fellow prisoners of war from the village, I would like to express my gratitude to our father, Rákosi, because this is the only word for the man who is so concerned about our fate." *Szabad Nép*, August 17, 1947.

representations were supposed to underline the image of Communist leaders as "men of the people." One article about Rákosi, written by Géza Losonczy, emphasized his unparalleled work ethic (he allegedly worked from early in the morning until late at night every day), his incredible memory, his mastery of chess, and even his swimming and rowing skills.[89] Losonczy also highlighted Rákosi's unshakable optimism and his sophisticated ("diplomatic" [*tárgyalóképes*]) sense of humor. The image of the benevolent leader who is concerned about the everyday matters of the people was clearly recognizable in Losonczy's appraisal of Rákosi:

> When traveling to mass meetings in the countryside, his car often stops next to the ploughed land, where people work, and it often stops in villages, in front of small shops, where he asks the owner about the prices and the cost of obtaining goods. He usually goes to the market at early dawn, talks to the housewives, looks into their baskets, inquiring about what can be bought, what not, and what the prices are. Sometimes, if he has time to spare, he sets out to visit towns in the countryside, villages, the suburbs of the capital, or mining regions, where he goes into the apartments to see what is being cooked for lunch or for dinner, and what is in the pantry.

Rákosi was presented as a caring leader who was interested in the tiniest details of everyday life and the smallest problems of the "little people" and who wandered around the country like a King Matthias.[90]

> Besides the most important political issues, he pays attention to the smallest things, because he knows that the price of potatoes is often more important for the working little man than the great political problems.

---

[89] *Szabad Nép*, August 10, 1947.

[90] King Matthias I, also known as Matthias Corvinus, was king of Hungary between 1458 and 1490. Despite his far from unproblematic legacy, he has remained one of the most uncontroversial figures in Hungarian collective memory to the present day. Matthias's rule is associated with every possible aspect of the notion of "grandeur": military feats, the spread of high culture (humanism and the Renaissance), and social justice. Matthias's figure also plays a prominent role in Hungarian folk traditions. He is the protagonist of numerous folk stories that depict him as a hero wandering in disguise. Tales about "Matthias the Just" portray him as a righteous ruler who remains mindful of the poor and delivers justice to the wrongdoers. For an assessment of Matthias's rule in a European context, see Tibor Klaniczay and József Jankovics, *Matthias Corvinus and the Humanism in Central Europe* (Budapest: Balassi, 1994).

In his conclusion, Losonczy called Rákosi "a prominent political asset to the whole nation" and a great "Hungarian statesman of a European caliber."[91] In general, *Szabad Nép*'s article provided a detailed summary of cultic images associated with Rákosi in Communist propaganda at the time of the 1947 elections. He was portrayed as a national politician of international reputation, a caring paternal figure, and an ordinary person —a "man of the people." At the same time, one must note the many personal, intimate details in the text and the tendency to pay more attention to mundane material problems (i.e., the price of potatoes) than to political matters. Such representations of the leader would have been considered inappropriate after 1948.

Rákosi's centrality in Party propaganda during the 1947 election campaign was apparent. However, other leading figures of the Communist Party were also represented in cultic terms and with a similar vocabulary. Révai, for instance, was characterized in a strikingly similar way to Rákosi when he was described as an "asset to the whole nation," and the descriptions of János Kádár and Mihály Farkas also included cultic images. Images of accessibility and immediacy, for example, were commonly used for these politicians. Farkas, for example, was described as a "good friend" who speaks "the language of the people" because he "never became detached from his roots."[92] Even some of the lesser Party leaders were lauded in the press during the coalition period. For example, Sándor Nógrádi, the leader of a small partisan contingent in northern Hungary in 1944, was portrayed by local newspapers as a war hero. *Szabad Magyarország* reported the great enthusiasm and the "lengthy celebrations" that allegedly accompanied Nógrádi's speeches in the northeastern corner of the country.[93] Despite the many similarities, however, the representations of lesser Communist leaders mirrored their actual position in the MKP. They were all portrayed as "friends" of the people; the position of the "father" was reserved for Rákosi. Nevertheless, there seems to have been a relatively balanced share of symbolic capital within the Party leadership during the coalition period. It should also be noted that the MKP was not

---

[91] *Szabad Nép*, August 10, 1947.
[92] Révai was praised in *Szabad Nép* on August 24, 1947. For Farkas, see *Szabad Nép*, August 20, 1947; for Kádár, see *Szabad Nép*, August 23, 1947.
[93] *Szabad Magyarország*, May 15, 1945.

the only party to rely on cultic images in its propaganda at this time. The National Peasant Party, for example, nurtured a distinctive cultic image of its leader, the writer Péter Veres. Furthermore, laudatory descriptions of Prime Minister (later President) Zoltán Tildy appeared in the newspaper of the more moderate Smallholders' Party.

By 1947 the diverse representations of Rákosi had merged into a coherent and unified leader image that remained more or less unchanged until 1953. Similarly, the patterns of describing the leader's speeches and his visits to factories and villages gradually assumed a standardized form in the coalition years and endured until the coming of the "New Course." The core aspects of Rákosi's imagery (i.e., the trials, the fifteen years in prison, and the reconstruction) even survived the first wave of de-Stalinization, and they continued to feature in representations of Rákosi until his resignation in July 1956. Although the discursive and ritual foundations of the Rákosi cult were laid down during the coalition period, the cult was limited to the Communist Party until 1948, and laudatory descriptions of second-rank Party leaders were also common. Nevertheless, the propagandistic adulation of Rákosi during the elections of 1947 demonstrated the potential to transform into a cult-building project of monumental proportions. One journalist at *Szabad Nép* aptly described the gradual intensification of Rákosi's exaltation at the time of the elections: "His figure is growing in the eyes of the working millions with every day, and, just like his prison guards some time ago, even his enemies salute him from afar."[94]

The Legitimization Offensive (1948–1949)

The changes on the Hungarian political scene in 1948–1949 entailed a significant shift in the priorities of Communist propaganda. The primary objective of propaganda in these years was to legitimize the new political system and the Party and its leaders. The centenary celebrations of the 1848–1849 Revolution and War of Independence created a unique opportunity to achieve these goals, but the 1949 elections also contributed significantly to the legitimizing efforts of the Communist Party. The nationalization and centralization of mass media that accompanied the

---

[94] *Szabad Nép*, August 10, 1947.

takeover process made it possible to extend the armory of Party propaganda. Although the press remained the main instrument to promote the Party's ideology, visual propaganda assumed a more prominent status in agitation campaigns. Posters and photos had been widely used before 1948, but after the takeover, newsreels, propaganda films, and paintings were also utilized in the popularization of the Party and its leaders. In addition, Communist propaganda increasingly exploited the mobilizing potential of music—particularly "mass songs"—and literature in its quest for legitimacy.

The Party's fixation on legitimacy further intensified the promotion of the Party leader. The centenary celebrations created a chance to integrate the Communist Party and its leaders into national historical traditions, while the elections of 1949 provided an opportunity to emphasize Rákosi's political achievements after the war. The election campaign, in fact, can be interpreted as the dress rehearsal for his full-blown leader cult.

Besides creating parallels between Rákosi and heroic figures from the nation's past, Communist propaganda enriched the imagery of the Rákosi cult in various other ways during 1948–1949. The attribution of political achievements to Rákosi remained an essential technique in the construction of the cult at the time: the Party leader was portrayed as the "Creator of the Constitution" in 1949, but he also became associated with the unification of the two workers' parties, the "unmasking" of the "conspiracy" of former minister of interior László Rajk, the launching of the first Five-Year Plan in 1950, and even with the Hungarian gold medals at the 1948 Olympic Games in London. *Szabad Nép* continued to supply the relevant material to justify all these associations. Readers' letters, in particular, were instrumental in creating the image of the leader as an omnipotent figure. Such letters expressed the people's gratitude to Rákosi for a new textbook, a renovated school, or the "unity of workers," as in the case of the workers of the Goldberger factory, who wrote their letter to "the leader of the working people," "in the happy hours of [the] unification" of the two Marxist parties.[95] Letters of gratitude were written by sportsmen and sportswomen as well. A group of Hungarian athletes at the London Olympics, for example, thanked Rákosi in a letter for providing the opportunity to take part in the event, where they had the chance to

---

[95] *Szabad Nép*, April 27, 1948.

demonstrate the "ardent fighting spirit" of the "Hungarian democratic youth."[96] Given that Hungary finished the Olympic Games in fourth place on the medal table, ahead of all the other "people's democracies," the propaganda value of this letter was enormous. Gratitude, happiness, and love for the leader continued to characterize popular responses to Rákosi in Communist propaganda at the time. Reports on Rákosi's speeches emphasized Hungarian society's real or imagined enthusiasm at being near him, and its love and trust for its wise leader. In an account of Rákosi's speech in Kecskemét on August 20, 1948, for instance, the papers noted a "labor competition" among those present to see who could applaud loudest after each remarkable announcement from the Party leader.[97]

"We Will Know Who Voted and Who Did Not": The Elections of 1949[98]

The propaganda campaign before the elections of 1949 saw the further intensification of the popularization of the MDP's leaders.[99] In comparison to the previous elections, the ongoing takeover provided a more centralized institutional background for the promotion of the Party's most influential figures. The reorganization of the Propaganda Department (the OPO) and the extension of its authority was followed by the nationalization of the media, which paved the way for a thoroughly organized election campaign.

The campaign began with Rákosi's speech at a Budapest mass meeting on April 19, and the propagation of the talk remained the focus of agitation activities for the entire period.[100] The speech was discussed in a wide range of newspapers and was broadcast on the radio. Weeks before the meeting, the OPO had already circulated detailed guidelines concerning the promotion of the speech,[101] and it carefully distributed the individual tasks among various newspapers. The Department's working plan for

---

[96] György Gyarmati, János Botos, Tibor Zinner, and Mihály Korom, *Magyar hétköznapok Rákosi Mátyás két emigrációja között 1945–1956* (Budapest: Minerva, 1988), 286–87.

[97] *Szabad Nép*, August 24, 1948. For Rákosi's speech, see Mátyás Rákosi, "A dolgozó parasztság a szövetkezés útján," in *Építjük a nép országát* (Budapest: Szikra, 1949), 281–315.

[98] MOL, 276. fond 108/9.

[99] On the elections of 1949, see István Feitl, "Az első népfrontválasztás," *Társadalmi Szemle* 49, no. 5 (1994): 73–85.

[100] "A választás: népünk kiállása a béke nagy eredményeinek és ötéves tervünk mellett," *Szabad Nép*, April 20, 1949.

[101] MOL, 276. fond 108/41.

Budapest dailies even prescribed the nature of articles each newspaper had to publish concerning the speech and made suggestions about their content.[102]

Besides planning the activity of the press with regard to Rákosi's speech, the OPO also supervised the distribution process. The reports sent to the department indicate the intensity and the strictly controlled nature of the campaign. According to these documents, during the two-week campaign in May 1949, the local newspapers—excluding *Szabad Nép*—published 323 articles that popularized the Party's most prominent figures and 330 other pieces that promoted the leaders more indirectly. By comparison, the same newspapers published forty-eight theoretical/ideological articles, 183 articles on "educating the people," twenty-two pieces on the village-visiting movement, fifty-one on Party organization, and twenty-one literary works.[103] The figures clearly imply the great effort invested in the popularization of the Party and its leaders at the time of the elections. The summary report of the OPO after the elections indicates the department's general satisfaction with the work of the newspapers and with the way they contributed to the promotion of the Party leader:

> Many articles were published in our newspapers concerning the popularization of Party functionaries ... especially at the time of the election campaign. They did a job of outstanding quality regarding the articles written about Comrade Rákosi, which reflected the burning love of our working people toward the leader of our Party.[104]

In addition to planning the activity of the press, the OPO also devised the radio program for the campaign period. The tasks of the radio mostly included the broadcasting of reports and interviews related to Rákosi's speech. The Propaganda Department expected lively interviews with people on the streets listening to the speech, and interviews with peasants about Rákosi, "the leader of all honest Hungarian workers."[105] Apart from the planning of media coverage, the OPO proposed disseminating the text of the speech itself, as a leaflet, in 300,000 copies.

---

[102] MOL, 276. fond 108/9.
[103] MOL, 276. fond 108/46.
[104] Ibid.
[105] MOL, 276. fond 108/9.

Rákosi's centrality in Communist propaganda was further underlined by election slogans that hailed the Party secretary or quoted his words,[106] and by the mass production of biographical flyers outlining the basic components of the myth of the "leader of the Hungarian people."[107] In general, Rákosi's persona maintained a central position at the time of the elections. He was intensely popularized by a wide range of propaganda instruments, which resulted in the cult assuming monumental proportions.

During the "Years of Turn," Communist propaganda made a significant appeal to all three categories of Max Weber's legitimacy ideal types.[108] The elections of 1949 were supposed to legitimize the Communist takeover through legal/rational means; the centenary celebrations of the Revolution of 1848 exploited national traditions for political purposes; and the intensification of the leader cult around Rákosi was supposed to fortify the sacral or charismatic aspects of the new regime. The MDP's legitimization offensive thus utilized a combination of legal, traditional, and charismatic methods to validate the claim of the Party—and that of its leader—to power.

The Full-Blown Cult (1949–1953)

The elections of 1949 signaled the beginning of a permanent propaganda and mobilization campaign. The elections in May were followed by the popularization of the constitution, and the constitution was followed by the propaganda of the Rajk trial in the autumn. A milestone in propaganda activities was the celebration of Stalin's seventieth birthday in December, but it was hoped that society could be kept mobilized through the promotion of the first Five-Year Plan, which was eventually launched

---

[106] "Long live the beloved leader of our Party and the Hungarian people, Mátyás Rákosi!"; "Under the leadership of Mátyás Rákosi, for welfare, peace, and a strong, independent Hungary!" MOL, 276. fond 108/9.

[107] One draft of Rákosi's biography meant to be distributed on fly sheets is of very low literary quality, full of spelling mistakes, grammatical errors, and mixed metaphors. See MOL, 276. fond 108/9. On the role of biographies in constructing the leader's cult, see Chapter 3.

[108] The expression "Years of Turn" is borrowed from the title of the book Éva Standeisky, Gyula Kozák, Gábor Pataki, and János M. Rainer, eds., *A fordulat évei. Politika – Képzőművészet – Építészet 1947–1949* (Budapest: 1956-os Intézet, 1998). It refers to the idea that the Communist takeover was a gradual process and its conclusion took several years.

in 1950. In addition to the mobilization of society, the launching of full-scale Sovietization in 1949 also contributed to the gradual ritualization of state-societal relations. Party life developed its own Soviet-style ritual system that included the establishment of Red Corners, the ritualization of meetings, and the spreading of denunciation practices. Communication within the Party and communication with the Party assumed a ritual format, manifested in the spreading of petitioning rites and in the ritualization of Party language.[109]

The implementation of the leader cult was the most important symbolic aspect of Sovietization, and it contributed both to the mobilization efforts of the regime and to the ritualization of social relations. The cult, in fact, became the key instrument to create and sustain popular enthusiasm for the regime and to confer a sacred aura on the Party and its leaders. Even before 1949, the orchestrated adoration of Rákosi reached a magnitude unparalleled in the Hungarian political scene. Although Rákosi's position at the apex of Party (and cult) hierarchy was already evident in 1945, the constant attribution of the country's achievements to his name in the coalition years gave him a unique image. As his popularization intensified during the takeover years, the degree of veneration reached unprecedented heights after 1949. Photos, portraits, and busts of the leader dominated the public sphere, suggesting Rákosi's omnipresence, and the press teemed with articles extolling his merits. Literary works also contributed to the exaltation of the leader: poems and short stories were published on a wide scale in the press and in literary anthologies.[110] Although Hungarian writers were expected to compose novels about the Hungarian leader as well, that ambition of Communist propaganda remained unaccomplished. Rákosi—like Stalin—only received episodic roles in the novels of the time.[111]

---

[109] On the characteristics of communication practices in totalitarian regimes, see Kirill Postoutenko, ed., *Totalitarian Communication: Hierarchies, Codes and Messages* (Bielefeld: Transcript, 2010).

[110] One of the most representative selections was the anthology of young writers *Fiatal írók antológiája* (Budapest: Szépirodalmi kiadó, 1951). A recent collection of poems from the 1950s: Attila Buda and László L. Simon, eds., *Munkás, paraszt, értelmiség munkaverseny lázában ég!* (Budapest: Korona Kiadó, 2002).

[111] On the novel of Illés (*Honfoglalás*) that reproduced the official image of the leader, see Árpád von Klimo, "'A Very Modest Man': Béla Illés or How to Make a Career through the Leader Cult," in Apor et al., *The Leader Cult*, 47–62. On Stalin, see Rosalind Marsh, *Images of*

Alongside the spreading of eulogies and the emergence of an ever-present image of the leader, the veneration of Rákosi became ritualized to a significant degree. Rhythmic applause and the chanting of the leader's name frequently punctuated meetings and speeches, and symbolic communication with the leader in the form of letter-writing became a standard practice.[112] Oaths, pledges, letters of gratitude, and requests were often published in the press and became indispensable parts of the cult. By the time of the 1952 Olympics, writing letters of gratitude had become a standard ritual of the Rákosi cult, such that most of the gold-medal winners in Helsinki deemed it necessary to express their gratitude to the Party secretary. The first two champions of the Olympic team, two gymnasts, Ágnes Keleti and Margit Korondi, wrote the following:

> Dear Comrade Rákosi!
> We are happy to report to you that today we won the Olympic championship. We are glad that the people did not trust us in vain, that Comrade Rákosi did not trust us in vain.
> We are grateful to the Party, to Comrade Rákosi, and to our working people for the support that enabled us to train under proper conditions. We hope that our success only signifies the beginning of our Olympic team's further victories.[113]

The Helsinki Games turned into the most successful Olympics in the history of Hungarian sport. Successive champions all followed the example set by the first medalists and sent telegrams of gratitude to the Party leader. Similar letters were written by the pentathlon team, the water-polo team, the soccer team, and individual athletes, including László Papp, the legendary boxing champion. After winning its tenth gold medal, the whole delegation composed a joint letter to the Party leader, crediting him

---

Dictatorship: Portraits of Stalin in Literature (London: Routledge, 1989); and Rolf Hellebust, "Reflections of an Absence: Novelistic Portraits of Stalin before 1953," in *Socialist Realism Revisited: Selected Papers from the McMaster Conference*, ed. Nina Kolesnikoff and Walter Smyrniw (Hamilton, ON.: McMaster University, 1994), 111–20.

[112] For a selection of letters addressed to Rákosi, see András Kő and Lambert J. Nagy, eds., *Levelek Rákosihoz* (Budapest: Maecenas, 2002).

[113] Gyarmati et al., *Magyar hétköznapok*, 290.

for their success.¹¹⁴ In the context of the Cold War, the regime exploited the successes of its athletes at the Olympics and interpreted their victories as proof of socialism's superiority over capitalist societies.

The process of transforming the cult of the Hungarian Party secretary into the master ritual of political participation went hand in hand with a campaign against the "cult of personality" on the lower rungs of the Party hierarchy. At about the same time that Rajk was expelled from the Party (June 11, 1949)—partly on the grounds of nurturing a cult around himself—*Szabad Nép* published articles denouncing the phenomenon. The paper argued somewhat paradoxically that the celebration of lesser leaders—which clearly imitated the veneration of Communist politicians on a national level—undermined the symbolic authority of those who truly deserved to be celebrated.¹¹⁵ This underlines the point, once again, that cult-building and cult criticism were parallel processes in Stalinist regimes and that the promotion of the Party leader's mythical persona at the top of the cult hierarchy was usually accompanied by the suppression of local mini-cults.

Rákosi's Sixtieth Birthday

The most monumental project of Communist propaganda in the process of cult construction was the campaign launched for the celebration of Rákosi's sixtieth birthday, which was modeled entirely on the 1949 festivities for Stalin's seventieth birthday.¹¹⁶ Both campaigns were overseen

---

[114] Ibid., 291.

[115] See, for example, the following issues of *Szabad Nép*: June 18, July 23, August 4. Special thanks to József Litkei for bringing these articles to my attention. The comments of the Party secretary in Budapest's Eighth District are worth quoting in detail: "Stop the cult of personality, comrades. Recently, in the Körling Factory, the manager—upon his arrival for a meeting—was celebrated with a standing ovation that lasted several minutes. Let's not stand up to celebrate so quickly, comrades. We do not stand up for the district Party secretary either. Sycophancy is one of the most disgusting things, and if somebody cannot make a difference between the significance of [ordinary] individuals and well-deserved respect for the greatest, that is a mistake." *Szabad Nép*, June 18, 1949.

[116] Given the exhaustive scholarly coverage of the birthday celebrations, the following discussion will focus on the institutional background of the preparations for the anniversary and will not provide a detailed account of the event. Information about the birthday will also be included in subsequent chapters. For Rákosi's sixtieth birthday, see Béres, "Születésnapok anatómiája"; Nemes, *Rákosi Mátyás születésnapja*; Pünkösti, *Rákosi a csúcson*, 424–41; Szücs, "Rákosi Mátyás Művek"; Piroska Kocsis, "Rákosi Mátyás hatvanadik születésnapjának megünneplése," *Archivnet* 6, no. 2 (2006), http://www.archivnet.hu/politika/rakosi_matyas_

by the Secretariat, which set up special birthday committees—the one for Stalin's birthday was headed by Rákosi himself—to supervise the propaganda work.[117] In the case of Stalin's birthday, the Secretariat decided on the quantity and the form of publications in Stalin's honor; the production of Stalin medals; the organization of an exhibition on Stalin's life; the labor competition launched before the birthday; the exact route of the train that carried the presents sent to the Soviet leader from Hungary; and even the program of the Opera, where the official celebration took place on December 20. The Secretariat also supervised the construction of the Stalin statue in Budapest, which became a symbol of the era; the erection of a Stalin statue in the city of Szeged; and the installation of several monuments to Soviet heroes.[118] However, given the symbolic significance of the event, the Hungarian Party leadership also requested Moscow's advice and assistance in organizing the birthday celebrations. The stakes were certainly high: Stalin's birthday signaled the ritual completion of Sovietization in the Soviet sphere of influence, and thus provoked a symbolic competition across the bloc in which no country wanted to be left behind. In a letter to Mikhail Suslov, for example, Rákosi asked the Soviet leader about "the correct Party line" and about how far Communist parties in the people's democracies were allowed to go in relation to the celebrations.[119] Getting hints about "the correct line" was imperative, because deviation from the standard Stalin imagery could result in stigmatization—or even expulsion—from the international cult community. In order to avoid the circulation of potentially subversive images about the generalissimo, the countries of the bloc—East Germany, Hungary, Romania, Poland, and

---

hatvanadik_szuletesnapjanak_megunneplese.html. (accessed April 23, 2012). See also the virtual exhibition of gifts sent to Rákosi at http://rakosi60.blogspot.com/p/sztarkiallitas-kossuth-teren.html (accessed April 23, 2012).

[117] The archival documents for Stalin's birthday are located at MOL, 276. fond 54/66; MOL, 276. fond 54/71–75 and 77.

[118] MOL, 276. fond 54/66; MOL, 276. fond 54/130. For the erection of Soviet memorials and statues, see János Pótó, *Az emlékeztetés helyei. Emlékművek és politika* (Budapest: Osiris, 2003). See also Piroska Kocsis, "'Sztálinhoz száll a hálaének, ki a jövőnk apja lett…' Sztálin 70. születésnapja Magyarországon," *Archivnet* 7, no. 6 (2007), http://www.archivnet.hu/politika/sztalin_70._szuletesnapja_magyarorszagon.html (accessed April 23, 2012).

[119] MOL, 276. fond 65/213. Quoted in Martin Mevius, *Agents of Moscow: The Hungarian Communist Party and the Origins of Socialist Patriotism 1941–1953* (Oxford: Oxford University Press, 2005), 256. I am indebted to the author for this reference.

Bulgaria—asked the All-Union Society for Cultural Ties with Foreign Countries (VOKS) to supply them with appropriate material about Stalin (biographies, images, sheet music, collected works, etc.).[120]

There is no sign of the Soviet Union's involvement in the organization of the birthday celebrations for the Hungarian leader; it seems that the MDP did not need the approval of the center to exalt its own secretary. The central decision-making bodies of the Party thus exercised complete control over the preparations for the event. Through the centralized nature of the campaign, there was a division of labor among these organs concerning the popularization of the leader. The APO and the Orgburo (*Szervező Bizottság*) were responsible for proposing and supervising a wide range of activities in relation to the popularization of the leader, but the hub of the campaign was the birthday committee. The committee was set up on August 29, 1951, by the Secretariat at the meeting in which the Poliburo's proposal to celebrate the event was discussed (in Rákosi's absence).[121] Under the leadership of Révai and his close associate Márton Horváth, it became the engine of cult-building at the time, and it monitored the production of the most important cult artifacts—such as the official biography of the leader—and the organization of the most significant cult rituals.[122]

The plan for the celebration of Rákosi's birthday, as approved by the Secretariat in August 1951, was carried out without substantial changes— although the idea of the labor competition was added later. However, the accepted version of the draft differed significantly from the Politburo's original proposal: the Secretariat, and Révai in particular, did not approve the making of a feature film about the leader's life, the installation of plaques at locations related to his life, the publication of his collected works, the publication of his prison notes, and the idea of drafting separate celebration plans for the DISZ and the army. (In the end, the only film released on the occasion was a documentary, entitled *Rákosi 60. születésnapjának megünnepléséről* [On the celebration of Rákosi's sixtieth birthday], that provided an overview of the key events of the

---

[120] Tikhomirov, "The Stalin Cult," 299 and 301.
[121] MOL, 276. fond 54/158.
[122] The other members of the committee were Mihály Farkas, István Kovács, and István Kristóf.

birthday celebrations.) Though the initial ambitions of the leadership were curbed, the most important suggestions went through. These proposals included a series of renamings, the publication of Rákosi's official biography, the preparation of gifts for the leader, the organization of exhibitions, the granting of awards to him, a party in the Opera House, the organization of celebrations by local Party committees and in schools, the painting of portraits, the commissioning of literary works depicting the Party secretary, and so on. Even the March 9, 1952, issue of *Szabad Nép* was discussed and agreed upon well in advance.

The day-to-day task of realizing these proposals was entrusted mainly to the APO. However, the Orgburo also had its share of the workload, as it supervised the labor competition—including the writing of congratulatory letters to the leader—organized for the Party secretary's birthday.[123] One of the main responsibilities of the APO was to direct the activity of newspapers and journals. It prescribed the type of articles to be published about Rákosi and selected the letters or pledges to appear in the press. The press was instructed by the APO to launch the birthday propaganda campaign two months before March 9 in order to prepare the much-anticipated event.[124] In accordance with the department's directives, a flood of articles and reports appeared in newspapers and journals extolling Rákosi. In addition, the press regularly reported on the pledges by factories, collective farms, or individuals and provided frequent updates on the labor competition launched for the event. On March 9, Rákosi's birthday, *Szabad Nép* gave a detailed account of the celebrations in the Opera House, and on the following days—together with *Magyar Nemzet* (Hungarian Nation)—it published the most important congratulatory letters Rákosi received from the Hungarian people and from abroad.

Besides the press, the APO also supervised the compilation of the literary anthology *Magyar írók Rákosi Mátyásról* (Hungarian Writers on Mátyás Rákosi).[125] The collection of poems, short stories, and one short drama, by a number of illustrious writers (such as Gyula Illyés, Péter Veres, Zoltán Zelk, and István Örkény), provided a comprehensive overview

---

[123] Reports about the labor competition MOL, 276. fond 55/194 and 198.
[124] MOL, 276. fond 89/193.
[125] Pál Réz and István Vas, eds., *Magyar írók Rákosi Mátyásról* (Budapest: Szépirodalmi kiadó, 1952).

of the cult's key components. The book included Sándor Nagy's short story representing the imagined continuity between Kossuth and Rákosi (see Chapter 4), István Örkény's interpretation of the Salgótarján myth (see Chapter 3), and a number of other writings on Rákosi's activity in the underground and his behavior before the court and in prison. Aside from the embellished representations of certain episodes in the leader's life, the book presented the monumental image of the benevolent father of the nation, the wise teacher of the people, and the omnipotent leader of the country. Béla Reményi's poem, for example, exemplifies the emotionally overwrought representations of Rákosi's image as a father. Through biblical allusions, the poet portrayed his relationship to Rákosi as an apprentice-master relationship similar to that of Peter and Jesus: "Now I have a real father! / Adopt me as your faithful son. / You who provide me with food—take care of me, / And make sure I am good and obedient. / I love you. You gave me / Your sixty years—what could I possibly give to you? / The one who loves me best, / Should kill me if I deny you."[126]

The literary anthology was complemented with the publication of a photo album—supervised by Rákosi's younger brother, Zoltán Bíró—on the leader's life.[127] The volume, which could be interpreted as the visual version of the leader's biographical narrative, extensively employed the Stalinist techniques of embellishment and falsification.[128] The creation of the photo of master and apprentice (i.e., Stalin and Rákosi), for example, required considerable creativity and innovation. Since no acceptable

---

[126] "Most van igazán apám! / Fogadj örökbe hű fiadnak. / Ki ennem adsz – vigyázz reám, / hogy jó legyek és szót fogadjak. / Szeretlek. Hatvan évedet / adtad nekem – hát én mit adjak? / Ki engem legjobban szeret, / az öljön meg, ha megtagadlak." Béla Reményi, "Mit adjak én?" in Réz and Vas, *Magyar írók Rákosi Mátyásról*, 139. The book is analyzed in detail in Czigány, "Neved ki diccsel ejtené...."

[127] *Rákosi Mátyás élete képekben* (Budapest: Szikra, 1952).

[128] According to Nemes, "the most important contributor, one might say 'inspired creator,' of this album was the retoucher, . . . [who] removed furrows and warts, softened hard features, turned soft ones into man-like hardness, or transformed them into a sympathizing character. He created backgrounds, and for persons whose existence became retrospectively undesirable due to political changes, he made them unrecognizable by applying beards, moustaches, and glasses." Nemes, *Rákosi Mátyás születésnapja*, 15. On the Stalinist practice of falsifying photos, see David King, *The Commissar Vanishes: The Falsification of Photographs and Art in Stalin's Russia* (New York: Metropolitan books, 1997).

pictures of the two leaders showed them side by side, the retoucher had to design an image almost completely from scratch, using the photo taken at the signing of the Soviet-Hungarian Friendship and Mutual Assistance Treaty.[129] The task was accomplished: the people between Rákosi and Stalin were removed, the Hungarian Party leader was magnified, and even his head was replaced with a more favorable portrait.[130]

The life of the Party secretary, in general, remained the center of cult-building at the time of the birthday celebrations. Besides establishing the editorial sub-committee for the completion of the official biography, the Party also focused on the publication and the utilization of the text for educational purposes. The task was coordinated by the APO, which also monitored popular reaction to the biography.[131] An exhibition entitled *Rákosi Mátyás harcos élete* (Mátyás Rákosi's Crusading Life) was organized in the *Munkásmozgalmi Intézet* (Institute of the Working-Class Movement), and it subsequently journeyed around the country as a traveling exhibition. The MDP leader's life was also celebrated in numerous articles published in newspapers and by the official biography, which was eventually written by Béla Illés (and not the editorial committee).[132] All these biographical pieces emphasized the exemplary nature of Rákosi's life and what made him ideal for his position. The enlightening effects of the Party leader's words and his contribution to the formation of the Communist historical master narrative were appraised in another eulogistic work—written by prominent historians—published by the Academy of Sciences.[133] The exhibition on the life of the MDP leader ran parallel with an exhibition of gifts that had been sent to Rákosi for his birthday. Such material expressions of gratitude included showcase products of the command economy, as well as objects bearing the traces of Hungarian folklore and Socialist Realism alike (bottles, embroidery, a carved wooden box, a flute, a walking stick, a whip, etc.).[134] Rákosi visited both exhibitions on

---

[129] The treaty was signed in Moscow on February 13, 1948.
[130] Nemes, *Rákosi Mátyás születésnapja*, 17.
[131] MOL, 276. fond 89/10. See also MOL, 276. fond 65/388.
[132] Béla Illés, *Népünk szabadságáért* (Budapest: Szikra, 1952).
[133] *Rákosi Mátyás és a magyar történettudomány* (Budapest: Akadémiai kiadó, 1952).
[134] The exhibition of gifts took place in the building of the Museum of Ethnography. For the interpretation of gifts, see Brooks, *Thank You, Comrade Stalin!* An anthropological approach

his birthday (March 9), after presiding over the opening of the Institute of the Working-Class Movement on the same day, providing a further indication of the close ties between the leader's life and the history of the Hungarian Communist movement.

The zenith of the birthday festivities was the celebration of the leader in the Opera House on March 8, 1952. Although his invitation card was only the two hundred and ninth (!) to be sent out, he certainly was the main attraction that night. He took center stage during the event—quite literally. Seated among prominent politicians, heroes of labor, and cultural celebrities, Rákosi received the congratulations of the various delegations (peasants, Pioneers, soldiers) that marched into the theater one after the other. Besides the orgy of song tributes—including the fake folk song "Gyertek lányok" (Come on Girls), addressed to him—that marked the evening's cultural program, Rákosi was praised by the president of the Presidential Council, István Dobi. However, it was Gerő's laudatory speech that epitomized the substance of the cult:

> We respect, honor, and love Comrade Rákosi, because every honest Hungarian, every true son of our country feels and knows that Rákosi and the Party are one! Rákosi and the Hungarian working class are one! Rákosi and the Hungarian people are one![135]

During the birthday celebrations, the archetypal aspects of Rákosi's persona—leader, teacher, and father—dominated his imagery. However, this was not the first time that that these images were associated with him, nor were they invented after the Communist takeover: they had been systematically attached to him since 1945. Communist propaganda thus

---

is provided by Nikolai Ssorin-Chaikov and Olga Sosnina, "The Faculty of Useless Things: Gifts to Soviet Leaders," in Heller and Plamper, *Personality Cults in Stalinism*, 277–300. On the gifts to Rákosi, see Miklós Bokor, ed., *Népünk szeretete. Népművészeink ajándékai Rákosi Mátyás 60 éves születésnapjára* (Budapest: Képzőművészeti Alap, 1952); Gábor Ö. Pogány, "Rákosi Mátyás és a művészet," *Szabad Művészet* 6, no. 3 (1952): 97–103; "Rákosi Mátyás elvtárs 60. születésnapja: az új magyar népi díszítőművészet fejlődésének hatalmas forrása," *Ethnographia* 53, nos. 1–2 (1952): 1–9; József Zelnik, "Miskakancsó R. M. apánknak," *Jel-Kép* 4, no. 3 (1983): 87–96. See also the virtual exhibition of gifts sent to Rákosi at http://rakosi60.blogspot.com/p/sztarkiallitas-kossuth-teren.html (accessed April 23, 2012).

[135] Sándor Balogh, ed., *Nehéz esztendők krónikája 1949–1953. Dokumentumok* (Budapest: Gondolat, 1986), 392. The newsreel coverage of the celebrations in the Opera is available at http://rakosi60.blogspot.com/p/kepek-1952.html (accessed April 27, 2012).

demonstrated a conscious effort to construct a cultic image for the Party leader(s) from the very beginning. The images they used were predominantly based on Soviet importation—the Stalinist model—but they also recycled Hungarian national traditions, and the vocabulary of cult-building that they adopted to construct the leader's mythical persona was consistent with the language of cultic representations in the interwar period. The significance of cult-building tendencies in Communist propaganda in 1945–1947 seems to reinforce the idea of "two-phase Sovietization." Even before the Communist Party gained complete control over Hungarian political life, it demonstrated a remarkable willingness to adopt Soviet cultural practices. Covert Sovietization coincides with the period of cult-building within the Communist Party (1945–1947), whereas overt Sovietization denotes the era of a full-blown leader cult (1948–1953).

Chapter 2
The Institutions and Agents of Cult Construction

Despite Rákosi's relative popularity in the coalition period, his cult did not emerge spontaneously: it was constructed for him. Moreover, his actual personality had very little to do with the monumental leader image that was forged in the furnaces of Communist propaganda. His depersonalized image was that of an omnipresent Stalinist Party leader with a national hue who came to personify the Party, the working-class movement, and eventually the whole nation. The construction of that image was a complex process that involved a range of institutions and individuals.[1] The creation of the cult of the Hungarian Party secretary involved the institutionalization of cult production, the centralized monitoring of the leader's image, the supervision of the production of cult artifacts, and the mobilization of functionaries willing to promote the image of the leader in all spheres of the cult. Nevertheless, the effort to exercise total control over the veneration of the leader sometimes failed, due to the fact that the cult was constructed at multiple institutional levels from the center to the periphery, and by various individuals with different social and professional backgrounds and with different perceptions of the cult's functions. At the same time, the moderation of the cult from the center often lacked consistency and regularity, resulting in the proliferation of locally modified—and thus unacceptable—images of the leader. Despite the Communist Party's intention to keep the development and manifestations of the leader's adulation under control, the cult involved a remarkable degree of spontaneity and happenstance.

---

[1] My initial ideas on the institutions of cult-building were published in Balázs Apor, "The Leader Cult in Communist Hungary, 1945–56: Propaganda, Institutional Background and Mass Media," in *War of Words: Culture and the Mass Media in the Making of the Cold War in Europe*, ed. Judith Devlin and Christoph Hendrik Müller (Dublin: UCD Press, 2013), 18–29. The following section is the result of further research on the subject.

Institutions of Cult-Building

The cradle of the cult was undoubtedly the Party. More specifically, the Party's Propaganda Department became the most important institution in the process of cult-building. The department utilized a wide range of tools, controlling the press, radio, the film industry, and book publishing, and it also had an influence over literature and the fine arts.[2] Apart from planning and supervising the construction of the cult, the department also monitored its reception.[3] The management of propaganda affairs was entrusted to the most reliable cadres from the highest strata of the Party elite. At one point it was directed by Révai himself, but other influential Party members, such as Sándor Nógrádi, László Orbán, Zoltán Bíró (Rákosi's brother), and Révai's right-hand man, Márton Horváth, also influenced the Party's propaganda affairs at different times.[4]

The institutional network of cult-building was gradually extended with the launching of full-scale Sovietization in 1948–1949. Apart from the various departments of the Party (the Department of Press, Orgburo, the Secretariat, etc.), government institutions, professional organizations, the media, publishing houses, and various nationalized companies were gradually enrolled in the production of cult objects and the execution of cultic practices. Before the media and various cultural institutions could participate in shaping the leader cult, cultural production had to be Sovietized; this was accomplished by the establishment of the Ministry of People's Education (*Népművelési Minisztérium*) in 1949.[5] The ministry

---

[2] The propaganda department of the MKP was called *Propaganda Osztály* (Propaganda Department). After the union with the Social Democrats and the formation of the MDP in 1948, the department was renamed *Országos Propaganda (Agitációs) Osztály* (Propaganda [Agitation] Department). After another reorganization in 1950, the name changed again, and the section was called *Agitációs és Propaganda Osztály* (Agitation and Propaganda Department; APO) until 1956.

[3] For more on monitoring propaganda, see Chapters 6–8.

[4] On the structural changes and functions of the MKP's Propaganda Department, see Julianna Horváth, Éva Szabó, and Katalin Zalai, eds., *A Magyar Kommunista Párt iratainak repertóriuma 1944–1948* (Budapest, 2001), 29–31.

[5] On the Sovietization of the cultural sphere, see Romsics, *Magyarország története*, 318–31, 357–74; Tibor Valuch, "A magyar művelődés 1948 után," in László Kósa, *Magyar művelődéstörténet* (Budapest: Osiris, 2000), 460–547. On aspects of cultural Sovietization, see Standeisky et al., *A fordulat évei*, 217–308.

was directed by Révai himself until July 1953, and its authority included the management of literary affairs; the coordination of the work of nationalized publishing houses; and the supervision of various matters in the fields of fine arts, the press, film propaganda, music, and so on. The ministry also supervised the process of creating cult relics, from the design phase to the actual physical manufacturing of the specific product.

Educational institutions also had a pivotal role in the transmission of cultic propaganda. Pictures of Rákosi were hung in classrooms; songs and poems praising him were taught; his life was included in the curriculum; and important anniversaries connected with him were celebrated in schools. The educational system was also meant to supply the regime with committed cadres who would contribute to the promotion of the leader's image and to the overall effort to inculcate the population with the Party's ideological tenets. Indeed, education was regarded as an important battlefield on which the indoctrination of the regime's values could be achieved. The leader's image as the teacher of the people clearly underlines the significance of education in Soviet-type political systems. The Communist conviction that society had to be "enlightened" and "civilized" in order to gain consciousness resulted in the radical transformation of traditional educational models and institutional structures in both the Soviet Union and in Central Eastern Europe. The Sovietization of education in Hungary included the nationalization of schools, the introduction of new curricula, and the rewriting of textbooks and other educational material.[6]

The replacement of members of the old intelligentsia in the schools with reliable cadres was also part of the transformation of the educational system. By prescribing compulsory ideological training for teachers, the Communist regime hoped to secure their loyalty and to enhance the transmission of political values to the students.[7] In addition to recruiting teachers, a wide range of training courses was organized to replenish the ranks of cult mediators with dedicated propagandists, agitators, people's educators (*népnevelők*), journalists, and so forth. In addition to the graduates of Party schools and crash courses for propagandists, many of the

---

[6] József Kardos, "Fordulat a közoktatásban," in *Fordulat a világban és Magyarországon 1944-1949*, ed. István Feitl, Lajos Izsák, and Gábor Székely (Budapest: Napvilág, 2000), 152–60; József Kardos, *Iskola a politika sodrásában, 1945–1993* (Budapest: Gondolat, 2007).
[7] Kardos, "Fordulat a közoktatásban."

rank-and-file promoters of the cult were trained by the Party Academy (*Pártfőiskola*) in Budapest in short courses (of a few months), or year-long courses. At the Academy, directed by the prominent ideologue László Rudas and the leading Muscovite historian Erzsébet Andics, the main instruction material was one of the most significant texts of the Stalin cult, the *Short Course*, which was complemented with classes on the history of the Hungarian working-class movement and the life of Rákosi.[8]

Affairs related to Party education were generally managed by the Party's Department of Education.[9] The Department was mostly responsible for the inculcation of the leader-centered historical narrative of the Hungarian labor movement, which was devised in the Institute of the Working-Class Movement under László Réti's directorship. The Department supplied the system of Party education with guidelines and syllabi for the compilation of curricula about the leader's mythical life and monitored the reception of Rákosi's biographical narrative.

As political socialization in the countries of the Soviet bloc involved the intense propagation of the worship of the local Party secretary, educational institutions, youth organizations, and journals for the younger generations became important vehicles of the leader cult.[10] Consequently, teachers, Pioneer leaders, and others became crucial promoters of the leader's image. The journals of youth associations, such as *Pajtás* (Fellow) and *Szabad Ifjúság* (Free Youth), were overloaded with representations of the Hungarian Party secretary, and children were often more exposed to the cult than adults. When Rákosi was elected prime minister, for example, *Szabad Ifjúság* called him "the wise leader of the *toilers of the world*," a designation that could not have appeared in the politically more cautious Party newspapers, such as *Szabad Nép*.[11] The intensive nature of

---

[8] Published in English as *History of the Communist Party of the Soviet Union (Bolsheviks): Short Course* (New York: International Publishers, 1939). The publication of the *Short Course* in 1938 marked the crystallization of the Stalinist historical narrative in the Soviet Union. A number of historians had worked on the manuscript, but Stalin assumed the role of chief editor of the text. For a detailed assessment of the Bolsheviks' search for a useable past, see Brandenberger, *Propaganda State in Crisis*.

[9] In 1951, at least one-third of the Party membership was enrolled in Party education. MOL, 276. fond 65/77.

[10] Ildikó Szabó, *A pártállam gyermekei. Tanulmányok a magyar politikai szocializációról* (Budapest: Új Mandátum, 2000).

[11] *Szabad Ifjúság*, August 15, 1952, in OSA 300/40/3/264. (Emphasis added.)

the Rákosi cult among children was also marked by the unusual frequency of pledges made to the leader by Pioneers or members of the DISZ. Children often swore an oath to Rákosi promising to study harder, to help the less-talented pupils, and to generally aim to become worthy Communist members of the new society.[12] During initiation rituals for children (such as to the Pioneer organization), the leader's name was frequently invoked; his accomplishments were also recited during collective events in Pioneer camps. The image of Rákosi transmitted to the young was that of a father figure. He was generally portrayed to children as a paternal mentor, a teacher, and an ideal whose example would show the young ones the right path to correct Communist behavior.

The Agents of the Cult

As the cult was transmitted through a complex institutional network—Party and government institutions, professional organizations, local councils, and so on—it was inevitably shaped by a wide variety of individuals of different social and political backgrounds. The intended message of the cult could thus be modified considerably in the institutional maze of the procedure of cult-building. As cases of excessive manifestations of the cult on a local level and their swift suppression by the center indicate, the function the cult was meant to fulfill was sometimes misinterpreted or distorted by the people involved in its construction and dissemination. Individual perceptions of the cult could therefore shape the representations of the leader to a certain extent.[13]

---

[12] See, for example, the reports submitted to the Department of Party and Mass Organizations at MOL, 88. fond 672–73.

[13] One example of the cult's excessive manifestations at a local level involved a Party secretary who prescribed the number of times the audience had to applaud at various meetings after the mentioning of the leaders' names. The overenthusiastic functionary even ordered that applause be rehearsed at membership meetings: "At every gathering, such as social gatherings, Party, factory, professional, district, and committee meetings, educational, theatrical, cinematic performances, and seminar lectures, it is absolutely compulsory: when Stalin's name is mentioned, the audience, the speakers, the Presidency, and the Secretariat leap to their feet from their seats and applaud twenty-five times. When Rákosi's name is mentioned, the audience stands up and applauds ten times. When Ernő Gerő's name is mentioned, the audience applauds ten times. At short meetings, the practice of showing respect [toward the leaders] should commence forthwith." OSA 300/40/3/264.

Virtually the entire Party elite was involved in the construction of the cult, but the major decisions were made by those functionaries who were responsible for running the key institutions of cult design. Therefore, the top Party leadership (Rákosi and his lieutenants) had indisputable responsibility in forming a divine aura around the leader. The second category of cult-builders incorporated a rather heterogeneous group of Party bureaucrats, intellectuals, artists, propagandists, teachers, and others who projected the centrally fabricated image of the leader toward the target audience or who were involved in the actual crafting of cultic objects. The task of propagandists, agitators, people's educators, and representatives of local Party authorities was to popularize the leader's image in a micro-environment and to inspire local manifestations of cult rituals (such as letter-writing or applauding).

Intellectuals played a considerable role in exalting Rákosi and bestowing divine characteristics upon him. Writers, journalists, musicians, historians, philosophers, actors, artists, and others were represented in Party organizations and in cultural institutions that gave them a certain influence over the flow of the cult. Therefore, Communist intellectuals constituted a substantial part of the cult's social base.[14] The role of the literary intelligentsia in the escalation of the cult of the Party secretary and in the promotion of his image was particularly notable. In addition to the "Muscovite" writers (Antal Hidas, Andor Gábor, Béla Illés, Gyula Háy, Sándor Gergely)—who returned to Hungary from the Soviet Union after the war—and some prominent "fellow travelers" (Péter Veres, Ferenc Erdei, József Darvas), the primary instruments of the MKP in the Sovietization of Hungarian culture were those known as the "young writers" (Tamás Aczél, László Benjámin, Ferenc Juhász, Péter Kuczka).[15] Although most of them joined the Party after the war, they enjoyed significant privileges from the beginning: they were granted financial support and publication opportunities as well as prestigious prizes (such as the Kossuth

---

[14] For the ambiguous attitude of Hungarian intellectuals to Communist ideology, see Lee Congdon, *Seeing Red: Hungarian Intellectuals in Exile and the Challenge of Communism* (DeKalb: Northern Illinois University Press, 2001).

[15] An intriguing overview on the Hungarian literary intelligentsia is Tamás Aczél and Tibor Méray, *The Revolt of the Mind: A Case History of Intellectual Resistance Behind the Iron Curtain* (Westport, CT: Greenwood Press, 1974).

clear idea of the function his fictitious persona was supposed to fulfill in Communist propaganda. He seems to have objected to an overtly "personal," or intimate, veneration of himself, while he advocated a largely depersonalized image that portrayed him as the symbolic representation of Communist ideals, the regime's achievements, and the multiethnic Soviet Union. Stalin's preference for "the cult of impersonality" was reflected in the way he intervened in cult affairs. He usually condemned the spreading of the leader cult at the periphery and the proliferation of sycophant careerists who were hoping for rapid social advancement through the cult.[25] The absence of images of Stalin in a family circle, and the banning of a book on his childhood, provide further evidence for the claim that the rise of the cult was engendered largely by pragmatic reasons and not only by Stalin's psychological need for self-aggrandizement. Stalin seems to have realized the mobilizing potential of representing Soviet power through a given individual in a culture that largely perceived politics in personalized terms.[26] He attempted to eliminate the personal characteristics from his official persona and promoted an image of the leader as the physical embodiment of Bolshevik rule, and as the representative of the construction of socialism.[27] The famous, although not necessarily true story of the row with his son, Vasily, about the name Stalin—"Stalin is Soviet power"—seems to underline this argument.[28] Nonetheless, since the cult was constructed on multiple levels, its boundaries changed constantly, lending an element of spontaneity to the worship of the leader. Even if there was a certain element of actual modesty or ideological consistency involved in the tempering of the cult by Stalin, the intention was lost spectacularly in the labyrinth of cult construction, and what appeared on the façade was one of the most monumental and ubiquitous leader cults of the twentieth century.

The closest associates of the leader often play a crucial role in his aggrandizement. As in Nazi Germany, where Göbbels took a decisive

---

[25] On leader cults in the Soviet periphery, see Rolf, "The Leader's Many Bodies."

[26] White, *Political Culture*.

[27] Erik van Ree argues that this was in line with the Soviet leader's perception of the Marxist tradition. Van Ree, *The Political Thought of Joseph Stalin*, 155–68.

[28] Stalin allegedly told his son: "You're not Stalin and I'm not Stalin. Stalin is Soviet power. Stalin is what he is in the newspapers and the portraits, not you, not even me!" Quoted in Plamper, *The Stalin Cult*, xiii.

role in formulating the Hitler myth, Stalin's entourage contributed to the master's exaltation and took the lead in publicizing and sustaining the codes and practices of his cult. As Benno Ennker argues, the cult became Stalin's instrument to secure the allegiance of his associates. By treating them with a combination of trust and mistrust, he generated competition for his confidence, which prompted members of his inner circle to try to outdo each other in praising him.[29] The prospect of possible downfall led to his lieutenants orienting toward what they perceived as "Stalin's will" in order to retain the master's trust. "Working towards the *vozhd*'" became a pervasive social routine in Soviet society, in the center as well as at the periphery.[30] With the exportation of the Stalin cult to the Soviet bloc, the "politics of trust and mistrust" was extended to the vassal countries. The position of satellite leaders was largely dependent on Stalin's will, which triggered a certain competition among the mini-Stalins for the master's favor. The countries of the Soviet bloc all vied in a ritual contest to demonstrate their progress in constructing socialism, as well as their enthusiasm in exalting Stalin. One of the cult's main functions—to keep Stalin's associates under control—was thus extended to regulating the Party leaders in Eastern Europe. The local Party secretaries took the leading role in praising Stalin in their countries, and "working towards Stalin" became typical of the way they communicated with each other and with Moscow.

Rákosi's Hungary also participated in the competition for Stalin's favor. As "Stalin's best Hungarian disciple," Rákosi was keen to prove to Moscow that the country he led was the most loyal of the people's democracies. In fact, he was not simply one of the best local disciples of Stalin; he was

---

[29] Ennker, "The Stalin Cult." Kaganovich was responsible for implementing elements of cultic language and practices even in the Politburo. As Ennker remarked, "The Bolsheviks came close to having a leader cult *within* the leadership": ibid., 93. For more on the relationship of Kaganovich and Stalin, see R. W. Davies, et al., eds., *The Stalin-Kaganovich Correspondence, 1931–1936* (New Haven, CT: Yale University Press, 2003). L. Beria is also considered one of those who made their fortunes by subscribing to the cult. The book on Stalin's activity in pre-revolutionary Transcaucasia, entitled *On the History of Bolshevik Organizations in Transcaucasia*, of which Beria claimed authorship, secured him a quick career in the region and later in Moscow as one of Stalin's closest companions. On Beria's contribution to the cult, see Amy Knight, "Beria and the Cult of Stalin: Rewriting Transcaucasian Party History," *Soviet Studies* 43, no. 4 (1991): 749–63.

[30] Ian Kershaw, "Working towards the Führer": 103–18. The concept has been adapted to the Soviet context by several authors such as Ennker, "The Stalin Cult"; and Rolf, "Working towards the Centre."

probably the most pedantic one. Rákosi was always quick to implement the policies required by Moscow. He was among the first to condemn Yugoslavia after the rift; he was ready to "overfulfill" Soviet requirements for military investment; he organized one of the biggest show trials (that of Rajk) in the bloc; and he even collected damning evidence against Rudolf Slánský and 600 other Communists in the people's democracies.[31] Like most of his colleagues, Rákosi contended for Stalin's favor, and he attempted to prove his preeminence among the competitors by seeking an informal relationship with the Soviet leader. He regularly sent telegrams to the Bolshevik Party secretary using a secure line, and he occasionally met Stalin in a less formal setting in one of his holiday dachas outside Moscow.[32] Nikita Khrushchev also remembers him showing up in the Caucasus on several occasions when Stalin was on holiday there, which allegedly annoyed the Soviet leader. Rákosi also participated at least once in Stalin's vicious drinking games, and although he claimed to have remained conscious, some memoirs recall him actually passing out in the end.[33] As part of the competition for Stalin's favor, Rákosi also criticized other countries for not representing the Soviet leader properly: after the SED's (*Sozialistische Einheitspartei Deutschlands*) 1951 congress in East Germany, he even wrote a letter to Suslov complaining that the Stalin

---

[31] Rákosi's diligence and his relationship with Stalin are analyzed by János M. Rainer, "Távirat 'Filippov' elvtársnak. Rákosi Mátyás üzentei Sztálin titkárságának 1949–1952," in Évkönyv VI: *1998*, ed. György Litván (Budapest: 1956-os Intézet, 1998), 103–18; and János M. Rainer, "Sztálin és Rákosi, Sztálin és Magyarország 1949–1953," in Ibid., 91–100. See also Gavlina Pavlovna Murasko, "Néhány ecsetvonás Rákosi Mátyás politikai portréjához," *Múltunk* 44, no. 2 (1999): 160–69. On the shift in the image of Yugoslavia in Communist propaganda, see Zoltán Ripp, "Példaképből ellenség. A magyar kommunisták viszonya Jugoszláviához, 1947–1948," in Standeisky et al., *A fordulat évei*, 45–62.

[32] See Rainer's articles above for more details.

[33] There are several accounts of the same incident. Nikita Khrushchev claims in his memoirs that Rákosi did not embarrass himself badly, but it seems that he told a different version of the story to other people—including his son—in which Rákosi passed out and had to be carried away. Sergei Khrushchev, ed., *Memoirs of Nikita Khrushchev*, vol. 2: *Reformer (1945–1964)* (University Park: Pennsylvania State University, 2006), 62–63. For the second version, see Veljko Micunovic's Moscow diary, quoted in Csaba Békés, Malcolm Byrne, and János M. Rainer, eds., *The 1956 Hungarian Revolution: A History in Documents* (Budapest–New York: CEU Press, 2002), 353, and Sergei N. Khrushchev, *Nikita Khrushchev and the Creation of a Superpower* (University Park: Pennsylvania State University, 2000), 169. For Rákosi's version of the story, see Rákosi, *Visszaemlékezések 1940–1956*, vol. 2, 751–52.

portraits decorating the event were too few and too small.[34] It is unlikely that Rákosi actually enjoyed special status in Stalin's eyes, given the Soviet dictator's growing paranoia and anti-Semitism in the last years of his rule. (Khrushchev claimed that Stalin had disliked the Hungarian leader.[35])

Although Rákosi never became the kind of dictator Stalin was, he assumed dictatorial powers nonetheless.[36] He became the general secretary of the Party in 1945, president of the People's Front in 1949, head of the informal Committee of Home Defense in 1950, and prime minister in 1952. He personally directed the functioning of the security police, the ÁVH: he interfered with the investigations, and he played a primary role in planning show trials against his political opponents. Despite his incontestable position in the Hungarian power structure, Rákosi remained dependent on Moscow (and Stalin), and his vulnerability became apparent after the death of the Soviet leader. Rákosi's dependence on Kremlin politics significantly shaped his attitude to Sovietization and turned him into an ardent supporter of the cult. Although he was first (allegedly) shocked by the magnitude of the Stalin cult when he arrived in the Soviet Union in 1940 after spending fifteen years in prison, he quickly became accustomed to it.[37] After his return to Hungary, he turned into the prime agent of the Stalin cult: he delivered the major announcements concerning Stalin, and he was the main organizer of the celebrations for the Soviet leader's seventieth birthday.[38]

Rákosi also actively promoted his own cult and accepted the public laudations of his mythical persona.[39] It is thus hardly surprising that his

---

[34] Tikhomirov, "The Stalin Cult," 315.

[35] See note 33.

[36] On Stalin as a dictator, see E. A. Rees, ed., *The Nature of Stalin's Dictatorship: The Politburo, 1924–1953* (Basingstoke: Palgrave, 2004); Oleg V. Khlevniuk, "Stalin as Dictator: The Personalization of Power," in Davies and Harris, *Stalin: A New History*, 108–120.

[37] According to Rákosi, after crossing the Soviet border in 1940, he wrote a letter of gratitude to Stalin that was amended with cultic epithets by the local officers. Rákosi, *Visszaemlékezések 1940–1956*, vol. 1, 13–14. In Moscow, he also tried to use his prestige to intervene in the release of Hungarian Communist émigrés who had been imprisoned during the Great Purges. He was soon informed of the new political realities, however, and stopped petitioning. Petrák, *Magyarok a Szovjetunióban*, 335–41.

[38] MOL, 276. fond 65/76.

[39] This partly had to do with his alleged inferiority complex. Pünkösti, *Rákosi a hatalomért*, 232–34.

cult became one of the most ubiquitous cults of the bloc during the Stalinist era. Rákosi's awareness of the importance of leaders in Communist propaganda was evident from the beginning. In a 1945 lecture to agitators, he stressed the importance of promoting the Party's leaders, including himself, although the call for the promotion of prominent individuals was tinged with irony:

> And a few words here on the popularity of the leaders of the Communist Party. It is not an exaggeration, nor a bias toward our Party, to claim that in the new Hungary, new, popular leaders were only produced by the Communist Party. . . . [W]e could refer to Comrade Vas, we could refer to Comrade Gerő, whose role in the reconstruction of the country does not need to be particularly underlined, and to Comrade Imre Nagy, whose name is connected with land reform (*Réti: And first and foremost to Comrade Rákosi*) and to Mátyás Rákosi. (*Excitement, long-lasting enthusiastic applause*) . . . [T]he Communist Party have their leaders coming from the people indeed, with whom if ordinary people talk, they feel as if the leaders were blood from their own blood, flesh from their own flesh, to whom they could reveal themselves and could talk to them as if they were at home in their family circle. To put it plainly, the popularity of the Communist Party is proper popularity—in the best sense of the word—because the people feel that the leaders are for them: work for them, feel for them, and stick with them through thick and thin, and this great capital should obviously be utilized during the elections, because this is a substantial part of our Party's capital.[40]

Rákosi's role in regulating the representations of his character is less documented than Stalin's interventions in similar matters. Although his personal files demonstrate that he often received documents related to the construction of the cult, the extent to which he actually controlled the process is difficult to assess. Nevertheless, Rákosi seems to have had a pivotal role in moderating his cult. He followed the editing process of his official biography and also contributed to the formulation of the historical narrative about the 1919 Hungarian Republic of Soviets. He sometimes judged works of art and literary pieces, intervened in renamings, and supervised certain aspects of the propaganda campaign for the celebration of his

---

[40] "Hogyan agitáljunk": Rákosi Mátyás előadása a pártnapi előadók és nagybudapesti vezető propagandisták értekezletén a választások előkészítéséről. September 8, 1945. PIL. 274. fond 21/4.

sixtieth birthday, including the preparation of the photo album of his life. (All photos had to be approved by him, and he removed some pictures of himself.)[41] In 1951, he approved the material about himself in a history textbook for ten-year-old children and also suggested changes to some of the eulogistic poems in the volume.[42] One of Rákosi's most remarkable contributions to the cult, however, was his emphasis on the supposed friendship between Lenin and himself.[43] His memoirs suggest that he remained faithful to that illusion—and to the idea of his own exceptionality—even after he left Hungary in 1956. Despite Rákosi's acceptance of his cult, the discursive example set by the Stalin cult prevented the worship of Rákosi from becoming too personal. The same pedantry in Rákosi's attitude toward Sovietization was also typical in his approach to the cult. Therefore, private and intimate details rarely became part of the MDP leader's imagery, and he was most often represented as an abstract symbol.

Like Stalin's associates, Rákosi's immediate circle was also deeply involved in the promotion of the Hungarian Party secretary's public adoration. The top Party leaders, known as the "troika" (Gerő, Farkas, and Rákosi) or the "quadriga" (the troika and Révai), were all trained in Moscow before 1945. Together with Zoltán Vas, Rákosi's former fellow prisoner, they were all familiar with the cult and with its functions, codes, vocabulary, and rituals. These individuals became the prime public promoters of the Rákosi cult, and they contributed significantly to its expansion. Gerő, for example, usually delivered the most important public announcements concerning Rákosi's image, including a speech at the Opera for Rákosi's sixtieth birthday. It was also Gerő who introduced the essential cult vocabulary to the Party membership in 1945. At the meeting of the first Budapest Party *aktíva*, he called Rákosi the "leader of our Party," a "great son of the Hungarian nation," and a "farsighted" and "wise leader," and he attributed prophetic skills to the MKP secretary.[44] Gerő highlighted the importance of Rákosi's speech at the same event and suggested that all Party members "should thoroughly study everything Comrade Rákosi has

---

[41] MOL, 276. fond 65/388. On the making of the photo album, see Nemes, *Rákosi Mátyás*, 21.
[42] MOL, 276. fond 65/343.
[43] See Chapter 3 for details.
[44] Mátyás Rákosi, *A pártaktíva feladatairól* (February 22, 1945), MKP szemináriumi füzetek, no. 2, p. 3. Party *aktívas* were regular meetings of Party activists at various levels of the institutional

talked about here."[45] Such a blatant use of the cult's language in 1945 paved the way for the further escalation of the leader in the Party.

Révai's role in the construction of the cult seems equally vital. As editor-in-chief of *Szabad Nép*, director of the Propaganda Department, and head of the Ministry of People's Education at different times, he became the main coordinator of the process of cult-building. With his close associate Horváth, he was also responsible for orchestrating the celebrations for Rákosi's sixtieth birthday. Nevertheless, Révai also occasionally tried to temper the cult's excesses. As for Farkas, he gave the cult his unconditional support, since he was also busy promoting his own cult in the army.

Because the nucleus of the Party leadership (Rákosi, Gerő, Révai, Farkas, Vas) had already been formed abroad, there was less positional infighting in the highest echelons of the MKP after the war. Thus what motivated the Muscovites to build up the myth of the leader was not so much their individual careerist desires as the attempt to adapt the Soviet example—deemed infallible—to Hungarian conditions. The Hungarian Party secretary's favor, however, became the point of orientation for the rest of the Party elite as well as for Hungarian society. The belief in the legendary leader's infallibility, coupled with the desire for rapid advancement in the Party hierarchy, encouraged second-rank Party leaders to get involved in the machine of cult construction. The degree to which individual career interests and group dynamics in the Hungarian Party elite were interrelated with the competition of praising Rákosi has not been scrutinized as thoroughly as the case of Stalin's lieutenants. Nevertheless, it can be asserted that Rákosi's inner circle (Gerő, Farkas, Révai), as well as his "outer circle" (the second-rank Party elite), took major responsibility in launching the cult of the Party leader into the Hungarian public arena.

The hub of support for the Rákosi cult was undoubtedly the Party bureaucracy, which owed its privileges and status to the Party leader and, in return, helped promote and participated in the cult. Rákosi's regular intervention in the selection of cadres created a solid base within the Party ranks for the cult, which had proven stable enough to outlast even the

---

structure of the state. Party and government organizations, as well as major industrial enterprises, all had a pool of committed Communist activists to rally for the successful realization of the Party's policies. Therefore, *aktívas* were pivotal to the Communist mobilizing campaign.

[45] Ibid., 30.

"New Course." The "Rákosi Youngsters" (István Dénes, Árpád Házi, László Piros, Lajos Ács, Béla Szalai, Rudolf Földvári, András Hegedüs, István Hidas, István Kristóf, Béla Vég, Gyula Egri, and János Matolcsi), whose careers began in the early 1950s, were grateful to Rákosi for their positions, displayed faith in the Rákosi myth, and retained unconditional loyalty toward the Party leader.[46]

An intriguing question concerning the development of the Rákosi cult is whether the MDP secretary actually had the potential to enter the highest echelons of the international Communist pantheon. Rákosi's past might have secured him a place at the top of the cult hierarchy. He participated in the revolutionary attempt to create the dictatorship of the proletariat in Hungary in 1919; he had a rapid, though short, career as secretary of the Executive Committee of the Comintern; he had two trials of remarkable international significance; and he spent fifteen years in the prison of a "reactionary" state. However, some flaws in his image hindered the wider international extension of his cult. Most importantly, his cult—unlike, for example, that of Dimitrov—did not posit him as a theoretician who contributed significantly to the development of Marxism-Leninism. Rákosi's published writings were only articles printed in newspapers and journals, and the transcripts of his speeches and orations. His one and only theoretical piece on Italian fascism—published in the 1920s—could not secure him a place among the theoreticians of Communism.[47]

---

[46] For a typology of careers in the Party, see István Szakadát and Gábor Kelemen, "Karriertípusok és mobilitási csatornák a Magyar Kommunista Párton belül (1945–1989)," in *Magyar társadalomtörténeti olvasókönyv 1944-től napjainkig*, ed. Tibor Valuch (Budapest: Argumentum, 2004), 664–77.

[47] Mátyás Rákosi, "Il fascismo italiano," in *Il fascismo. Le interpretazioni dei contemporanei e degli storici*, ed. Renzo de Felice (Rome and Bari, 1998), 95–105.

Chapter 3

"The Biography is a Very Serious Issue": The Role of Biographies in Constructing the Rákosi Cult

Biographies and Stalinist Political Culture

Biographies are essential to the process of cult construction. The extensive proliferation of such writings became one of the most typical manifestations of the cultic veneration of monarchs, emperors, and revolutionaries, as well as leaders of modern political movements. Communist cults also relied heavily on biographies. The life stories of Stalin, Mao, Dimitrov, Thorez, and others were published in great numbers and were used for a multitude of propaganda purposes. The lives of leaders were studied by schoolchildren, at courses and seminars in Party schools, and at all levels of education. They became a central point of reference: journalists referred to them in their articles, speakers at mass demonstrations mentioned the exemplary deeds of the Party leader, and academics—historians, philosophers, and so on—emphasized the given leader's contribution to the ideological development of the Party and the historical changes in the nation's existence. Besides official biographies, which were usually published as a separate book or booklet, biographical material was circulated in the form of pamphlets, leaflets, or even novels. Biographical information was frequently incorporated into history books, general course descriptions, and syllabi. Motion pictures (newsreels or feature films) were effective ways of conveying biographical elements—although not in Rákosi's case—and even sound recordings, such as interviews, were employed to portray the events of a specific person's life. No matter what form they took, biographies of leaders were normally used for two main purposes in Communist propaganda. Shorter biographies (in pamphlets, flyers, newspaper articles, etc.) were disseminated during intense agitation periods, when the leaders' biographies were popularized as part of a broader mobilization campaign (such as elections). Apart from fulfilling immediate agitational needs, biographies played a pivotal role in the Party's indoctrination efforts. The exemplary life of the leader was used as instruction material in educational institutions, and it was exploited to promote the core values and ideological tenets of the regime.

Biographical writing had a certain tradition in the working-class movement before Stalinist times, even if the Bolsheviks were initially dismissive of the value of such writings.[1] Nevertheless, life stories were used by most Russian parties at the time of the 1917 revolution, and biographies contributed to the rise of the "cult of the freedom fighter" at the time. Socialist parties also published pamphlets, poems, songs, and short biographical sketches promoting their own leaders while trying to consolidate their status on the unstable political scene.[2] Although the early years of Bolshevik rule, with its focus on the masses as the driving force of history, downplayed the role of the individual, the central place of the Bolshevik Revolution and the Russian Civil War in Bolshevik mythology soon prompted the publication of a number of (auto)biographical anthologies of veterans and heroes of 1917–1921.[3] The beginning of the "heroic age" in the late 1920s was also manifest in the celebration of the lives of socialist heroes (Stakhanovites, heroes of labor, explorers, aviators, and so on) through the circulation and popularization of biographical writings. The mid-1930s ideological shift toward Russian national myths and symbols further boosted the use of biographies. The emergence of "national Bolshevism" significantly reshuffled the pantheon of Soviet heroes, rehabilitated pre-revolutionary Russian historical figures (Ivan the Terrible, Peter the Great, Kutuzov, etc.), and resulted in the large-scale dissemination of their biographies, especially during the war.[4]

---

[1] Pennetier and Pudal, "Stalinism," 24.
[2] Orlando Figes and Boris Kolonitskii, *Interpreting the Russian Revolution: The Language and Symbols of 1917* (New Haven, CT: Yale University Press, 1999), 75.
[3] Pennetier and Pudal, "Stalinism," 24.
[4] David Brandenberger, *National Bolshevism: Stalinist Mass Culture and the Formation of Modern Russian National Identity, 1931–1956* (Cambridge, MA, and London: Harvard University Press, 2002), 145. On the rehabilitation of historical figures, see Maureen Perrie, *The Cult of Ivan the Terrible in Stalin's Russia* (Basingstone: Palgrave, 2001).

As Katerina Clark has argued, the roots of Stalinist biographical representations can be found in nineteenth-century radical fiction and, to a lesser extent, in medieval hagiographic writings about Orthodox saints.[5] As she points out, the plot structure of literary works that functioned as models for the Socialist Realist writers of the 1930s generally followed the pattern of a biography. The biographical perspective remained the unifying theme of the Socialist Realist master plot as it crystallized in the early 1930s. A typical novel in High Stalinism was, in fact, a ritualized representation of the Marxist-Leninist interpretation of history, portrayed in biographical terms. The development of a typical hero's character in the Soviet novel of the 1930s—as the protagonist gradually acquired "consciousness"—epitomized the Bolshevik perception of historical progress.[6] As Socialist Realism and Soviet political discourse merged in the years of Stalinism, the biographical perspective became an essential building block of the Bolshevik historical narrative. Generally, the flow of events in historical works of the 1930s centered on "great events" and the lives of "great men," as opposed to the abstract social categories of Marxism of the 1920s.[7] Furthermore, historical biography became a popular genre. The majority of literary works or films released in the late 1930s were biographies, either of Russian historical figures (Brusilov, Peter the Great, Aleksandr Nevskii, Kutuzov, Suvorov, etc.) or of top Communist leaders (Stalin, Kirov, Voroshilov, or Ordzhonikidze).[8] As Clark remarks: "It was an age when it seemed that virtually everyone who put pen to paper was writing a heroic biography of one of the official heroes (a member of the Stalinist leadership, a Civil War hero, a leader figure from the national past, like Emelian Pugachev, or a symbolic hero)."[9] Ordinary citizens encountered biographies on a daily basis, but the ability to write one also became an important skill in Stalinist political culture. People were required to submit autobiographies when dealing with Party and government institutions, but such institutions—particularly cadre departments and the secret police—were also busy collecting biographical information about

---

[5] Clark, *The Soviet Novel*.
[6] Ibid., 15–16.
[7] Brandenberger, *National Bolshevism*, 52–53.
[8] Ibid., 145; Clark, *The Soviet Novel*, 124.
[9] Ibid., 118.

the people who came under their radar. Thus the embellished life stories of Communist leaders emerged in a political culture that was centered on biographical narratives.[10]

The Stalinist culture of biographical representations was transferred to Eastern Europe after the war as part of the Sovietization process, and the circulation of the life stories of heroes and Party leaders also became a routine practice of Communist propaganda in the region. The centrality of biographies in Communist cult-building projects is underlined by the fact that all Eastern European Party leaders had their official biographies published—and translated into several languages—in the early 1950s, irrespective of the degree of cultic veneration around the individual leaders. (The one exception was Dimitrov, whose first biography was published in the Soviet Union in 1934.)[11] The biographies of Pieck and Gheorghiu-Dej were released in 1951; Bierut's and Rákosi's were published in 1952 for their sixtieth birthdays; and Tito's came out in 1953.[12] Although Gottwald's official biography was only published in 1954, a year after his (and Stalin's) death, there were two biographical publications—in multiple languages—available about him during his lifetime. (Both were written by the same author who eventually completed the official biography.)[13] The last biography modeled on the Stalinist biographical narrative was that of Ulbricht in the GDR, published—somewhat paradoxically—during the period of de-Stalinization in 1958.[14] The tendency to represent the Party leadership in biographical terms continued in the post-Stalin period, as shown, for example, by Erich Honecker's biographical projects. However, the republication of Tito's first biography in 1980—without any changes in the original text and with two more volumes added—signifies the lasting

---

[10] This was also observed by Pennetier and Pudal, "Stalinism," 25.

[11] The English version is Stella Dimitrova Blagoeva, *Dimitrov: A Biography* (New York: International Publishers, 1934).

[12] *Gh. Gheorghiu-Dej* (Bucharest: Román Munkáspárt, 1951); Fritz Erpenbeck, *Wilhelm Pieck: Ein Lebensbild* (Berlin: Dietz, 1951); Józef Kowalczyk, *Bolesław Bierut: Życie i działalność* (Warsaw, 1952); Vladimir Dedijer, *Josip Broz Tito: prilozi za biografiju* (Zagreb, 1953).

[13] The first one was published as early as 1946: František Nečásek, *Klement Gottwald: Communist Premier of Czechoslovakia; A Biography* (London, 1946). The second one was about his youth: František Nečásek, *Mládí Klementa Gottwalda*, 2nd ed. (Prague, 1951). The official biography is František Nečásek, *O Klementu Gottwaldovi (náčrt životopisu)* (Prague, 1954).

[14] Johannes R. Becher, *Walter Ulbricht: Ein deutscher Arbeitersohn* (Berlin, 1958).

importance of biographies in Communist representations of power and leadership across Eastern Europe.[15]

The compilation and publication of the official biographies of Stalin and the "lesser gods" was not an easy task. As the biographies of Stalin, Rákosi, and even Lenin show, these projects took a long time and involved the participation of numerous high-ranking Party officials in the research and editing process, and even the intervention of the Party leader himself. Nevertheless, in spite of the great effort invested, some biographies were still rejected.[16] As in the cases of socialist heroes and Russian national figures, the biographies of Stalin and the "mini-Stalins," or local Party leaders, also fused (Party) history and the life story of the leader. In effect, these official biographies became the personalized representations of the history of national working-class movements, offering an individualized account of the local Party's struggles and sacrifices while demonstrating the transformation of "class instinct" into "class consciousness."[17] At the same time, biographies summarized the official values and ideological tenets of the regime and provided an example of the idealized behavior that it hoped to instill in the public. They were, in fact, "apprenticeship manuals" that functioned as guidelines to living like a real Communist.[18] The official biographies of local leaders could thus be regarded as cross-sections of local Party history and introductory texts to Communist lore in general. But the biographies of Communist leaders could also be considered cross-sections of their own cults. The biography was a summary or outline of the myths about the particular leader in a simplified, condensed form. At the same time it functioned as a guideline to, or map of, the cult, from which one could master the symbols and the language of the leader cult. The official biography also had a legitimizing function,

---

[15] His official biography—*Erich Honecker: Skizze eines politische Lebens* (Berlin: Institut für Marxismus-Leninismus, 1977)—was followed by an autobiography written by a ghostwriter: Erich Honecker, *Aus meinem Leben* (Berlin, 1980). On the continuation of Stalinist patterns in the representations of Communist leaders in the GDR and Poland, see Jan C. Behrends, "Nach dem Führerkult. Repräsentationen des Generalsekretärs in Polen under DDR," in *Medien und Imagepolitik im 20. Jahrhundert. Deutschland, Europa, USA*, ed. Daniela Münkel and Lu Seegers (Frankfurt am Main: Campus, 2008), 57–83. On the republished Tito biographies, see László Rehák, "Tito életrajzának első kötete," *Létünk*, May 20, 1981, 987–91.
[16] On Stalin's official biography, see Brandenberger, "Stalin as Symbol."
[17] Pennetier and Pudal, "Stalinism," 21.
[18] Ibid., 23.

as it strove to explain why and how the leader in question became the ideal person to steer the country toward a better future. As the boundaries blurred between personal life story and Party history, as well as between the leader's personality and the collective identity of the Party, the official biography also contributed to the strengthening of the legitimate basis of the regime and Party.

Biographies' complex character and multifunctionality were acknowledged and consciously exploited by Stalin. In the mid-1930s, he intervened in history-writing, advocating recognition of the role of "great men" in advancing historical progress, and he also helped rehabilitate pre-revolutionary, tsarist historical figures.[19] Stalin contributed to the editing process of a number of historical works—the *Short Course* chief among them—as well as some biographies (e.g., that of Suvorov).[20] The dictator gave his explicit view of biographies while he was revising the second edition of his own biography in 1946. At a meeting he convened for the authors involved in the process, he argued that "the toiling masses and simple people cannot begin the study of Marxism-Leninism with Lenin's and Stalin's writ[ings]. They should start with the biography. The biography is a very serious issue—it has enor[mous] mean[ing] for the Marx[ist] enlight[enment] of the simple people."[21]

Given the importance of the biographical perception of history in Stalinist political culture—along with the facts that Stalin deemed biographies crucial to mass mobilization campaigns and to the construction of his own cult, and that Khrushchev, in his "secret speech" in 1956, also referred to Stalin's short biography as a significant manifestation of "the cult of personality"—there is a strong case to be made for the study of biographies in the process of constructing the cult of Communist leaders in the Soviet Union and the peripheries of the Soviet empire.[22]

---

[19] This was as part of the critique of the Pokrovskii School of historiography. For Stalin's role in shaping history-writing, see Perrie, *The Cult of Ivan the Terrible*; Tucker, *Stalin in Power*, 530–50. See also Brandenberger, *National Bolshevism*. On Stalin's role in the construction of his own cult, see Davies, "Stalin and the Making of the Leader Cult."

[20] Brandenberger, *National Bolshevism*, 148.

[21] As cited in Brandenberger, "Stalin as Symbol," 265. See also van Ree, *The Political Thought of Joseph Stalin*, 162–65.

[22] For Khrushchev's speech, see Nikita Sergeevich Khrushchev, *The "Secret" Speech: Delivered to the Closed Session of the Twentieth Congress of the Communist Party of the Soviet Union*

The Biographies of Rákosi

The first biography of Mátyás Rákosi was published well before he could influence Hungarian politics in any significant way. Written by György Szamueli, it came out in Moscow in 1935 with a foreword by Béla Kun.[23] Due to the Great Purges, however, the book suffered the same fate as many other publications of the time. As it contained references to leading figures of the Comintern (including Kun) purged in 1936–1938, it was re-edited and re-released in 1937 with a different foreword.[24] Even the name of the author was changed: Szamueli was given the pseudonym "E. Téglás."[25] The first biography of Rákosi was published at the time when Soviet political discourse was teeming with heroes, and the biography was the dominant genre used to publicize them. The immediate context of the publication of the biography, however, was the second Rákosi trial (in 1934–1935) in Budapest, which the Comintern exploited for propaganda purposes, as it had with Dimitrov's trial in Leipzig a few years earlier.[26] The publication of the biography of the "illuminating beam of light," as Henri Barbusse once called Rákosi, was an essential part of this process.[27]

The Szamueli/Téglás book did not (yet) portray a father figure in the mold of the Stalinist "great family."[28] Although Rákosi was given mentor-like qualities in the book, and he was depicted as a banner for the working class to rally around at the time of his trials, his portrayal remained close to that of an ordinary Communist hero, in this case the

---

(Nottingham: Spokesman Books, 1976). As Erik van Ree remarked, "the cult rested importantly on hagiographies": *The Political Thought of Joseph Stalin*, 162. David Brandenberger also noted that "biography as a genre lies very close to the heart of the personality cult": Brandenberger, "Stalin as Symbol," 251.

[23] Georg Samueli, *Rakoshi, Matias* (Moscow: Molodaia gvardiia, 1935).

[24] Pünkösti, *Rákosi a hatalomért*, 12. On the effect of the purges on the Comintern, see Chase, *Enemies within the Gates?*

[25] E. Téglás, *Rákosi Mátyás* (Moscow, 1937). The author himself fell victim to the Great Purges. Chase, *Enemies within the Gates?* 496.

[26] Rákosi was first put to trial in Hungary in 1925 and was sentenced to eight-and-a-half years' imprisonment. In 1934, instead of releasing him, the Hungarian authorities brought Rákosi to court again (for his activity in the 1919 Hungarian Republic of Soviets). This time he received a life sentence. On the rise of the Dimitrov myth, see Markus Wien, "Georgi Dimitrov: Three Manifestations of His Cult," in Apor et al., *The Leader Cult*, 194–207.

[27] *Rákosi elvtárs élete. Szakszervezeti Ismeretterjesztő előadások* (Budapest, 1952), 11.

[28] Clark, *The Soviet Novel*, 114–36.

"hero of the Comintern." Interestingly, the biography was never again published after 1945 and was not used for propaganda purposes in postwar Hungary. Thus, unlike Dimitrov, whose 1934 biography remained an essential component of the cult-building process in Bulgaria after the war, Rákosi returned to Hungary from the Soviet Union without an approved Stalinist biographical narrative. One can only speculate why the post-1945 leadership discarded Rákosi's first biography. It was probably because of the book's tendency to represent him as an "ordinary hero" instead of a father figure, but it could have been because of the manuscript's tainted past and the references to purged Communists.

The first biographical material published on Rákosi after the war was a printed version of a short radio interview recorded on October 4, 1945.[29] The image of Rákosi presented in the interview was heavily influenced by the leader cult discourse, and it provides a further example of cult-building tendencies in the Communist Party in the coalition period:

> The difficult years spent in the penitentiary did not break his will, nor did they dim his judgment. His sheer existence meant permanent menace and a mortal threat to the Horthy reactionaries.[30]

Although no officially approved biography of Rákosi was available during the coalition years, the dissemination of biographical texts of Communist leaders in the form of pamphlets, leaflets, or newspaper articles was a standard practice at the time. Such publications were mostly distributed during intense agitprop periods—such as election campaigns—on the initiative of central Party organs.[31]

One of the first proposals by the MKP's Propaganda-Agitation Department to publish biographical pamphlets popularizing political leaders—the top twelve Communist candidates—was implemented for the 1945 elections. The pamphlets contained a picture and a short biography of the leader as well as his address to the constituency where the

---

[29] *Egy nagy harcos életéből. Rádióbeszélgetés Rákosi Mátyással 1945. október 4-én* (Budapest: Szikra, 1945).

[30] Ibid., 1.

[31] Short biographies of political leaders were used for propaganda purposes by other Hungarian political parties as well.

material was distributed.[32] The leaders of the Party became more prominent in Communist propaganda at the time of the next elections, in 1947. At its meeting on July 31, the Politburo commissioned *Szabad Nép* and *Magyar Nap* (Hungarian Sun) to publish a series of short biographical articles popularizing Communist leaders.[33] The first article published in the series was about Rákosi, and it was followed by similar writings on Farkas, Révai, Erik Molnár, Kádár, and others. Despite the instructions of the Politburo, however, the biographical information was overshadowed by lengthy praise for the leaders. Nevertheless, the portrayal of the Party's prominent figures in Communist newspapers provides another example of the uniformity of leader representations in Communist political discourse at the time. In all cases, the articles' main focus was on the leaders' approachability, their commitment to work, and their qualities as leading politicians—images that the various authors conveyed through the use of a standardized cultic vocabulary.

The publication of short biographies of Communist leaders was also part of the electoral campaign of 1949. This time, the Agitation Department's proposal to publish propaganda leaflets about the Party's key figures included detailed guidelines for the structure and content of such biographies.[34] The document suggested that the leaflets follow a thematic structure instead of a chronological one (how the candidate fought the imperialists, his activity in the working-class movement, his loyalty to the people, etc.), and it outlined a number of virtues to be emphasized in the biographies (heroism, firmness, devotion). Naturally, the flyer about Rákosi was supposed to be longer and more colorful than those for other leaders.

Apart from mobilization campaigns, Communist propaganda also used Rákosi's biographies in Party education. One proposal of the MDP's Orgburo in November 1948, for example, authorized the Association of Hungarian Freedom Fighters to give lectures on the lives of Rákosi, Lenin, and Stalin as part of its two-month-long evening course.[35] As the instruction in the life of the leader was considered a serious matter, in 1950 the

---

[32] PIL, 274. fond 21/5.
[33] PIL, 274. fond 3/99.
[34] MOL, 276. fond 108/9.
[35] MOL, 276. fond 55/39.

APO published a number of guidelines on the proper way to teach about Rákosi's life at courses and seminars in Party schools. At the same time, classes on Communist biographies were integrated into the curricula of various Party-affiliated institutions. In early 1951, for example, the department proposed teaching the biographies of Lenin, Stalin, and Rákosi at the one-year journalism course in two blocks of three lessons.[36]

The "Year of the Turn" saw the beginning of the inclusion of biographical material about the leader in history textbooks for schoolchildren. The first such textbook was published in 1948, for fourteen-year-old primary-school pupils. It was followed by similar publications for nine- and ten-year-olds, ten- and eleven-year-olds, and seventeen- and eighteen-year-olds in subsequent years.[37] Biographical information on Rákosi, however, never constituted a separate chapter in any of the history books; the leader's life remained embedded within the greater thematic structures of Hungarian history.[38] The way in which Rákosi was presented to the children was also adjusted to the age of the pupils. The textbook for nine- and ten-year-old children, for example, contained morality tales from the leader's childhood and portrayed him as the most talented and committed pupil at school.[39] The books for older children focused more on his qualities as conductor of the Hungarian working-class movement and his exemplary behavior during his trials.

Apart from presenting the model life of the Hungarian Party leader, textbooks for children became vehicles of the leader cult in many other ways. The textbook written for secondary-school children, for example, included eight volumes of Rákosi's collected speeches in the recommended-reading section, as well as three other publications on him. References to Rákosi or quotations from his speeches also featured extensively in

---

[36] MOL, 276. fond 89/10.

[37] For primary-school students: László Zsigmond, Klára Fejér, and Béla Karácsonyi, *Történelem. Az általános iskolák VIII. osztálya számára*, 5th ed. (Budapest, 1952). For secondary-school pupils: Lajos Lukács, *A magyar nép története III. rész (1849-től napjainkig)* (Budapest, 1951). The material for technical schools: Endre Kovács, Gyula Simon, and Béla Bellér, *Történelem. A Szakiskolák IV. osztálya számára* (Budapest, 1954).

[38] In a 1952 primary-school textbook, the biographical information on Rákosi appeared in three different chapters. *Történelem. Az általános iskolák VIII. osztálya számára* (Budapest, 1952).

[39] Similar fictitious moral stories from Lenin's and Stalin's childhood were also included in the same book. Éva Kovács, "Vezérekről, példaképekről gyermekeknek," *História* 9, nos. 5–6 (1987): 42.

textbooks for younger children. Apart from the leader's frequently quoted statements on the political and economic state of the country, his remarks on or evaluations of the nation's past were also regularly incorporated into the text.[40] The leader's "revealing" comments on the reasons for the Hungarian defeat in the 1849 War of Independence, and his assessment of the historical significance of the peasant leader György Dózsa in 1514, for instance, were usually included in the teaching materials.[41]

The endurance of cultic textbooks for children is fairly remarkable. The primary-school history book, for example, was awarded the silver Kossuth Prize in 1949, and it also survived the first wave of de-Stalinization in 1953–1954, with the material on Rákosi remaining untouched. The ambiguity and restricted scope of the "New Course" (1953–1955) in Hungary was also marked by the fact that none of the other books had been modified significantly. The Rákosi cult was only purged from history textbooks after 1956.

The changes in the use of Rákosi's biographies highlight a shift in the nature of Communist propaganda in Hungary after 1948. Before the "Year of the Turn," the most important goal of propaganda was to mobilize the population to rebuild the country, and to popularize the MKP's beliefs and political objectives. In this context, the biographies of leaders were used primarily for agitation purposes, usually within the framework of a broader campaign (e.g., elections). As soon as the Party's position on the political stage was unchallenged, Communist propaganda underwent a remarkable metamorphosis that also triggered a change in the function of leader biographies. Besides retaining its mobilization aspect, propaganda served primarily to endorse the regime's indoctrination efforts. With the aim of integrating society under the banner of socialism, the biographical representations of the Hungarian working-class movement (i.e., the life stories of Rákosi) were utilized to inculcate the ideological tenets of the regime and the behavioral patterns it expected from its citizens.

---

[40] Ibid., 43.
[41] E.g., Béla Karácsonyi, *A magyar nép története. I. rész 1526-ig* (Budapest, 1954), 105; Péter Hanák, ed., *Történelem. A középiskolák II. osztálya számára* (Budapest, 1949), 168–69.

The Official Biography

In January 1948, the Propaganda Department suggested publishing a series of leaflets on Hungarian and international Communist leaders and martyrs such as Rákosi, Dimitrov, and Tito.[42] However, the proposal was never implemented. Additionally, just as in the Soviet Union, some intellectuals offered their services. One of them, who continually bombarded Rákosi with petty appeals, was the Muscovite writer Sándor Gergely. In a letter to the leader—a mixture of flattery, requests, and intrigues—he volunteered for the task of writing the biography of Rákosi.[43] Other writers also tried to gain the privilege of representing certain periods or events in the life of the leader. Sándor Rideg, for instance, contemplated writing a book on Rákosi's childhood; Gyula Háy requested that the Party secretary allow him to compose a drama about the Rákosi trials; Lőrinc Kovai submitted a film script about the 1919 Republic of Soviets to the Rákosi Secretariat; and Lajos Barta suggested writing a screenplay on Rákosi's life that "would give sense to our entire history."[44] These proposals were either rejected straightaway or simply left unrealized.

The decision to publish Rákosi's official biography was eventually made at the August 29, 1951, Secretariat meeting, when the proposal to celebrate the Party leader's sixtieth birthday was approved. The proposal suggesting the publication of Rákosi's biography and the organization of an exhibition on his life was put forward by Révai. The idea of making a film and a documentary on Rákosi's life, *Rákosi Mátyás 60 éves* (Mátyás Rákosi: Sixty Years Old), was also discussed at the meeting, but it was rejected.[45] The task of preparing the writing and publication of Rákosi's biography was assigned to László Réti, director of the Institute for the History of the Working-Class Movement, and Ferenc Karinthy, a well-known writer. A few weeks later, the APO set up an editorial board to write and edit

---

[42] PIL, 274. fond 21/1.
[43] Gergely's letter to Rákosi was sent on March 6, 1950, MOL, 276. fond 65/332. ő.e.
[44] Despite its emphasis on the Tsarytsin-Salgótarján parallel, Kovai's script was turned down without hesitation, because the Party authorities did not appreciate the degree of violence and "sadistic details" in the text. (Kovai was simply called "abnormal" by the reviewer of his script.) Ibid.
[45] The rejection of the film on Rákosi's life by the Secretariat: MOL, 276. fond 54/158. For the idea of making a documentary on the Party secretary's life, see MOL, 276. fond 65/388.

Rákosi's biography.⁴⁶ The committee consisted of twelve people, each of whom was responsible for editing different chapters of the draft. The symbolic significance of the biography was demonstrated by the fact that the editorial board included senior members of the Party: two members of the troika (Gerő, Farkas); the ideological chief, Révai; the head of the Agitation and Propaganda Department, Márton Horváth; and Rákosi's brother, Zoltán Bíró. The actual manuscript was written by Réti and was reviewed by the APO. It was most likely seen by Rákosi himself, but his precise involvement in the process is unknown. A leaflet based upon the Réti text was translated into several languages, and the Ministry of Foreign Affairs sent the translations to Hungarian embassies abroad.⁴⁷ However, Réti's biography was never published—either in the leaflet version or the full text—because the publication process was suddenly halted. According to a letter Horváth wrote to Gerő, the editorial board finally decided not to disseminate Réti's text, as it needed to be "substantially reworked."⁴⁸ Although the relatively late stage at which the biography was canceled might indicate Rákosi's personal intervention, the role of the Party leader in the cancellation remains unclear.⁴⁹ The birthday committee seems to have regarded the withdrawal of Réti's work as a temporary decision. Horváth's June 6, 1952, letter to Gerő, which was also forwarded to Révai, Farkas, and Vas, indicates that the editorial board planned to revise Réti's text and publish it later as the official biography.

Although it remains unclear why the Réti manuscript was never published, some hypotheses can be formed. Like the biography of Stalin, the text was saturated with outright falsifications and exaggerations of the leader's role in historical events. In Réti's case, however, historical distortions apparently went beyond the limits, and there was also a risk that the leader would become an object of ridicule. For instance, the description of the young Rákosi eating a whole package of food at British customs because the officers would not let him bring it through is more

---

⁴⁶ MOL, 276. fond 89/163.
⁴⁷ Nemes, *Rákosi Mátyás születésnapja*, 29.
⁴⁸ MOL, 276. fond 65/389.
⁴⁹ It may have been Révai who eventually decided to withdraw the biography, as he often curbed the excesses of the Rákosi cult. However, the fact that he was deeply involved in the editing process of the Réti biography from the beginning weakens this argument.

an indication of greed than alleged poverty. Moreover, the portrayal of "the handsome young Hungarian lad with sleek black hair" who "made the girls' hearts beat whenever he danced the *csárdás*" makes Rákosi sound more like a dandy than a devoted Communist and future leader.[50] The description of an impoverished Rákosi with his toes poking out of his shoes and the claim that he was the first to teach Hungarian demonstrators the lyrics of the *Internationale* (in March 1912) are further anecdotes that might potentially have made the leader look ridiculous. In addition, the structure of the manuscript was rather uneven. Moreover, it was overburdened with lengthy quotations from Rákosi and Stalin and with extensive elaboration of the historical context. Réti's prose style was also tediously turgid and effusive—resembling Stalin's official biography in this regard.[51] No matter how tempting, Réti's abandoned biography can hardly be used as a representative example of what constituted excess in the construction of the Rákosi cult. Apart from some ridiculous statements, the style, the structure, and even the editing process of the text was very similar to Stalin's official biography, and with little effort it could have been adjusted to the standard of the Soviet leader's life story. The fact that the biography was rejected in the end, therefore, does not demarcate the limits of the leader cult. Instead, it implies that the moderation of the Rákosi cult was spontaneous and that the cult's perimeters were constantly shifting.[52]

As the date of Rákosi's birthday—March 9—was looming, an emergency solution was found. Illés, a writer loyal to the regime, was entrusted with the task of composing Rákosi's biography under immense time pressure.[53] He met Rákosi on January 15, 1952 (at 9 p.m.), to discuss the leader's life, and a month later the biography was already being distributed as the primary material for teaching Party courses on the life of the leader.[54] (Illés did rely on Réti's work, however.) As soon as Illés finished writing

---

[50] Réti's manuscript can be found at MOL, 276. fond 65/389.
[51] Brandenberger, "Stalin as Symbol," 269. For the Hungarian translation of Stalin's biography, see *J. V. Sztálin. Rövid életrajz* (Budapest: Szikra, 1949).
[52] This endorses David Brandenberger's argument about the ad hoc nature and inconsistency of the organization of the Stalin cult. Brandenberger, "Stalin as Symbol," 251.
[53] Pünkösti, *Rákosi a csúcson*, 424–38. On the position of Illés in the Hungarian literary scene after 1945, and his relationship with Rákosi, see von Klimo, "'A Very Modest Man': Béla Illés."
[54] For the notes about the meeting, see MOL, 276. fond 65/332. For Rákosi's notes to Illés, see PIL, 720. fond 1.

the manuscript, it was rapidly translated into a number of languages and was eventually published as the official biography of Rákosi in February 1952, with the title *Népünk szabadságáért* (For Our People's Freedom). At the same time, Illés's text was authorized by the Orgburo—on Horváth's proposal—as the sole interpretation of Rákosi's life, while the distribution of biographical material unapproved by the APO was prohibited.

> Given that recently certain provincial Party committees, lower-level Party committees, and mass organizations prepared, printed, and distributed various materials on Comrade Rákosi's life that were not checked by any higher-level Party organizations, and thus gave rise to the emergence of incorrect influence in the line of propaganda of the preparation of Comrade Rákosi's birthday, the Orgburo will not permit the publication and distribution of any material on Comrade Rákosi that was not checked and approved by the Agit. Prop. Department [APO] beforehand. The Party committees of the counties should submit any related material for approval before further distribution. The biography of Comrade Rákosi will be published and will be processed at political seminars of Party schools and evening political schools. The propaganda campaign of Comrade Rákosi's birthday should be based exclusively on this material and also on the material published in the Party press. Márton Horváth[55]

Once Illés's booklet was ready, the MDP launched a campaign within the framework of the birthday celebrations to popularize the life of Rákosi. An outline of the new biography was translated into several languages (English, German, French, Russian, Romanian, etc.), while newspapers and journals were ordered to publish complimentary reviews and abstracts of the work.[56] Apart from the official biography, other publications and events also celebrated Rákosi's life at the time of his birthday, including an anthology of photos from his life and an exhibition in the Institute for the History of the Working-Class Movement entitled *Rákosi Mátyás harcos élete* (Mátyás Rákosi's Crusading Life).[57]

---

[55] The meeting of the Orgburo took place on February 11, 1952, MOL, 276. fond 55/193.

[56] MOL, 276. fond 89/193. The English-language leaflet, based on Illés's text, is *Mátyás Rákosi: On the Occasion of His Sixtieth Birthday* (London: Hungarian News and Information Service, 1952). A review of Illés's text was published in the official newspaper. Károly Kiss, "Rákosi elvtárs életéről," *Szabad Nép*, February 24, 1952.

[57] *Rákosi Mátyás élete képekben*. This book was also translated into a number of foreign languages.

A few weeks before the Party leader's birthday, the Party organized short evening courses on Rákosi's life.[58] In addition, seminars and lectures dedicated to the Hungarian Party leader's life took place at all levels of education during the month of Rákosi's birthday. (The APO even designated which sections of Illés's biography should be read aloud.)[59] Most of the biographical outlines and teaching materials were also updated in accordance with the new biography.[60] In some cases, course outlines were changed to include separate classes on Rákosi's life, based on the official biography.[61] Although the material on the Party leader's life in school textbooks remained more or less intact after the publication of Illés's book—though it was very often quoted—guidelines based on the text were published illustrating the proper way to teach the leader's life in Party seminars and in school classrooms.

Besides prescribing the method of teaching Rákosi's biography, the Propaganda Department also tried to influence how the people would perceive the life of the leader. The press published reports about students speaking of the inspiration provided by Rákosi's example, and emphasizing the special, festive atmosphere in the classroom when Rákosi's life was discussed: "It is impossible to talk about the life of Rákosi in a dirty, untidy room; it is impossible to give a boring, dull lecture on the topic."[62] Similar articles were published about teachers, too. One instructor of a propagandist seminar, for example, said the assignment was the greatest challenge of his life and had an unforgettable, enlightening effect.[63]

Public response to the biography was cautiously monitored by the APO during the birthday campaign. According to one report, Illés's book was extremely popular among Party members and quickly sold out.[64] The document emphasized that at least half a million people had studied the life of the Hungarian dictator in evening classes before his birthday, and another half a million had participated in public meetings or reading

---

[58] MOL, 276. fond 89/10.
[59] Pünkösti, *Rákosi a csúcson*, 427.
[60] Some examples: *Rákosi elvtárs élete*; and *Rákosi elvtárs harca*, 3 vols., (Sztálinváros, 1952).
[61] As in the case of the Stalin Academy for Political Officers in October 1952. MOL, 276. fond 89/123.
[62] *Szabad Ifjúság*, November 16, 1952.
[63] "Hogyan készültem a Rákosi elvtárs harcos életéről szóló szemináriumra?" *Szabad Nép*, March 2, 1952.
[64] MOL, 276. fond 89/10.

circles on the same theme. The report also noted the unexpected success of Rákosi's life story among the peasantry. Lectures on the life of the leader allegedly stimulated a significant increase in the number of applications to evening courses and Party schools in the countryside, and in the number of pledges at collective farms and machine stations.[65] Similar reports were submitted from industrial plants, where the biography was usually said to have energized the labor competition and invigorated political activism. In the Nitrokémia factory the lecture on Rákosi's life supposedly attracted three times as many spectators as usual.[66] There were even priests who responded positively to Illés's book. A "peace priest" writing a letter to Rákosi praised the originality and clarity of the writing style, adding that he was so moved by the leader's life story that he became a devotee of the cause.[67]

The Biographical Narrative

The biographical narrative applied two major techniques to underline Rákosi's position as the leader. The biographies either exaggerated Rákosi's impact on history or diminished—and often erased—the significance of other historical actors (e.g., Béla Kun) who could potentially eclipse the leader as the conductor of Hungarian history.[68] According to Rákosi's biographical narrative, as presented in a crystallized form in Illés's booklet, the leader came from a working-class family with a long revolutionary tradition that constantly had to struggle for its daily bread. Due to his poverty-stricken background, Rákosi started to show an interest in the plight of the deprived as a child and was already participating in workers' demonstrations at an early age. He became committed to the cause of the working-class movement as a teenager and, at the age of fourteen, participated in the protest marches of 1906 in Szeged. Immediately after completing his secondary-school studies, he joined the Social Democratic

---

[65] Ibid.
[66] MOL, 276. fond 89/612.
[67] Kő and Nagy, *Levelek Rákosihoz*, 71–72. Peace priests were members of the movement organized by the regime to diminish the spiritual influence of the churches.
[68] This was also a typical feature of the biographies of Communist leaders, as observed by Pennetier and Pudal, "Stalinism," 25.

Party, and as the secretary of the leftist-radical Galilei Circle in Budapest, he "prepared himself for the hard and dedicated life of the revolutionary fighter."[69] As a result of years of study in London and Hamburg and the prisoner-of-war camp in Russia during World War I, Rákosi became a devoted Bolshevik and, in November 1918, was "one of the founders" of the Hungarian Party of Communists (KMP) (no other founders were normally mentioned in his biographies).

One of the core elements of Rákosi's biographical narrative was his activity during the Hungarian Republic of Soviets of 1919, especially the feat of defending the mining town, Salgótarján, a victory credited exclusively to him. The battle, in which the invading Czech troops were stopped and driven back by miner militias and the Hungarian Red Army, was compared to Stalin's defense of Tsaritsyn in the Russian Civil War. The narrative of the event was utilized to emphasize Rákosi's heroic virtues, his "enormous organizational talents," his dynamism, and his intransigence toward the enemy, all of which ensured that he emerged triumphant from the conflicts he faced.[70]

Although the myth of Salgótarján remained an essential building block of the Rákosi cult, the focus of all biographical depictions of the leader was undoubtedly his trials in 1925–1926 and 1934–1935.[71] The trials in front of the "Fascist Blood-court" and the fifteen years he spent in prison elevated Rákosi above ordinary members of the Comintern, making him the most esteemed figure of the Hungarian working-class movement and, later, the indisputable leader of the Communist Party.[72] The descriptions of the trials in Rákosi's biographies focused mainly on the behavior of the accused in the court. The life stories of the leader emphasize that Rákosi presented an example of "grim courage," "Communist fortitude," "unbreakable willpower," "Marxist-Leninist discernment," "superior knowledge," "insights of a genius," and "great tactical skills."[73] In general, the event was presented in an exceptionally theatrical, dramatized way. The descriptions, for example, of the executioner watching the trial, and the sounds of the

---

[69] Illés, *Népünk szabadságáért*, 5.
[70] On Rákosi's role in Salgótarján, see Hajdu, "Kérdőjelek R. M. hiányzó portréjához."
[71] Rákosi faced five different courts altogether in fifteen years.
[72] Győrffy, *A Rákosi-per*, 3–11.
[73] Illés, *Népünk szabadságáért*, 31–43.

construction of the gallows reverberating in the courtroom, were all meant to portray the dramatic atmosphere of the trials.[74] Similarly, the claim that "when he looked at the panel of judges, he was looking into the eyes of death"[75] was also meant to paint the whole event with melodrama and histrionics.

The account of the trials provided an opportunity to highlight Rákosi's prophetic abilities and timeless wisdom. When Rákosi asserted that land would only be distributed by the Communists, the judge reprimanded him: "Rákosi, do not be a prophet!"[76] As Communist propaganda attributed the 1945 distribution of land to Rákosi and the Communists, it became possible to claim that what the Communist leader once foretold finally became true. All in all, the trials were presented as a moral victory for the Hungarian working-class movement, where the accused, Rákosi, became the accuser, and the counter-revolutionary, "reactionary" Horthy regime, and "predatory imperialism" in general, was placed in the dock. Due to his extraordinary virtues and the exemplary Communist behavior he showed at the trials, Rákosi—at least according to the biographies—proved that he possessed the abilities of an ideal revolutionary fighter and thus became *the* leader of the Hungarian workers.

The narrative of the trials and Rákosi's activity in the Comintern had an international dimension. The biographies of the leader underlined the "great respect" Rákosi enjoyed as a secretary of the Comintern's Executive Committee and referred to his missions as the Comintern's emissary, which helped in the ideological cleansing of some Communist parties (Italian, German, French) in Europe.[77] Rákosi's imagined worldwide significance was further enhanced during the trials, as Illés illustrated in the following way:

> From the shores of the Arctic Ocean to the palm groves of the south, the Polish border to the Yellow Sea, thousands of towns, a hundred million people of a hundred thousand villages shouted in a hundred languages, with one heart: "Set Rákosi free!"[78]

---

[74] Ibid., 33. See also *Rákosi elvtárs élete*, 9.
[75] Illés, *Népünk szabadságáért*, 36.
[76] Győrffy, *A Rákosi-per*, 129.
[77] Illés, *Népünk szabadságáért*, 26.
[78] Ibid., 33.

The embellished representations of Rákosi's struggles, sacrifices, and sufferings were all meant to demonstrate that the leader was the right person for his post. The illustration of Rákosi's intellectual development, and the way he acquired his "superior knowledge," was the second pillar of the justification of Rákosi's leadership and his image as the teacher of the nation. In his biographies, education played a central role. No matter how difficult the circumstances were, Rákosi always studied hard and was always the best pupil of each institution he attended. He was "one of the most outstanding students" of the secondary school in Szeged, and he also earned an honors degree at the Eastern Academy of Commerce in Budapest. With the help of scholarships, Rákosi continued his studies abroad in Hamburg and London, which further broadened his "remarkable theoretical knowledge" and international focus.[79] Rákosi also fully utilized his time as a POW during World War I and in the prisons of the Horthy regime and studied further. Besides being shown as a pupil, he was also portrayed as a teacher who willingly shared his knowledge with his less-educated comrades and companions. He helped his less-talented schoolmates in secondary school, he organized study groups in the POW camps, and he taught the principles of Marxism to his fellow inmates in prison. His biographies emphasized that Rákosi turned his prison cell into a Party school, where he lectured about the theoretical basis of Marxism-Leninism and correct Communist behavior. However, his image as the teacher of the entire nation was linked to the trials, when he turned the convict's bench into a pulpit from which he preached the ideas and goals of the Communist movement and showed the way toward a better future for the Hungarian people.

Apart from focusing on his qualities as leader and teacher, the biographical narrative conferred an additional aura of authority on Rákosi by emphasizing his links with prominent figures of the international working-class movement and Hungarian history. Illés's book suggested Rákosi's affinity with the eighteenth-century Hungarian freedom fighter, Ferenc Rákóczi, by stressing that his family lived for a while in the courtyard of an inn in Sopron (*Fehér Ló*) in which Rákóczi had stayed two

---

[79] Ibid., 7. This aspect of the cult is discussed in more detail in the following chapter.

centuries before.⁸⁰ Illés also highlighted that in London, Rákosi regularly visited the British Library, "the great library in which Marx once worked."⁸¹ Nevertheless, the most significant link was with Lenin, the major source of legitimacy within the Communist movement. Illés, who also portrayed the first meeting of the young Rákosi and Lenin in 1920 in a separate short story, likened the encounter in his book to that between a master and his apprentice.⁸² Despite emphasizing Lenin's qualities as a mentor, Illés tried to suggest an equal relationship between the two politicians: Lenin sat next to Rákosi, and instead of Lenin listening to the Hungarian Communist's report about the events of 1919, they had a "friendly" talk. In the end Lenin was pleased by the performance of his pupil: "The mighty eagle taught the young eagle to fly and was satisfied with its apprentice."⁸³

Rákosi himself contributed significantly to the proliferation of legends and myths about his life. In a 1945 radio interview, for example, he explained how he convinced some delegates traveling to the Congress of the Soviets in St. Petersburg to accept Lenin's proposal to sign the Brest-Litovsk Peace Treaty in 1918.⁸⁴ The story gave the impression that a former POW returning from Siberia was better informed on international matters than Russian politicians or even the Bolshevik leadership. More remarkable was Rákosi's input to the construction of the "Lenin link." The minutes of the January 1952 meeting between Rákosi and Illés indicate that the Hungarian leader's relationship with the spiritual father of the Communist movement featured prominently in the interview.⁸⁵ Apart from a detailed account of their first meeting, Rákosi described Lenin as his main patron in the Comintern in the early 1920s. He claimed that Lenin never forgot him and that due to the Soviet leader's personal intervention, Rákosi was elected to various committees of the Comintern. Rákosi characterized their relationship as one of equals and recalled a few times when he actually criticized Lenin for his views.

---

⁸⁰ Ibid., 4.
⁸¹ Ibid., 7.
⁸² Illés, "Történelmi lecke," in Réz and Vas, *Magyar írók Rákosi Mátyásról*, 80–92.
⁸³ Ibid., 89.
⁸⁴ *Egy nagy harcos életéből*.
⁸⁵ MOL, 276. fond 65/332.

Rákosi, in his autobiographical remarks to Illés, also exaggerated his personal impact on the international working-class movement and portrayed himself as one of the most prominent leaders of the Comintern in the early 1920s.

> I was the first of the Hungarian Communists with whom it was possible to have a meaningful conversation. I was the first real Communist about whom one could tell that he read Marx and Lenin, who was adept at military affairs, had traveled a lot, and knew languages. I was highly esteemed.[86]

It is interesting to note that at the meeting with Illés, Rákosi rarely referred to the events that constituted the core elements of his cult (1919 and the trials). Whether this is an indication of his modesty is doubtful,[87] even though he is said to have once warned historians not to give him credit for what he did not do.[88] It seems more likely that he simply regarded his connections to Lenin as being of higher symbolic value. He was very proud of his link with the Soviet leader—even though their relationship was not particularly strong—and he never stopped emphasizing his alleged close comradeship with Lenin. He remained true to this myth even after 1956, when he used it as a symbolic shield against the accusations of the Kádár regime concerning his responsibility for the 1956 revolution.

In contrast with the official biographies of Stalin, Dimitrov, or even Gottwald, Rákosi's life stories never exploited the image of the great theoretician. Although he was portrayed as a wise teacher whose pronouncements enlightened the way to socialism, revealed the future, and gave meaning to the past, Rákosi's lack of interest in theory ruled out a portrayal of him as a great Marxist theorist. The biographies made no reference to Rákosi's Jewish background either. Even the Rákosi family's suffering during World War II—Rákosi's father, his brother Béla, and his sister Hajnal died in a Nazi concentration camp—was left out of the leader's biographies. The omission of Rákosi's origins in the biographical narrative partly had to do with the atheism of the Communist movement,

---

[86] PIL, 720. fond 1.
[87] According to Pünkösti, Rákosi longed for his biography to be written. Pünkösti, *Rákosi a hatalomért*, 12.
[88] Pünkösti, *Rákosi a csúcson*, 426.

but an equally important factor was the rise of Communist anti-Semitism in the late Stalinist era.⁸⁹ Rákosi himself occasionally made anti-Semitic statements. Moreover, he had no issues with parroting the Soviet leaders' anti-Semitic remarks—expressed during the "consultations" in June 1953—concerning the dominance of "non-Hungarian" Party members in the Party leadership.⁹⁰ The popular perception of the Communist Party in Hungary as a "Jewish party" was another possible reason for concealing the leader's Jewish origins.

Rákosi's biographical narrative was composed according to Stalinist conventions; thus it is similar to the official biographies of other Stalinist leaders published in the Soviet bloc.⁹¹ All these leaders were portrayed as men of the people coming from a poor working-class background. Gheorghiu-Dej, for example, had allegedly never seen his father in new clothes, and he could only guess the original color of those his father was wearing. Likewise, Gottwald's hands had supposedly become calloused when he was a little child from the hard work he did in the fields.⁹² Another compulsory component of the biography was early commitment to the cause. Pieck became a member of the German Social Democratic Party at the age of nineteen, Gheorghiu-Dej started organizing strikes when he was eighteen, and Gottwald was only sixteen when he joined the working-class movement.⁹³ The struggles and the sufferings of the given leader and the way he acquired his supreme theoretical knowledge and the attributes of a Communist leader received special attention in the biographies. Clashes with the authorities, arrests, and trials gained particular prominence in such texts. When Gheorghiu-Dej was arrested—and allegedly tortured—after the strikes in Galați in February 1933, he was put

---

⁸⁹ On the Jewish question and the rise of Communist anti-Semitism in the Rákosi era, see Róbert Győri Szabó, *A kommunizmus és a zsidóság az 1945 utáni Magyarországon* (Budapest: Gondolat, 2009), 157–253.

⁹⁰ For Rákosi's anti-Semitic comments during the Rajk trial, see Győri Szabó, *A kommunizmus és a zsidóság*, 207. See also György Kövér, *Losonczy Géza, 1917–1957* (Budapest: 1956-os Intézet, 1998), 180–81. For more details on the "consultations," see Chapter 9.

⁹¹ This section is based on a comparison of the official biographies of Gheorghiu-Dej, Gottwald, and Pieck. I have used the Hungarian editions of these biographies.

⁹² *Gh. Gheorghiu-Dej*, 8; František Nečásek, *Klement Gottwald. Rövid életrajz* (Bratislava: Polit. Kiadó, 1955), 9–10.

⁹³ Fritz Erpenbeck, *Wilhelm Pieck. Egy harcos élet útja* (Budapest: Szikra, 1953), 16; *Gh. Gheorghiu-Dej*, 9; Nečásek, *Klement Gottwald*, 10.

on trial, during which he assumed moral superiority over the regime. His trials were described almost identically to the Dimitrov and Rákosi trials: he became the accuser instead of the accused, unmasking the wrongdoings of the capitalist system and the exploiting classes.[94] Like Rákosi, Gheorghiu-Dej was imprisoned after his trial—which triggered an "immense" international response, including the usual letter from Henri Barbusse—and used his time there to educate himself and teach other prisoners the correct Party line. His cell functioned as a quasi-Party school, and he turned the infamous Doftana prison camp into a "Red University," at least according to his biography.[95] Neither Gottwald nor Pieck had to go through such ordeals during their careers in the Party and the Comintern, except for the times when they were forced to emigrate to the Soviet Union—where they got the chance to meet Lenin or Stalin. Although they both protected women protesters from aggressive policemen at some stage—Gottwald was even injured—the trope of the emergence of their supreme knowledge was linked more to education and intellectual work rather than direct confrontations with "reactionaries."[96] Gottwald was naturally the best child in his school, but his role as a propagandist, and particularly his contribution to the development of the Communist press in Slovakia, were used to demonstrate the evolution of his theoretical knowledge. Pieck's image as a theorist was less important (though he was posited as a disciple of Franz Mehring). However, he was still described as an "intellectually vibrant" child and a "bookworm" who would complete any task he took on in school superbly. He was also portrayed as a shrewd and canny character in the book, always outsmarting his opponents in difficult situations. From this point of view, his portrayal shows more similarities to the ideal-type of a quick-witted folk hero who always manages to escape from the enemy Münchausen-style than to stereotypical representations of a fierce Communist leader.

The biographies of Pieck, Gheorghiu-Dej, and Gottwald were closely linked to the history of the nation and the working-class movement in their respective countries. Gheorghiu-Dej's biography was completely

---

[94] *Gh. Gheorghiu-Dej*, 26–33.
[95] Ibid., 34–35.
[96] Nečásek, *Klement Gottwald*, 40; Erpenbeck, *Wilhelm Pieck*, 32.

subordinated to the history of Romanian Communism, whereas Gottwald's claimed that the leader's life was "identical to the history of our Party and our working-class movement, and it is identical to the struggle of our people for national independence and for the construction of a new socialist society."[97] In the case of Pieck, the history of the German nation came first and the workers' movement second, which stems from his position as president of the GDR and his image as a national politician and not a Party man.[98] The merging of Party history with the biographies of Communist leaders is largely responsible for the dominance of the constructed impersonal persona over the actual personality of the leader. Generally, the life stories of the leaders did not include many references to their private lives.[99] The one exception is Pieck's biography, which at times is shockingly intimate. The harmonious relationship of the Communist leader with his family is described extensively, and we also learn about Pieck's love of theater and music, about his dancing skills, his first date with his future wife, and even the fact that they got married in a church (!). Again, the biography's lengthy treatment of Pieck's private life, which was a deviation from the standard Stalinist hagiographical narrative, could have been related to his position and his image as the embodiment of the (East) German nation.

Following the Stalinist model, Eastern European Party leaders were generally described as exemplary role models and representatives of ideal Communist values in their biographies. Gheorghiu-Dej, for example, was said to possess the virtues of Party discipline, decisiveness, fortitude, modesty, vigilance, anti-bureaucratism, and an uncompromising attitude toward the enemy. He understood the importance of criticism and self-criticism and of maintaining close links with the masses and the young, and his life generally provided an example of how a Communist should live and fight. Gottwald was described as a leader of the Leninist-Stalinist type; a statesman and a strategic thinker (a "helmsman"); a great theoretician with great foresight; and a leader with a strong hand

---

[97] Nečásek, *Klement Gottwald*, 157.
[98] Erpenbeck, *Wilhelm Pieck*, 89.
[99] Gottwald's biographer briefly acknowledges the role of the leader's wife in creating "a clean and harmonious" domestic environment that enabled the Communist politician to devote his life to the working-class movement. Nečásek, *Klement Gottwald*, 167.

("a marble rock") who retained close ties with the masses and the younger generation, and thus remained righteous and modest. Both leaders were praised for continuing to lead the struggle for the creation of socialism after the "liberation" (examples included rebuilding, the creation of a new constitution, the implementation of industrialization and collectivization, and the unveiling of "conspirators," "wreckers," and other imaginary enemies of Communism). For all this, they deserved the gratitude and love of the people, at least according to their biographers.

Behind the Constructed Façade

Even without much scholarly scrutiny, the falsifications in Rákosi's biographies seem overwhelming. To begin with, Rákosi did not come from a poor peasant background. His father was a Jewish merchant who gave his children a rural petty-bourgeois upbringing.[100] Rákosi's role in the working-class movement before 1919 was also distorted in the narratives about his life. Despite his activity in radical political circles, he had no connections to the organized workers, and he was not fighting on the barricades, as Illés and other authors suggested. Nor was Rákosi a war hero. His unit was captured as soon as it arrived at the Eastern Front (April 1915), and he remained in a POW camp until February 1918, without actually trying to escape. He did not organize any significant Marxist discussion groups there, and he did not become a mentor of any kind, as he was himself uninformed about what was going on in the world at the time.[101] After finally escaping from the camp in February 1918, he failed to get in touch with the Hungarian Communists in St. Petersburg, and he did not become a revolutionary conspirator in Hungary after his return.[102] Rákosi's political career started in November 1918, with the founding of the Communist Party. He was one of its most talented organizers, but he was not among the key figures of the Hungarian Republic of Soviets of 1919, despite his position as people's commissar. He spent

---

[100] His father once went bankrupt, however, which resulted in a few years of hardship for the family.
[101] Feitl and Sipos, "Előszó," xvi–xvii.
[102] József Szekeres, "Egy dokumentum története. Rákosi Mátyás 1925. évi rendőrségi és ügyészségi vallomásainak jegyzőkönyve." Történelmi Szemle 33, nos. 1–2 (1991): 93.

most of his time at the front, although his military activities were not particularly successful. The retreat of the Hungarian Red Army from the area of Csap-Munkács-Sátoraljaújhely, which he was meant to oversee, was a disaster—even Rákosi admitted as much in his memoirs—and his role on the Southern Front was not remarkable either. However, he did participate in the Battle of Salgótarján, which marked the beginning of the Red Army's triumphant northern campaign. Rákosi was a political commissioner of a retreating military unit in the battle, and although he was active in the defense of the town, he was not responsible for turning the tide, as his biographies suggested.[103] The actual leader of the miner militias defending Salgótarján was Gyula Hevesi,[104] and the battle was eventually decided by the arrival of the Sixth Division of the Red Army, which was ordered to protect the coal resources in the area.[105]

After the collapse of the Hungarian Republic of Soviets, Rákosi left for Moscow, which marked the beginning of his career in the international movement. He was among the first Hungarian exiles to arrive in the Soviet Union, the "state of the proletariat," where membership in the Hungarian Party of Communist—a party that once implemented the dictatorship of the proletariat—proved to be a good reference. He became secretary of the Comintern in 1921, which made him one of the leading figures of the working-class movement. However, his missions as an agent of the Comintern to Italy, France, Germany, and Czechoslovakia were not as successful as his biographies—and he himself—later claimed. His activity in Italy, for instance, led to more conflict than compromise and could generally be regarded as a failure.[106] His dogmatism and inflexibility have also been

---

[103] Hajdú, "Kérdőjelek R. M. hiányzó portréjához."

[104] People's commissar in 1919. He emigrated after the fall of the Soviet Republic and returned to Hungary in 1948. He worked in academia thereafter and never again got involved in politics. Rákosi, *Visszaemlékezések 1892–1925*, vol. 2, 865.

[105] The two people's commissars (Hevesi and Rákosi) and the other political commissioners sent to the town by the revolutionary government were rather unpopular among the miners and industrial workers, who eventually sent a deputation to the people's commissar of military affairs asking for the replacement of Rákosi and his comrades. The deputies complained about the unequal treatment of worker militias and regular troops, and they demanded the appointment of "old, well-known steel-worker comrades," whom they could trust more. PIL 720. fond 2/II.

[106] His main task was to foster the unification of the left wing of Serrati's Socialist Party and the Italian Communist Party. While trying to achieve that goal, he sometimes acted against the Comintern's directives, and due to his impatient behavior, the Italian Communist leaders repeatedly asked for his replacement. On Rákosi's activity in Italy, see András Fejérdy,

highlighted by historians. István Feitl and Levente Sipos note: "Rákosi in the 1920s, as at home previously, continued to represent a hard, stubborn, intolerant policy, with which he often caused the most harm to his own movement, especially when, as a delegate of the Comintern, he interfered in the affairs of the Italian, the German, and the Czechoslovakian Party."[107]

Even though Rákosi was an influential leader in the Communist movement, the claim that he became some sort of an apprentice and close associate of Lenin was groundless. Although he met Lenin often, they did not have a special relationship. Rákosi's closest colleagues—and patrons—in the Comintern were Zinoviev, Radek, Bukharin, and the ex-leader of the Hungarian Republic of Soviets, Béla Kun.[108] (As all of them were executed during the Great Terror, there was no mention of them in any biographical texts on Rákosi.) The Lenin link was essentially used as symbolic leverage in the 1950s to highlight Rákosi's significance in the history of the Comintern and thereby to improve his international prestige.

Like Rákosi's international significance, his activity as the Comintern's agent in Hungary to reorganize the illegal Communist movement was exaggerated. For example, the leader's biographies never mentioned the critical comments of Jenő Landler—one of the most prominent Hungarian émigrés in Moscow at the time—on Rákosi's nomination for the task: "He has no experience in basic organization, he failed in Livorno, he became conceited and eccentric, he has a haughty attitude toward the proletariat, and like a spoiled child, he often turns headstrong."[109] While Landler's conflicts with Kun and his supporters (including Rákosi) were one reason for the negative judgment, his concerns about Rákosi's qualities turned out to be well-founded. Rákosi was unable to revitalize the illegal Communist movement, and he got himself arrested on September 22, 1925, due to a "conspiratorial error." In addition, his disgraceful behavior during the interrogations almost ended his political career. Even though he was not tortured or beaten, he provided detailed information about both the

---

"Rákosi Mátyás és az olasz munkásmozgalom (1920–1923)" (MA thesis, Eötvös Loránd Tudományegyetem, Budapest, 2001). My thanks to the author for sending me the manuscript.

[107] Feitl and Sipos, "Előszó," xxi. He was not elected to any of the central organs of the Comintern at its Fifth Congress.

[108] Ibid., xix. See also Pünkösti, *Rákosi a hatalomért*, 16.

[109] Feitl and Sipos, "Előszó," xlvi.

Hungarian underground movement and the Comintern. Among other things, he talked about the August 20, 1925, re-foundation congress of the Hungarian Party of Communists in Vienna, naming the participants (and their pseudonyms), listing the members of the new Central Committee, and summarizing the speeches of the delegates.[110] He went on to describe how the Communist movement was funded, and how they tried to transform the legal Socialist Party into a cover party for the Communists. He informed the police about the meetings that took place with the Socialist leaders, about the people he met and what they talked about. Altogether, he provided incriminating evidence on twenty-eight people in the working-class movement.[111] While his testimony to the police focused on the secrets of the Communist Party, he gave more information on the Comintern to the public solicitor. He outlined the structure of the Comintern, the authority of the Executive Committee, the role of the secretaries and Zinoviev, and described how the most important decisions were made. He even revealed how much the leaders of the organization earned each month. The significance of his testimonies in general, as József Szekeres put it, was that "he was the first to provide authentic information to the police of a capitalist state about the organization and functioning of the Comintern, about the way the international Communist movement and individual Communist parties were managed, and about the financial resources of the Communist movement."[112]

Rákosi's behavior in front of the Hungarian authorities seriously undermined his standing in the Comintern. Kun and his comrades expressed their displeasure to Rákosi through his lawyers, but he was also quick enough to realize the consequences of his "chatter." As a result of this, Rákosi withdrew his police testimony in front of the court.[113] When explaining his decision to the judge, he claimed that he merely wanted to place his comrades under legal protection in order to prevent them from being tortured by the police.

---

[110] For Rákosi's confessions with a commentary, see Szekeres, "Egy dokumentum története." The reference in the archives: PIL 720. fond 3.
[111] Szekeres, "Egy dokmentum története," 102.
[112] Ibid., 163.
[113] *Pesti Napló*, November 15, 1925. He never withdrew his testimony to the public solicitor.

"The only reason I confessed to the police in the way I did was that I knew that my comrades were being beaten up. I did not get any beatings ..." Rákosi says that he wanted to get to the Public Prosecution Authority as soon as possible, in order to attain legal protection and to acquire a defense lawyer.[114]

The recognition that the forthcoming trial was of great propaganda value in popularizing Communist ideas contributed to the spectacular transformation of the Comintern's agent. Thus the Rákosi who appeared in front of the court was radically different from the one who revealed the most intimate secrets of the international working-class movement. Even though Rákosi's despicable behavior while in custody was well-known at the time, the incident was left out of his biographical narratives, for understandable reasons. Even the records of his interrogation—found by accident in 1954—were confiscated by the secret police from the archives, and they remained hidden until the late 1980s.[115]

The trials and the fifteen years spent in prison restored Rákosi's damaged prestige in the working-class movement and made him the incontestable leader of the Hungarian Communist Party after World War II. Nevertheless, though the descriptions of the trials contained an element of truth, Rákosi's biographies highly exaggerated the international response to the events. Since the campaign was directed by Kun and the Comintern, spontaneous expressions of popular support for Rákosi were certainly less extensive than the biographies claimed.

The biographical narrative closely resembles a hagiography. It portrays Rákosi as the man for whom the suffering nation had been waiting, the one who could bring redemption. Besides resembling stories of salvation from the Christian tradition, biographies were also reminiscent of a prototypical Socialist Realist novel.[116] The humble background of the leader; his early commitment to the cause; his superior intellect; and his ordeals, sacrifices, and martyrdom were fundamental components of the Socialist Realist master plot. Rákosi's biography is a typical manifestation of the life story of a father figure in the Stalinist "great family," whose entire life,

---

[114] Ibid.
[115] Szekeres, "Egy dokumentum története," 91.
[116] As outlined in Clark, *The Soviet Novel*.

from his early childhood on, and his extraordinary qualities as a mentor proved he was qualified to guide the people toward socialism.[117] Like the prototypical Socialist Realist hero, the life of Rákosi was embedded in the history of the working-class movement. Indeed, the biography was the personalized history of the Hungarian Communist Party. As the biographies represented an idealized life totally dedicated to the idea of Communism, no aspect of Rákosi's life was described apart from his activity in the Communist movement. There were no details of his private life (such as family relations, love, and marriage) in his life story, and his individual characteristics also remained obscured. In addition, the virtues attributed to Rákosi were the basic exemplary values of an ideal-typical revolutionary hero. His standard descriptors ("serious," "stern," "intent," "calm," etc.) were, in fact, those predominantly used to depict father figures in Socialist Realist novels.[118] The lack of reference to Rákosi's personal features and the extreme idealization of his qualities made the biographies of the leader impersonal. He lost his individual characteristics and became the embodiment of officially professed values. In his biographies, Rákosi personified all the ideals, principles, and aspirations of the Communist state. He became a complex symbol with a collective face—the epitome of officially celebrated, ideal values. Rákosi's "cult of personality," as manifested in his biographies, was based not on the leader's individual merits but rather on the highly abstract, impersonal values of the Communist movement.

The regime created a de-individualized and extremely idealized biography of the leader in order to present a behavioral pattern for society to emulate.[119] By disseminating and teaching Rákosi's life story, Communist propaganda sought to inculcate the core values of Communism in society, in accordance with the monumental strategy to remold social identities and create the socialist "New Man." The production and distribution of Rákosi's biographies, therefore, contributed not only to the construction of the "cult of impersonality" of the leader but also to the grandiose endeavor to implement Communism.

---

[117] Rákosi's biography, just like Stalin's, is distinct from a *Bildungsroman* in the sense that there is no real conversion with the leader: Rákosi is endowed with timeless qualities.

[118] Clark, *The Soviet Novel*, 301.

[119] On de-individualized heroes representing "Bolshevik virtues," see Clark, *The Soviet Novel*, 46–47, 70. Even Stalinist autobiographies depersonalized the leader, as Maurice Thorez's "memoirs" demonstrate. For an analysis of his *Fils du peuple*, see Pennetier and Pudal, "Stalinism," 26–27.

Chapter 4
"He Was Created by a Thousand Years": Nationalism and the Leader Cult

A key component of the imagery of cultic leaders is the claim that the monarch, the emperor, or the Party chairman represents the best interests of a certain political community. With the rise of nationalism in modern times, political communities have increasingly been defined in national and ethnic terms; consequently, aspiring leaders have increasingly been portrayed as personifications of the national cause. By the twentieth century, nationalism had emerged as an inescapable frame of reference that shaped representations of political communities and political leaders alike, culminating in the excessive veneration of nationhood in right-wing authoritarian regimes in the interwar period. Nonetheless, Stalinist leader cults in postwar Central and Eastern Europe are rarely interpreted from the perspective of nationalism. In fact, a common stereotype about such cults is that they were imposed upon the respective societies and were thus completely alien to local, national traditions. To the casual observer, the cults of satellite leaders might seem like poor copies of the Stalin cult at best, with no connections to national traditions at all. Nationalism, however, was an important part of the imagery of Soviet-type leaders, and significant attempts were made to portray Communist Party secretaries as leaders of the nation in this period. The use of nationalism was partly a pragmatic decision that had to do with the legitimacy deficit of the Communist Parties (especially the Hungarian, the Polish, and the Romanian ones), but it was also related to the Communist movement's recognition of the structural framework of nationalism. By World War II, Communists generally accepted the validity of political communities formed on an ethnic basis, and they considered the nation-state a useful instrument to further their utopian goals.

Nationalism and Communism

Internationalism and nationalism both constituted significant parts of postwar Communist ideology throughout the entire sphere of Soviet military and political influence.[1] Nationalism, in fact, became the most important component in the Communists' quest for legitimacy in the Central and Eastern European countries after World War II. However, the attempt to graft nationalism onto Communist ideology was not an innovation of the Communist parties of the region; the initiative came from the Soviet Union. After the encouragement of cultural nationalism under the label *korenizatsiia* ("indigenization" or "nativization") in the 1920s, the Soviet leadership introduced vigorous Russo-centric propaganda with a strong emphasis on state-building and Russian national traditions in the 1930s.[2] During World War II, Soviet propaganda became blatantly nationalistic, and with the dissolution of the Comintern in 1943, the Eastern European Communist parties also adopted a national stance. Thus it is not at all surprising that the postwar period saw the remarkable emergence of nationalist tendencies in the ideology of Eastern European Communist parties. In some cases, such tendencies reached surprisingly high levels, as in Czechoslovakia, Hungary, and Poland. The Communist parties of the region sought to portray themselves as "heirs" to the traditions of their nation through a radical (Marxist) reinterpretation of history, the rearrangement of the canon of national heroes, and the introduction of new events to commemorate, along with new rituals.[3]

---

[1] On the relation between Marxism-Leninism and the national question, see Walker Connor, *The National Question in Marxist-Leninist Theory and Strategy* (Princeton: Princeton University Press, 1984); and Peter Zwick, *National Communism* (Epping: Bowker, 1983). A good analysis of the historiography of the subject is provided by Martin Mevius in his "Reappraising Communism and Nationalism," *Nationalities Papers* 37, no. 4 (2009): 377–400.

[2] Brandenberger, *National Bolshevism*. On the policy of *korenizatsiia*, see Francine Hirsch, *Empire of Nations: Ethnographic Knowledge and the Making of the Soviet Union* (Ithaca, NY: Cornell University Press, 2005); Terry Martin, *The Affirmative Action Empire: Nations and Nationalism in the Soviet Union, 1923–1939* (Ithaca, NY: Cornell University Press, 2001); Yuri Slezkine, "The USSR as a Communal Apartment, Or How a Socialist State Promoted Ethnic Particularism," *Slavic Review* 53, no. 2 (1994): 414–52.

[3] On the nationalist tendencies in the Czechoslovak Communist Party, see Walter A. Kemp, *Nationalism and Communism in Eastern Europe and the Soviet Union: A Basic Contradiction?* (Basingstoke: Palgrave, 1999). The relationship of the Hungarian Communists to the national question has been analyzed in detail by Mevius, *Agents of Moscow*.

The MKP, like many of its fellow Communist parties in the zone of Soviet influence, also adopted the national line after the war. It incorporated elements of a nationalist discourse into its ideology; it pursued policies of "national interest" (land reform, the return of prisoners of war from the Soviet Union, the introduction of the new currency, the proclamation of the republic, and so on); and its propaganda relied heavily on national symbols.[4] Révai's remark that "someone who denies the national past ... denies the Hungarian people" also demonstrates the Communist Party's dedication to the construction of a useable past through the incorporation of elements of the national tradition.[5] The key themes in the Communist version of Hungarian history were national independence and "progressive traditions." "Progressive traditions" included the peasant revolt of György Dózsa in 1514, the Jacobin conspiracy in the late eighteenth century, the "plebeian democratic" trends of the 1848 Revolution, and the Republic of Soviets of 1919.[6] Primarily due to Révai's work in the 1930s, the idea of "progressive traditions" emerged as the most notable link between the Communists and Hungarian history.[7]

Besides the formation of a historical narrative, the Communist Party appealed to national sentiments in various other ways. They used national symbols (the tricolor flag); they celebrated national holidays, including August 20 (the date commemorating the foundation of the Hungarian state) and March 15 (the anniversary of the Revolution of 1848); and they put portraits of national heroes such as Rákóczi, Kossuth, and Petőfi next to the pictures of the Party's leaders.[8] The nationalist tendencies in the

---

[4] For an analysis of the use of national traditions in Communist propaganda after the war, see Éva Standeisky, "A kígyó bőre. Ideológia és politika," in Standeisky et al., *A fordulat évei*, 151–71.

[5] Quoted by Standeisky, "A kígyó bőre," 158.

[6] Miklós Lackó, "A magyar kommunista mozgalom és a nemzeti kérdés 1918–1936," in *Gazdaság, társadalom, történetírás*, ed. Ferenc Glatz (Budapest: MTA Történettudományi Intézet, 1989), 269. On the cult of history in Hungarian political culture, see Árpád von Klimo, *Nation, Konfession, Geschichte: zur nationalen Geschichtskultur Ungarns im europäischen Kontext (1860–1948)* (Munich: Oldenbourg, 2003).

[7] Miklós Szabó, "Magyar nemzettudat-problémák a huszadik század második felében," in Miklós Szabó, *Politikai kultúra Magyarországon 1896–1986* (Budapest: Medvetánc, 1989), 230–31.

[8] The MKP also tried to present socialist holidays (May 1 and November 7) as national festivities. Róbert Szabó, "Politikai propaganda – történelmi ünnepek 1945–1956" (PhD dissertation, ELTE, Budapest, 1988); Vilmos Voigt, "Éljen és virágozzék... (A budapesti május elsejékről)," in "Kultuszok és kultuszhelyek," special issue, *Budapesti Negyed* 2, no. 1 (1994): 166–86.

MKP's ideology were already apparent in 1945, but the centenary of the Revolution and War of Independence of 1848–1849 further emphasized the national allure of the MKP. In fact, the centenary of 1848 became the ideological framework of the takeover: the Hungarian Communist Party "reinvented" one of the most important building blocks of Hungarian national traditions to justify the introduction of the Soviet-type political system.[9] The slogan "The heir of Kossuth, Petőfi, and Táncsics is the Hungarian Communist Party!" expressed the Party's objective to define itself as the only political force able to accomplish the unfinished reforms of 1848.[10] Communist historians created historical parallels between the past and their own age in order to bolster the Party's claim that "the people's democracy in Hungary ... is the modern successor to the Hungarian War of Independence."[11] The Communists, representing themselves as the bearers of revolutionary continuity, claimed they had always acted in the spirit of 1848. In their view, rebuilding; the Three-Year Plan; the union of the two labor parties; the nationalization of factories, mines, and banks; and even the cadre policy of the Party were rooted in the spiritual soil of 1848. At the same time, Révai and other ideologues called for a continuing evolution of these achievements. They argued that the need to protect the principles of 1848 made the transition from the period of people's democracy toward socialism inevitable. Thus the legacy of 1848 was not only

---

[9] András Gerő, *Az államosított forradalom. 1848 centenáriuma* (Budapest: Új Mandátum, 1998), 15. The notion "invention of tradition" was coined by Eric Hobsbawm in Eric Hobsbawm, "Introduction: Inventing Traditions," in *The Invention of Tradition*, ed. Eric Hobsbawm and Terence Ranger (Cambridge: Cambridge University Press, 1983), 1–14.

[10] Rákosi made it clear in his 1948 New Year's speech that the Party "should use the centenary of 1848 in order to demonstrate through action that it is we in Hungarian democracy who most consistently and most successfully realize the ideals and desires of Kossuth, Petőfi, and Táncsics: the creation of a free, powerful, and prosperous people's Hungary." *Szabad Nép*, January 1, 1948. On the centenary celebrations, see Róbert Szabó, "Politikai propaganda és történelmi ünnep. Adalékok az 1948. márciusi centenáriumi ünnepségek történetéhez," *Történelmi Szemle* 40, nos. 3–4 (1998): 215–27. On the history of the commemorations of March 15 and the anniversary's significance in the formation of Hungarian national identity, see Gyarmati, *Március hatalma*; Gerő, "March the Fifteenth"; and Gerő, *Képzelt történelem*, 163–80.

[11] *Szabad Nép*, March 18, 1948. "1848/49 is much more than a simple ideal. Despite the hundred-year gap, '48/49 is the foundation of the new democratic Hungary in both a moral and a physical sense, and the precondition of our modern national existence." Quoted in Gerő, *Az államosított forradalom*, 33. The most significant attempts to reinvent the history of 1848 include József Révai, *48 útján* (Budapest: Szikra, 1948); and Márton Horváth, *Lobogónk, Petőfi* (Budapest: Szikra, 1951).

used to justify the politics of the MKP after 1945; it was also exploited to foreshadow the future, with socialism as the only possible political system that could be based on the principles of 1848.

Stalin, the Mini-Stalins, and National Traditions

Despite the prevalence of nationalism in postwar Communist propaganda, there was little attempt in the countries of the Soviet bloc to adjust the image of Stalin to national traditions. In postwar Central and Eastern Europe, the Soviet leader was first and foremost a supranational symbol, the man who was the sole embodiment of the universal project of building socialism. The origins of this image go back to the mid-1930s, when the Party leader was turned into the prime symbol of the multiethnic Soviet federation. Although Stalin's image made an appeal to national traditions on the Soviet peripheries to some extent, mainly through the use of folk art and folk poetry, he remained an abstract symbol beyond national affiliations: he was the essence of the idea of the "friendship of peoples" and the symbolic father of the "fraternal community."[12] Stalin's image as the "father of peoples" was extended after World War II to incorporate the countries of the enlarged Soviet sphere of influence. For the newly formed people's democracies, the initiation ritual to join the "fraternal community" was Stalin's seventieth birthday in December 1949.[13] During the celebrations, the Soviet leader emerged as the most powerful symbol of socialism across the globe. The postwar Stalin cult thus became the most important symbolic component of the Sovietization process—the vehicle to advance the political, cultural, social, and economic integration of the countries of the Soviet bloc.

Stalin's persona as "the father of peoples" was a composite one. In postwar Eastern Europe, he was most often portrayed as the best friend of the

---

[12] Richard Stites observed that Stalin's face in visual images distributed in the peripheries of the Soviet Union was adjusted to fit national stereotypes. Richard Stites, "Utopian or Antiutopian? An Indirect Look at the Cult of Personality," in *The Cult of Power*, 87. The "father of peoples" image of Stalin is analyzed in detail by Plamper, "Georgian Koba."

[13] On the emergence of the Stalin cult in the GDR and Poland, see Behrends, "Exporting the Leader." See also Alexey Tikhomirov, "The Stalin Cult," 297–321.

nation and the most ardent supporter of national interests on the international level. At the same time, he was celebrated as a military genius who saved the world from the Nazi beast, and he was gradually turned into a universal symbol of peace (and the "fight for peace") after the onset of the Cold War. These images were applied in a fairly consistent and standardized way across the countries of Eastern Europe. He was described as "the best friend of the German people," "the best friend of the Hungarian people," "the unbending friend of Poland," and he was described as the guarantor of independence and freedom in the countries of the bloc. At the same time, he was hailed as the protector of the interests of those nations. For example, in the GDR he was hailed as the architect of German unity, whereas in Poland he was portrayed as the defender of Poland's Western borders.[14]

Despite the attempt to link Stalin to national interests, the images associated with the Soviet leader were supranational, portraying him as the embodiment of the collective—the "fraternal community"—rather than its individual parts. Nevertheless, the adaptation of the Stalin cult to national cultural contexts through the use of specific techniques, genres, and vocabulary taken from the pool of national traditions inevitably conferred a certain national coloring on the image of the Soviet leader in the countries of the Eastern bloc. In addition, the historicization of Stalin's image as a friend could also be considered an attempt to integrate the Soviet leader into the nation's past. Communist propaganda did not simply present him as the best friend of the nation in the present; it also claimed that he had *always* been a friend and the representative of the nation's true interests, in contrast with Hitler, Piłsudski, Horthy, and other "traitors."[15] Adding a historical perspective to Stalin's image as a friend made it possible to claim that it was the Soviet leader who made possible the realization of the nation's unfulfilled goals.

The image of the leader of the Soviet Union as "the great friend" of the nation remained an emphatic part of his cult in Hungary too. The attempt to add a national color to the Stalin cult, and to incorporate the Party secretary into the corpus of Hungarian national traditions, reflected similar

---

[14] Behrends, "Exporting the Leader," 164, 169.
[15] For the Polish case, see ibid., 164–65.

tendencies in the Soviet bloc and among the diverse nationalities in the Soviet Union. Stalin was usually portrayed by Communist propaganda as the man who gave meaning to Hungarian history, as well as the one who brought salvation to the Hungarian people by liberating them from Nazi oppression and showing them the way toward a better future. After the unveiling of the Stalin statue in Budapest on December 16, 1951, *Szabad Nép* described Stalin as the greatest figure in Hungarian history, who had realized the dreams and aspirations of national heroes of the past.

> He is also the greatest individual in Hungarian history. The state-founding work of King Stephen, the dauntless patriotic struggles of the Zrínyis and the Hunyadis, Rákóczi's heroic fight for liberty, Lajos Kossuth's glorious revolution of 1848–49, the dream of Petőfi, Ady, Attila József, the colossal endeavor of the Republic of Soviets, the three-decade-long fight—rich in martyrdom—of the Hungarian Communists—has been won with the victory of the Soviet army.[16]

Révai, in his appraisal of the statue, called the monumental likeness of the Soviet leader a "Hungarian statue" that had emerged "from the soul of our nation."[17]

The effort to integrate Stalin into the pantheon of national heroes in Soviet-bloc countries was perceived by the respective societies in a fairly ambiguous way. Although the Stalin cult was meant to reconcile Communist internationalism with specific national traditions, the distance between official discourse and the lived experience was far too obvious. Communist propaganda hailed Stalin as the liberator of Eastern Europe, but wartime memories of the Red Army and the continuing Soviet military presence in the region gave rise to feelings of oppression. Throughout the bloc, there were rumors that the countries of Eastern Europe would be incorporated into the Soviet Union, and historical parallels were made between Sovietization and nineteenth-century Russian imperial expansion (especially in Poland).[18] Deeply rooted national antagonisms and legacies of prewar authoritarian leader cults also made the merging of

---

[16] Quoted by Pótó, *Az emlékeztetés helyei*, 172.

[17] *Magyar Nemzet*, December 18, 1951.

[18] Archival records demonstrate that this was a frequent rumor in Hungary. For Poland, see Behrends, "Exporting the Leader," 167.

the Stalin cult and national traditions difficult. At the same time, Stalin remained a distant leader from both a physical and a symbolic point of view. He never visited the newly founded people's democracies, and he never received official delegations from the countries of the bloc either.[19] This certainly amplified the perception of the Soviet leader as a distant foreign ruler. Thus the cult of Stalin was never really able to reconcile Communist internationalism with national traditions.[20]

Although Stalin remained "the best friend" of the nations of Central and Eastern Europe, he was not turned into a "true" national hero. It was the task of satellite Party leaders to assume that role. Eastern European Party leaders were all portrayed as the representatives of national interests and the "best sons of the nation." Bierut, for example, was celebrated as the "Helmsman of the Polish Nation," the "Re-constructor of Warsaw," and the guarantor of the safety of Poland's "regained" western territories. His role as president of Poland was emphasized to buttress the idea that he was the embodiment of the whole Polish nation.[21] Gottwald was described by his biographer as the "first among the greatest sons of the Czechoslovak people," the man who represented the most glorious chapters of the history of the Czech and Slovak nations. The Czechoslovak leader supported the expulsion of Germans from the country after the war, and he made frequent appeals to the Hussite traditions of the nation to underline his national credentials.[22] When he assumed the position of president in June 1948, he proudly marched into the historic Prague castle, into the "ancient seat of state power."[23] He remained a "true patriot" even in death, as his funeral concluded in the National Memorial on Vítkov Hill, near the site of a historic Hussite battle. Gheorghiu-Dej was described in similar terms. He was called "the best son of the motherland" who demonstrated "proud patriotism" during his trials in 1933 and whose whole life was an

---

[19] Ibid., 172.

[20] Martin Mevius claims that such reconciliation only worked at a dialectical level. Mevius, *Agents of Moscow*, 267.

[21] Main, "President of Poland."

[22] For example, in Parliament in October 1938, he declared: "Believe me: as a Communist I have always been proud to be Czech and proud to be a son of the nation of Hussites." Nečásek, *Klement Gottwald*, 71.

[23] Ibid., 127.

example of Communist patriotism and internationalism.[24] Dimitrov was hailed as the inventor of national roads to Communism, and as a Bulgarian patriot,[25] but Pieck was also portrayed as the embodiment of the (East) German nation and leader of the country's reconstruction after the devastation of the war. As with Bierut in Poland, Pieck's position as president of the country was heavily emphasized to support his image as a representative of national interests.

In general, the images of Communist leaders in Central and Eastern Europe revolved around the ideals of national independence and freedom, and the notion that the Party leader was the representative of true national interests. At the same time, the arguments that the goals of Communist internationalism could be harmonized with national aspirations and that true patriotism also meant unwavering loyalty to the Soviet Union were not particularly credible and did not convince the societies in question. These societies commonly associated satellite Party leaders with Communist oppression; they regarded them as loyal representatives of Stalin and rarely perceived them as national heroes.

Rákosi, the Ultimate Freedom Fighter

Like his colleagues in the Eastern bloc, Rákosi was frequently labeled "the best son of the motherland," and one of the most frequent titles for him in the 1950s was "the best son of the Hungarian people." His image, however, displayed notable national traits from 1945 on. He was regularly depicted as a defender of national interests: his name was associated with land reform (together with Imre Nagy); he was dubbed the "father of the forint"; he interceded with Stalin for the return of the prisoners of war, and he was engaged in diplomatic struggles with the Czechoslovak government concerning the deportation of Hungarians from Czechoslovakia.[26] Besides incorporating the image of a national politician, the cult absorbed national traditions in various other ways. The "Rákosiana" recycled several

---

[24] *Gh. Gheorghiu-Dej*, 28–29 and 58.
[25] Wien, "Georgi Dimitrov," 194–207.
[26] On the POW situation and the Czechoslovak affair, see Mevius, *Agents of Moscow*, 124–27, 176–78.

components of the most significant hero cults in Hungarian history and added them to the core imagery of the Communist Party leader. By adopting a set of common Hungarian, as well as European, folklore tropes, the Rákosi cult took a significant step toward adapting the principally Soviet leader cult to local conditions. Despite the recasting of such traditions, however, the Hungarian Party leader never became part of Hungarian folklore traditions, and the efforts of the Agitprop Department to enforce such a cultural fusion remained insignificant when compared to similar endeavors in the Soviet Union regarding Lenin and Stalin.[27]

One of the curious features of the Rákosi cult was that the representations of the leader's persona rarely involved references to significant statesmen in Hungarian history. Although the persona of—for example— the founder of the state, King Stephen I, would have provided a ready parallel for the Rákosi cult, reverence for the first king among the Hungarian population was scarcely played upon by the Communist regime. Unlike the Stalin myth, which from the mid-1930s operated through the creation of close historical analogies with great state-building rulers— Ivan the Terrible and Peter the Great—the cult of Rákosi was not backed up substantially by comparisons with significant Hungarian kings, such as Stephen I, Béla IV ("The Second Founder of the State"), or Matthias Corvinus, who were appreciated for their state-building talents.[28] As for the lack of significant attempts to link King Stephen and Rákosi, this is most likely explained by the fact that the first king's cult was seen as discredited, due to its relationship in the interwar period with the ideology of territorial revisionism.[29]

Among the few (implicit) historical parallels drawn with Hungarian monarchs, those established between King Matthias Corvinus and Rákosi

---

[27] Frank J. Miller, *Folklore for Stalin: Russian Folklore and Pseudofolklore in the Stalin Era* (Armonk: M.E. Sharpe, 1990).

[28] On the function of the image of Ivan the Terrible in the Soviet Union, see Perrie, *The Cult of Ivan the Terrible*.

[29] The attempt to diminish the symbolic significance of St. Stephen was reflected in the way St. Stephen's Day—the holiday dedicated to the foundation of the Hungarian state—was reformatted. August 20 was renamed Constitution Day in 1949, and it was remodeled as a fertility feast at the same time, when the harvest and the baking of the "new bread" were celebrated. While the Communist Party abandoned the tainted Stephen cult after 1945, the positive evaluation of the first Christian ruler remained intact.

were the most remarkable. Such associations usually exploited the fact that both figures had the same given name.[30] Rákosi was occasionally called "Mátyás the Just" (*igazságos*), which previously had been used exclusively for King Matthias, but the title "Mátyás the Liberator of Prisoners" (*fogolyszabadító*), which was given to the MKP secretary at the time of the return of the prisoners of war, could also evoke popular associations with the image of the Renaissance king. While Communist propaganda generally avoided strong emphasis on analogies between Rákosi and King Matthias, such a correlation still seems to have triggered a few affirmative responses. One "peace priest," for example, in a letter to the MDP leader in June 1950, claimed that the loss of justice and truth after King Matthias's death was finally restored by Rákosi:

> I have been trying to compare our Mátyás Rákosi to Mátyás Hunyadi, since if truth had gone with the latter, with you this long-lamented truth has finally returned to our nation's life![31]

Occasionally, Communist propaganda appealed to folk traditions when suggesting similarities between the Renaissance ruler and the leader of the Communist Party. The image of Rákosi, as a benevolent father figure walking among the people and listening to their complaints, was to some extent resonant with the folkloristic representations of King Matthias that portrayed the ruler as a wanderer, meandering about the country disguised, attentive to the hardships of ordinary people.

The relative insignificance of national etatist traditions in the process of sculpting Rákosi's persona was countered by the cult's reliance on revolutionary traditions and the tendency to construct parallels between Rákosi and freedom fighters or rebel figures of the past. For example, some aspects of the myth of Ferenc Rákóczi, the leader of the eighteenth-century anti-Habsburg uprising, resurfaced with regard to Rákosi, enriching the cult of the Party leader with another layer of national character. Although the tales about Rákóczi's legendary hair could not have been applied to the MDP leader for obvious reasons, several other components of the Rákóczi cult were recycled. The stories of the Rákosi speech that supposedly

---

[30] Mátyás is the Hungarian version of Matthias.
[31] Kő and Nagy, *Levelek Rákosihoz*, 71–72.

changed the course of events in the Battle of Salgótarján in 1919 generally emphasized the fact that the oration took place under the tree Rákóczi planted. As well as the obvious allusion to the cult of trees, which had been a vital part of the Rákóczi myth in earlier centuries, Rákosi worship also appropriated some other holy places of the Rákóczi cult, such as the Fehér Ló inn in Sopron.[32] The resanctification of such places was meant to emphasize continuity and symbolic proximity between the two leaders and thereby aimed to confer absolute spiritual authority onto Rákosi. The early phase of the Rákosi cult also witnessed the recurrence of the bell motif, which remained a powerful element of the Rákóczi myth after the defeat of the War of Independence of 1703–1711. In the years of postwar reconstruction, Rákosi—like Rákóczi—was portrayed several times as a caring leader, who personally retrieved a lost church bell or granted a new one to a particular religious community.

Among the recycled revolutionary traditions, the myth of 1848 became the most important component of the Rákosi cult. The historical interpretation of 1848 as articulated by Révai and his companions added new national building blocks to the myth of the first secretary. The re-evaluation of the Revolution included a reassessment of the role of its leader, Lajos Kossuth, who was presented as the forefather of the people's democracy and was compared to Rákosi.[33] Continuity between Kossuth and the Communist Party secretary was established by linking the otherwise different political agendas of the two political leaders. In fact, the political endeavors of the Communist Party shaped the historical interpretation of Kossuth considerably. Communist historians projected the Party's political agenda onto the past and presented these principles as the ideals of the leader of the Revolution of 1848. Such interpretations of Kossuth suggested that the policies of the Party since 1945 were attempts to realize Kossuth's unfulfilled political goals. Rákosi, as the leader of the Party and the symbol of its successes, was portrayed as the person who was personally responsible for accomplishing Kossuth's unachieved aims.

---

[32] Illés, *Népünk szabadságáért*, 4.
[33] For the historical interpretation of Kossuth, see György Spira, *Kossuth Lajos a szabadságharc vezére: Útmutató városi és falusi előadók számára* (Budapest: Művelt Nép, 1952); *Emlékkönyv Kossuth Lajos születésének 150. évfordulójára*, 2 vols., (Budapest: Akadémiai kiadó, 1952); and various studies and articles by Aladár Mód and Miklós Gimes, also collected in Gerő, *Az államosított forradalom*.

The Kossuth-Rákosi relationship was represented in a similarly indirect manner by paintings that depicted Rákosi in an orator's pose while delivering a recruitment speech in 1919: this was a typical image of Kossuth in late-nineteenth-century Romantic paintings.[34] However, in literary works the connection between the two leaders was represented in a more straightforward way. In short stories and poems that attempted to merge Hungarian folklore with Communist ideology, Kossuth was presented as the spiritual forefather of the Hungarian Communist leader. The short story by Sándor Nagy entitled *A nép reménysége* (The Hope of the People) was one of the most blatant efforts to establish continuity between the two leaders.[35]

The story's protagonist is an old man, a veteran of 1848–1849. All his life, ever since the fall of the Revolution, he believed that Governor Kossuth would someday return. Excited by the rumor in 1919 that Kossuth had come home and arrived in Szeged, the old man sets off with his grandson to see the legendary governor one last time. On their arrival in Szeged, they enter a mass meeting and witness a heated debate between the speaker and two skeptics in the audience. The speech of the orator, whom the old man cannot yet see in the crowd, convinces the veteran that the leader of the Revolution of 1848 has finally come home. Touched by the speech, the grandfather wants to shake the speaker's hand, at which point he realizes that the orator is an unknown young man, not Kossuth. The old man, however, feels no disappointment after meeting Rákosi, the mysterious speaker, because he believes that if the two leaders' goals are the same, there can be no difference between them: "he was called Kossuth before; now his name is Rákosi!"[36]

Nagy's novella recycled a common trope of Hungarian folklore: the longing for the return of Kossuth. As a reviewer remarked, the author demonstrates how "the wait for the return of Kossuth by the simple sons of our people turns into a fulfillment of joy when Mátyás Rákosi appears."[37] The belief in the return of the hero who brings about salvation on his

---

[34] László Bencze's painting *Comrade Rákosi Delivering a Recruitment Speech in Vérmező in 1919* is a typical example of the type. Stalin and Lenin also appeared in such postures on Socialist Realist paintings.

[35] Sándor Nagy, "A nép reménysége," in Réz and Vas, *Magyar írók Rákosi Mátyásról*, 45–63.

[36] Nagy, "A nép reménysége," 63.

[37] *Kis Újság*, April 6, 1952.

return is a well-known trope of Hungarian, as well as European, folklore traditions (such as the King Arthur legend). The leitmotif also had remarkable antecedents in ancient religious belief systems (the ever-dying and resurrecting gods in Mesopotamia and Egypt) and in Christian faith. The folklore variant of the myth, as also expressed in Hungarian folktales, is based on the popular belief in the immortality of the hero. It suggests that certain kings or freedom fighters do not die but only go to sleep in a secret location—often a cave under the hill, where their beard keeps growing—and will return to fight for their people in case of dire need. Similar narratives have been recorded in Hungary with regard to Saint Stephen, Saint Ladislaus (who allegedly returned once), and King Matthias. The traditional belief in the return of the hero was also emphatically manifest in the myth of Rákóczi, as well as in the legends of Kossuth. Popular belief in the leaders' return was already expressed soon after the prince and the governor went into their respective exiles (Rákóczi in 1711, Kossuth in 1849), and such beliefs remained essential parts of the cults of these revolutionaries. Moreover, when the myths of the two undying anti-Habsburg rebel heroes started to blend into each other at the time of the War of Independence in 1849, Kossuth was often described as the re-embodiment of Rákóczi. An old man near Szeged, for example, was reported to have expressed his faith in Rákóczi's immortality to the commissioner of Southern Hungary:

> But, my lord, Rákóczi is not dead. When he left the country for exile, he swore that he would return once. And so he did. You, my lords, could call him Kossuth if you wish, but he is Rákóczi still.[38]

Whether Nagy's short story was actually inspired by this episode is uncertain, although the location—Szeged—is identical in both narratives, and the monologue of the veteran in Nagy's story is also suspiciously similar to the description of Rákóczi and Kossuth in the anecdote cited above. Whatever the case, Nagy's short story reinvented an important component of Hungarian folk tradition in order to establish a firm continuity between Kossuth—whom the author called "socialist" at one point—and Rákosi. Instead of the legendary ex-governor, who was expected to return,

---

[38] Quoted by Magyar, *Rákóczi a néphagyományban*, 196.

Rákosi appears on the scene, providing spiritual fulfillment and a sense of redemption to the Hungarian people. The figures of Kossuth and Rákosi thus merged into one—into the all-encompassing image of the ideal-typical freedom fighter.

The tendency to depict Rákosi as the personification, the ultimate outcome, and the accomplishment of 1,000 years of Hungarian history and its freedom-fighter traditions can also be observed in a poem by Endre Vészi. It describes Petőfi and Kossuth as Rákosi's precursors, whose spirit endured and was re-embodied in the figure of the MDP secretary: "He was created by a thousand years / Petőfi and Kossuth passed over / Their hearts and their words to him / Thus they continued to exist."[39] Endre Darázs's poem "Rólad beszélünk" (We Are Talking about You) linked Rákosi's figure to Hungarian freedom-fighter traditions in a similar way. The first two stanzas compare the journey into exile of Rákóczi, Kossuth, and Rákosi. The poet claims that Rákosi left the country under the worst conditions, but he was the only one to return. He has thus proven that he can accomplish what his predecessors could not for 300 years: "Rákóczi looked back one last time / The horses were impatient / And took their knight / With his head turned down far away, never to return. / Kossuth was also taken to his doom / By the slow boat at Orsova. / The third one held his head high / At the border between two bayonets. The first one left in a nice gown, / The second was already poor, / The third took the most: / The sufferings of his prison. / Besides that, all three took / The bitterness of their people, weighty as a stone, / Three men of three centuries / Carried the repressed strength of the nation."[40]

Literary works that addressed the issue of continuity between Hungarian freedom-fighter traditions and Rákosi's persona suggested the existence of an ideal-typical image of the "hero of the people" subsisting in an abstract sphere, whose avatars were the great individuals of Hungarian

---

[39] "Egy ezredév alkotta őt, / Szívét, szavát / Petőfi, Kossuth adta át, / Hogy így folytassa önmagát!" Cited in László Kardos, "Rákosi Mátyás alakja a magyar költészetben," *Irodalomtörténet* 34, no. 2 (1952): 138.

[40] "Rákóczi utólszor visszanézett. / Türelmetlenkedtek a lovak / És örökre messzire ragadták / Lehajtottfejű lovagjukat. / Kossuthot is pusztulásba vitte / Orsováról a lassú ladik. / Két szurony közt került a határra, / Felemelt fővel a harmadik. // Az első még szép köntösben ment el, / Szegénységben csak a második, / A harmadik a legtöbbet vitte: / Börtönének szenvedéseit. / Mind a három vitte ráadásul / Nép keservét, nehéz, mint a kő, / Három század három

history who became incorporated into the Communist historical canon (such as Dózsa, Rákóczi, Petőfi, and Kossuth). Rákosi was portrayed as the heir to this tradition, but at the same time, he was also depicted as the one who had accomplished what his predecessors could not. As Tibor Méray remarked in *Szabad Nép* in an appraisal of Rákosi's election speech of May 10, 1953: "The people of a new Hungary, those who realized the most beautiful dreams of the past, have come here to meet the greatest son of the homeland, who has accomplished and continued the work of Rákóczi, Kossuth, and 1919: Comrade Rákosi."[41] The idea that Rákosi realized everything the nation had ever fought for lent a certain supreme aspect to his image and posited the Party secretary as the fulfillment of the course of Hungarian history. The attempt to integrate the leader into the national pantheon therefore corresponded with Rákosi's official biographies that portrayed his life as a salvation story. The depiction of Rákosi as the ultimate freedom fighter, the one who would bring redemption to the people, emerged as an emphatic element of the cult and added a unique Hungarian color to his persona. While Stalin's image was constructed by exploiting Russian state-building traditions, Rákosi's claim to a position as a lesser messiah was linked to the attempt to integrate the Party leader into the pantheon of Hungarian freedom fighters, and to portray him as the terminus of the nation's history. This complex image, however, was not an invention of Communist propaganda. The Horthy cult had a similar dimension in the interwar period: the regent was frequently portrayed as the man capable of completing the work of Rákóczi and Kossuth.[42] Thus an important component of Hungarian cultic traditions was recycled in order to enhance the national aspects of the Communist leader's constructed persona.

The main motivation behind adding a national dimension to the predominantly Soviet-type leader cult was the attempt to posit Rákosi as the embodiment of the entire (national) political community. In the process of weaving threads of the national tradition into the texture of the cult, Communist propaganda exploited revolutionary traditions, recycled

---

emberében / Egy nemzetnyi elfojtott erő." Endre Darázs, "Rólad beszélünk," in Réz and Vas, *Magyar írók Rákosi Mátyásról*, 138.

[41] *Szabad Nép*, May 11, 1953.

[42] Turbucz, "A Horthy-kultusz kezdetei."

common folkloristic tropes, created historical parallels, and constructed continuities between the leader of the Party and important historical figures. Alongside Stalin, Rákosi received the label "our father" (*apánk*), a title that only two figures had earned before: the chieftain Árpád and Kossuth. The Party's effort to integrate its leading politicians into the heroes' pantheon was also expressed through visual means. As early as 1945, portraits of the leaders of the MKP frequently appeared alongside the pictures of prominent national figures (Kossuth, Dózsa, and Rákóczi). During the celebrations of the centenary of the dethronement of the Habsburgs in Debrecen (April 14, 1849), the main street of the town leading from the station to the church, where Kossuth delivered his dethronement speech, was decorated with pictures of Kossuth, Petőfi, and Táncsics, side by side with those of Communist politicians such as Lenin, Stalin, and Rákosi.[43] The location of Communist political demonstrations and festivities was also meant to reinforce the alleged connection between the leaders of the Party and prominent individuals from Hungary's past. Heroes' Square—with the Millennium Monument—marshaled the entire Hungarian historical pantheon as a background for the regime's most important holidays, while in Kossuth Square, in front of the Parliament, the Party leadership was seated on a dais between the statues of Rákóczi and Kossuth, erected on the two sides of the square, during political demonstrations or election meetings.[44] Besides the staging of the regime's rituals close to the monuments of historical figures, the attempt to integrate the heroes of the Communist movement into the national tradition was also manifest in the idea to create a burial place for Communist martyrs in Kerepesi Cemetery, among the mausoleums of Count Lajos Batthyány and Kossuth.[45]

---

[43] MOL, 276. fond 108/26.

[44] The Millennium Monument in Heroes' Square, completed in 1906, consists of statues of Hungarian kings and the seven legendary chieftains who led the conquest of the Carpathian Basin (*honfoglalás*) by the Hungarian tribes in 895–96. The construction of the monument was part of the celebrations marking the thousand-year anniversary of the event. The choice of setting was meant to reinforce the Party's interpretation of the achievements of the people's democracy as a second *honfoglalás*. The concept *honfoglalás* was used with a wide semantic field in Communist political rhetoric and could refer to the land reform of 1945, as well as to the "liberation" of the country by the Soviet Army—as represented in the novel *Honfoglalás* by Béla Illés. For more details, see von Klimo, "'A Very Modest Man': Béla Illés," 48–51.

[45] The construction of the pantheon of the working-class movement is analyzed by Péter Apor, "The Eternal Body: The Birth of the Pantheon of the Labor Movement in Budapest," *East*

The pantheon of working-class heroes was built only after the 1956 revolution (in 1959), however, and the cult of the heroic dead remained less emphasized during the Rákosi era.

Although it would be wrong to claim that the cult of Rákosi was based predominantly on national symbolism, the strong presence of such symbols nevertheless must be acknowledged. The Communist leader cult in Hungary, however, in terms of visual appearance, rituals, and rhetoric, remained, for the most part, a Soviet import, even if it had significant continuities with Hungarian—mostly prewar—cultic traditions. Nonetheless, the reinvention of the traditions of 1848 at the time of the centenary celebrations did influence the representations of Rákosi and altered his evolving cult considerably. Rákosi was represented as the new Kossuth, who—like his predecessor—would lead the nation to a better future.

The Soviet-Yugoslav rift and the CPSU's 1948 criticism of the Hungarian Communist Party's "nationalist deviations" led to a certain tempering of national propaganda.[46] The symbolic significance of March 15 gradually became overshadowed by the celebrations of April 4 and May 1, and in 1951 it was declared a normal working day.[47] The change in the hierarchy of cults was symbolized by the unveiling of a Petőfi statue in the village of Bogyiszló: the event took place on March 9, 1952—on Rákosi's sixtieth birthday—instead of the anniversary of the 1848 revolution.[48] Nevertheless, despite the devaluing of the commemorations of 1848, the reinvented myth of the revolution retained its remarkable status in Communist propaganda during the Stalinist years in Hungary. The most expensive cultural investment of the time, for example, was the film *Föltámadott a tenger* (The Sea Has Arisen, 1953), which was based on the events of 1848-1849. The film was based on the novel by the distinguished writer Gyula

---

Central Europe / L'Europe du Centre Est 31, part 1 (2004): 23-42; and Péter Apor, *Fabricating Authenticity in Soviet Hungary: The Afterlife of the First Hungarian Soviet Republic in the Age of State Socialism* (London: Anthem Press, 2014): 125-64.

[46] "Az SZK(b)P KV Külügyi Osztályának jelentése a Magyar Kommunista Párt vezetésének nacionalista hibáiról és a magyar kommunista sajtóbán érvényesülő burzsoá befolyásról," in Standeisky et al., *A fordulat évei*, 205-8. The context and the effect of the CPSU's and the Comintern's critique is discussed by Mevius, *Agents of Moscow*, 213-36; and by Ripp, "Példaképből ellenség," 45-62.

[47] Gerő, *Képzelt történelem*, 173.

[48] Pótó, *Az emlékeztetés helyei*, 140.

Illyés and featured the top Hungarian actors of the time. Besides the enormous financial support the film received, Révai personally supervised the shooting, making sure that the script followed the official interpretation of events. However, whether the film's appeal to national sentiments—along with the national aspects of the Rákosi cult—triggered a more sympathetic attitude toward the Communist regime is doubtful.

Chapter 5
"Comrade Rákosi Lives with Us": The Visual and the Spatial Aspects of the Rákosi Cult

Leader cults tend to rely heavily on visual propaganda techniques. The design and the production of images, as well as the spatial arrangement of portraits, have been pivotal to the construction of cultic representations of dominant political figures in the past. Stalinist leader cults also had a significant visual dimension that generally contributed to Soviet attempts at reconfiguring the meaning of symbolic spaces. Communism, in fact, displayed a certain obsession with spatial reorganization that was manifested in monumental construction projects and renaming rituals.[1] Spatial transformation was linked to the idea of social change and thus resulted in the permeation of the concept of space with an element of sacredness. As Clark has argued, "Sovietized space" was arranged in concentric circles based on "spheres of relative sacredness" all pointing toward the center of centers, Moscow.[2] With the emergence of the Stalin cult in the mid-1930s, the sacred center became personified by one man, the secretary of the Communist Party, surrounded by his closest companions, who also benefited from the leader's public veneration. The emergence of the image of Stalin as the focal point of Soviet symbolic space is exemplified by Barbusse's description of the Soviet leader in 1935: "He is the very center,

---

[1] Insights into the structure of Soviet space and Soviet spatial politics are provided by Evgeny Dobrenko and Eric Naiman, eds., *The Landscape of Stalinism: The Art and Ideology of Soviet Space* (Seattle and New York: University of Washington Press, 2003).

[2] Katerina Clark, "Socialist Realism and the Sacralizing of Space," in Dobrenko and Naiman, *The Landscape of Stalinism*, 8–19. On the spatiality of the Stalin cult, see Plamper, *The Stalin Cult*, 87–116. See also his "The Spatial Poetics of the Personality Cult: Circles around Stalin," in Dobrenko and Naiman, *The Landscape of Stalinism*, 20–45. On the role of the Stalin cult in center-periphery relations, see Behrends, "Exporting the Leader"; Rolf, "Working towards the Centre." See also Tikhomirov, "The Stalin Cult."

the heart of all that radiates from Moscow through the entire world."³ The centrality of the leader was constructed by promoting his image as the main inspiration and driving force behind the building of socialism. In eulogies the leader was frequently described in terms of spatial metaphors. In paintings and public cult rituals, he was often depicted as an "artist-creator," or the "unmoved mover" who made the whole world turn while he himself stood still at the center like an indestructible rock or an all-powerful giant.⁴ The association of socialist construction with Stalin was also manifested in the spread of the leader's name. The numerous renamings in honor of Stalin were supposed to function as symbolic signposts indicating the distance traveled on the road to socialism. Naming collective farms, industrial plants, and the 1936 constitution after the head of the CPSU was meant to buttress the slogan: "we are building socialism with Stalin's name."

Apart from representations of the leader as the epitome of socialist construction and the sacred center of Soviet space, and as a distant and abstract mystical entity possessing superhuman powers, he was also portrayed as an approachable and accessible person, a "man of the people," someone who paid attention to the everyday problems of the "little people." The image of the ever-caring, omniscient, omnipotent, and omnipresent leader was enhanced to a large extent by the wide-scale proliferation of leader images (paintings, posters, photos, and statues) and the placement of portraits at all possible locations in private and public spaces alike. In general, the relative success of the Stalin cult was essentially indebted to the spatial organization of cult artifacts and cult practices, and to the subtle manipulation of the distance between leader and led. The constant shifting of emphasis between the remoteness and the closeness of the leader, in fact, became a fundamental method of constructing the cult of the Soviet leader.⁵ The Sovietization of symbolic spaces and the expansion

---

[3] Henri Barbusse, *Stalin* (Moscow, 1935), 5. Quoted in Tikhomirov, "The Stalin Cult," 297.

[4] The image of the artist-creator is analyzed by Boris Groys, *The Total Art of Stalinism: Avant-Garde, Aesthetic Dictatorship and Beyond* (Princeton: Princeton University Press, 1992). The Aristotelian concept of the "unmoved mover" (also used by St. Thomas Aquinas) is applied to the Soviet context by Rolf, "Working towards the Centre."

[5] This phenomenon also characterized the cult of saints. Peter Brown, *The Cult of Saints: Its Rise and Function in Latin Christianity* (Chicago: University of Chicago Press, 1981).

of the leader cult were thus closely linked in Stalinist political culture. This chapter will explore this connection by analyzing the spatial dimensions of Rákosi's organized veneration and the visual propaganda techniques implemented by the Hungarian Communist regime to promote the image of the omnipresent Party secretary.

The Sovietization of symbolic space in Central and Eastern Europe started with the arrival of the Red Army in the region during the war. Soviet propaganda claimed that the soldiers' sacrifices conferred a sacral aura upon the territories for which they had fought. In order to create a visual testimony of its struggles, the Red Army commissioned the erection of war memorials in the countries of the soon-to-be bloc, including Hungary. The location, the size, and the design of these monuments were often decided upon in the army headquarters and were intended to occupy the most important symbolic spaces of the countries "liberated" by the Soviet Union. The task of local authorities was to realize the Soviet plan. For example, the location of the Liberation Monument in Budapest was selected by none other than Marshal Voroshilov, and the construction of the monument was supervised by his client, the artist A. Gerasimov.[6]

Besides copying the methods of representing the *vozhd'* in the Soviet Union, the adaptation of the leader worship to Eastern European Party secretaries also involved emulating the cult's spatial organization. Party leaders in the Eastern bloc normally stood in the center of mass demonstrations and festivities, towering above the masses on their podium or stage. Their portraits (paintings, posters, photos) and statues were ubiquitous, visually dominating the national public sphere and leaving an impact on the appearance of private spaces as well. As in the Soviet Union, countless institutions, streets, collective farms, and industrial units were named after the Party leader, providing clear markers for the citizens who tried to orientate themselves in the Soviet(ized) cosmos. Even though local Party secretaries were portrayed as omnipresent and were described as the architects of socialist transformation in their own country, the peripheral nature of their cults remained apparent. The status of Moscow, or "the Stalinist Rome," as the sacred center and the symbolic dominance of Stalin

---

[6] Pótó, *Az emlékeztetés helyei*; Reuben Fowkes, "The Role of Monumental Sculpture in the Construction of Socialist Space in Stalinist Hungary," in David Crowley and Susan E. Reid, *Sites of Everyday Life in the Eastern Bloc* (Oxford: Berg, 2002), 65–84.

were beyond question.⁷ The construction of monumental Stalin statues in the countries of the bloc—most notably, in Prague and Budapest—functioned as permanent visual reminders of the hierarchical relationship of leader cults within the Soviet empire.⁸

Rákosi, the "Sacred Center"

Just as Stalin was portrayed as the architect and conductor of the building of Communism in the Soviet Union, Rákosi was frequently described as the heart and soul of socialist transformation in Hungary, which contributed to the shaping of the image of the omnipotent leader. Although the idea of Rákosi as the fountainhead of social, economic, and cultural changes was a powerful image in Communist propaganda, depictions of Rákosi as the "artist-creator" possessing divine characteristics were less frequent than in the case of Stalin. Nonetheless, there were some literary attempts to bestow god-like qualities upon the Party leader. One of the best-known examples is a poem by László Benjámin that portrayed Rákosi as an all-powerful poet (an artist) who created the world (a work of art) out of nothingness: "The poem is also praising only him, the work of art praises its master. / He created the world and the sky out of nothingness, / He gave subject to ambitious poets, he gave the voice for songs, / Strength to the voice, he is the number one in the line of poets, / And he is the greatest of all."⁹ Another young poet of the time, Tamás Aczél, depicted Rákosi as a god-like figure who granted the Hungarian people the essential prerequisites of existence: "Because he gave strength to do

---

⁷ On the notion of Moscow as the fourth Rome in Stalinist culture, see Katerina Clark, *Moscow, the Fourth Rome: Stalinism, Cosmopolitanism, and the Evolution of Soviet Culture, 1931–1941* (Cambridge, MA: Harvard University Press, 2011).

⁸ On the transformation of space in the Hungarian context, see György, "A mindennapok tükre,"; and András Ferkai, "A sztálinizmus építészetéről," in György and Turai, *A művészet katonái*, 24–33. See also the relevant chapters of Standeisky et al., *A fordulat évei*.

⁹ "Csak őt dicséri most a vers is, / dicséri mesterét a mű. / A semmiből formált világot / és eget, nagylélekzetű / költőknek tárgyat, dalra hangot, / erőt a hangra ő adott a / legelső a költők sorában / köztük is a legnagyobb." László Benjámin, "Mindennap győzelem" [Every Day Is a Victory]. The poem was first published in an anthology of "progressive" poets: *Hét évszázad magyar versei* (Budapest: Szépirodalmi kiadó, 1951), 972. It was later republished in the literary anthology compiled for Rákosi's sixtieth birthday in 1952.

things, / Clean air to breathe, / Sense to the growing, great days, / Solid material for the workbench, / And he also gave fresh water, so that this anguished, bleeding Hungary, / Could slake her thirst. / He is standing on the gleaming peaks of the country / And opens up the large gates of its history."[10]

In addition to the scarcity of descriptions of Rákosi as a creator, literary representations of him only rarely employed spatial metaphors. Stalin was often compared to mountain peaks, indestructible rocks, or even the sun, but Rákosi was hardly ever portrayed in such a way.[11] The Hungarian leader was occasionally presented as a larger-than-life figure (a giant, for example), but divine features were only occasionally attributed to him in literary representations.[12] The core image of Rákosi transmitted by communist propaganda was that of the wise teacher and the father of the nation; the god-like characteristics of the Party secretary were less emphasized.

Although Rákosi was not represented as an "artist-creator" as much as Stalin was, the Hungarian leader's position as the sacred center and the motor of socialist transformation in the country was often enacted in the rituals of the cult, especially at festivities culminating in mass demonstrations. Scholars of Soviet rituals tend to agree that the leader's position was crucial to the organization of such events: he was usually placed in the center of all activities standing on a podium, watching the crowd marching in front of him.[13] Thus mass festivals with the leader placed in a stationary position above the people, watching the endless movement

---

[10] "Mert a dologra Ő adott erőt, / a lélekzethez tiszta levegőt, / értelmet a növekvő, nagy napoknak, / kemény anyagot a munkapadoknak, / friss vizet is, hogy oltsa kínzó szomját / ez a meggyötört, véres Magyarország, / amelynek fénylő csúcsaira állva, / történelme nagy kaputi kitárta!" Tamás Aczél, "Az első szóról" [About the First Word], in Réz and Vas, *Magyar írók Rákosi Mátyásról*, 192–96.

[11] One example is the poem by Géza Képes about the Rákosi trials in the interwar period. It compares Rákosi to a granite rock that withstands the "lapping of the filthy tides," i.e., the accusations of the court. Géza Képes, "A szabadság dala," in Réz and Vas, *Magyar írók Rákosi Mátyásról*, 177–81. On the use of spatial metaphors in the construction of the Stalin cult, see Plamper, *The Stalin Cult*, 91–95.

[12] "He is our kind. He stands out among us; he is much taller than us and is large enough to embrace all of us." Lajos Mesterházi, "Személyes segítség," in Réz and Vas, *Magyar írók Rákosi Mátyásról*, 273.

[13] Petrone, *Life Has Become More Joyous, Comrades*; Lane, *The Rites of Rulers*; Rolf, "Working towards the Centre."

of the crowd, reproduced the image of the "unmoved mover," the great director of the building of socialism. In addition, the Party secretary's position during rallies clearly indicated the hierarchical relationship of the leader to the people, and that of the leader to the rest of the Party leadership.

During the Stalinist period in Hungary (1949–1953), the most imposing mass demonstrations took place on April 4 (Liberation Day) and on May 1.[14] The official celebrations in both cases were held in Heroes' Square (*Hősök tere*), at the meeting point of the magnificent Andrássy Avenue (renamed for Stalin in 1949) and almost-as-wide György Dózsa Avenue. The square was a symbolically laden place. The grandiose Millennium Monument, with statues of Hungarian kings and the seven legendary chieftains who led the Hungarian tribes into the Carpathian Basin in the ninth century, saturated the square with the air of history and national traditions and turned it into a site with a symbolic value that proved difficult to supersede. It is no wonder that the square became the main spot for Communist celebrations, a place where social relations were ritually re-enacted within the framework of mass demonstrations. The status of Heroes' Square as the prime location of festivals was only challenged in December 1951 with the erection of the Stalin statue on György Dózsa Avenue, a few hundred meters from the square. Stalin Square, however, never became the new sacred center. Although it was the site of Communist mass demonstrations from 1953 on, the death of the Soviet leader, and the ensuing waves of de-Stalinization campaigns, left the square bereft of its symbolic aura. Ultimately, Stalin's statue was torn down during the 1956 Uprising.

The celebrations taking place on Heroes' Square and on Stalin Square (from 1953) followed a fairly standard ceremonial routine. The ranks of demonstrators, arranged according to various social categories (occupation, age, gender), were already positioned on Stalin Avenue and on György Dózsa Avenue by the time Rákosi and members of the Politburo usually arrived. The Party leaders were greeted with the rhythmic chanting of "Éljen Rákosi! Éljen a Párt!" (Long live Rákosi! Long live the Party!),

---

[14] On August 20 and November 7, no official demonstrations were held; these holidays were usually celebrated at the Opera, with the participation of the Party elite and distinguished foreign—mostly Soviet—guests.

and then the procession began.[15] (The April 4 celebrations started with a military parade and were opened by Minister of Defense Mihály Farkas.) Rákosi and members of the Party elite were located on a monumental stage erected in the middle of Heroes' Square, generally in front of the Monument of the Seven Chieftains. From 1953 on, the Party leadership stood on the tribune in front of the Stalin statue. The placement of Party functionaries or members of the government clearly reflected the hierarchies of power. In the middle stood the leader, Rákosi, surrounded by his closest companions (Gerő, Farkas, Révai), members of the Politburo, and a few ministers. On occasion, distinguished Soviet guests, such as Voroshilov on the fifth anniversary of the "liberation," were placed next to the Hungarian Party secretary.[16] Delegations from abroad, lesser Party functionaries, generals of the army, leaders of trade unions and mass organizations were normally seated on smaller podiums close to the main stage. From their richly decorated pulpit, dominated by the giant portraits of Lenin, Stalin, and Rákosi, the MDP's general secretary and his entourage watched the endless rows of demonstrators carrying pictures and expressing loyalty and devotion toward the leaders. Because of the sheer number of leader portraits people were carrying, Rákosi and the Party leadership were continually looking at their own faces. The image of the masses marching with the face of the Leviathan Rákosi was meant to symbolize the inseparable unity of the leader and the led. The endless flow of Rákosi portraits added a ritual emphasis to the idea of the leader as the personification of the nation and the cause.

Reports in the Communist press about mass celebrations tried to emphasize the leader's centrality. This was often done by contrasting Rákosi's static posture with the dynamism of the masses. "Everything is on the move," *Szabad Nép* informed its readers on its front-page coverage of the April 4 celebrations in 1950, and continued by portraying the festive crowd as a "colorful waving meadow."[17] Metaphors taken from nature were frequently employed by journalists to emphasize the vibrant character of demonstrations. The processions were most frequently compared

---

[15] *Szabad Nép*, May 3, 1949.
[16] *Szabad Nép*, April 6, 1950.
[17] Ibid.

to forces of nature, especially to water. *Szabad Nép*'s article on the May 1 celebrations in 1949, for example, called the first, early-morning gathering of demonstrators a "brook," which slowly turned into a "stream," continued to grow into "four mighty rivers," and eventually became a "sea" "flowing through the entire country from Zala through Somogy."[18] The same newspaper also described subsequent May 1 demonstrations as "flooding rivers," "rolling tides of men,"[19] or "endless tides."[20] However, because water was uncontrollable, unpredictable, and spontaneous, such metaphors gradually disappeared, giving way to images implying discipline, order, and consciousness.[21] Descriptions of incidents when the procession was disrupted because someone wanted to take a closer look at Rákosi, or passages illustrating the "tide of love" that almost toppled the stage of the leaders,[22] became less common and were gradually replaced by metaphors comparing festive demonstrations to military parades. Guidelines for demonstrators were published instructing them how to behave and how to march as a disciplined mass that displayed political consciousness. Such guidelines warned demonstrators not to break the line, not to giggle, and to act as if they were the atoms, or constituents, of the utopian socialist community.[23]

For the participants, the highlight of the demonstrations, at least according to Communist propaganda, was when the individual, after walking for a long time (some demonstrations lasted for more than five hours), caught a glimpse of the Party leader on the podium. Communist newspapers often reported on incidents (fictitious or real) when the sight of the leader triggered emotional outbursts and the slackening of discipline among the marching crowd.[24] Some people started to dance in front of the MDP secretary, while others started to play music happily. Women usually raised their children in the air to show them to Rákosi,

---

[18] *Szabad Nép*, May 3, 1949.
[19] *Szabad Nép*, May 3, 1950.
[20] *Szabad Nép*, May 3, 1951.
[21] On the spontaneity-consciousness dialectic, see Clark, *The Soviet Novel.*
[22] *Szabad Nép*, May 3, 1949.
[23] György Szücs, "A képfelség elve," in György and Turai, *A művészet katonái*, 53.
[24] For more on the effect of seeing the leader during mass demonstrations in the Soviet Union, and the constant disorder at festivities, see Petrone, *Life Has Become More Joyous, Comrades*, 26–27, 40–43.

their collective and symbolic father, and Pioneers normally sang songs or cried out spontaneous slogans invoking his name. As the rows of demonstrators were always moving, expressions of devotion to the leader were continuous, further intensifying the whirl around him. Amid all the commotion, he remained static, merely waving and smiling at the people who went past.

Visualizing the Leader

The wide-scale proliferation of pictures is normally regarded as the stereotypical manifestation of the Rákosi cult. Historians have analyzed the role of visual images in Communist propaganda at great length, but contemporaries also perceived the dissemination of pictures as the essence of the cult.[25] One of the first attempts to rein in the Rákosi cult in 1954, for example, was a Politburo decision that ordered the removal of Rákosi's images from walls.[26] After 1956, when trying to eliminate vestiges of the cult, Kádár paid special attention to the problems associated with leader pictures.[27] Society's view of portraits as the primary transmitters of the cult was signified by acts of iconoclasm through which certain groups or individuals expressed their resistance to the Rákosi cult during the 1950s.[28] Bonfires of Rákosi's photos in October 1956 by the revolutionaries are further examples of the popular perception of the cult and its visual manifestations.

Portraits of Rákosi—painted or photographed—were indeed produced and disseminated in large numbers and were installed at a wide variety of locations, creating the illusion of omnipresence. He featured in paintings and posters, appeared on cinema screens in newsreels, and also became the subject of sculpture, resulting in the mass production of busts, and sometimes full-size statues. While his portraits dominated the spectacle

---

[25] For scholarly treatment of the subject, see subsequent footnotes in this chapter.
[26] "A Politikai Bizottság határozata a személyi kultusz maradványainak felszámolására," in Lajos Izsák, ed., *A Magyar Dolgozók Pártja Határozatai 1948–1956* (Budapest: Napvilág, 1998), 258.
[27] Sándor Balogh et al., eds., *A Magyar Szocialista Munkáspárt ideiglenes vezető testületeinek jegyzőkönyvei*. 4 vols., (Budapest: Intera Rt, 1993–1998).
[28] See Chapter 7.

of mass celebrations from 1945 on, it was the Communist takeover that prompted the centralization of the production of visual cult artifacts. The Orgburo's decree on April 25, 1949, prohibited the publication of photos of Hungarian and international leaders in the press without authorization from the Propaganda Department.[29] Another resolution, four months later, forbade the manufacturing of leader statues without the permission of the Ministry of Internal Affairs (!).[30] The establishment of the Ministry of People's Education in September 1949 concluded the centralization of the production and circulation of visual depictions (portraits, statues, reliefs) of Hungarian as well as international political figures.

Photographs of the leader published in newspapers or installed in various public locations remained the most important visual transmitters of the Rákosi cult. The majority of photos of Rákosi were portraits, but there were many showing him delivering a speech at mass demonstrations or Party meetings, or talking to the people during his visits to factories, collective farms, or Pioneer camps. These pictures bolstered Rákosi's image as the teacher of the nation and as a benevolent father/friend. One of the most emblematic images of the cult was a photograph portraying Rákosi in a field of wheat, holding a stalk of wheat in his hand. Aczél and Méray capture the essence of the picture in an expressive way:[31]

> This picture—so the faithful thought—expressed with the utmost concentration and perfection all the benevolence that radiated from Mátyás Rákosi toward the people, whether the people desired his benevolence or not. All these qualities were evident: the serenity emanating from the man standing in the middle of the wheat field; the strength and tenderness with which he grasped the tough, yet fragile stalks; the serenity promising a secure future; the solicitude and responsibility for the new bread, the new future; the goodness of heart with which, with the loving eye of the farmer, he scanned the stalks; and the expert knowledge he had of the crop, because it was quite evident in the photograph that, apart from being deeply moved by the stalks of wheat, his quick eye had immediately noticed the quality

---

[29] MOL, 276. fond 55/68.
[30] MOL, 276. fond 55/78.
[31] On the motif of grain in visual arts, see Miklós Peternák, "Az államosított látás. Kísérlet az allegorikus dokumentarizmus megteremtésére," in György and Turai, *A művészet katonái*, 80–90.

of it and had calculated the quintals per acre and added up the quintals to get the national average. And beyond all that, this picture summed up in its straight-forward symbolism, the important truth that this man had deep roots in the Hungarian soil, as deep as the wheat itself, and that this soil fed him and made him strong as steel, so that he was at once son and father of the Hungarian land and the Hungarian village.[32]

In contrast to photographic images, works of art depicting the Hungarian Party leader remained few. Although busts of Rákosi were omnipresent—mass-produced—a monumental Rákosi statue was never built, and there were relatively few plaques, bas-reliefs, sketches, or drawings featuring him in circulation at the time. Moreover, the way in which Rákosi was portrayed in such media was unimaginative and monotonous. The uniformity of representations had to do with the stylistic framework that determined depictions of the leader in the fine arts (painting, graphic arts, and sculpture): Socialist Realism. The adoption of "*szocreál*" in the Hungarian cultural sphere was marked by the opening of the first exhibition of Soviet paintings in Budapest in October 1949.[33] Following the example of the Soviet Union, paintings and statues featuring the leader were subsequently displayed at annual nationwide exhibitions that presented the achievements of Socialist Realist art.[34]

Some of the most prominent artists of the time, including József Csáki-Maronyák, Bertalan Pór, György Konecsni, and Pál Pátzay, received state requests to paint portraits of Rákosi, usually on the basis of official

---

[32] Aczél and Méray, *The Revolt of the Mind*, 163.
[33] András Székely, "Az 'ötvenes évek' művészetéhez," *Mozgó Világ* 10, no. 3 (1984): 23–28. The most representative studies on Socialist Realist art include Matthew Cullerne Bown, *Art Under Stalin* (Oxford: Phaidon, 1991); Matthew Cullerne Bown, *Socialist Realist Painting* (New Haven, CT: Yale University Press, 1998); Igor Golomstock, *Totalitarian Art in the Soviet Union, the Third Reich, Fascist Italy and the People's Republic of China* (New York: IconEditions, 1990); Groys, *The Total Art of Stalinism*; Geb Prokhorov, *Art under Socialist Realism: Soviet Painting, 1930–1950* (East Roseville: Craftsman House, 1995); Richard Taylor, *The Aesthetic Arsenal: Socialist Realism under Stalin* (New York: Institute for Contemporary Art, 1993); On the role of painting in the construction of the cult, see Plamper, *The Stalin Cult*.
[34] The first exposition of such kind, the First Hungarian Fine Arts Exhibition, was organized in August 1950. *I. Magyar Képzőművészeti Kiállítás*, Műcsarnok, Budapest, 1950. Subsequent exhibitions of Socialist Realism with a number of Rákosi images on display were held November 4–December 2, 1951, and in December 1952.

photos.[35] However, the Party center remained generally unhappy with the various works the artists submitted. As the official arts journal, *Szabad Művészet*, complained in 1953, none of the painters had actually managed to produce a satisfactory portrait of the leader up to that point.[36] While the power balance between artists and the state remained lopsided, some painters dared to approach the Party secretary for permission to paint him. One of them was Sándor Ék, the well-known Socialist Realist painter, who pestered the Party with letters asking to paint Rákosi in person and not from photos.[37] Although Révai never grew fond of Ék, the artist's paintings of Rákosi were reproduced and circulated in various formats, and he was eventually granted his own exhibition in November 1952, where his monumental portrait of the leader was also displayed.[38]

As was the case with paintings, posters and placards depicting Rákosi were highly monotonous and uniform, and were less diverse than Stalin's visual images.[39] Rákosi appeared mostly on posters that were designed as bulletin boards, but his persona was also invoked through his words—quotations of his on color posters. The few posters that did portray the Party secretary used more conventional methods of portraiture. The poster by István Czeglédi and Tibor Bánhegyi that announced the 1950 congress of the Communist Youth Organization (DISZ), for example, portrays Rákosi on a podium in a lecturing pose, with notes—signifying wisdom—in his hand.[40] The leader is shown standing in front of a national flag and pointing toward the distance with his right arm. Three young figures—typical representations of the working class, the peasantry, and the intelligentsia—are standing in front of the stage, all looking in the direction in which Rákosi is pointing. Rákosi's posture represented the image

---

[35] György, "A mindennapok tükre," 14.
[36] "Imre István beszámolója az I. Országos Képzőművészeti Tanácskozásról," *Szabad Művészet* 7, nos. 3–4 (1953): 63. Quoted by Szücs, "A képfelség elve," 56.
[37] MOL, 276. fond 65/337.
[38] Révai sent Rákosi a note about Ék in December 1951 that said: "He has painted you once. Badly." Ibid.
[39] Katalin Bakos, "Folyamatosság és törés a plakátművészetben," in Standeisky et al., *A fordulat évei*, 239–64. On political posters in the Soviet Union and in Central and Eastern Europe, see Bonnell, *Iconography of Power*; Stephen White, *The Bolshevik Poster* (New Haven, CT: Yale University Press, 1988); and James Aulich and Marta Sylvestrová, *Political Posters in Central and Eastern Europe 1945–95* (Manchester: Manchester University Press, 2000).
[40] OSZK GP, 11/1950, F408.

of the leader showing the way toward socialism and a brighter future. The dedication and dynamism of the three figures expressed unity, trust, and the common will to follow the road of the leader and the Party. The characteristics of Socialist Realist painting can also be observed on György Konecsni's poster promoting the Second Congress of the MDP in 1951.[41] The artist depicted Rákosi as a jovial, caring father figure, standing in the circle of three figures symbolizing typical social categories (the worker, the peasant woman, and the soldier). Rákosi is captured in a teaching pose, while the people around him listen carefully, with happiness, contentment, and affection on their faces.

Like the "still images" of the leader (posters, photos, and paintings), newsreels provided additional visual material for underlining the leader cult discourse. Although the project to immortalize Rákosi in feature films failed, he remained the most frequently portrayed Hungarian politician in newsreels and propaganda films shown by cinemas all around the country.[42] According to records concerning *Magyar Filmhíradó* (Hungarian Newsreel), the Party secretary featured in at least seventy newsreels in 1945–1951.[43] Most of them reported on Rákosi's speeches in the Parliament or other forums, as well as his visits to factories and the countryside. Some of the newsreels depicted the leader's less important public appearances: dedicating his books, distributing Party membership cards, voting at elections, having a paternal chat with workers or peasants, visiting Pioneers, accompanying prominent foreign statesmen, or participating in the inauguration of monuments. The newsreels never showed Rákosi's private life.

Since the primary function of newsreels was illustration and not information, whatever appeared on the screen was loaded with symbolic content. These films viewed politics and society through a utopian perspective,

---

[41] OSZK GP, 21/1951, F520.

[42] There was one instance, however, when an actual scene was shot depicting the leader for Zoltán Várkonyi's film, *A harag napja* (*The Day of Anger*). The scene, in which the famous actor Imre Soós played Rákosi, depicted the Party leader on horseback (a fairly unusual image) at the Salgótarján Front. However, the beginning of the "New Course" in the summer of 1953 made such overtly cultic representations of Rákosi inappropriate, and after a directive from above, Várkonyi eventually altered the script. The showing of the movie was also canceled by the Secretariat in 1954. Árpád Pünkösti, *Rákosi bukása*, 82.

[43] MOL, 276. fond 89/280.

and instead of describing the present, they portrayed an idealistic future, as imagined by Communist ideologues and propagandists.[44] Newsreels and propaganda films presented ideal-typical situations, as well as ideal-typical people who represented clichéd social categories (the "working woman," the "soldier," the "peasant," etc.), lacking any individual traits. Rákosi was also shown in typical postures—as a teacher speaking to or educating the people, or a father/friend fraternizing with them—and was portrayed through standardized images. Propaganda films and newsreels featuring Rákosi usually reiterated the standardized representations of the Hungarian Party leader, as they also appeared in other media. They portrayed Rákosi as the benevolent father-figure or the teacher of the nation, whom the population supported without hesitation. Teaching, in fact, was one of the most frequent topics of such programs. Teachers taught children; workers were taught by other, more experienced workers; but the super-teacher, or the "wise and benevolent teacher of the nation," was Rákosi himself. The proper way to react to the Party leader's pronouncements or "teachings" was also illustrated in newsreels. Shots of the audiences of Rákosi's public appearances (visits, speeches, lectures) showed the spectators en masse, applauding enthusiastically. Such images represented the alleged unity and unconditional support of the people for the Party secretary.

Visual representations of the leader generally relied heavily on the stylistic armory of Socialist Realism and reflected the basic attributes of the visual language of the Stalin period.[45] Therefore, one of the most common features of the visual images depicting the leader was utopianism. The themes and characters depicted in posters, photos, paintings, and reliefs were usually placed in an imagined, ideal future, showing the people what they could become if they followed the course of the Communist Party. Within this framework the function of Rákosi's visual representations was twofold: to underline the idea of the leader's omnipresence and to provide visual endorsement for the leader cult discourse. The primary aim of the

---

[44] An analysis of newsreels in Hungary is provided by András Bálint Kovács, "Adalékok az ötvenes évek magyar filmhíradóinak ikonográfiájához," in György and Turai, *A művészet katonái*, 91–98.

[45] Those attributes, according to György, were homogeneity, limited vocabulary, and simplistic grammar. György, "A mindennapok tükre," 20.

mass production of busts, photos, and paintings was to make the leader's mystical body omnipresent through the proliferation and dissemination of his likenesses. The visual representations of the leader should thus be interpreted as cult objects, rather than works of art with remarkable aesthetic qualities.[46] Since functionality prevailed over aesthetic considerations in the production of Rákosi pictures, the boundaries between stylistic categories (posters, paintings, and photos) were blurred, resulting in uniformity and monotony. Because all forms of visual art were supposed to convey the same meaning, while the availability of acceptable images was limited, the representations of the leader became repetitive, eventually decreasing the symbolic value of Rákosi's portraits.[47] From a functional point of view, the visual images of Rákosi came to resemble religious icons, much like the pictures of Lenin and Stalin in the Soviet Union.[48] At the same time, the leader's individual characteristic features were largely overshadowed by the symbolic aspects of his persona, adding a further element of impersonality to representations of him.

The Spatial Allocation of Rákosi's Images

Attempts to fill public spaces with the portraits of the Party leader were already remarkable before 1948. Guidelines and instructions regarding the distribution and placement of Rákosi portraits were usually issued by the Agitprop Department or the Orgburo at the time of general elections (1945 and 1947), or before mass festivities, such as the May 1 celebrations. However, the occupation of Hungarian symbolic space by the Communists

---

[46] As also suggested by Sinkó, "A politika rítusai."

[47] Malte Rolf compares the self-referentiality of Stalinist culture to a hall of mirrors: "Soviet culture in the 1930s might be thought of as a hall of mirrors. Cultural items constantly reflected other bits of the rhetoric, symbols, or ritual of the Soviet cultural canon. Although extensive in quantity, these reproduced images were limited with regard to subjects, themes, and composing elements. Official culture under Iosif Stalin allowed no or little reference to anything outside the sanctioned Soviet symbolic cosmos. This monad-like unity resulted in the widespread standardization and dull monotony of the cultural landscape. It was not a rare incident for workers to compose a letter to Stalin during a meeting in the Stalin House of Culture of the Stalin Factory on Stalin Square in the city of Stalinsk." Malte Rolf, "A Hall of Mirrors: Sovietizing Culture," *Slavic Review* 68, no. 3 (2009): 601.

[48] Ulf Abel, "Icons and Soviet Art," in Arvidsson and Blomqvist, *Symbols of Power*, 141–62.

was signaled by the 1947 decree of the Ministry of Religion and Public Education that ordered the removal of undesirable images (irredentist pictures such as the map of Greater Hungary; portraits of pre-1945 politicians; images related to Habsburg rule; etc.) from public institutions and schools. A subsequent decision forbade the decoration of public premises without the permission of the Ministry.[49] Besides purging public spaces of the visual remnants of the past, the distribution and arrangement of images of the new power were prescribed by central directives. The Agitprop Department submitted in-depth proposals on the positioning of leader portraits during major festivals or political events. The pictures of Rákosi were always to dominate over the portraits of regional Party leaders, in order to prevent the emergence of a cult of "mini-Rákosis."[50] On occasion, the Secretariat and government organizations also intervened in the way leader portraits were installed.[51] For example, the Council of Ministers, in a 1951 decree, laid down general guidelines regarding the decoration of public spaces at the time of national holidays and other festivities. The resolution that actually codified the existing practice declared that "full decoration," including the placement of gigantic leader portraits, could only be used for decoration purposes for important anniversaries, such as April 4, May 1, and November 7.[52]

One of the first examples of well-coordinated central planning with regard to the placement of leader portraits was the election campaign of 1949. The OPO, apart from ensuring the uniformity of leader portraits, defined precisely how and where the various types of images should be placed. Before launching the agitation campaign, the OPO compiled packages of propaganda material for local Party organizations that included officially approved portraits of Communist leaders (Marx, Engels, Lenin, Stalin, and Rákosi) as well as figures of the Communist historical canon

---

[49] Sinkó, "A politika rítusai," 55 and 69.

[50] "We should make sure that the erroneous cult of personality does not prevail at the demonstrations of mass organizations, offices, or certain Party organizations in the provinces." MOL, 276. fond 108/26.

[51] The fifth anniversary of the "liberation" in 1950 and the festivities on May 1 in the same year were two occasions when the Secretariat significantly modified the Propaganda Department's proposal concerning the placement of leader portraits. MOL, 276. fond 54/89; MOL, 276. fond 54/94. The original proposal for April 4 can be found at MOL, 276. fond 108/46.

[52] Quoted by Szűcs, "A képfelség elve," 55.

(Petőfi, Kossuth, Táncsics, and Dózsa).[53] As soon as the position of the Communist Party was cemented in the Hungarian power structure, the APO put forward another initiative to centralize the production and dissemination of leader portraits. In a proposal from 1950, the department argued for the primary importance of leader portraits and considered them to be "the most effective tools of agitation and propaganda toward the politically backward masses in particular."[54] The proposal emphasized the need to standardize the pictures of leaders carried at mass demonstrations or used as decoration in offices "in order to avoid political mistakes and manifestations of bad taste, and to eliminate occasional manifestations of the personality cult."[55] As in 1949, the APO advocated the publication of a centrally designed set of portraits for the popularization of leaders. The portraits were to be installed mostly in Party and government offices, and in the premises of police departments, as well as military buildings.

Instructions from the Party and government organs, as well as published guidelines written by professional decorators, usually prescribed the way in which the portraits of Lenin, Stalin, and Rákosi were to be installed at various meetings or celebrations.[56] Although the images of the three leaders would appear occasionally on the same level in the coalition years, the Sovietization of symbolic space also entailed the introduction of a cult hierarchy expressed through visual means. The arrangement of the portraits of the major figures of the Communist universe came to resemble an iconostasis, with the images arranged according to a triptych pattern. Lenin's portrait was normally placed on the left-hand side of the viewer, taking the first place in the row of images. The picture of Stalin was on the same horizontal line, which indicated the equal significance of the Soviet dictator and the founding father of the Soviet state. The portrait of Rákosi was generally hung in the center, with the picture of Lenin on its left and Stalin on its right, but the image of the Hungarian leader

---

[53] MOL, 276. fond 108/9.
[54] MOL, 276. fond 108/2.
[55] Ibid.
[56] Szücs, "A képfelség elve," 55. Instructions of the Propaganda Department regarding the arrangement of leader images: MOL, 276. fond 108/2; MOL, 276. fond 108/9; MOL, 276. fond 108/26.

was placed lower than the other two. The visual syntax of leader portraits (i.e., the way they were arranged in relation to each other) fostered the visual reproduction of the international leader cult hierarchy and designated the local Party leaders' position in it.[57] Although the centrality of Rákosi's picture could be interpreted as an indication of his central position in the Communist pantheon, the obvious vertical inferiority of his portraits overtly indicated the boundaries of the Party leader's sub-cult.

The number of Rákosi portraits and busts produced and disseminated in 1945–1956 is difficult to estimate. As pictures of the leader were ubiquitous, even the most conservative estimate would run into the millions. One record from the Szikra publishing house, sent to the MKP Propaganda/Agitation Department in October 1945, states that at a time when paper was still extremely scarce, the Party had ordered 50,000 copies of the leader's portraits to be used during the 1945 general election campaign.[58] For the 1947 elections, the Bureau suggested 130,000 prints of the official photographs; for the 1949 elections, the number was 160,000.[59]

Rákosi pictures were also manufactured for commercial purposes. In 1946 the Orgburo accepted the proposal to print and sell 10,000 postcards bearing the MKP leader's face.[60] The well-known picture of Rákosi in the grain field was also published on 50,000 postcards for the Unification Congress in 1948.[61] Two years later, when the cult was flourishing, a proposal to produce leader portraits for sale was naturally much more ambitious. Referring to the high interest in the portraits of Communist Party leaders in the country, the Agitprop Department suggested the production of five different types of Rákosi images, designed for various purposes—altogether 270,000 copies of the leader's likeness.[62]

The absurdity of the sheer number of leader portraits in circulation paralleled the absurdity of the locations where many of these images were placed. They were hung in offices and in school classrooms, where

---

[57] The concept "visual syntax" is used here in the same way Victoria Bonnell defined it, i.e., "the positioning of figures and objects in relation to each other and the environment." Bonnell, *Iconography of Power*, 10.
[58] PIL, 274. fond 21/1.
[59] PIL, 274. fond 21/9; MOL, 276. fond 108/9.
[60] PIL, 274. fond 5/15.
[61] PIL, 274. fond 21/1.
[62] MOL, 276. fond 108/46.

they replaced the images of Horthy.⁶³ Thousands of leader portraits were carried at festivities and mass demonstrations, and they were also used as decoration for public holidays, dominating the scene at such events. Workplaces—especially factories—were supposed to install their own Red Corner, which functioned as a local shrine of Communism, like the Lenin Corners in the Soviet Union.⁶⁴ Besides displaying the portraits of the factory's privileged shock workers, Red Corners overflowed with portraits of, and quotations from, Rákosi, Lenin, and Stalin.⁶⁵ According to contemporary memoirs and reminiscences, photos or small busts of Rákosi were present in hospitals and at sporting events, and they could even end up "on the top of a pyramid of fat" at a butcher's, or among women's underwear in clothes shops.⁶⁶ The portraits of Stalin, Lenin, and Rákosi even featured at fashion shows, overlooking the parade from above the stage.⁶⁷ The memoirs of Ákos Major, an ex-judge of the People's Tribunals, recalled the time a Budapest butcher sculpted a bust of Rákosi and displayed it in his window in order to promote his shop. His initiative caught on, and busts of the leader started to appear in the windows of neighboring shops. As winter turned to spring, however, the sculpture started to melt, revealing the material the butcher used: pork fat. In order to prevent public ridicule, and more importantly, the authorities' intervention, the butcher quickly removed the great leader's image and sold the rest of the fat.⁶⁸ The ubiquity of Rákosi's portraits was described by Aczél and Méray in the following way:

> All that we knew for certain was that there was not an office, or a schoolroom, or a shop or shop window, or a railway waiting room, or small inn or coffeehouse without that portrait on the wall. Neither was there a local Party office, nor a trade union center, nor an editorial room, nor a factory

---

⁶³ Teachers were encouraged to hang up pictures of Lenin, Stalin, and Rákosi during the 1949 elections. According to a report sent to Rákosi, they did a good job. MOL, 276. fond 65/175.
⁶⁴ On the Lenin Corners, see Tumarkin, *Lenin Lives!*
⁶⁵ The first proposal to set up Red Corners in factories was submitted by the Propaganda Department on November 8, 1948. MOL, 276. fond 108/26.
⁶⁶ OSA, 300/40/3/264.
⁶⁷ Valuch, "A magyar művelődés," 489.
⁶⁸ Ákos Major, *Népbíráskodás – forradalmi törvényesség. Egy népbíró visszaemlékezései* (Budapest: Minerva, 1988), 441–43. Miklós Szabó remembered a similar incident, in which a butcher placed a bust of Rákosi in his shop window for the leader's sixtieth birthday. Miklós Szabó, "Hétköznapi sztálinizmus Magyarországon," *Századvég*, nos. 6–7 (1988): 162.

workshop or gate, nor dressing room, nor sports field, nor hospital room, nor ship's cabin, nor health service consulting room, nor tractor station, nor cinema, nor cloakroom, nor open-air theater, nor supermarket, nor garage, nor museum in Hungary without a portrait.[69]

Besides featuring mass celebrations and Communist festivities, the representations of the leader were tightly linked to everyday collective rituals. Party membership meetings, commemorations, and agitation briefings normally took place in places sanctified by the image of the leader: in a Red Corner, next to a Rákosi bust, in front of wall newspapers or "glory boards," and so forth. The images of Rákosi could also become the objects of individual cult rituals. As one young poet argued after the unveiling of the Stalin statue in 1951, effigies of Communist politicians could be communicated with in the leader's physical absence. People were meant to turn to the visual representations of leaders in their misery, in their happiness, when in need of advice, or after the fulfillment of individual plans.[70] Indeed, in the Soviet Union, pictures of Lenin and Stalin replaced the icons of saints in many houses and inherited the mystical function of Orthodox Christian images.[71] While examples of such quasi-religious admiration of Rákosi's portraits are rare, Communist propaganda conferred a certain spiritual aura upon his pictures. Newspapers such as *Szabad Nép* frequently reported Pioneer children swearing an oath to his portrait, or workers offering pledges to it, in the physical absence of the subject of veneration. Márta Gergely's one-act play from 1952, *Az ígéret* (The Promise), also endorsed the idea of the ever-present leader in the private sphere through his image.[72] The drama, which depicts a family moving into their new apartment, reaches its high point when the little girl hangs a picture of Rákosi on the wall and asks her mother: "Comrade Rákosi lives with us too, doesn't he?"[73]

---

[69] Aczél and Méray, *The Revolt of the Mind*, 162.
[70] Tamás Aczél, "Sztálin szobra – a béke jelképe," *Szovjet Kultúra* 4, no. 1 (1952): 6.
[71] The turning of Lenin's images into icons is analyzed by Tumarkin, *Lenin Lives!*
[72] Márta Gergely, *Az ígéret*. Műsorfüzet, Dolgozó Ifjúság Szövetsége – Úttörő Mozgalom (Budapest, March-April-May 1952), 71–73. The play was clearly influenced by A. Laktionov's painting *Moving Into a New Flat* (1951).
[73] The play is analyzed in detail by Szűcs, "A képfelség elve," 46.

Signposts of Progress: Renamings

Renaming rituals were emblematic manifestations of the leader cult. Street or place names, and markers of socialist progress such as factories, collective farms, cultural and educational institutions, were renamed after the Party secretary—and some of his close lieutenants—to establish symbolic signposts for the citizen who wished to orientate him- or herself in the realm of Sovietized space.[74] Despite the increasing number of renamings, the redrawing of the country's symbolic geography remained a sensitive issue throughout this period. Although it is difficult to discern any careful planning of, or a consistent policy toward, renamings, the Party organs responsible for authorizing name changes generally tried to avoid the devaluation of the leader's name and declined a number of proposals that they saw as inappropriate.

A flurry of name changes swept through the country's symbolic scenery soon after World War II, eradicating the remnants of fascist influence and conservative authoritarianism. Squares and streets named after Hitler and Mussolini were no longer acceptable, and the names of historical figures, mostly from the leftist depository of heroes (Táncsics, Petőfi, Dózsa, Kossuth), emerged in their place. There were also examples of local authorities—mostly those affiliated with the MKP—choosing Soviet military and political figures as eponyms. As a result of some prodding in 1948 from Rajk, the minister of internal affairs, by the end of the year, the country's symbolic map was sprinkled with place names honoring Marx, Lenin, Stalin, Voroshilov, Malinovskii, and Molotov.[75]

One of the first institutions to be named after Rákosi—apart from the Hungarian "Rákosi Brigade" that fought in the Spanish Civil War—was an orphanage founded in 1945, but the coalition years witnessed several other renamings for the Party secretary. A newly built residential district in the city of Debrecen, for instance, came to be known as "*Rákosi-prolitelep*" (proletarian neighborhood). Moreover, one of the first ships renovated after the war was christened "Mátyás Rákosi." Even sports events

---

[74] A thorough linguistic analysis of name changes in Soviet-type regimes is offered by Szergej Tóth, "Nyelvhasználat egy totalitárius rendszerben (Nyelvszociológiai megközelítés)" (PhD dissertation, Eötvös Loránd Tudományegyetem, Budapest, 1999).

[75] Mevius, *Agents of Moscow*, 253.

(chess and soccer tournaments) became associated with Rákosi's name at the time.[76] Although the renaming of institutions—especially those under MKP control—after prominent politicians was an established practice in the coalition years, the process became standardized only after the Communist takeover.[77] Alongside the flurry of proposals that were meant to centralize cult production, the Agitprop Department outlined the general policy of name changes in late 1949 and also suggested a pool of names to choose from (Soviet and Hungarian Party leaders, socialist heroes, national heroes, etc.). According to the proposal, the main function of renaming rituals was to strengthen loyalty and dedication toward the regime among the population and to enhance the masses' political consciousness by setting exemplary figures before them.

> We will use the name changes to deepen in the laborers a new patriotic sentiment, proletarian internationalism, loyalty to the Soviet Union and to the great leaders of the working-class movement. Setting great exemplary figures and glorious historical events before the laborers would educate them to take a worthy part in the battles fought at the frontlines of production, following the example of those whose names were given to their factory.[78]

Renamings were to be organized so that they would seem to be initiatives from below. If the requested name was that of a living leader, the workers were supposed to write him a letter explaining the achievements of the factory and describing the pledges they would make if granted the honor of bearing such a revered name. Renaming rituals were preceded by an intense agitation campaign in the respective factories, in which the workers were expected to grasp the significance of the renaming and to recognize the new duties that the name change would bring about. Since the precondition for permission to use a name was outstanding production, the laborers were expected to perceive the renaming as a reward for

---

[76] The chess competition was authorized by the Orgburo: PIL 274. fond 5/28. It was the official newspaper that reported about the soccer tournament called the "Rákosi Cup." *Szabad Nép*, August 23, 1947.

[77] One of the first examples that marked the beginning of the tide was the request of the Szeged Party Committee in December 1948 asking for the Orgburo's permission to rename the newly rebuilt bridge over the Tisza River after Rákosi. MOL, 276. fond 55/50.

[78] MOL, 276. fond 108/2. It first was discussed at the meeting of the Secretariat on October 26, 1949. MOL, 276. fond 54/68.

their good performance. The regime also anticipated that the workers at factories that received such a privilege would express their gratitude by stepping up their work efforts.

The procedural routine established by the Propaganda Department was closely followed by factory committees that sought to acquire the leader's name. Workers, encouraged by local Party officials, wrote letters to the leader requesting name changes, and, at the same time, offered pledges to the Party if permission were given. A typical example was the letter of a brigade in Sztálinváros that applied for volunteer work and requested that Rákosi allow them to bear his name. "We craftsmen from the private sector will have to show our affection with more gratitude to Comrade General Secretary and the Party through this voluntary work, because we can only thank Comrade General Secretary, and the great Party under his guidance, for being able to work in peace."[79] The Party's approval was followed by the intensification of the workload and the reinvigoration of the ongoing labor competition, as the case of the factory on Csepel Island demonstrates: "This decree triggered genuine enthusiasm and happiness among the workers, which they expressed through pledges offered en masse."[80]

The renaming of what was then Hungary's largest factory complex (the former Manfréd Weiss Works on Csepel Island) after Rákosi (*Rákosi Mátyás Művek*) in 1950 signaled the beginning of the most symbolically laden name changes. The use of the Party leader's name was particularly common in the sphere of production. The number of Rákosi Brigades in factories and collective farms increased, and they all participated in the nationwide "Rákosi shift" in anticipation of the leader's sixtieth birthday. The name of the Party leader was also linked to culture and education. Apart from the Mátyás Rákosi House of Culture in Budapest on Attila József Square, the central school of the Trade Union Council was granted the name of the leader in August 1949.[81] Furthermore, the special college for officers at the armored divisions of the army took Rákosi's name in 1951 (*Rákosi Mátyás Páncélos Tiszti Iskola*).[82] Following a similar pattern, a secondary school was named after the Party secretary in Tatabánya,

---

[79] Kő and Nagy, *Levelek Rákosihoz*, 108.
[80] MOL, 276. fond 108/19.
[81] MOL, 276. fond 54/58.
[82] *Szabad Nép*, August 20, 1949.

and a "Rákosi Room" was established in Sopron, in the primary school that the leader once attended.⁸³ The most significant renamings, however, were implemented for Rákosi's sixtieth birthday in 1952. The university in the city of Miskolc, which specialized in training mining and mechanical engineers, was christened *Rákosi Mátyás Nehézipari Műszaki Egyetem* (Mátyás Rákosi Technical University for Heavy Industry). At the same time, the Party established a Rákosi Study Contest (*Rákosi Mátyás Tanulmányi Verseny*) for secondary-school students, a Rákosi Grant for outstanding university students, and a Rákosi Award for exceptional academic activity.⁸⁴ By 1953 at least thirty collective farms across the country bore Rákosi's name, and several cities had a Rákosi Street (such as Kalocsa, Kiskunfélegyháza, and Szarvas).⁸⁵

The renaming process also had a remarkable international aspect. The practice of renaming institutions after Communist leaders from the Eastern bloc—the most common example being Stalin—was widespread in the countries of the "peace camp" in the 1950s. Hungary was no exception: it had factories named after Gheorghiu-Dej and Wilhelm Pieck, as well as Klement Gottwald, not to mention the dozens of streets that bore the name of Lenin, Stalin, or the Red Army. Such name changes were meant to symbolically endorse the cults of Party secretaries in the bloc, but they also helped promote the idea of friendship and unity in the Soviet empire.⁸⁶ The frequency of the appearance of a Party leader's name on the symbolic maps of foreign countries indicated his significance in the hierarchy of mini-Stalins, and it also designated his position in the constantly changing international pantheon of leaders.⁸⁷

---

⁸³ *Szabad Nép*, November 1, 1949.

⁸⁴ The renamings for the leader's sixtieth birthday were decided by the Secretariat in August 1951. MOL, 276. fond 54/158. The Rákosi Study Contest was the predecessor of the *Országos Középiskolai Tanulmányi Verseny* (National Study Contest of Secondary-School Students), which continues to the present day.

⁸⁵ There were slight variations in the names of kolkhozes: "Rákosi," "Mátyás Rákosi," "Rákosi Csillaga" (Rákosi's Star). OSA, 300/40/3/264

⁸⁶ On the idea of friendship, see Jan C. Behrends, *Die erfundene Freundschaft: Propaganda für die Sowjetunion in Polen und in der DDR (1944–1957)* (Cologne: Böhlau, 2006).

⁸⁷ In Hungary, proposals to name a place or a particular institution after a non-Hungarian leader were put forward by the Central Committee's Department of Foreign Affairs (*Külügyi Osztály*). In 1949, in honor of the deceased Georgi Dimitrov, for example, the department came up with the idea to rename one of Budapest's large squares after the Bulgarian Communist leader. Of the three options in the proposal (Fővám Square, Kálvin Square, or Kálvária Square), the Secretariat chose Fővám Square. MOL, 276. fond 54/54.

Following the pattern of mutual renamings in the Soviet bloc, the name of Rákosi was also exported, which—to a limited extent—transferred his cult beyond the country's boundaries. For instance, in 1952 *Szabad Ifjúság* (Free Youth) reported the christening of a machine station in the GDR (in Mecklenburg), as well as the renaming of a collective farm in Bulgaria (in Uzundzhovo), after Rákosi.[88] At the same time, a factory in Romania (in Bucharest) was given the name "Rákosi Works." War-stricken North Korea also expressed its gratitude for Hungarian—mostly medical—aid and renamed a hospital after the leader of the MDP.[89] In one case a Soviet newborn—a girl—was christened Matiasa, in honor of the Hungarian leader, in February 1952.[90] Renaming requests from abroad were submitted to the Hungarian government even after the Rákosi cult had reached its peak in 1952. The Andreas School in Berlin, for example, asked the Hungarian government for permission to rename itself after Rákosi in March 1955.[91]

The process of renaming institutions was meant to convey symbolic allegiance and absolute loyalty to the leader. By adopting the leader's name, the workers of the chosen factory or kolkhoz expressed their commitment to and full association with the goals of the leader, without the possibility of deviance or doubt. Those industrial units or collective farms honored by the name of Rákosi were also expected to perform better than the rest. In fact, it was assumed they would set an example in production that could be emulated by other, less (or more?) fortunate, institutions. The drive to match the expectations of the Party was compensated by the rise of the renamed institution to a semi-privileged status. Those industrial or educational units that were named after Rákosi received widespread publicity in the press, and more attention from the Party, which could result in easier access to scarce commodities. Indeed, such potential economic advantages were often a major incentive for requesting permission to rename a place or an institution after Rákosi or other Communist leaders on the local level.[92]

---

[88] *Szabad Ifjúság*, August 16, 1952.
[89] OSA 300/40/3/264.
[90] Pünkösti, *Rákosi a hatalomért*, 22–23.
[91] MOL, 276. fond 65/343.
[92] This aspect, however, would need to be researched further. Such studies exist in the Soviet context. Malte Rolf, for example, called the attempt of local Party organs to gain the privilege

Despite their distinguished status, institutions carrying the leader's name did not always demonstrate extraordinary accomplishments. Attaching Rákosi's name to a Budapest orphanage, for example, could not save the institution from the management's notorious financial lapses.[93] Shortcomings were also reported in the functioning of other educational institutions bearing Rákosi's name. A report that addressed what it referred to as early-age manifestations of sexuality at the Maxim Gorky School claimed that such problems were observed mostly among children from the Rákosi Kindergarten in Budapest.[94] The Hungarian Party leader also complained in 1954 about the bad reputation of Rákosi kindergartens in the country. He allegedly blamed Árpád Szakasits for suggesting such renamings and claimed that the former leader of the Social Democrats simply wanted to ridicule him.[95]

The sensitive nature of the reconfiguration of symbolic space in Hungary was signified by the occasional rejections of name changes, especially in the coalition period. A suggestion in 1945, for example, to rename a mine (St. Stephen's Mine) after the MKP leader was rejected by the Orgburo without much hesitation.[96] Rejections, however, also occurred after the conquest of symbolic space in 1948–1949. The suggestion of the Nagykanizsa Party Committee to rename the town's main street after Rákosi, for example, was also vetoed by the Orgburo in November 1948.[97] A more ambitious proposal, submitted by the Székesfehérvár Party Committee for the leader's sixtieth birthday, suffered a similar fate. Révai swiftly rebuffed the request to rename the new theater and György Dózsa Square after Rákosi: "It is not desirable: 1. What kind of an idea is that, to suggest the renaming of György Dózsa Square or the renaming of a theater after Comrade Rákosi? 2. We don't do such things in Budapest;

---

of using the leader's name the "colonisation of the leader's name." Rolf, "The Leader's Many Bodies," 197–206.

[93] The orphanage's regular requests for financial aid were sent to the Orgburo.

[94] MOL, 276. fond 65/343.

[95] Pünkösti, *Rákosi a csúcson*, 293. Árpád Szakasits was a politician and a prominent member of the Hungarian Social Democratic Party. He was general secretary of the party between 1939 and 1948, and after the unification of the two leftist parties he became president of the newly-formed MDP. He became the second (and last) president of the Hungarian republic in 1948, and the first chairman of the Hungarian Presidential Council in 1949. He was arrested on trumped up charges in 1950 and was only released in March 1956.

[96] Mevius, *Agents of Moscow*, 103.

[97] MOL, 276. fond 55/44.

therefore, it is not possible to rename streets in the provinces after him either. It is impossible to check if worthy streets or squares would be selected."[98] On occasion the Secretariat even refused requests to rename institutions after Stalin. The Party Academy's December 5, 1950, appeal to adopt Stalin's name, for example, was turned down despite the director's heavy use of cultic language in her request letter.[99] While the Party tried to retain the symbolic value of Communist leaders' names by rejecting certain renaming proposals, it also attempted to root out any potential ambiguities in relation to Rákosi's name. For instance, a species of viper that was common near the Rákos stream and was thus called the "Rákosi viper" was renamed the "fallow viper" in order to prevent subversive uses of the leader's name.[100]

Despite the many occasions when renaming proposals were rejected, the number of place names, educational institutions, collective farms, and factories bearing Rákosi's name increased rapidly. Although no towns were named after the Hungarian Party leader (unlike Gottwaldow in Czechoslovakia, Gheorghiu-Dej in Romania, or Dimitrovgrad in Bulgaria[101]), the renaming of the indicators of Socialist transformation after the Party secretary, and the permanent association of achievements with the leader in Communist propaganda, significantly reinforced the image of Rákosi as the sole embodiment of socialist transition in Hungary.

The "leaderization of space" was therefore a fundamental part of the Sovietization of symbolic space in postwar Hungary. The politics of renaming and the allocation of leader images were meant to bolster the image of the leader as the epitome of progress and socialist transformation. Through the depiction of the leader as the focal point of symbolic space, Rákosi was represented as the great director of the building of socialism in Hungary. However, in contrast to the cult of Stalin in the Soviet Union,

---

[98] Quoted in Pünkösti, *Rákosi a csúcson*, 429.

[99] "We are convinced that if the name of Comrade Stalin could glitter on the façade of our school, it would inspire all the teachers and students of the school to work harder, to make more sacrifices, and to study more deeply. We would aspire more intensely to become worthy of executing the tasks set by Comrade Stalin and his best Hungarian apprentice, Mátyás Rákosi." The letter was written by Erzsébet Andics. MOL, 276. fond 54/122.

[100] Information on the snake is available at http://www.rakosivipera.hu/en/hungarian-meadow-viper/ (accessed June 8, 2012).

[101] Anders Åman, "Symbols and Rituals in the People's Democracies During the Cold War," in Arvidsson and Blomqvist, *Symbols of Power*, 52.

the notion of the omnipresent leader was almost exclusively promoted through the distribution of Rákosi's images. Although the Rákosi cult was transmitted partly through painting, sculpture, and posters, the idea of the leader's ubiquity was communicated primarily through photographed —and retouched—portraits or their poster counterparts. Such portraits —along with copies of the busts of the leader—were supposed to function as icon-like cult objects, representing the leader's mystical body, and thus should be assessed from a functional point of view and not on the basis of their artistic qualities. The religious connotations of the leader's images were further endorsed by the spatial arrangement of the pictures of major Communist saints in a triptych-like way. Some of these images—such as wall newspapers at workplaces—even featured in collective rituals on occasion. Nevertheless, the role of visual arts, with the exception of photography, in the process of cult-building was far less significant than in the case of the Lenin and the Stalin cults. The limited application of visual arts in the construction of the Rákosi myth was coupled with the small number of images such representations depicted. The leader was mostly portrayed in a teacher pose while speaking in front of an audience, or as a father/friend having a paternal talk with workers, peasants, children, or foreign politicians. Pictures from Rákosi's private life or his childhood were not in circulation. The Hungarian Party secretary's visual representations, in accordance with the cult discourse, lacked any intimate details and remained largely impersonal.

PART II

RESPONSES TO THE CULT'S EXPANSION

Chapter 6
"Love for Comrade Rákosi Has Become Deeper": The Communicative Influence of the Cult

Popular Opinion and the Stalinist "Source Lens"

Since the cult was not constructed by a single institution, its expansion was not monitored by a single department either. Party and government departments, professional organizations, and newspapers that participated in the creation of the Rákosi myth were all expected to provide feedback on the process of cult-building and on the commitment and proficiency of the cult's agents. At the same time, they were instructed to observe the population's general reaction to the organized veneration of the leader. The monitoring of the performance of propaganda bodies and the political attitudes of society was integrated into the surveillance strategies of the regime and was part of the attempt to establish a Soviet-type "culture of surveillance" in a Hungarian context: the secret police, Party and government organs, and indeed every citizen were supposed to stay "vigilant" at all times and report any suspicious activity or rumor to the appropriate institution. Summary reports on the attitudes of the public were dubbed "mood reports" in official parlance and were among the most common documents produced by the Communist regime. "Mood reports" were compiled by the Agitprop Department of the Communist Party based on accounts submitted by local Party organs, mass organizations, and the letters departments of newspapers. However, industrial units, collective farms, and public institutions were also required to reflect on the general political atmosphere in their immediate social surroundings.[1]

---

[1] As well as the various Party departments, the secret police continuously monitored the mood of the population, through its extensive network of informers and spies. However, letters addressed to the leader, readers' letters to *Szabad Nép*, and—on occasion—even judiciary

As Katherine Verdery has observed, practices of surveillance resulted in the mass production of files and dossiers and contributed to the emergence of a parallel economic system whose function was to produce reports.[2] Part II of this book relies heavily on documents created by the paper-producing economic sub-system as it sets out to address the impact of the cult on society and the overall efficiency of cult propaganda.

Judging by the mood reports, the Rákosi cult was only infrequently commented upon by the Hungarian population. Whether the scarcity of reflections on the cult indicates popular ignorance toward the phenomenon, or instead occurred because the propaganda staff deemed unwise the forwarding of cult-related (especially negative) comments, remains impossible to determine. Therefore, it is difficult to measure the different perceptions of the MDP secretary's adoration in Hungarian society. Did the rituals and the language of the cult meet with support, or did they provoke mainly hostility? To what extent did people remain indifferent to the adoration of the Party leader? Did the cult have any significant impact on the population at all?

The reception of the cult of Rákosi is connected to the problem of popular opinion in totalitarian regimes. The issue of social support for the cult cannot be separated from the questions of how the establishment of the Communist dictatorship was generally perceived and whether, in

---

documents testified to the attitudes of the people toward the establishment and its leaders. Unfortunately, many informant reports collected by the secret police (ÁVO, later ÁVH) in 1949–1956 were destroyed in 1956. Hence research on Hungarian society's attitude toward the Communist system must primarily be based on propagandists' mood reports—also decimated at the time of the revolution—which generally display a lower heuristic value. For more on the destruction of secret police files, see Magdolna Baráth, "Az állambiztonsági iratok selejtezése, megsemmisítése," in György Gyarmati, ed., *Trezor 3. Az átmenet évkönyve* (Budapest: Állambiztonsági Szolgálatok Történeti Levéltára, 2004), 255–80. Accounts of the popular mood, especially at the time of the Communist takeover in 1948–1949, were frequently forwarded to the Party center by telephone. Secretaries of local Party sections, regional and city councils, and factories in particular submitted their reports to the Propaganda Department in person by other means of telecommunication. On the basis of the information extracted from the reports of regional Party institutions and mass organizations (such as trade unions and youth and women's organizations), the agitprop section of the Central Committee prepared a written summary and forwarded this to the central Party organs, and often to some prominent members of the Party leadership. Rákosi, for example, usually read the general mood report summaries collected by the Agitprop Department.

[2] Katherine Verdery, *What Was Socialism and What Comes Next?* (Princeton: Princeton University Press, 1996), 24.

Soviet-type societies, one could identify spheres of limited social autonomy where unofficial views could be expressed. Although the study of popular opinion in totalitarian systems has recently gained some popularity among historians, the field is littered with debates about the credibility of primary sources—the "source lens"—and the actual value of the information they contain.[3] Nonetheless, scholars tend to agree that the notion of popular opinion is complex and cannot be reduced to a consent/dissent binary.[4] While support and resistance were both manifest in Soviet-type societies, such attitudes were merely part of a "wide continuum of societal responses."[5] It is generally acknowledged that popular opinion is shaped by a number of factors—subjective and collective experience, memories, and attitudes. Therefore, it is often ambivalent, ambiguous, and controversial, and it is something that is impossible to quantify.[6] Despite the volatile nature of the phenomenon, historians concur that communication along unofficial lines remained possible even in the Stalinist context, and dissenting opinions could be articulated in a variety of different ways.

What historians tend to disagree about is the credibility of the "totalitarian source lens" and whether documents such as mood reports echo the

---

[3] Among the most important studies on public opinion in totalitarian systems, including the Soviet Union, are those of Paul Corner, ed., *Popular Opinion in Totalitarian Regimes: Fascism, Nazism, Communism* (Oxford: Oxford University Press, 2009); Sarah Davies, *Popular Opinion in Stalin's Russia: Terror, Propaganda and Dissent, 1939–1941* (Cambridge: Cambridge University Press, 1997); Walter D. Connor and Zvi Y. Gitelman, eds., *Public Opinion in European Socialist Systems* (New York and London: Praeger, 1977). See also the relevant sections of Brandenberger, *National Bolshevism*; Polly Jones, "Strategies of De-Mythologisation in Post-Stalinism and Post-Communism: A Comparison of De-Stalinisation and De-Leninisation" (PhD dissertation, University of Oxford, 2002); and Polly Jones, "'I've Held, and I Still Hold, Stalin the Highest Esteem': Discourses and Strategies of Resistance to De-Stalinisation in the USSR, 1953–62," in Apor et al., *The Leader Cult*, 227–45. In the German context, see Ian Kershaw, *Popular Opinion and Political Dissent in Third Reich, Bavaria, 1933–1945* (Oxford: Clarendon Press, 1983); and Ian Kershaw, *The "Hitler Myth"*. See also Peter Holquist, "'Information Is the Alpha and Omega of Our Work': Bolshevik Surveillance in Its Pan-European Context," *Journal of Modern History* 69, no. 3 (1997): 415–50. On the reception of the Stalin cult in the GDR, see Plamper, "The Hitlers Come and Go…."

[4] For a discussion of the Stalinist "source lens," see Lynne Viola, "Popular Resistance in the Stalinist 1930s: Soliloquy of a Devil's Advocate," in *Contending with Stalinism*, ed. Lynne Viola (Ithaca and London: Cornell University Press, 2002), 25 and 35. On the issue of binaries, see Jan Plamper, "Beyond Binaries: Popular Opinion in Stalinism," in Corner, *Popular Opinion in Totalitarian Regimes*, 64–80.

[5] Lynn Viola, "Introduction," in *Contending with Stalinism*, 1.

[6] On the variety of factors shaping popular opinion, see Jill Stephenson, "Popular Opinion in Nazi Germany: Mobilization, Experience, Perceptions: The View from the Württemberg Countryside," in Corner, *Popular Opinion in Totalitarian Regimes*, 107–21.

"true" opinion of the population. Sarah Davies, in her seminal study on popular opinion in the Soviet Union, argued that some sort of an "impressionistic" overview of popular responses, or rather, a "collection of diverse popular reaction,"[7] to Stalinist policies can be reconstructed on the basis of reports. However, other scholars remained more skeptical, claiming that such reports tell us more about the regime's surveillance practices than about the actual attitude of society toward the Communist Party and its leaders.[8] While the debate about the value of primary sources has not reached a conclusion, there seems to be a general agreement on how to conceptualize what these documents do or do not discuss. Thus most authors use the idea of "popular opinion" instead of "public opinion," indicating the difficulties of measuring and reconstructing the latter on the basis of available sources. Popular opinion is a more fluid category than public opinion: it is spontaneous and subject to sudden changes; it can be ambiguous and even controversial; and it is unquantifiable. However, even if historians discussing the subject acknowledge the inconsistent nature of popular opinion in a totalitarian context, the very word "opinion" suggests a certain degree of consistency. This book instead advocates the use of the term "popular mood," which conveys the spontaneous, elusive, and unpredictable aspects of popular responses to the regime's policies in a more appropriate way.

There is a fundamental difference between public opinion and popular mood. In totalitarian regimes the government sought to suppress dissenting opinions and unofficial channels of communication. While the Party eliminated the means to systematically measure public opinion, it remained obsessively preoccupied with gathering information on what people thought. In its paradoxical struggle to both suppress and gather knowledge about popular political attitudes, which was partly fueled by fear of dissent, the regime required workplaces, Party departments, government institutions, its army of informants, and the secret police to constantly report on the "mood" of the population.[9] However, the process of gathering information about the popular mood produced a distorted

---

[7] Davies, *Popular Opinion in Stalin's Russia*, 8.
[8] Holquist, "Information Is the Alpha and Omega of Our Work."
[9] Paul Corner, "Introduction," in Corner, *Popular Opinion in Totalitarian Regimes*, 3.

picture of citizens' overall political views. This process was partly responsible for the regime grossly miscalculating the consequences of certain policies. Due to the elusive nature of the popular mood, and also due to the way it was measured and evaluated, it is questionable whether the Party ever gained an accurate overview of political attitudes in society.

The interpretation of mood reports poses a number of methodological concerns for historians. The general atmosphere of unpredictability in Stalinist society—including the frequent rotation of cadres, the absurd expectations of the Party leadership, the threat of being purged, and so on—could and did result in the creation of fictitious opinion reports. The information department of the ÁVH, for example, filtered and evaluated the daily mood reports before forwarding them and often submitted only those pieces of information that they considered to be in accord with the Party's expectations.[10]

In addition to the problem of falsification, there was the issue of the regime's Manichean worldview, shown by the binary labeling of all opinions in the mood reports as either positive or negative. This approach excluded the possibility of recording and reporting complex or ambivalent attitudes, even if such views were articulated in public. Moreover, since the regime demanded affirmation from its subjects, the sections enlisting expressions of support for the Party's goals and policies tended to dominate in the reports, and often marginalized negative opinions, which were labeled "hostile opinions" or "the influence of the enemy." The dominance of positive opinions in mood reports, however, can hardly be interpreted as proof of widespread support for, or acceptance of, the Communist regime. Affirmative statements in the documents were articulated in the official discourse, which could be attributed in part to the creative intervention of the propaganda staff editing the reports. At the same time, the similarity of the vocabulary of the cult and the language of the reports could be interpreted as a demonstration of the discursive influence of the Communist master narrative on society and on the Hungarian vernacular. In the mood reports, positive statements about Rákosi

---

[10] At the time of the New Course, Gerő, as the new minister of internal affairs, criticized the ÁVH's practice of feeding the Party sifted mood report summaries. Müller Rolf, "A politikai rendőrség tájékoztató szolgálata 1945–1962," in *Trezor 2. A Történeti Hivatal évkönyve, 2000–2001*, ed. György Gyarmati (Budapest: Történeti Hivatal, 2002), 116–17.

usually parroted the official image of the leader as it appeared in the media. However, whether such statements were articulated by devout supporters of the cause, invented and inserted by Party functionaries, or uttered by non-believers who simply learned how to "speak Bolshevik" cannot be determined from the documents.[11] As with affirmative views, the significance of negative opinions should not be exaggerated, and one must not interpret these opinions as indicators of the existence of organized resistance movements under the Communist regime.[12]

The binary categorization of opinions was congruent with the Communist idea of social transformation and historical progress advanced by class warfare. Nevertheless, it hindered the possibility of identifying complex or ambivalent political attitudes to the regime. The matrix of diverse political attitudes is obscured by the painfully simplistic taxonomy adopted in the reports. It is possible, for example, that some people supported certain government policies while rejecting others. People could also take different standpoints in different spheres of social life (workplace, social circle, home, and so on) or articulate inconsistent views due to their being politically less informed or ideologically less trained than others. Sometimes people exploited the dominant political discourse and used the language of the Party in the hope of achieving material benefits or avoiding retribution. There was also a tendency in Soviet-type societies to subvert the official discourse and to express disapproval or criticism through the vocabulary of Party rhetoric.[13] Mood reports, however, are not particularly informative about the individual motifs behind the articulation of a certain opinion, and they remain silent about incidents in which complex or inconsistent political views were uttered.

Besides the difficulties of analyzing ambiguities and shifts in people's attitudes toward the regime, the "process of silencing"—to use Sarah Davies's term—and the various communication strategies citizens used during Rákosi's rule further complicate the attempt to outline social

---

[11] The concept of "speaking Bolshevik" was developed by Kotkin, *Magnetic Mountain*, 198–237.

[12] Jan Plamper observed the problem in the context of East Germany: Plamper, "The Hitlers Come and Go," 326.

[13] One example was the Stalin constitution in 1936 as elaborated by Petrone, *Life Has Become More Joyous, Comrades*, 176–84. A similar trend of using the official rhetoric of the constitution of 1949 to express dissatisfaction with the regime can also be identified in Hungary.

attitudes to the system and the leader cult. Due to the omnipresence of coercion and state violence in Hungary in the 1950s, the spreading of dissenting opinion was reduced to informal communication channels (word of mouth), or else such opinions were masked by Aesopian language and were shrouded in jokes, rumors, and *chastushki*.[14] The use of Bolshevik-speak in everyday communication with the authorities was another strategy to hide one's actual opinion about the Party and its leaders. Non-verbal ways of expressing political support (such as applauding) or opposition (such as iconoclasm), which remained a specific feature of Stalinist culture, also obscured the complexity of political attitudes toward the regime and the cult.

Apart from labeling opinions as either "positive" or "negative" and thus dividing society into supporters and enemies, the editors of mood reports further obfuscated social diversities by adopting a schematic (and dogmatic) categorization of society. Whenever informants indicated the respondents' social background, they employed catch-all concepts such as "peasant," "kulak," "worker," and "intellectual." Moreover, respondents, or those who wrote letters to Rákosi or to newspapers, also tended to identify themselves with the same, all-encompassing social categories.[15] Considering the extensive restructuring of Hungarian society in the 1950s, sparked off by breakneck industrialization, collectivization, mass urbanization, social mobilization, and the Party's haphazard cadre policy, such categories are not always helpful when trying to establish which social groups supported or rejected the regime's policies. The constant shifts in individual social positions in the Stalinist "quicksand society" hindered the possibility of linking certain political attitudes to specific social groups.[16] Because it is problematic to determine how the regime

---

[14] On informal communication strategies in the Soviet Union, see Raymond A. Bauer and David B. Gleicher, "Word-of-Mouth Communication in the Soviet Union," *Public Opinion Quarterly* 17, no. 3 (1953): 297–310. A *chastushka* is a type of Russian folk song that is usually distinguished by its humorous, satirical content.

[15] On the use of schematic social categories in political discourse, see Sándor Horváth, "Munkás, paraszt, értelmiség munkaverseny lázában ég," in *Mérlegen a XX. századi magyar történelem –értelmezések és értékelések*, ed. Levente Püski and Tibor Valuch (Budapest: Debreceni Egyetem Törénelmi Intézete és az 1956-os Intézet, 2002), 345–57.

[16] There are only a few historical works in Hungarian that address the popular perception of the regime. See, for example, Szabó, "Hétköznapi sztálinizmus"; György Gyarmati, "A társadalom közérzete a fordulat évében. Közvéleménykutatások és ÁVO hangulatjelentések 1948-ban,"

was popularly received based on the information in surveillance documents, it remains difficult to establish which social groups supported, rejected, or ignored the Rákosi cult. Opinions about the cult reached the Party leadership through a number of filters within the Party bureaucracy, where they were sifted, simplified, and rephrased, further complicating the interpretation of such documents.

While surveillance documents continue to cause problems of interpretation, they remain valuable sources for historians, as they shed light on the discursive expansion of propaganda in society and indicate the extent to which the language of the cult infused day-to-day communicative practices. Did ordinary people use the vocabulary of the cult when communicating with the regime? To what extent did the codes and messages of the leader cult define communication within the Party bureaucracy? In addition to highlighting the communicative influence of the cult, surveillance documents also attest to the role of agency in the dissemination of the cult's codes and are thus indicative of the overall efficiency of propaganda. Agency, in fact, is crucial to the study of the cult's reception. The commitment, education, and socio-cultural background of propagandists and agitators influenced the way ideology was transmitted and the extent to which the original message was transformed or distorted by the time it reached its target audience. The regime's functionaries at the lower end of the bureaucratic hierarchy thus had an important role in shaping the way society perceived the cult.[17] Mood reports generally provide useful information about the way ideologies are transmitted and internalized in closed societies by highlighting how the agents of totalitarian propaganda contributed to the regime's indoctrination efforts. Part II of this book is concerned with both agency and the popular reception of cultic messages.

Mozgó Világ 24, no. 10 (1998): 95–111. Some hints concerning the perception of the system are also included in Tibor Valuch, *Magyarország társadalomtörténete a XX. század második felében* (Budapest: Osiris, 2001); and in Gyarmati et al., *Magyar hétköznapok*. The term "quicksand society" was coined by Moshe Lewin in "Introduction: Social Crises and Political Structures in the USSR," in *The Making of the Soviet System: Essays in the Social History of Interwar Russia* (London: Pantheon Books, 1985), 44.

[17] The importance of Party functionaries in influencing the efficacy and the perception of the regime's propaganda has been discussed extensively in Petrone, *Life Has Become More Joyous, Comrades*; and in Malte Rolf, *Soviet Mass Festivals, 1917–1991* (Pittsburgh: University of Pittsburgh Press, 2013).

The communicative influence of the cult will be addressed on the basis of documents that informed the Party center of the spreading of affirmative attitudes to the cult and reported on (allegedly) successful rituals or promotion campaigns. The discussion of the problem of resistance to the veneration of the leader relies on sources lamenting outbursts of criticism and dislike of cultic objects and messages. The question of agency will be analyzed in conjunction with popular indifference and records of frustrated attempts at promoting the leader's image.

The Popularity of the Leader

According to the surveys of the Hungarian Institute of Public Opinion (*Magyar Közvéleménykutató Intézet—MKI*), which functioned between 1945 and 1949, Rákosi enjoyed remarkable popularity among the Hungarian population in the postwar years, especially among the petty bourgeoisie, the intelligentsia, and the industrial workers of Budapest.[18] In January 1946 he was the country's second most popular politician (after the Smallholder prime minister, Zoltán Tildy), and he rose to first place a year later. He was considered the most skillful leftist orator in May 1948, and an August 1947 poll showed that the majority of respondents regarded him as the person best qualified to be prime minister.[19] Although Rákosi became prime minister a few years later (in August 1952), his popularity had vanished by then. The establishment of the communist dictatorship; the launching of the First Five-Year Plan in 1950, with its forced industrialization and collectivization campaigns; the rapid worsening of living conditions; and the intensification of coercion and terror all contributed to the decline of Rákosi's reputation from 1949.

Given the difficult circumstances in which the MKI functioned in the coalition years, one might have doubts about the accuracy of the survey

---

[18] On public opinion research in the coalition period, see Ádám Levendel, "A Magyar Közvéleménykutató Intézet (1945–1949)," *Jel-Kép* 4, no. 3 (1983): 134–39; András Lénárt, "'Nevet nem szabad kérdezni!' Közvélemény-kutatás Magyarországon 1945 és 1949 között," in *A demokrácia reménye: Magyarország 1945*, ed. János M. Rainer and Éva Standeisky (Budapest: 1956-os Intézet, 2005), 146–75; Gyarmati, "A társadalom közérzete a fordulat évében"; Robert Blumstock, "Public Opinion in Hungary," in Connor and Gitelman, *Public Opinion in European Socialist Systems*, 132–66.

[19] Levendel, "A Magyar Közvéleménykutató Intézet (1945–1949)."

results.[20] However, even if Rákosi was never the country's most popular politician, he was certainly among the most popular ones in the coalition period. Rákosi's relative popularity during those years is normally attributed to his—and the MKP's—role in reconstruction after the war. The Party's popularity was partly reflected in the sudden growth of its membership after the war. Many of the newcomers joined the Party because of the role it played in reconstruction: land distribution, the introduction of the new currency, and price reductions for basic commodities were popular measures for which the MKP often claimed credit. Many also chose the Party in the hope of better career opportunities and rapid advancement on the social ladder. It seems plausible to suggest that many of those who chose the Communist Party did so due to the Party's "performance attainment" and not because they had a comprehensive understanding of Marxist philosophy and its complex terminology.[21] Despite the increase in the Party's membership, Rákosi's popularity was not matched by the popularity of the Party.[22] As the 1945 and 1947 election results indicate, Communist propaganda generally failed to turn the reputation of its leader into genuine support for the Party.

Even if Rákosi's relative popularity seems genuine enough, it remains questionable whether the population enthusiastically welcomed the expansion of the leader cult. Although the Communist press was full of expressions of loyalty and support for the MDP secretary, the representative value of such opinions should be seriously questioned. Instead, it seems that even as the cult grew after 1949, Rákosi's reputation withered. This indicates that a cult can grow even when the leader is actually unpopular. Nonetheless, the Rákosi cult could be considered a successful venture in the sense that it functioned: its textual and visual manifestations dominated the public sphere, and the regime ensured popular participation in its rituals. The cult thus worked, irrespective of popular perceptions of the phenomenon and Rákosi's popularity. Whether it fulfilled the functions it was meant to fulfill, however, is an entirely different matter.

The successful operation of the Rákosi cult depended on two factors:

---

[20] For more details on the difficulties and the problems the MKI had to face, see Lénárt, "Nevet nem szabad kérdezni!"

[21] The concept of "performance attainment" has been developed by Rees, "Leader Cults," 4.

[22] A similar distinction existed in relation to Hitler and the Nazi Party. Kershaw, The "Hitler Myth", 1.

a centralized institutional system for the construction of cult images and objects, and a core group of followers (Party functionaries, idealist intellectuals, etc.) who firmly believed in the Party secretary's capabilities or were simply grateful to him for their careers. The question of why society participated in the cult's rituals is a more complex one. Some historians argue that group dynamics and the desire to integrate into the collective encouraged (some) citizens to take part in cultic practices irrespective of their individual views of the phenomenon.[23] Participating in the regime's rituals created a sense of identity and belonging and allowed individuals to adjust to the new political culture by refashioning themselves as good socialist citizens.[24] While social integration appealed to some, one should not underestimate the role of coercion and soft pressure in the process of creating an audience for the cult. One unusual source—a private letter from a woman to her husband, intercepted by the ÁVH in 1951—demonstrates the discrepancy between participation in, and subjective views of, the cult and highlights the importance of social pressure to integrate into the community through ritual means.

> You tend to skip meetings—good for you. But for me, who is not even a member of the Party nor the Emndsz [sic—MNDSZ], I still had to go to the famous democratic woman's day on Wednesday. They were here for me, and I had to go, I did not want to, but they said that I must. I went, but oh, it was such a nuisance! Especially when they started cheering and applauding to the rhythm of "long live Rákosi Stalin Rákosi" [sic]. First, I looked around to check if everybody was applauding, but unfortunately everybody applauded, so I had to do so, too. But I refused to say "long live," and I thought of nice things and wished good things for us. You've never seen so many people with a long face in one place before; for that it was worth going there. On top of all that, there were no seats left when I got there, so I had to stand there for two-and-a-half hours, and my back hurt like hell in the end, so I cursed the celebration and the one who decided that I should go along too. I'm already afraid of March 15; I will surely have to go along again and listen to all that nonsense.[25]

---

[23] See, for example, Juliane Fürst, *Stalin's Last Generation: Soviet Post-War Youth and the Emergence of Mature Socialism* (Oxford: Oxford University Press, 2010), 153.

[24] Jochen Hellbeck, "Liberation from Autonomy: Mapping Self-Understandings in Stalin's Time," in Corner, *Popular Opinion in Totalitarian Regimes*, 49–63.

[25] ÁBTL 3.1.5 O-9558.

Creating the illusion of social consensus and reaffirming the image of unity through ritual means was pivotal to the regime's mobilization strategy.[26] Ensuring popular involvement in rituals of affective consensus was thus crucial for the Communist leadership. By respecting its codes and rules, the participants—including the woman above—contributed to the maintenance of such practices, irrespective of their personal views of the Party and its leaders. The writing of enthusiastic reports about propaganda events was also integrated into the process of imagining consensus. Documents noting the enthusiastic reception of the leader were thus ritualized components of the regime's discursive strategies to construct the illusion of unity. As participants in the same matrix of ritual practices, the people who applauded the leader at Party meetings and the propagandists who wrote enthusiastic reports about such events had no alternative but to master the language of the leader cult, at least to a certain extent. The cult thus had a remarkable impact on communicative practices, verbal and non-verbal alike, even if it generally failed to turn Hungarian society into a community of believers.[27] Using the cultic narrative was part of the social adjustment—whether intentional or enforced—to the new political and cultural environment, with its system of myths and ritual practices.

This chapter will address the effect of the cult on communication within the Party bureaucracy, as well as between citizens and the leadership, on the basis of sources that recorded (or invented) expressions of love and gratitude toward Rákosi. Affirmative responses in such reports were usually linked to a speech or announcement of the leader that either preceded or followed the implementation of certain Party policies. Such reports described the reactions of people listening to the speech on the radio, or noted the atmosphere of Party meetings where the words of the leader were discussed. Letters written to Rákosi also indicate the extent to which the language of the cult was internalized. Often written in desperation, such petitions occasionally employed the vocabulary of the cult in making a variety of requests of the leader.

---

[26] On the "cult of consensus" and the importance of "staged rituals of consensus" in the GDR, see Martin Sabrow, "Consent in the Communist GDR or How to Interpret Lion Feuchtwanger's Blindness in Moscow 1937," in Corner, *Popular Opinion in Totalitarian Regimes*, 168–83; and Thomas Lindenberger, "Tacit Minimal Consensus: The Always Precarious East German Dictatorship," in Corner, *Popular Opinion in Totalitarian Regimes*, 208–22.

[27] Polly Jones has also reflected upon the impact of the cult on communicative practices in the Soviet Union. See Jones, "I've Held, and I Still Hold, Stalin in the Highest Esteem," 228.

The Elections of 1949

This book has argued before that the general elections of 1949 signaled a significant advance in the development of the Rákosi cult and paved the way for the excessive exaltation of the Hungarian Party secretary in subsequent years. The leader and his words occupied center stage during the campaign; the use of applause and other social practices associated with his persona assumed a ritual character; and cultic propaganda was aimed at the entire population for the first time. Rákosi's speech on April 19 in the Thirteenth District of Budapest signaled the beginning of the election campaign, but his subsequent speeches, as well as his visits to factories, also received wide-scale coverage. It was yet another Rákosi speech, broadcast on the radio on May 14, that marked the end of the campaign.[28]

The shift in the promotion of the Party leader was indicated by the enormous efforts the Agitprop Department made in organizing and monitoring the reception of Rákosi's public appearances. The number of reports the department prepared and received from regional Party committees about the public radio broadcasts for Rákosi's speech on April 19 demonstrate this.[29] One such report remarked that "such a widespread tuning in on a national level has never happened before," while another boasted that in 60–62 percent of Hungarian villages, arrangements were made so that the entire village could hear the broadcast speech.[30]

The OPO closely monitored the popular reception of Rákosi's speech, highlighting the overall interest and enthusiasm with which it was allegedly received. Reports submitted to the department underlined that Rákosi's announcement was widely discussed in factories and in the countryside. The letters department of *Szabad Nép* pointed out, for example, that in some villages in the Dráva region, villagers spontaneously formed discussion groups and talked about the speech until nightfall and for several days afterwards.[31] The OPO was generally pleased with the way the campaign speech of the Party leader was received, and it proudly declared that "the talk was being discussed everywhere." One worker from the Ganz

---

[28] "Előre a Népfront győzelméért!" *Szabad Nép*, May 15, 1949.
[29] "A választás: népünk kiállása a béke nagy eredményeinek és ötéves tervünk mellett," *Szabad Nép*, April 20, 1949.
[30] MOL, 276. fond 108/7; MOL, 276. fond 108/11.
[31] MOL, 276. fond 108/17.

factory expressed amazement over "how the Rákosi speech changed the mood of the entire plant in a single day."[32]

Similar reactions to Rákosi's speeches were observed throughout the entire campaign period. Reports after his visit to Celldömölk (May 8), for example, spoke of peasants converted to the cause by his oration and enthusiastic teachers expressing faith in his promises.[33] Rákosi's visits to industrial units had an equally positive resonance, at least according to Communist propagandists. Reports from the Ganz factory, for example, described excited workers talking about the "unforgettable moment" when they shook hands with the leader.[34]

Besides expressions of awe and admiration for Rákosi, propaganda reports discussed the supposedly spontaneous spread of cult rituals, including applause and the chanting of Rákosi's name. Celebrations of the leader were reported from all around the country. In the Ózd factory, for example, István Kossa's speech on Liberation Day (April 4) was interrupted by lengthy applause and rhythmic chants after every mention of Stalin or Rákosi.[35] As the election approached, applauding and chanting rituals featured more frequently in reports. On the day of the election, festive demonstrations organized by the Party usually culminated in the participants rhythmically chanting the slogan "Éljen Rákosi! Éljen a Párt!" (Long live Rákosi! Long live the Party!).[36]

Propaganda reports indicate the overall satisfaction of the Party leadership with agitation during the elections and with the population's perception of propaganda messages. General evaluations of propaganda activities at the time of the elections declared that the primary goals—to create and/or intensify affection for the leader—had been achieved and popular devotion for Rákosi had increased. As one report in June 1949 declared: "One of the immediate consequences of the elections was the immense increase of the Party's influence and the overall deepening of love for the

---

[32] MOL, 276. fond 108/7.
[33] MOL, 276. fond 108/11. The report on teachers—prepared by the Ministry of Religion and Education—emphasized that the speech signaled a "breakthrough on the pedagogical front." MOL, 276. fond 65/175.
[34] MOL, 276. fond 108/17.
[35] István Kossa was a member of the Central Committee and the Politburo of the Communist Party from 1945–1951 and was the general secretary of the Council of Trade Unions from 1945 to 1948. In 1949 he first became minister of industrial affairs, then minister of finance.
[36] MOL, 276. fond 65/61.

Sándor Ék: Mátyás Rákosi at the front in Salgótarján in 1919 (1951).
Published in *Rákosi Mátyás élete képekben*. Budapest: Szikra, 1952. 27. HUNGART © 2017.

Rákosi as Secretary of the Comintern's Executive Committee in 1921.
Published in *Rákosi Mátyás élete képekben*. Budapest: Szikra, 1952. 29. HUNGART © 2017.

Rákosi in 1934, after the conclusion of his first prison sentence.

Published in *Rákosi Mátyás élete képekben*. Budapest: Szikra, 1952. 37. HUNGART © 2017.

Rákosi on trial in Budapest in January 1935.

Published in *Rákosi Mátyás élete képekben*. Budapest: Szikra, 1952. 39. HUNGART © 2017.

The Szemerei collective: Comrade Rákosi among prisoners of war (1951).
Published in *Rákosi Mátyás élete képekben*. Budapest: Szikra, 1952. 59. HUNGART © 2017.

Rákosi meeting with former prisoners of war in Debrecen after their return from the Soviet Union, 1947.
Published in *Rákosi Mátyás élete képekben*. Budapest: Szikra, 1952. 83. HUNGART © 2017.

Rákosi and peasants (1):
Checking the scythe of a smallholder in 1945.
Published in *Rákosi Mátyás élete képekben*.
Budapest: Szikra, 1952. 71. HUNGART © 2017.

Rákosi and peasants (2):
Rákosi receives a sheep as a gift
before an election speech in
the countryside in 1947.
Published in *Rákosi Mátyás élete képekben*.
Budapest: Szikra, 1952. 82. HUNGART © 2017.

Rákosi and peasants (3): Rákosi cutting bread
after his speech in Kecskemét on August 20, 1948.
Published in *Rákosi Mátyás élete képekben*.
Budapest: Szikra, 1952. 101. HUNGART © 2017.

Rákosi and peasants (4):
Rákosi meeting peasant delegates
at the Second Congress of the MDP
in February 1951.
Published in *Rákosi Mátyás élete képekben*.
Budapest: Szikra, 1952. 127. HUNGART © 2017.

Rákosi and workers: Rákosi enjoying a beer with workers after the nationalization of industrial enterprises in the spring of 1948.
Published in *Rákosi Mátyás élete képekben*. Budapest: Szikra, 1952. 86. HUNGART © 2017.

Rákosi and soldiers: Rákosi visiting an army camp with Mihály Farkas (facing the camera) in 1951.
Published in *Rákosi Mátyás élete képekben*. Budapest: Szikra, 1952. 130. HUNGART © 2017.

Rákosi and children (1): Rákosi with a baby, 1950.
Published in *Rákosi Mátyás élete képekben*. Budapest: Szikra, 1952. 117. HUNGART © 2017.

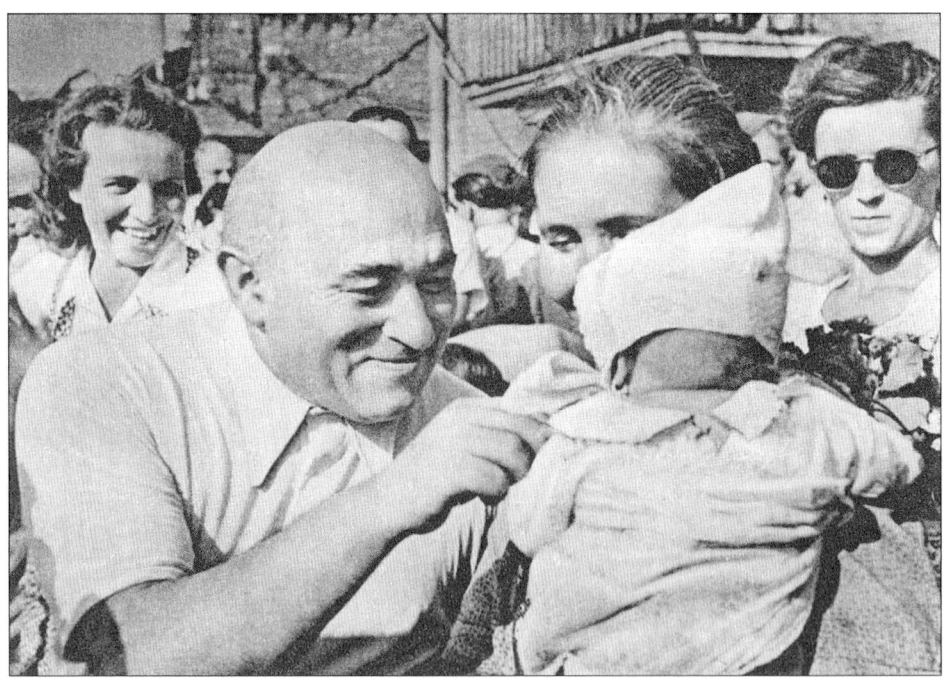

Rákosi and children (2): Thanking Rákosi for "a happy childhood," 1948.
Published in *Rákosi Mátyás élete képekben*. Budapest: Szikra, 1952. 87. HUNGART © 2017.

Rákosi and children (3): Rákosi at the pioneer camp of Parád, 1950.
Published in *Rákosi Mátyás élete képekben*. Budapest: Szikra, 1952. 116. HUNGART © 2017.

Rákosi and children (4): The "father of the people" among schoolchildren in Budapest.
Published in *The Life of Mátyás Rákosi in Pictures*. Budapest: Szikra, 1952. 137. HUNGART © 2017.

Rákosi and children (5): Watching the May 1 parade on Stalin Square in 1955.
84057:FORTEPAN/FORTEPAN.

Under Stalin's gaze: Rákosi and Gheorghiu-Dej at the Stalin exhibition in Bucharest in 1948.
Published in *Rákosi Mátyás élete képekben*. Budapest: Szikra, 1952. 92. HUNGART © 2017.

The "two Dimitrovs": Rákosi and Georgi Dimitrov after the signing of the Bulgarian-Hungarian friendship treaty in 1948.
Published in *Rákosi Mátyás élete képekben*. Budapest: Szikra, 1952. 91. HUNGART © 2017.

Stalin and his "best Hungarian apprentice" in Moscow, after the signing of the Soviet-Hungarian friendship treaty in February 1948.
Published in *Rákosi Mátyás élete képekben*. Budapest: Szikra, 1952. 89. HUNGART © 2017.

The symbolic triumvirate: policemen carrying the portraits of Lenin, Stalin, and Rákosi at a mass parade in 1950. 16502:FORTEPAN/Magyar Rendőr.

May 1 parade on Heroes' Square, Budapest, 1950. 67623:FORTEPAN/Magyar rendőr.

The building of the Ministry of Internal Affairs in 1951. The portraits of Lenin, Stalin, and Rákosi are arranged according to a triptych pattern. 16609:FORTEPAN/Magyar Rendőr.

May 1 parade on Andrássy Avenue in Budapest, 1949. 32909:FORTEPAN/Kovács Márton Ernő.

May 1 parade at Oktogon in Budapest, 1946.
79197:FORTEPAN/Berkó Pál

Sándor Ék: Portrait of Mátyás Rákosi (1952).
7690:FORTEPAN/FORTEPAN.

The symbol of the Stalinist leader cult in Hungary: the portrait of Rákosi in the field of wheat (1948).
Published in *Rákosi Mátyás élete képekben*. Budapest: Szikra, 1952. 85. HUNGART © 2017.

leaders of the Party, especially for Comrade Rákosi. The change was also manifested in the expressions of affection for the Soviet Union."[37] A different account emphasized that claims linking Rákosi's name to the country's achievements and his image as a man of his word—a leader who always kept his promises—were received positively in the villages.[38]

The "Rákosi Constitution"

The way the mood reports represented the perception of the leader's statements became standardized (ritualized) during the elections. By the time the MDP secretary announced the new constitution in August 1949, the editors of such reports were more or less aware of what aspects of the responses should be emphasized.[39] The documents usually stressed that Rákosi's speech was preceded by "suspenseful anticipation" all around the country and brought together an "unexpected number of people" for the broadcast at various locations.[40] The speech itself was described in the reports as a "decisive event" that explained the constitution in simple terms, clarified the political situation, and raised the consciousness of the population. A worker in the Arms Factory talked about the enlightening effect of listening to the oration, but many intellectuals were also reported to have defined the event as a "clear, reassuring reply" to all problematic questions.[41] Many reports emphasized the allegedly spontaneous outbursts of joy stimulated by the words of the leader: they spoke of "inexpressible happiness," "boundless enthusiasm," and "tears of joy" during the speech. Lengthy applause and the rhythmic chanting of the names of Rákosi and Stalin were essential components of these reports.[42]

---

[37] MOL, 276. fond 108/11.
[38] Ibid.
[39] The text of the bill was published in *Szabad Nép*: "A Magyar Népköztársaság alkotmányáról szóló törvényjavaslat," *Szabad Nép*, August 7, 1949. Rákosi's speech about the constitution: "Rákosi elvtárs nagy beszéde a Magyar Népköztársaság alkotmányáról," *Szabad Nép*, August 18, 1949. The Communist newspaper also published Rákosi's proposal in the Parliament: "Rákosi Mátyás elvtárs beterjesztette az országgyűlésen a Magyar Népköztársaság alkotmányáról szóló törvényjavaslatot," *Szabad Nép*, August 11, 1949.
[40] See the report from Nógrád County, for example, in MOL, 276. fond 108/7.
[41] Ibid.
[42] Ibid.

Like the Party secretary's earlier addresses to the people, the announcement of the constitution remained the subject of discussions at various forums in the subsequent weeks. According to the narrative of these meetings, the participants associated the constitution with Rákosi and rewarded the leader with their gratitude and ever-deepening love. One man, in a letter to *Szabad Nép*, argued—using the oxymoron in the title of this book—that the constitution should be attributed to both Rákosi and Stalin: "next to the name of Stalin, the name of Rákosi radiates invisibly between the lines of the constitution." Inspired by the Soviet example, one employee of the Ministry of Internal Affairs even suggested naming the constitution after Rákosi.

> In the Soviet Union, they call the basic laws that secure progress the Stalin constitution. We could rightly name our people's constitution the "Rákosi constitution," since it was his wise foresight that gave birth to our law of great importance, which, for the first time in the course of history, is the constitution of the people.[43]

The expected (and reported) emotional reactions to the linking of Rákosi's name to the constitution were gratitude, trust, and love. Trust and fidelity in Rákosi's announcements concerning the constitution were usually expressed in comments like "whatever Rákosi wants can only be good for the working class," or in assertions that because the constitution was Rákosi's creation, it could only be good, since whatever the leader had said before always turned out to be true and right.[44]

Besides manifestations of loyalty to and belief in the leader, sentiments of love and affection toward him were also reported during the constitution campaign. One document reported triumphantly: "The deepening of love toward Comrade Rákosi and the Soviet Union is evident everywhere. At the meetings, enthusiastic and enduring celebrations of Comrade Rákosi and Stalin can be experienced, and Rákosi's unquestionable merits in the creation of the constitution are the subject of discussions everywhere."[45] The journalists at the letters department of *Szabad Nép* were

---

[43] MOL, 276. fond 108/17.
[44] MOL, 276. fond 65/71; MOL, 276. fond 108/17.
[45] MOL, 276. fond 108/7.

equally impressed by popular reactions to the constitution and reported on the increasing devotion toward the MDP secretary as reflected in letters and telegrams of gratitude sent to the newspaper. "The thankfulness and gratitude that the workers feel for our Party and our wise leader, Comrade Rákosi, because of the creation of the new constitution, is expressed in every letter."[46]

Expressions of gratitude were often combined with oaths promising to follow the path outlined by the leader, or pledges to increase productivity. Peasants from the countryside and workers from the factories were reported to have promised to work harder in order to express gratitude to the leader for the constitution.[47] The emphatic link between gratitude, deepening love, and economic productivity is aptly illustrated by a comment from a worker in Borsod County:

> Thus far we, the Hungarian working people, haven't had a constitution. We can thank the great Soviet Union, our Party, and Comrade Rákosi for the first constitution of the Hungarian working people. The constitution gives us strength for production, for the successful fulfillment of our Three-Year Plan, and it increases our loyalty and love toward the great Soviet Union, our Party, and Comrade Rákosi.[48]

General assessments of Party propaganda during the constitution campaign reflected the satisfaction of the OPO once again. It is hard to find a report from the first two weeks of August 1949 that did not highlight expressions of gratitude and ever-deepening love toward Rákosi, Stalin, and the Soviet Union. Reports submitted after *Szabad Nép*'s August 7 publication of the draft of the constitution continuously referred to the intensification of "love for the Soviet Union, the Party, and Comrade Rákosi."[49] Outbursts of adoration culminated on the day of the enactment of the constitution, August 20. Originally the day of St. Stephen, August 20 was restyled Constitution Day (or the Day of the New Bread). Traditional religious processions were replaced by festive demonstrations expressing gratitude and love toward the leader. The OPO reported enthusiastically:

---

[46] MOL, 276. fond 108/17.
[47] See, for example, MOL, 276. fond 108/7; MOL, 276. fond 108/17.
[48] MOL, 276. fond 108/7.
[49] MOL, 276. fond 65/71.

The celebrations of August 20 were generally successful. We were able to accomplish our goals in terms of mobilization and popular mood, and as a consequence, love for the Soviet Union, our Party, and Comrade Rákosi has become deeper, proletarian internationalism was deepened, and the worker-peasant alliance has strengthened.[50]

"For Rákosi, thanks; for Rajk, the gallows!"

Devotion to the leader meant inexorable hatred of his enemies. After László Rajk was arrested in 1949, he was portrayed as Rákosi's nemesis. According to reports on the popular mood, the (invented) "Rajk conspiracy" to assassinate Rákosi infuriated the people. The documents talked about "overwhelming outbursts of hatred" provoked by the "evil plan" of Rajk and his henchmen to restore the "reactionary" past.[51] Shock and fury triggered demands for death penalty for the convicts. The Party Center and *Szabad Nép* were flooded with memoranda, letters, telegrams, and decrees of local gatherings from all over the country requesting the execution of Rajk. Collective declarations were accompanied by reports of outbursts of individual rage and demands for execution through mob law or lynching. One worker suggested executing Rajk with a tilt hammer. Another proposed tying him between cars "to test his tensile strength."[52] A shock-worker in Sümeg demanded "indescribable punishment" for the convicts, who dared to attack "the freedom of the people, and its dear leader, Comrade Mátyás Rákosi."[53]

In the ritualized narrative of mood reports, expressions of hatred toward the enemies of the leader were coupled with demonstrations of gratitude and affection toward Rákosi for unveiling the conspiracy. A worker on a collective farm in Mezőcsát thanked Rákosi "for spotting the plot of the treasonous scoundrels in time," while another peasant in the Csorna area was grateful that "the beloved leader of our Party and our people . . . exposed these villains." One Party member in Szolnok even invented a new slogan: "*Rákosinak köszönet, Rajkéknak kötelet*" (For Rákosi, our

---

[50] MOL, 276. fond 108/7.
[51] MOL, 276. fond 108/7.
[52] Ibid.; MOL, 276. fond 108/18.
[53] MOL, 276. fond 108/7.

thanks; for Rajk, the gallows).⁵⁴ Letters and telegrams of gratitude that were submitted to the Rákosi Secretariat and *Szabad Nép* also thanked the MDP leader for his vigilance.⁵⁵ Expressions of gratitude and love, as usual, were combined with pledges in factories and collective farms. Industrial and agricultural workers promised to intensify their work efforts and meet their quotas as a sign of their gratitude to Rákosi for uncovering the Rajk conspiracy and "saving them from this immense danger."⁵⁶

"Even the Air Changes": Narratives of Rákosi's Words

Reports on the reception of the constitution and election campaigns of 1949 provide a representative overview of the type of responses that Rákosi's speeches or articles allegedly evoked among the population. Such documents assumed a highly standardized format by mid-1949 and retained a ritual character until the summer of 1953. The narrative in the reports that crystallized after the consolidation of Communist rule consisted of a relatively stable set of themes and images that were regularly associated with reactions to Rákosi's "enlightening words." Such themes included the popular anticipation that preceded a particular announcement of the leader ("Something important is about to happen whenever Comrade Rákosi talks to us"⁵⁷); the enthusiastic and heated discussion of the topics and ideas raised in his speech (one factory was compared to a "busy anthill"⁵⁸); the radical transformative effects of his words ("even the air changes in the following days"⁵⁹); and the audience's ritualized reactions to the oration manifested in applause and celebrations. By portraying Rákosi's words as having extraordinary powers that could bring about revolutionary transformations, the mood reports adhered to the strategy of cult-building that bestowed extraordinary—even magical—qualities upon Rákosi's utterances. The leader's statements were represented as

---
⁵⁴ Ibid.
⁵⁵ MOL, 276. fond 108/17–18; MOL, 276. fond 65/71.
⁵⁶ MOL, 276. fond 108/18; MOL, 276. fond 65/71; MOL, 276. fond 108/7.
⁵⁷ MOL, 276. fond 89/267.
⁵⁸ MOL, 276. fond 108/17.
⁵⁹ MOL, 276. fond 108/19.

"words of conversion" that could enlighten individuals and cause a sea change in the development of class consciousness.

The key aspect that emerged in narratives of support and consent was the energizing impact of Rákosi's words on the audience. His speeches were generally reported to have inspired enthusiastic debates and discussions among the population. People were generally reported to have said that Rákosi revealed the mistakes and showed the right way to correct them, and that, in general, he pointed the way to a brighter future. Respondents—or those writing the reports—also tried to adapt the particular problems raised by Rákosi's announcements to the local context. After the leader's speeches, they zealously started to look for kulaks or wreckers in their own environment and tried to figure out to what extent the problems mentioned by Rákosi affected their factory or collective farm. In addition, the words of the Hungarian Party secretary were regularly reported to have clarified ideological matters, defined social categories, and highlighted the fronts of political struggle. Rákosi's March 1949 report to the Central Committee declaring war on the kulaks, for example, was often interpreted, at least according to the reports, as a guideline that "cleared up the fronts of rural class war," strengthened the consciousness of the peasantry, and put fear in the hearts of wreckers and class enemies.[60] One document described two terrified kulaks who were overheard talking at a railway station about their inescapable downfall: "we are facing the gallows."[61]

The idea of Rákosi's words as morale boosters and crucial factors in propelling production was constantly reaffirmed in reports on the popular mood. Such accounts enthusiastically described how the leader's speech prompted a sharp increase in production and helped intensify the labor competition underway at the time. The reports after Rákosi's speech on February 10, 1950, for example, noted a sudden improvement of labor morale in the factories, manifested in the revitalization of labor competition, and noted a drastic change in the mentality of workers and their attitude to work in general.[62] One worker even defined the speech as

---

[60] Mátyás Rákosi, "Pártunk feladatai," in *Építjük a nép országát*, 399–450.
[61] MOL, 276. fond 108/7.
[62] MOL, 276. fond 108/8.

a second liberation.⁶³ Other reports followed the same pattern. Rákosi's speech to the Party *aktíva* in September 1949 was reported to have given a new impetus to the ongoing labor competition in the Óbuda Furnishing Factory, while the Party leader's announcement on November 30, 1951, allegedly raised the working morale of the workers in the Kecskemét Tinned Foods Factory.⁶⁴ Eruptions of enthusiasm, combined with a rapid increase in the number of pledges in state farms, machine stations, and kolkhozes, were also reported after the same speech.⁶⁵ The workers of the Lamp Factory, for example, pledged to accomplish the Five-Year Plan ahead of the deadline.⁶⁶

While reports on the galvanizing effects of the leader's speeches can be doubted, there was one instance when Rákosi's words inspired genuine political activism. His talk on the importance of criticism and self-criticism at the meeting of the Central Committee on February 10, 1950, like Stalin's similar announcements, struck a chord with the workers and provoked a flood of denunciation letters complaining about corruption and the abuse of power by local factory managements or Party committees. The torrent of letters that reached the Party center indicates that Rákosi's invitation to participate in criticism/self-criticism rituals was partially successful, and it did spur a sudden increase in the number of critical comments about various issues.⁶⁷ The leader's attempt at introducing the Stalinist ritual of *kritika/samokritika*, however, turned out to be a double-edged sword, as it prompted genuine complaints about the regime. Such complaints were normally regarded as manifestations of hostility and led to the denunciation of the letter-writer.

In addition to the revitalization of political activism, the rise in labor morale, and a general improvement of class consciousness, the narrative of positive reactions to Rákosi's speeches included descriptions of intense emotions—gratitude, trust, and love—among the audiences of the cult.

---

⁶³ Ibid.

⁶⁴ "Nagyobb munkafegyelemmel, fokozott egyéni felelősséggel a termelékenység emeléséért. Rákosi elvtárs beszéde a Nagybudapesti Pártválasztmány értekezletén," *Szabad Nép*, September 2, 1949. MOL, 276. fond 108/18; MOL, 276. fond 89/10.

⁶⁵ MOL, 276. fond 89/267.

⁶⁶ MOL, 276. fond 89/612.

⁶⁷ MOL, 276. fond 108/19.

The Party leader's declarations generally aroused the "utmost gratitude" among the people, who allegedly described him as a man of his words and as a trustworthy figure with exceptional managerial talents.[68] Since important policies (almost always announced by Rákosi) were generally presented as gifts, the population was expected to demonstrate its gratitude with deepening fidelity, loyalty, and love toward the Party and its leader. Not surprisingly, then, the accounts of the popular responses to Rákosi's speeches always reported the deepening of love for the Hungarian Party secretary. The frequency of claims such as "love for the Party and Comrade Rákosi has been strengthened" in mood reports indicates a high degree of standardization and the ritualization of the structure and vocabulary of such accounts. In 1949, for example, the Budapest Party Committee reported on the gradual intensification of devotion toward Rákosi almost every week.[69]

If the ritualization of the format and narrative of mood reports could be interpreted as a barometer of the expansion of the cult, then the increasing frequency of cult rituals in mood reports from 1949 further indicates the spread of the phenomenon. By 1950, accounts of the ritual celebration of Rákosi during speeches, festivities, and holidays became essential components of mood reports. During the celebrations of the fifth anniversary of Liberation Day, for example, most of the regional reports emphasized the recurring ritualistic salutations to the Hungarian and Soviet Party leaders by those attending the festive gatherings. In the town of Körmend, the demonstrators marched to Soviet army headquarters to celebrate Liberation Day and chanted the names of Stalin and Rákosi together with the Soviet soldiers.[70] Descriptions of the ritualistic celebration of leaders continued to feature in mood reports even after the proclamation of the "New Course." The first time steel flowed from the smelter of the Stalin Steel Works in Sztálinváros in November 1953, the gathering burst out in enthusiasm and applauded Rákosi and Stalin for a long time.[71]

---

[68] MOL, 276. fond 65/71.
[69] Ibid.
[70] MOL, 276. fond 108/26.
[71] MOL, 276. fond 89/163.

"Comrade Rákosi, Listen to My Problems as If You Were My Father": Letters to the Leader

Writing letters to the leaders of the Communist Party was a widespread phenomenon in Soviet-type regimes. The unreliability of legal institutions and the total absence of representative institutions, as well as the bureaucratization of the regime, coupled with a general atmosphere of unpredictability and arbitrariness, turned letter-writing into a popular strategy whereby citizens attempted to establish informal communication channels with the Party and government authorities.[72] As Sheila Fitzpatrick has argued, letters, petitions, and denunciations became important elements of popular culture in the Soviet Union during the Stalin era.[73] Letters to Stalin and to other leaders were often motivated by pragmatic and utilitarian considerations and relied heavily on the language of propaganda. They also exploited the rhetoric of the leader cult on occasion, although the proportion of cultic letters remained relatively low.[74] Even if writing letters to the authorities was a common practice in the Rákosi era, as the thick files of the Rákosi Secretariat and the readers' letters department of *Szabad Nép* demonstrate, such letters have only recently received historical scrutiny.[75] Nevertheless, an assessment of cultic letters in a Hungarian context might provide clues as to the degree to which the population internalized the verbal aspects of the cult, and which images of the leader letter-writers appealed to in order to achieve their goals. The stylistic, structural, and functional similarities between the letters written

---

[72] On letter-writing practices in the Soviet context, see Sheila Fitzpatrick, "Signals from Below: Soviet Letters of Denunciation of the 1930s," in "Practices of Denunciation in Modern European History, 1789–1989," special issue, *Journal of Modern History* 68, no. 4 (1996): 831–66; Sheila Fitzpatrick, "Readers' Letters to *Krest'ianskaia Gazeta*, 1938," *Russian History / Histoire Russe* 24, nos. 1–2 (1997): 149–70; Sheila Fitzpatrick, "Supplicants and Citizens: Public Letter-Writing in Soviet Russia in the 1930s," *Slavic Review* 55, no. 1 (1996): 78–105; Sarah Davies, "The 'Cult' of the *Vozhd'*: Representations in Letters, 1934–1941," *Russian History / Histoire Russe* 24, nos. 1–2 (1997): 131–47.

[73] Fitzpatrick, "Supplicants and Citizens," 93.

[74] Davies, "The 'Cult' of the *Vozhd'*," 132.

[75] The one exception is a volume that contains a collection of letters written to Rákosi: Kő and Nagy, *Levelek Rákosihoz*. See also Árpád Pünkösti, "Névtelen leveleket forgatva," *Jel-Kép* 4, no. 3 (1983): 74–86. While in the Soviet Union letter-writing in the 1930s followed pre-revolutionary patterns of appealing to authorities, the historiographical gap in the Hungarian context makes it difficult to assess to what extent letter-writing in the 1950s had its origins in pre-war political culture.

to Rákosi and those addressed to Stalin add further arguments to a brief overview on letter-writing practices in Hungary in the Stalin era.

As in Soviet Russia, request letters, petitions, denunciations, and letters of gratitude were sent not only to the first secretary (Rákosi) but also to members of the core Party leadership (such as Farkas, Gerő, and Révai).[76] The typical letter that landed on the desk of the Hungarian Party leader was a request for material resources or privileges. People would turn to Rákosi asking for a visa, or permission for themselves or relatives to travel abroad. Another common request was connected to the housing shortages of the time. Intellectuals enjoying Rákosi's patronage would ask for a new flat or request the leader's permission to sell or swap their apartments. On occasion, intellectuals, especially writers and artists, asked for an audience or a personal meeting with the Party secretary. A more common type of request letter was an appeal to the leader in favor of an arrested or deported relative. Most of these letters emphasized the relative's innocence and begged that his or her case be re-examined. Other requests also reached the Rákosi Secretariat. The editorial board of the satirical weekly *Ludas Matyi*, for example, asked for a new car; one Pioneer expressed his desire to receive a North Korean war refugee as his adopted brother; and a sportswoman asked the Party to allow her to marry a Bulgarian man.[77] One peasant simply wanted to slaughter his swine and asked for the leader's approval.[78]

Besides petitions, Rákosi's Secretariat received numerous letters of denunciation. Denunciations were essential components of criticism/self-criticism rituals and became a characteristic feature of Stalinist political culture. The practice of denouncing was encouraged by the Communist regime in order to keep state and Party bureaucracy under some sort of social control.[79] Letters of denunciation were often composed by "little people" who felt it necessary to inform the Party leadership about the wrongdoings of local authorities or to unveil what they perceived—or wanted the Party to perceive—as enemy activity. The majority of such

---

[76] The major collection of the letters sent to Rákosi is held in MOL, 276. fond 65/375–85. The ones sent to Révai can be found at MOL, 276. fond 68/110–13. His ministerial letters are at MOL, XIX-I-3-e 1–6.
[77] Kő and Nagy, *Levelek Rákosihoz*, 100, 103, 111.
[78] Ibid., 121–22.
[79] Fitzpatrick, "Signals from Below," 833.

letters were addressed to newspaper editorial offices: *Krest'ianskaia Gazeta* in Soviet Russia and *Szabad Nép* in Hungary.[80] In fact, a large proportion of readers' letters to *Szabad Nép* complained about systematic abuses of power by Party authorities or local factory managements. Such denunciation letters, however, were rarely addressed to Rákosi, although the most exceptional cases were usually forwarded to his Secretariat. Likewise, the MDP secretary became the addressee of everyday denunciations only on occasion (one such letter was from a peasant who accused his neighbor of not fulfilling his requisition quota).[81] The type of denunciations normally written to Rákosi involved intra-Party intrigues or personal infighting and mutual accusations among members of the government. Piroska Szabó's accusations against Anna Ratkó, who allegedly faked illness in order to miss the mourning session of the Parliament after Stalin's death, or the case of István Szirmai, who was removed from the radio and was arrested on trumped-up charges, are examples of this.[82]

Like Soviet letter-writers, the authors of letters to Rákosi usually identified themselves by the schematic social categories and stereotypes promoted by Communist propaganda. Such self-assignment of social identities often involved "self-cadreization," which meant the inclusion of short autobiographies that informed the leader of—real or invented—past activities (usually resistance during World War II) and political affiliations. The letters also included a section of ritual self-criticism in cases where one's record was seen as politically tainted. As in the Soviet case, Hungarian letter-writers sending requests to the leader tended to identify themselves as victims and as weak and powerless supplicants.[83] They often emphasized their desperate situation and referred to Rákosi as their last hope. One female writer who wanted to share with Rákosi the "great tragedy" of her life described herself as "the most unfortunate woman," "a broken woman," and even "a living corpse."[84] Other writers approached the MDP secretary similarly and addressed him in "final desperation,"

---

[80] The *Szabad Nép* readers' letter files are at MOL, 276. fond 108/17–19.

[81] Kő and Nagy, *Levelek Rákosihoz*, 166–67.

[82] Ibid., 157–67. Anna Ratkó was minister of people's health until 1953. István Szirmai was the director of the national radio from 1949 to 1953.

[83] Fitzpatrick, "Supplicants and Citizens," 83–84; Davies, "The 'Cult' of the *Vozhd*'," 139.

[84] Kő and Nagy, *Levelek Rákosihoz*, 47.

"great financial misery," "greatest sorrow," or "absolute helplessness."[85] The authors of such letters would usually describe Rákosi as the last man they could trust, or, as one writer called him, "the last refuge."[86] The petitioner often attempted to play on emotional chords and tried to establish a relationship of intimacy with the leader, while continuing to emphasize the author's dependent status. Intellectuals who sent letters to the leader employed intimate flattery, according to the logic of a patron-client relationship, in the hope of access to material resources.[87] Letters of this kind were sent to Rákosi by Tibor Déri and Kálmán Sándor, and especially by Sándor Gergely and Béla Illés.[88]

Although the cult did not feature in letters to Rákosi as frequently as one might expect, many petitions did appeal to the cult vocabulary and exploited the language of the cult. Such letters employed the conceptual tools of the cult, evoked Rákosi's most frequent images, and utilized the standard epithets of the leader as projected by Party propaganda. Besides being called a wise and caring person, Rákosi was usually termed the "leader of our Party" or the "deeply loved leader of Hungary." One writer even compared him to the legendary king Matthias Corvinus, while another claimed that "Comrade Rákosi is our Lenin."[89]

The most frequent image that letter-writers appealed to was the image of the Hungarian Party leader as a benefactor and an omnipotent father figure. Whether letter-writers actually believed Rákosi was all-powerful or if they simply exploited the image for pragmatic reasons is impossible to determine. Nonetheless, letters of request addressed to Rákosi evoked the image of a caring leader willing to aid his people in their time of need. Passages such as "I know that whoever turns to Rákosi with a request has all of his/her problems resolved" and "the prudent wisdom of Mr. Vice-Prime Minister has solved numerous cases that no one else could have solved" exemplify the argument.[90]

The leader's paternalistic benefactor image was also invoked in letters

---

[85] Ibid., 49, 197–98, 217–18.
[86] Ibid., 53.
[87] Fitzpatrick, "Patronage and the Intelligentsia," 92–111.
[88] MOL, 276. fond 65/332; von Klimo, "'A Very Modest Man': Béla Illés," 47–62.
[89] Kő and Nagy, Levelek Rákosihoz, 71–72, 134.
[90] Ibid., 40–41, 141–42.

that called Rákosi the nation's father. One letter-writer begged the MDP secretary: "Comrade Rákosi, listen to my problems as if you were my father."[91] Those writers who asked Rákosi to be the godfather of their child hoped the leader's benevolence would be extended to their family. These people often wished to gain advantages in the distribution of resources by linking Rákosi to the family and nominating him as the honorary *pater familias*. In the beginning, especially in the coalition years, the Rákosi Secretariat would approve such requests, and the MDP secretary became the godfather to several children in the country. However, the pragmatic motivations behind such invitations soon became apparent, and from 1948 on, the Party leadership usually rejected similar appeals.

A typical cult letter was a letter of gratitude sent by individuals, groups, or institutions to the leader, thanking him for a certain gift, a particular achievement, or the progress in building socialism in general. People would thank the MDP secretary for the replacement of a lost church bell, school textbooks, a new radio set, an Olympic gold medal, or simply the "achievements of our Party." Many such letters were published in the press, especially for Rákosi's birthday. For example, on Rákosi's fifty-ninth birthday in 1951, the ÁVH expressed its gratitude for the Party leader's help in unmasking the "enemy within."[92] While letters and telegrams of gratitude were essential parts of the cult, they should be interpreted as ritualistic public demonstrations of gratitude toward the leader, rather than individual attempts to establish informal communication channels with him. Letters of this type were encouraged by the authorities on a daily basis, and therefore they can hardly be used to assess subjective perceptions of the cult.

Replies to the letters and petitions submitted to Rákosi did not follow a set pattern. Denunciations were normally acted upon, but the requests of "little people" were sometimes left unanswered. Still, the frequency of interventions by the Rákosi Secretariat was relatively high, which indicates that the Secretariat paid attention to maintaining the image of the leader as a benefactor. Nevertheless, the outcome of letter-writing was uncertain, and—as in the Soviet Union—it could occasionally backfire

---

[91] Ibid., 47.
[92] Ibid., 146–47.

on the author.⁹³ The man who asked for financial assistance from Rákosi, the godfather of his twin children, was fired from his workplace because, as the ÁVH revealed, he had previously asked Horthy, as well as the leader of the fascist Arrow Cross movement, Ferenc Szálasi, to become the godfather of two of his other children.⁹⁴

It seems that, as in the Soviet Union, the leader cult was not an essential component of petitions and denunciations sent to the Hungarian Party secretary. The language of the cult, however, was exploited occasionally by letter-writers. Cultic letters were usually composed for pragmatic reasons, and in such cases the cult was used as a communication code between the citizens and the state.⁹⁵ Flattering the leader for utilitarian reasons was not a strategy unique to letter-writers; calculated flattery was part of the communication strategy of Stalinist political culture as a whole. Struggling for Rákosi's soul, or—to paraphrase Ian Kershaw—"working towards Rákosi," was an essential component of those schemes that aimed to obtain privileges from the center and gain wider access to material resources.⁹⁶

Positive responses to the Rákosi cult usually appealed to the leader's paternalistic image as a powerful benefactor. Such reactions tended to describe the people as dependents, in constant need of guidance in all walks of life, including production, politics, and intellectual development. The words of the leader defined to them what was right and what was wrong, and laid out the path that they were supposed to follow. The image of society that the reports or letters frequently evoked reflected Communist propaganda's propensity to portray the population as being in a permanent state of infancy. The relationship of the "infant society" and its father was ritually re-enacted in thanking rites, which were usually, but not exclusively, connected to political achievements such as the constitution. Expressions of gratitude, when linked to the emergence of threat and menace (during the time of the Rajk trial, for example), also represented the dichotomy of the immature people and their teacher-father. According to the narrative of the mood reports compiled at the time of the Rajk trial, Rákosi, the nation's father, by unmasking the conspirators, demonstrated

---

[93] Fitzpatrick, "Supplicants and Citizens," 103; Davies, "The 'Cult' of the *Vozhd*'," 132.
[94] Kő and Nagy, *Levelek Rákosihoz*, 18.
[95] Rolf, "Working towards the Centre."
[96] Kershaw, "Working Towards the Führer."; Benno Ennker, "The Stalin Cult, Bolshevik Rule."

to his naive children the potential dangers of the outside world, which made the infants realize their vulnerability. They, in turn, responded to the father-leader by strengthening emotional ties to him and expressing increasing rage against his enemies.

Like opinions published in Communist newspapers, the reactions recorded in mood reports or inscribed in letters represented the "gift economy" at work.[97] Respondents who used the codes and practices of the Rákosi cult usually described labor as a moral duty, done in return for the leader's "gifts" to society. It was not potential material reward or the hope for upward social mobility that boosted production figures; gratitude to the leader became the primary motivation for the doubling of work efforts. In exchange for what were portrayed as the Party secretary's achievements, the Hungarian population made pledges, boosted production, and surrounded Rákosi with an ever-deepening affection. The concept of "gift" had a wide semantic range into which literally anything could fit: the constitution, the lowering of prices, the unmasking of enemies, Olympic medals, or peace loans. The functioning of the "gift economy" was aptly described by a Csepel worker who, in November 1949, asserted, "it is OK if they deduct the peace loans [from our salary], since Comrade Rákosi gives it back every day. Meat, fat, potatoes, and silk are cheaper, and through this we get back the money that has been withheld from us."[98]

Affirmative responses to the cult, as represented in mood reports, were closely aligned with the official cult discourse and in many cases were strikingly similar to the actual guidelines of the Propaganda Department that detailed the way the leader's pronouncements were to be interpreted. The informants of the Agitprop Department in the villages and factories often simply reaffirmed the official propaganda image of the leader in their reports. The fact that reports on the popular mood tended to mirror the language of the cult seriously questions the credibility of such documents and impedes attempts to reveal the subjective motivations behind positive responses to the leader worship. It is also questionable whether such reports say anything about supporters of Rákosi. The mood reports suggest that individuals responded to the cult with equal enthusiasm in

---

[97] Brooks, *Thank You, Comrade Stalin!*
[98] MOL, 276. fond 65/71.

public and private contexts, which was clearly not the case. The similarity of newspaper reports and mood reports on the reception of the Rákosi cult could most likely be explained by the "creative intervention" of the authorities, newspaper editors, propagandists, or individual informants in sorting, editing, and (re-)structuring such replies. The remarkable similarity between the two types of documents could also be explained by a certain level of awareness of the codes and conceptual armory of the Bolshevik language in Hungarian society. Whatever the reasons for the resemblance between published propaganda materials and reports on the popular mood, a high degree of linguistic and structural ritualization appeared in responses to the Rákosi cult, which ran parallel with the expansion and consolidation of the leader worship in 1949. The spread of ritualized language use was partly caused by the centralization of propaganda activities, but it could also have been related more generally to the social adjustment triggered by the stabilization of Communist rule.

Due to the way positive replies were selected/invented, forwarded, and interpreted in mood reports, it is difficult to reveal consistent affirmative attitudes to the cult, or to decipher people's actual opinions about the phenomenon. Those respondents or letter-writers who reacted positively to the cult often did so for pragmatic reasons. Strategic flattery was usually used when trying to achieve material advantages or career goals, but the reiteration of the conceptual set of the cult discourse could also be interpreted as a survival tactic to avoid the attention of the authorities. Besides the aspects of calculation and fear, however, the responses to Rákosi's speeches did involve an element of spontaneous enthusiasm, even after the Communist takeover. Since many of Rákosi's speeches culminated in festivities in which access to goods became easier and people could forget about material shortages for the moment, some surely looked forward to the leader's appearances. The "festival effect" was thus one factor that encouraged audiences to listen to the MDP secretary's announcements. The use of the radio in broadcasting speeches was probably another. Since the major transmitter of the leader's voice, the radio, was a rarely seen technological device, especially in the countryside, people would often go to public listening rituals simply to observe the machine. Irrespective of the many possible reasons why people attended the leader's speeches or why they wrote him a letter—out of calculation, coercion, fear, the desire to integrate into the community, or interest in the radio set—a substantial part of Hungarian society was indeed aware of the practices and the rhetoric of the leader cult. Whether wholeheartedly, insincerely, or out of fear, people participated in the cult's rituals. They also tended to appeal to the leader cult discourse, but the relative rarity of references to it in the sources suggests that in the Hungarian context, the cult failed to emerge as the dominant narrative in communicative encounters between citizens and the state.

Chapter 7
"Death to Uncle Rákosi!"
Negative Perceptions of the Cult

References to "enemy activity" in mood reports occasionally included critical remarks on the leader cult. While it may be tempting to interpret such references as part of archival rituals—as demonstrating the continuing influence of the "enemy" (in small doses) justified the Party line—ÁVH documents attest that many such incidents were indeed real and that people expressed their discontent with the leaders and the regime and its policies in many different ways. Whether sporadic manifestations of dissatisfaction could be encapsulated by the term "resistance," however, is a more complex matter.

The notion of resistance enjoys considerable popularity among historians, yet it remains a remarkably fluid concept. The flexibility of the term has to do with the alleged ubiquity of resistance—"where there is power, there is resistance"—and its association with a number of equally elusive notions, namely agency, intentions, and context.[1] It is not just theoreticians of power (and resistance) who see subversion and defiance everywhere. The Stalinist regime, with its paranoid mindset, was also inclined to attribute criticism to the influence of the enemy and perceive practices of day-to-day survival as manifestations of hostility. Wearing the wrong kind of dress, dancing to "inappropriate" music, going to church, cracking jokes about politicians in a pub, or stealing wood from the forest

---

[1] Foucault's famous quote is from Michel Foucault, *The History of Sexuality*, vol. 1, *An Introduction* (New York: Pantheon books, 1978), 95. Definitions of resistance have largely been influenced by James C. Scott's ideas on the subject, as elaborated in his seminal book *Domination and the Arts of Resistance: Hidden Transcripts* (New Haven, CT: Yale University Press, 1990).

could all be defined by the Communist authorities as acts of sabotage.[2] As theoretical treatments of resistance are relatively close to the regime's own perception of the phenomenon, historians of the Stalinist past tend to treat the notion with extra care.[3] While it is clear that actual acts of defiance were more common than has been previously assumed and that "hidden transcripts" continued to exist during the Stalinist period, the doubtful credibility and general silence of the sources about individual motivations and the historical context make the application of the term a challenging task. Therefore, any discussion of resistance will inevitably include a hypothetical element.

The scarcity of archival sources makes it impossible to provide a representative overview of negative social attitudes toward the Rákosi cult in Hungary. Yet the documents demonstrate that it was indeed possible to reject the cult and express dissatisfaction with its manifestations. A closer look at examples of defiance and subversion will thus highlight (some of) the boundaries of cult construction and offer a glance at the possible spaces and contexts of disobedience. While the examples of non-compliance discussed in this chapter should not be considered representative, such cases underscore the possibility—rather than the commonality—of "resistance" toward the cult.

Due to the irregularity of sources indicating anti-Rákosi dissent, it is not feasible to reconstruct counter-narratives to the cult. Moreover, the relationship between narrative and counter-narrative in general, and between cultic discourse and resistance in particular, was far from straightforward in Soviet-type societies. Discontent with the leader myth, for example, was not always expressed through an alternative narrative. Dislike of the cult could be articulated within the confines of the official discourse, and with the help of the language and vocabulary of the cult. In such cases, it was the context in which such views were voiced and the way they were expressed that could make them subversive. The boundary between resistance, accommodation, and collaboration, therefore, was

---

[2] Marcin Kula, "Poland: The Silence of Those Deprived of Voice," in Corner, *Popular Opinion in Totalitarian Regimes*, 150.

[3] The most sophisticated theoretical and methodological discussion of the notion of resistance in the Stalinist context is offered by Lynne Viola. See Viola, "Introduction," and Viola, "Popular Resistance in the Stalinist 1930s."

sometimes a blurry one.⁴ The definition of resistance largely depends on the context of, and the intentions behind, individual acts. Since those aspects are often not revealed in archival sources, it remains difficult to outline coherent attitudes and consistent strategies against the cult, even if subversive activities in Rákosi's Hungary were more widespread than has been assumed in the past.⁵ Therefore, this chapter defines examples of discontent as "spontaneous manifestations of dissatisfaction" instead of using the elusive notion of "resistance."

Although the reconstruction of narratives of defiance is impeded by many obstacles, we can identify certain patterns in criticism of the cult. Dissatisfaction with the cult was expressed in various distinct forms.⁶ While negative opinions about the leader were purged from the public sphere, critical and insulting remarks spread through unofficial communication channels and were conveyed through rumors, jokes, rephrased *chastushki*, anonymous makeshift fliers, and graffiti. Non-verbal expressions of discontent, especially vandalism of the leaders' portraits, were also reported frequently to Party organizations and the ÁVH. Although individual motivations behind such subversive acts are difficult to reconstruct, it seems that apart from religious convictions, it was primarily the hardships of everyday life that triggered the condemnation of the leaders' privileges and of Rákosi's image as a benefactor and a paternal figure. It is equally problematic to identify spaces where dissatisfaction could be freely expressed. Rather unsurprisingly, in a number of documents,

---

⁴ On the practice of expressing discontent through the official discourse, see Juliane Fürst, "Prisoners of the Soviet Self? Political Youth Opposition in Late Stalinism," *Europe-Asia Studies* 54, no. 3 (2002): 353–75. See also István Rév, "Az atomizáció előnyei," *Replika* (1996), nos. 23–24: 141–57. In her book *Stalin's Last Generation*, Fürst demonstrates the prevalence of pro-regime yet anti-Stalinist attitudes among Communist youth and highlights the significance of the official discourse in transmitting oppositionist ideas. She argues that successful indoctrination could also nurture defiance.

⁵ In his doctoral dissertation, Karl Brown has convincingly argued that resistance in Stalinist Hungary was more widespread than had been assumed. This was partly because of the inefficiency and the incompetence of Communist authorities. Karl Brown, "Regulating Bodies: Everyday Crime and Popular Resistance in Communist Hungary, 1948–1956" (DPhil dissertation, University of Texas at Austin, 2007). I am grateful to the author for sending me a copy of his dissertation.

⁶ On various forms of resistance during the Rákosi era, see Margit Balogh, "Kommunizmus és egyházi ellenállás Magyarországon," in Püski and Valuch, *Mérlegen a XX. századi magyar történelem*, 271–85; István Rév, "Paraszti ellenállás a klasszikus szocializmusban," in *Múltunk Jövője. Szabadelvűek a népi kultúráról* (Budapest: T-Twins, 1993), 75–84; and Rév, "Az atomizáció előnyei".

slander against the leader was recorded in pubs (especially in the countryside). While the courage to malign the leader often came from a bottle, sometimes those who were caught by the authorities merely claimed drunkenness as an excuse—they were fully aware of the potential consequences of their actions if they were sober.[7]

Criticism of the regime usually caught the attention of the authorities and was met with legal retribution. The framework of legal prosecutions was provided by the infamous Article VII, ratified in March 1946, which regulated the protection of the establishment against "criminal offenses."[8] Due to the vague definition of what constituted a "criminal offense against the republic," the bill was later applied in the show trials of denounced Communist politicians (including Rajk), in trumped-up court cases against the Party's non-Communist political opponents, and even against "little people" who were reckless—or just drunk—enough to criticize the Party and its leaders in public. The extent of Communist influence over judicial and legal affairs was shown by the relatively high number of cases, even in the coalition period, in which ordinary people were prosecuted for expressing their disapproval of Communist leaders.

Critiques and Iconoclasts

Many of the bold remarks criticizing the cult questioned the validity of the components of the leader's imagery as promoted by Communist propaganda. It was the image of Rákosi as a benefactor that was challenged most often, in remarks that contrasted his privileges and wealth with the desperate social and economic conditions of the postwar countryside.[9] A man from Sarkadkeresztúr, for example, was sentenced to three years in prison in 1947 for commenting upon the "kingly riches" of Rákosi and other members of Parliament.

---

[7] About one-fifth of the ÁVH documents that were examined (78) contain references to alcohol consumption.

[8] On Article VII and its abuse by the Communists in their struggle for power, see Mária Palasik, *Chess Game for Democracy: Hungary between East and West, 1944–1947* (Montréal: McGill-Queen's University Press, 2011), 57–61, 146–53.

[9] Mária Palasik, "A szólásszabadság deklarálása és korlátainak kezdete Magyarországon (1946–1949)," *Századok* 132, no. 3 (1998): 585–606.

I know what they are doing in the Parliament, they are not interested in the fate of the poor at all; they all have cars. Rákosi has so many cars that he sits in one of them in the morning and sits in another one in the afternoon. You have no idea—Rákosi has a seven-story palace with ninety rooms. Why doesn't he live in a house with thatch like you do?[10]

Peasant women, with their heightened sensitivity toward the hardships of the family, were also among those who criticized Party leaders for their privileges and for being out of touch with the countryside's problems. A woman in Gyula, for example, was put on trial for criticizing Rákosi's high salary.[11] Three other women in the Szeged region were also prosecuted for expressing their worries about their family's well-being in a vulgar way, while complaining about the requisition of livestock and questioning the image of the Party leader as the liberator of prisoners of war: "May God fuck Mátyás Rákosi's mother; he only came to Bácsalmás to take away the sheep, and the prisoners still haven't come home."[12]

Rákosi's official image as a benefactor—the man always receptive to the problems of the people—was not the only aspect of the cult narrative that the population doubted. The idea that "Rákosi always keeps his promises," for example, became a target of criticism. Factory workers in Budapest, for example, were reported to have complained throughout 1954 that Rákosi had not implemented the promised price reductions for meat and fat.[13] In such cases, it was not disbelief in the leader's cultic image but affirmative references to the cult's claims that the regime perceived as acts of hostility. To be fair, the Party was right to maintain a degree of skepticism toward seemingly positive responses to communist propaganda. There were certainly people who used the language of the cult opportunistically and appealed to its codes in order to avoid obligations such as participating in political meetings or attending Party seminars. One commenter in 1950 bitterly reported the widespread rumor in Budapest that attending meetings was no longer obligatory, because Rákosi had said so.[14] One woman from the MÁVAG foundry explicitly cited Rákosi in an attempt

---

[10] Ibid., 591.
[11] Ibid., 594.
[12] Ibid., 594–95.
[13] MOL, 276. fond 65/72.
[14] MOL, 276. fond 108/8.

to evade her educational obligations: "Comrade Rákosi has proclaimed that no coercion can be applied in any line [i.e., aspects of social life]. [Therefore] no one can force me to attend seminars."[15] When subjective interpretations of the leader's announcements were presented sarcastically, retaliation followed. In the Keltex textile factory in January 1953, a foreman referring to a speech of Rákosi suggested the workers pledge to boost population growth, telling his female colleagues, "we men would shoulder the more difficult part." The unfortunate foreman paid the price for his sexist comment: he was expelled from the Party in February and was arrested by the ÁVH soon afterwards.[16]

The language of the cult was thus used in everyday communicative situations between state and society, and it often provided the linguistic tools for the articulation of critical views of Rákosi and the regime's policies. Further examples of subverting the discourse of the cult include critical remarks about the leader's close relationship to Stalin, or negative reflections on his announcements. As has been highlighted in the previous chapter, Rákosi's utterances were represented in Communist propaganda as turning points that signified the coming of changes and transformations of historical significance. As some of the mood reports testify, many people indeed accepted the official idea that the leader's statements served as markers of political change. However, contrary to official intentions, some people believed that Rákosi's speeches actually signaled the coming of something menacing. One example concerns Rákosi's pronouncement that the elections of 1949 would bring about a sea change in Hungarian history. Many people were convinced that he was actually hinting at the collectivization of agriculture—this was indeed launched in 1949—or Hungary becoming a republic of the Soviet Union. A peasant near Szerencs bitterly exclaimed in April 1949: "Let's not vote, because if we do, there will be kolkhozes. Surely there will be kolkhozes, because Rákosi announced that after the elections, the situation will change."[17] The image of the Party leader as the man who enjoyed the confidence and trust of Stalin ("Stalin's best Hungarian disciple") was also frequently subverted.

---

[15] MOL, 276. fond 108/19.
[16] MOL, 276. fond 65/72.
[17] MOL, 276. fond 108/11.

The narratives of the cult linked the symbolic legitimacy of the leader to Moscow's—and Stalin's—support; therefore the idea that Rákosi was the guarantor of Hungary's commitment to the Soviet path to socialism remained a central component of cultic texts. However, Rákosi's close adherence to the Soviet model and the intimate link between him and Stalin were considered harmful by many. Rákosi was often described as a mere puppet or servant of Moscow.[18]

While the language of the cult could be used to express dissatisfaction with the cult, in many cases it was completely ignored, especially when criticism of Rákosi took the form of pure slander and cursing. In fact, about half of the anti-Rákosi incidents that are recorded in the ÁVH archives were spontaneous outbursts of rage or cursing, sometimes anti-Semitic in nature, invoking the name of the leader.[19] Comments such as "Comrade Rákosi is a piece of shit," "Rákosi is a fat-headed Jew, a stupid scoundrel, and an imbecile," "I shit in Uncle Matyi's mouth and on his cock," and Rákosi is a "miscreant, blackmailer, and a blood-sucking lowlife" illustrate the complete lack of sophistication in such references.[20] One similar inscription on a school wall in Budapest—supposedly written by orphans—was even accompanied by drawings of the fascist Arrow Cross symbol and read: "Drop dead, Uncle Matyi Rákosi!" (Dögöljön meg Rákosi Matyi bácsi!)[21]

Those people who expressed disapproval of the images of Party leaders did not appeal to the language of the cult either. Although they were attacking the most emblematic manifestation of the cult, their individual motivations for destroying or mutilating portraits and statuettes did not always reflect an overall anti-Communist attitude.[22] Whether the defacing of pictures could be linked to traditions of iconoclasm or to popular Bakhtinian rituals (explained in the next section) to topple authority relations is difficult to determine on the basis of the sources. Notwithstanding the

---

[18] MOL, 276. fond 65/70.
[19] I have found a total of seventy-eight cases in ÁBTL in which the secret police carried out an investigation.
[20] The location of the references in order: ÁBTL 3.1.9. V-22093; ÁBTL 3.1.9. V-91 111; ÁBTL 3.1.9. V-6597; Palasik, "A szólásszabadság deklarálása és korlátainak kezdete," 596.
[21] MOL, 276. fond 65/359.
[22] Juliane Fürst has shown that iconoclastic acts in the Stalinist Soviet Union did not necessarily indicate an anti-Soviet political stance. Fürst, *Stalin's Last Generation*, 124–25.

difficulties of interpretation, it could be argued that vandalizing or distorting the leaders' portraits was one of the most common ways of expressing irritation with the Rákosi cult. Spectacles of the 1956 revolution included the burning of piles of pictures of Rákosi on the street, but incidents of iconoclasm were also common throughout the 1950s, as reports on the popular mood demonstrate. A remarkable number of such cases were reported to the Party from all over the country in 1950. In February, one Rákosi portrait was damaged in Algyő. In April, giant portraits of the leader decorating Hódmezővásárhely were torn down after the April 4 celebrations. In May, pictures of Rákosi were vandalized in Monostorapáti.[23] Schools, where portraits of Rákosi were hung in almost every classroom, became frequent sites for iconoclastic acts. A report on the "activity of clerical reaction" informed the Rákosi Secretariat in March 1950 of a school in Budapest's Seventh District where someone had scribbled on the leader's portrait and scratched its eyes out, even though the image was "hung so high that it could only be reached using a ladder."[24] Similar incidents were reported in several schools throughout the country.

The symbolic significance that the regime attributed to iconoclastic acts is demonstrated by the occasional involvement of the ÁVH in the investigations, although it is difficult to reconstruct a pattern among the cases that were eventually referred to the security police.[25] The participation of the ÁVH was requested in a diverse range of inquiries: when someone tore down or spat at images, or when fascist symbols were sketched on pictures of the Party leader, as in the case of a (drunken) man who, on his way home from a village pub fight, drew a swastika on a Rákosi portrait using a leaf.[26]

Although the reports often tried to blame "clerical reaction" for iconoclasm in schools, it seems more plausible to consider such incidents acts of teenage impudence and deviant behavior triggered by a general disrespect for authority figures, rather than symptoms of early-age political

---

[23] MOL, 276. fond 108/26. The document recording the incident in Monostorapáti is stored in MOL, 276. fond 108/8.

[24] MOL, 276. fond 65/359.

[25] Fifteen percent of the anti-Rákosi cases kept in the ÁVH archives were related to the defacing of the leader's portraits. Note that this figure also includes iconoclastic incidents that took place during the Uprising in 1956.

[26] ÁBTL 3.1.9. V-2319.

consciousness and consistent resistance practices.[27] The portrait damage reported from the Rákosi Secondary School in Tatabánya, where the eyes of a Stalin painting were pierced and the shoulder badges of the Soviet leader cut out, seems to reinforce this point.[28] Nevertheless, there were several cases when citizens perceived leader portraits as insulting to their religious convictions. For example, women in Tápiószentmárton who disrupted the meeting of the local MNDSZ cell in January 1950 demanded that the cross once again be displayed in schools, and they linked this to the removal of pictures of Lenin, Stalin, and Rákosi from the walls.[29]

The rejection of the leader cult for religious reasons not only was apparent in acts of iconoclasm but also was a recurring motif in reports that noted opposition to Rákosi's cultic persona. Often those in congregations, influenced by priests, expressed dislike of the cult. Disparaging statements were also uttered by the clerics themselves. At the time of Stalin's seventieth birthday, for example, many clergymen criticized the adulation of the Soviet leader and the devaluing of the Christmas celebrations. One Catholic priest from Békéssámson lamented that "they want to overshadow the celebration of Christ by exalting great men."[30] Some of the priests who were forced to deliver a speech for Stalin's birthday used similar Aesopian language to criticize the adulation of him; instead of praising Stalin, they talked about the evanescence of the power of pharaohs and emperors.[31] The parish priest in Abavár went even further and was reported to have called Stalin's birthday "the day of Doubting Thomas." Another cleric, teaching in the village school of Bucsa, questioned Stalin's demi-god image in a fairly direct way: "Who is the greater lord, God or Stalin? In whose eyes would you spit?"[32]

The continuing influence of Christianity and the legacy of Christian nationalism that dominated the ideological landscape of interwar Hungary

---

[27] About similar attitudes of adolescent cynicism toward the leader in the Soviet Union, see Catriona Kelly, "Grandpa Lenin and Uncle Stalin: Soviet Leader Cults for Little Children," in Apor et al., *The Leader Cult*, 102–22. One of the documents that linked continuing clerical influence in schools to the destruction of images is "Feljegyzés a klerikális reakció tevékenységéről," May 6, 1950, MOL, 276. fond 65/359.
[28] Ibid.
[29] MOL, 276. fond 108/8.
[30] MOL, 276. fond 65/359.
[31] MOL, 276. fond 108/19.
[32] MOL, 276. fond 108/8.

were partly responsible for the re-emergence of anti-Semitic themes in expressions of discontent with the regime and its leaders. The continuity of popular anti-Jewish attitudes in Hungary is demonstrated by the regularity of anti-Semitic slander targeting the Party leader.[33] It was often emphasized that Rákosi was "not Hungarian": he was mostly depicted as the main representative of "Jewish rule" in the country or simply a "Jewish henchman." He was described as "stupid," "dirty," a "swindler," a "scoundrel," or simply a "bold Jew," and he was deliberately called "Roth" instead of Rákosi by several people, even if his original name was actually Rosenfeld.[34] To many, it seems, Rákosi's Jewish background was simply incompatible with the image of the wise leader of the (Christian) Hungarian nation. As one crude flyer put it: "How could a vile Jew become the wise teacher of a civilized Christian people?"[35]

The survival of elements of prewar political culture in Hungary was also reflected in the continuation and/or emergence of alternative cults or counter-cults. The very existence of such counter-cults challenged the legitimacy of the Rákosi cult and Rákosi's authority. At the time of the general elections in 1949, for example, Communist propagandists grumbled about the "cult" and the enduring popularity among the peasantry of the writer and National Peasant Party leader Péter Veres. The villagers of Miske allegedly declared that they wanted "to be the soldiers of Péter Veres and not of Rákosi," while the inhabitants of Enying addressed the writer as "the leader of the people."[36] In addition to the "Veres worship," remnants of the Horthy cult also occasionally collided with the emerging adoration of Communist leaders. Horthy portraits appeared randomly at various locations, including Soviet war monuments and schools, and some workers even compared Stalin's cult unfavorably with Horthy's, especially at the time of Stalin's seventieth birthday.[37] Infrequently, criticism of Rákosi

---

[33] Twenty-three percent of the "anti-Rákosi" cases in the secret police records included anti-Semitic slander.

[34] The references are from the following archival files: ÁBTL 3.1.9 V-77842; ÁBTL 3.1.9 V-5073; ÁBTL 3.1.9. V-13793; MOL, 276. fond 108/11; MOL, 276. fond 65/70; and Palasik, "A szólásszabadság deklarálása és korlátainak kezdete," 594.

[35] ÁBTL 3.1.9 V-144220/1.

[36] MOL, 276. fond, 108/11.

[37] MOL, 276. fond, 108/8; MOL, 276. fond, 65/359. The workers noted that the people even received gifts on Horthy's name days.

was combined with praise of Hitler and even Szálasi.³⁸ Dissatisfaction with Rákosi's symbolic standing manifested itself not only in reverence for authority figures of the not-so-distant past but also in the admiration of those politicians who were stigmatized as "enemies of the people" after the Communist takeover. Such figures included Cardinal Mindszenty, Rajk, and even Marshal Tito. Considering Mindszenty's popularity in the early postwar years, the Communist authorities' concern over such expressions is not surprising. Reports on "reactionary activities" in the country in 1948–1949, for example, often recorded positive remarks about the cardinal and even inscriptions on walls such as "Long live Mindszenty, death to Rákosi!"³⁹ Critical attitudes toward the Rákosi cult could also be detected in popular attempts to invert the official narrative of the "Tito-Rajk conspiracy" and honor the protagonists of the trial instead of the Party's leader. Rajk, for example, was often praised for his alleged attempt to create "national Communism," as opposed to Rákosi, who was perceived as a loyal servant of Stalin and the representative of Soviet-type socialism.⁴⁰ Graffiti praising Rajk, Tito, and even President Truman demonstrated the spread of contrary interpretations of one of the most monumental show trials in the Stalinist Eastern bloc.⁴¹

Jokes and Political Rumors

Until recently, jokes have been considered indicators of the existence of hidden forms of resistance in Soviet-type societies. This interpretation owes much to the substantial theoretical literature on satire, laughter, and humor. Sigmund Freud, for example, claimed at the beginning of the twentieth century that humor enabled the psyche to break free from social norms and regulations. Mikhail Bakhtin famously interpreted laughter as

---

[38] ÁBTL 3.1.9. V-34839.
[39] MOL, 276. fond, 65/359; MOL, 276. fond 65/61.
[40] MOL, 276. fond 108/17.
[41] One of the reports from September 1949, for example, informed the Party headquarters about graffiti on a train near Balassagyarmat that read: "To the gallows with the Jews Rákosi and Gerő; long live Tito and Rajk. Don't believe the Soviet Union." MOL, 276. fond 108/7. Similar incidents were reported in other parts of the country. MOL, 276. fond 108/8.

a weapon of the oppressed to oppose the establishment and turn power relations upside-down in carnivalesque moments.[42] The association of irony and laughter with resistance to authority seems to have endured throughout the twentieth century, as demonstrated by an influential theoretical work on satire published in the mid-1990s that defined the genre as a form of "resistance to cultural and political hegemony."[43] In Soviet-type societies, the totalitarian paradigm gave rise to the assumption that making jokes (and, in fact, any form of resistance) was impossible in an atomized, fragmented, and terrorized society. Recent scholarship on Soviet wit and political humor in the Stalin era has demonstrated that laughing at the regime was indeed possible, and despite the repressive nature of the political system, jokes actually flourished.[44] Wisecracks subverting official propaganda claims spread like wildfire even during the Great Terror, and they helped strengthen shattered social bonds.[45] Moreover, it is now clear that private and official humor were not two separate realms; they were connected in various ways.[46] Laughter in Stalinist political culture, therefore, was not necessarily an act of resistance: it was possible to laugh at and laugh with the regime at the same time.

While it is doubtful that the act of joke-telling in Communist Hungary was a way of promoting an oppositionist agenda, it is notable that anecdotes about dictators (such as Hitler, Stalin, Rákosi, and Ceauşescu) actually comprise the majority of political jokes collected in the country in the second half of the twentieth century.[47] Furthermore, many of these

---

[42] Sigmund Freud, *Der Witz und Seine Beziehung zum Unbewussten* (Vienna: Deuticke, 1905); Mikhail Bakhtin, *Rabelais and His World* (Cambridge, MA: MIT Press, 1968).

[43] Brian A. Connery and Kirk Combe, *Theorizing Satire: Essays in Literary Criticism* (Basingstoke: Macmillan, 1995), 11.

[44] Robert Thurston, "Social Dimensions of Stalinist Rule: Humor and Terror in the USSR, 1935–1941," *Journal of Social History* 24, no. 3 (1991): 541–62; David Brandenberger, ed., *Political Humor under Stalin: An Anthology of Unofficial Jokes and Anecdotes* (Bloomington: Slavica, 2009). It must be underlined that the importance of joke-telling tends to be inflated retrospectively by those who lived through the period: Kula, "Poland," 163.

[45] Fitzpatrick, *Everyday Stalinism*, 166; Thurston, "Social Dimensions," 550.

[46] Thurston, "Social Dimensions," 554; Serguei Oushakine, "Laughter under Socialism: Exposing the Ocular in Soviet Jocularity," *Slavic Review* 7, no. 2 (2011): 247–55.

[47] The anthologies used for the book were the following: Imre Katona, ed., *Viccek Sztálinról, Rákosiról és Ceauşescuról* (Budapest: Új Aurora Könyvek, 1989); József Bényei, *A személyi kultusz humora* (Debrecen: Csokonai, 1989); and János Botos, *Politikai humor, 1945–1948* (Budapest: Reflektor Kiadó, 1989). Unfortunately, none of these volumes describes the methodology

jokes were indeed straightforward expressions of dissatisfaction with the regime, or blunt judgments about Rákosi's personal and physical qualities. Nonetheless, it would be an oversimplification to claim that jokes or rumors functioned as transmitters of counter-narratives to the official discourse. Apart from the difficulties of reconstructing individual motivations for telling such stories, the question of authenticity might lead to another methodological dead end. The original source of anecdotes and the date of their first recording are often difficult—if not impossible—to identify, which impedes any attempt to contextualize such texts. Jokes constantly evolve—their content and form change, and the protagonists are replaced over time—which makes the interpretation of witticisms problematic.[48] In addition, the documents (secret police reports, memoirs, ethnographic collections) in which anecdotes and gossip were recorded usually omit the context in which such stories were uttered (when, where, in what social environment, etc.) and say very little about the performative aspects of joke- or gossip-telling (i.e., the way they were uttered). Despite the scholarly rigor with which the jokes were selected and presented in some Hungarian anthologies, such volumes say close to nothing about the factors—intention, context, performance—that would help to locate anecdotes on the "continuum of popular responses" to the regime.[49] The historian is thus mostly left with nothing but the texts themselves.[50]

---

used in the selection of jokes, and they say very little about the time and the context of recording such stories.

[48] Marcin Kula has also highlighted the difficulty of reconstructing the chronology and the geographical movements of jokes. Kula, "Poland," 163.

[49] David Brandenberger's anthology of Stalinist-era jokes makes a remarkable attempt at contextualizing the process of joke-telling in the Soviet Union on the basis of interviews conducted with Russian émigrés after World War II (the Harvard Interview Project). The author claims that jokes were mostly spread in social circles bound together by trust and affinity (family, close friends, colleagues, etc.). This argument is plausible, but it does not really account for the spontaneous "export" of jokes and joke-types beyond the borders of the Soviet Union. The transnational dimension of joke-telling seems to have been more important than has been assumed so far, and it would certainly merit detailed scholarly scrutiny. Brandenberger, *Political Humor*, 3–9.

[50] There is, of course, a range of suitable methods and analytical approaches (textual and discourse analysis, inter-textual relations, philology, etc.) that could be employed in the exegesis of jokes. The analysis of dictator jokes would certainly benefit from an ethnographic approach focusing on inter-textual relations between anecdotes. Since jokes often traveled across borders, the problem of authenticity and transfer could also be addressed from that perspective. Such an approach would be highly relevant to the study of Rákosi jokes, since many of the

The question of interpreting jokes and rumors is related to the broader historical problem of intentions and perceptions. The Stalinist authorities saw the influence of the enemy behind even the simplest forms of daily survival tactics. Thus a careless comment could easily be labeled "anti-Soviet agitation" (or "whispering propaganda"). Political jokes and rumors, too, were perceived by the Stalinist regime as symptoms of anti-Soviet attitudes in society and were treated accordingly. As David Brandenberger has shown, the Soviet leadership perceived jokes as threats to the stability of the key myths supporting the establishment, including the myth of Stalin.[51] The Bolshevik leaders were not merely humorless; they were paranoid about the destructive potential of satire. While the regime perceived jokes as acts of resistance, the intentions of those who spread them were not necessarily oppositionist. Jokes and rumors are largely spontaneous products of popular imagination, and their transmission follows traditional patterns of tale-telling. It thus remains difficult to decipher the actual attitude to politics, the Communist regime, or the leader cult of the people who passed on such narratives.

Despite the doubtful political intent involved in inventing and spreading rumors or jokes, cracking a joke about Rákosi could provoke a swift response from the authorities, as memoirs and archival records testify. Some of the anecdotes in Imre Katona's anthology were also recorded in agents' reports to the security police, and a few of those were even followed by legal action.[52] There were people who were arrested for telling a Rákosi joke as early as 1947, and there were some who ended up in the infamous Recsk concentration camp for the same reason, at least according to former inmates' recollections.[53] The spreading of unfounded

---

anecdotes about the leader, it seems, were "imported" narratives. Such a complex methodological treatment of jokes, however, lies beyond the scope of this chapter. Katona, *Viccek*, 21.

[51] Brandenberger, *Political Humor*, 21.

[52] ÁBTL 3.1.2 M-20596/1 (October 1955). In a different case, a man who told a satirical joke about Hungary's inferior status to the Soviet Union was arrested and sentenced to four months in prison. ÁBTL 3.1.9. V-5775 (August 1949).

[53] László Borhi, "Stalinist Terror in Hungary, 1945–1956," in *Stalinist Terror in Eastern Europe: Elite Purges and Mass Repression*, ed. Kevin McDermott and Matthew Stibbe (Manchester: Manchester University Press, 2010), 120. For memories of Recsk, see György Faludy, *My Happy Days in Hell* (London: Penguin, 2010), and Géza Böszörményi, ed., *Recsk* (Budapest: Széphalom Könyvműhely, 2006). While people could end up in jail for cracking a joke about the leader, it seems that jokesters in Rákosi's Hungary were punished less often than

rumors—especially war rumors—could also bring the unwary narrator to court or, much worse, to the ÁVH.⁵⁴ Nevertheless, jokes and gossip about the MDP leader were rarely recorded in police documents or reports on the popular mood.⁵⁵ One possible explanation for the scarcity of Rákosi jokes in the archives is that the functionaries who wrote the reports did not have access to circles where critical jokes were told, or if they did, they did not have the courage to forward the jokes.⁵⁶ There is evidence to suggest that mood reports and police records were occasionally filtered and that abusive comments or anecdotes were deleted from the documents submitted to the Party center. In one such case from 1950, the reviewer crossed out a (very) vulgar *chastushka* and an equally vulgar joke in the police report and replaced them with the phrase "slander against the Soviet Union and the leader of our people." The *chastushka* read as follows: "Come with me to my little Russian village, / I await you there with open arms, / Because we have no lavatory there, / People shit all over the place, / And wipe their ass with leaves. / I won't go to your Russian village, / I won't go into your open arms, / Because we have lavatories here, / People shit on Rákosi, / And wipe their ass with *Szabad Nép*."⁵⁷

According to Katona, there were relatively few jokes in circulation about the MDP leader in 1945–1956.⁵⁸ Moreover, most of the wisecracks about Rákosi were rather bland, unsophisticated, judgmental, and even vulgar.⁵⁹ There is a limited variety of themes in such stories, and most of

---

their colleagues in the Stalinist Soviet Union. This aspect of joke-telling, however, needs further research.

⁵⁴ Palasik, "A szólásszabadság deklarálása és korlátainak kezdete," 598.

⁵⁵ One incident of spreading satirical jokes about Rákosi and calling Party decisions "fudges" was reported from Nyíregyháza in May 1955. MOL, 276. fond 65/70.

⁵⁶ Another possible explanation is that people simply did not make many jokes about Rákosi.

⁵⁷ "Gyere velem kicsi orosz falunkba, / Oda várlak ölelő két karomba, / Mert minálunk nincs árnyékszék. / Szerte széjjel szarik a nép / Falevéllel törli a picsáját. // Nem megyek én a te orosz faludba, / Nem megyek ölelő két karodba / Mert minálunk van árnyékszék / Rákosira szarik a nép / Szabad néppel törli a picsáját." As for the joke: "Rákosi couldn't do his thing in the toilet, and a Gypsy told him to put a hat on his head. Rákosi went home, put a hat on his head, and then he could do his thing in the toilet. Rákosi then asked the Gypsy how he knew that this would work. The Gypsy replied: You needed the hat, because it [i.e., the excrement] was not sure which way to come out." ÁBTL 3.1.9 V-10222.

⁵⁸ He identifies 116: Katona, *Viccek*, 14.

⁵⁹ For Katona's discussion of Rákosi jokes, see Katona, *Viccek*, 14–21.

them contain simple and blunt criticisms of the leader.⁶⁰ Rather unsurprisingly, there is not a single joke in which Rákosi appears in a positive light. Simplicity of content matched simplicity of structure and form. There were many one-liners that ridiculed the leader, but more "proper" jokes also typically lacked complexity and sophistication. At the same time, there was no such thing as a popular Rákosi joke. The wisecracks that were widely spread were variations of dictator jokes in which Rákosi simply replaced other leaders, such as Stalin, Hitler, or Mao, as the protagonist. The most original witticisms were the ones that made fun of Rákosi's name or his physical appearance. Moreover, many of the jokes about the Hungarian leader were actually "imported" from Stalin's Russia. How and when these jokes crossed the borders of the Soviet Union, and who "smuggled" them across, remains unclear.⁶¹ Nor do we know much about how such stories were domesticated and adapted to the Hungarian cultural context. However, the fact that subversive narratives created about the Soviet dictator were also recycled in Hungary demonstrates the potency and vigor of informal communication channels in postwar Eastern Europe.

One of the most widespread anecdotes of the dictator-joke type was about a man who buys the official newspaper (such as *Pravda* or *Szabad Nép*) every morning, glances at the front page and then immediately throws it away. When the news vendor asks why he is doing so, the man replies that he is only interested in the obituaries. When the news vendor tells him that obituaries are normally published on the back page, the man responds that the one he is looking for would be on the front page.⁶² Although popular anecdotes about the MDP secretary in the 1950s closely resembled those told about Stalin, some of the stories invented about Rákosi were specifically adapted to his personality. Whereas the bulk of Stalin jokes mocked the boot-licking and deification of the Soviet

---

⁶⁰ The majority of anecdotes ridiculed the Party secretary's character and/or his physical appearance (this was not very common in the case of Stalin). The second most common topic was his imagined death or disappearance; the third was the cult. Other, less frequent themes included terror, poverty, Rákosi as the lackey of Moscow, etc. Katona, *Viccek*, 17.

⁶¹ One can only guess at the identity of such "joke smugglers": former POWs, Russian émigrés, journalists, employees of trading companies, diplomats, Hungarian émigrés in the Soviet Union, etc.

⁶² For the version with Rákosi's name, see Bényei, *A személyi kultusz humora*, 55.

leader, most of the Rákosi anecdotes ridiculed the Hungarian leader's physical qualities or referred to his anticipated removal.[63] In other words, while jokes about Stalin tended to ridicule the absurd dimensions of his cult, wisecracks about his "best Hungarian disciple" mostly made fun of his unfortunate looks. The cult of Rákosi was parodied less often, but his height, the shape of his head, and his baldness were common targets of such jokes. This is exemplified by the story about a drawing class in school where the children are supposed to draw Rákosi's portrait, and someone asks the teacher if they can use a compass to sketch the dear leader's head.[64] In a more vulgar joke, Rákosi is taking a bath when a domestic servant accidentally opens the bathroom door and mistakes the leader's bottom for his head.[65]

Although jokes about Rákosi's physical appearance dominate the collection of anecdotes about him, several jokes in the same corpus made fun of the leader cult and its absurd manifestations. Some of these jokes overtly ridiculed the language of the cult and questioned the validity of the epithets given to Rákosi in the Communist media. In one such story, which had many variants, the complex set of images associated with the leader in Communist propaganda became the target of biting humor. The story, spread in the late 1940s, is about a caricaturist who is reprimanded by Rákosi for mocking the leader in his drawings. Lecturing him, Rákosi says: "How dare you make up jokes about the first man of the Party, the idol of the Hungarian people, whom they think of as their father?" The caricaturist responds: "But Comrade Rákosi, that wasn't my joke!"[66]

Apart from the jokes ridiculing Rákosi's conceitedness and the leader cult discourse in general, there were wisecracks that singled out specific aspects of the cult, such as the father image, for mockery. In a conversation between two stock joke characters about the introduction of the

---

[63] Katona, *Viccek*, 9, 17.
[64] Ibid., 45; Bényei, *A személyi kultusz humora*, 41.
[65] Katona, *Viccek*, 45.
[66] Ibid., 14. In a different version, collected in the early 1950s, Uncle Kohn is spreading jokes about the leader, for which he has to face Rákosi's wrath. "You will have to pay 500 forints for showing no respect for the first man of the country, who is the hope of the workers, the ideal of the people, and Stalin's best apprentice. Do not dare tell jokes like that anymore!" Kohn replies: "You will give me 500 forints for the previous joke, Comrade Rákosi—then we are square." Ibid., 15.

new currency in 1946, Grün says to Kohn: "They say that Rákosi is the father of the forint." Kohn replies: "Then it must have been its mother who was nice."[67] The image of Rákosi as "the father of the nation" was also undermined by jokes in which people (schoolchildren, "the Jew," "the Gypsy," etc.), after learning the identity of their collective "father," express their desire to become orphans.[68] Along with the jokes that parodied the language of leader worship, there were those that satirized some of the cult's manifestations, such as the proliferation of portraits or the endless applause at Party meetings after every mention of Rákosi's name. The endless celebration of the leader at festivities, gatherings, and cinematic or theatrical performances or during public radio broadcasts was often derided. One such joke, recorded in 1951, highlighted the absurdity and monotony of applauding rituals. The speaker at a meeting had to halt his speech every three minutes, because at the mention of Rákosi's name, the crowd would stand up and cheer for a long time. When the local Party secretary criticizes him for referring to the MDP secretary too often and thus interrupting the talk, the speaker replies: "At least I kept the audience awake."[69] Several jokes of a different type expressed loathing for the omnipresence and/or the aesthetic qualities of leader portraits. One concerned a man who is emigrating and takes a Rákosi picture with him to use as a cure whenever he feels homesick. Another was a story in which the father of the family places the leader's picture on the cupboard in order to keep the children away from the candies.[70] A joke that was widespread around the time of Rákosi's sixtieth birthday described the desecration of the leader's images. According to the story, Rákosi's Secretariat receives several complaints that the stamps bearing Rákosi's portrait do not stick. When Rákosi questions the designer (or goes to the post office), it turns out that people are spitting on the side with the leader's face on it instead of the side that was glued.[71] Besides jokes that ridiculed the language or the manifestations of the leader cult, there were others that cast aside subtle irony and portrayed Rákosi in an openly vulgar way. Nevertheless,

---

[67] Bényei, *A személyi kultusz humora*, 38.
[68] Ibid., 53; Katona, *Viccek*, 21.
[69] Ibid., 42.
[70] Bényei, *A személyi kultusz humora*, 50, 51.
[71] Ibid., 46; Katona, *Viccek*, 42.

anecdotes that compared the MDP secretary to a penis or to a bucket of human feces were mostly collected in 1955 and 1956, when ridiculing the leader did not necessarily result in the intervention of the authorities, and criticism could be expressed without Aesopian linguistic skills.[72]

Rákosi was also a frequent subject of unflattering gossip and rumors.[73] However, whether this gossip actually represented the political stance of the individuals who spread it or was forwarded due to the narrative tradition of popular communication is difficult to deduce. Rumors about Communist leaders frequently alleged that they had disappeared, fled the country, been arrested, or even been killed (by "the Russians"). The rift with Yugoslavia in 1948 and the subsequent war hysteria fed the popular imagination and, in particular, sparked the proliferation of fantastic stories and apocalyptic rumors about an imminent war, the collapse of the regime, and the disappearance of Communist leaders.[74] After the denunciation of Rajk, for example, there were rumors that Rákosi had fled to the Soviet Union and that he had been expelled from a UN meeting by none other than Churchill.[75] The mysterious disappearance of the Hungarian Party secretary continued to feature in mood reports in the early 1950s. A 1951 report from Kőszeg, for example, recorded the belief that the Party secretary was deported by Soviet soldiers because he refused to attack Yugoslavia.[76] Apart from the imaginary stories about Rákosi's disappearance and arrest, largely sparked by the war hysteria of the early 1950s, there were also rumors of a fistfight between the Party secretary and Rajk, as well as invented stories about his resignation and new job at the Cominform (recorded in 1955).[77] While some rumors questioned

---

[72] "WC-ben egy penis rajza, a vége Rákosi fejévé alakítva, alatta a következő felirat: Rákosi a fasz, vagy lógjon, vagy menjen a picsába!" (1955): ibid., 42.

[73] On rumors and gossip during the Hungarian Republic of Soviets of 1919, see Boldizsár Vörös, "'Szamuelli repülőgépen Oroszországba szökött.' Álhírek Budapesten a Magyarországi Tanácsköztársaság idején," *Budapesti Negyed* 13, nos. 1–2 (2005): 31–62. For a systematic assessment of theories of rumors, see Zsuzsanna Szetelszky, "A pletyka pszichológiája" (PhD dissertation, Pécsi Tudományegyetem, Pécs, 2010).

[74] The following rumor, reported from Monok in April 1949, is a good example of popular apocalyptic mysticism: "At one corner of the street there was a chest. Once, when a man opened it, a man-sized rubber gendarme jumped out of it. In the meantime a burning joist crossed the sky. That was a sign of God, because the English are coming." MOL, 276. fond 108/11.

[75] MOL, 276. fond 108/7.

[76] MOL, 276. fond 89/267.

[77] MOL, 276. fond 65/71; MOL, 276. fond 65/78.

aspects of Rákosi's constructed persona, the cult hardly ever featured in such stories.

Although archival documents reported expressions of dislike for the cult and its subject, such accounts in the corpus of sources are overshadowed by more mundane themes, related to the day-to-day operation of the government (issues of production, reaction to government and Party decrees, etc.). Coverage of the negative reception to leader worship seems to be the exception rather than the rule in these reports. Besides the inconsistent way in which such incidents were reported to the authorities, criticism of the cult was also expressed unsystematically by the population, making it difficult to discern a pattern in it or to reconstruct a certain popular conception of the leader cult. Even so, some conclusions could be drawn as to the overall perception of the cult among its opponents. These people generally criticized the language of the leader cult and often questioned the sanctified image of Rákosi projected in propaganda. The official representations of the MDP secretary as a benefactor and as an omnipotent, paternal leader who cared about the problems of the "little people" were usually contrasted with perceptions of Rákosi as a distant tyrant bathing in wealth and privilege. A similar logic subverted the concept of Rákosi's words as the markers of progress and positive changes. The declarations of the leader were often understood as signifiers of something ominous; they were also exploited for utilitarian purposes, and in attempts to escape obligations. Rákosi's symbolic standing was further undermined by the (re-)emergence of counter-cults. On the whole, verbal disagreement with the cult conveyed radically different emotional feedback toward the leader than the regime expected. Instead of expressing gratitude and love, such statements expressed discontent, rage, and loathing and blamed Rákosi for social and economic hardships.

Since our sources are mostly silent about the intentions behind, and the context of, passing on jokes, it remains difficult to determine whether political anecdotes were told merely for (self-)entertainment or to erode the regime's discursive authority. The Stalinist leadership, however, perceived satirical reflections of its policies as enemy propaganda. The Party, which desperately tried to engender a constant flow of positive emotions towards its leaders, considered joking harmful and politically subversive. In its view, ironic anecdotes steeped in disdain did not simply undermine the Communist master narrative but also hindered the establishment of affective bonds between state and society.

While joke-telling was not always a political act, jokes and rumors about Rákosi often represented a certain perception of politics and expressed simple political desires and expectations. The rising number of rumors and jokes about Rákosi's presumed removal or death indicated the leader's declining popularity. Alternately, jokes that ridiculed the omnipresence of portraits and mocked ritual applause suggest that those who came up with such stories perceived such manifestations of the cult as absurd or hideous, or they found the idolization of its aesthetically unappealing subject ludicrous. While cracking a joke was not necessarily a conscious act of resistance, anecdotes about the Hungarian Party leader are imbued with a sense of disdain and loathing. The themes of Rákosi jokes reflect a straightforward and fundamentally negative attitude to the leader: there is very little ambiguity, sophistication, or double meaning in those texts. The humor in the anecdotes, while it makes people laugh, is rather bitter and vile. These jokes were thus meant not to provoke liberating laughter but to release frustration, anger, and even hatred and to function as verbal painkillers to ease confrontation with everyday hardships. Rákosi jokes were jokes not of resistance but of frustration and disdain that fostered social adjustment to the changing political environment.

While blunt aesthetic judgments and vulgar one-liners do not constitute a coherent counter-narrative to the leader myth, Rákosi seems to have been portrayed as something like the villain from traditional folk tales. He was generally represented as a mean, paranoid character completely alienated from the people and society. Jokes and rumors about the leader, therefore, could also be interpreted as communicative mechanisms of creating psychological boundaries between the leader and the led, and verbal strategies of exclusion that aimed at removing the Party secretary from popular conceptions of the national community.[78]

---

[78] Gossip and wisecracks often function as tools to strengthen the norms of a social group. Individuals who are perceived as violators of such values are symbolically excluded from the community through gossip. One of the pioneering works on the function of gossip is Max Gluckman, "Gossip and Scandal," *Current Anthropology* 4, no. 3 (1963): 307–16.

Chapter 8
Ignorance is Bliss: Popular Indifference and the Shortcomings of Communist Propaganda

The phenomenon of popular indifference in totalitarian regimes has received surprisingly little attention from historians so far. Apart from Ian Kershaw's seminal book on popular opinion in Nazi Germany (specifically, in Bavaria), which included a detailed examination of the relationship between indifference and the Holocaust, very few scholars have addressed the significance of apathy, unconcern, and impassivity in the formation of popular attitudes to authoritarian political systems.[1] The reason is that most scholars regard the concept of "indifference" as generally incapable of providing credible explanations for the stability of dictatorial regimes or for the failure of their policies and ideological agendas. Historians trying to account for the (temporary) stability of totalitarian political systems focused their attention on the social base of such regimes, affirmative attitudes in society, and areas of consensus between the state and the population. On the other hand, scholars interested in the endurance of spheres of (relative) autonomy in subjugated populations are normally concerned with opposition and dissent and are inclined to study such phenomena through the broad conceptual lens of James Scott. Thus popular indifference—that indefinable gray area of inarticulate opinions—has, to

---

[1] Kershaw, *Popular Opinion and Political Dissent*. Several authors have commented on indifference and political apathy in Soviet society. John Scott, in his famous memoirs, observed an acute lack of interest in the election of Party functionaries, and he also described the low quality of education at evening courses in Magnitogorsk. John Scott, *Behind the Urals: An American Worker in Russia's City of Steel*, enlarged edition prepared by Stephen Kotkin (Bloomington: Indiana University Press, 1989), 35, 45–47. Juliane Fürst has commented on how the dullness of Komsomol meetings in the 1950s triggered absenteeism and boredom. Fürst, *Stalin's Last Generation*, 100–102, 111. Sarah Davies has also reflected on how the Stalin cult was ignored in her book *Popular Opinion*, 120, 167.

date, met mostly with scholarly indifference. This is partly related to the paradoxical nature of the phenomenon. Indifference implies neither dissent nor consent; moreover, it could both augment and thwart the regime's attempts at the same time. As Ian Kershaw has argued, it created a "moral vacuum" in Nazi Germany and thus paved the way for the realization of Hitler's murderous goals.[2] By contrast, depoliticization and widespread political apathy in the Italian provinces prevented the accomplishment of the Mussolini regime's ultimate goal: the creation of the Fascist New Man.[3]

Sources containing references to the "silence of the people" and political apathy are notoriously difficult to interpret. Although people often switch off their political sensors in times of repression and economic hardships while trying to "muddle through," they also tend to feign indifference to avoid the watchful eye of the state.[4] In addition, the Communist Party, which hoped to achieve its aims through mass mobilization and expected political activism from its citizens (especially industrial workers), was all too ready to affix the label "indifferent" to attitudes and behavior that it believed was not enthusiastic enough. While interpreting manifestations of popular indifference—as seen through the regime's eyes—could be problematic, this chapter argues that indifference examined in conjunction with agency and incompetence in the dissemination of Communist propaganda could nonetheless shed some light on subjective perceptions of the regime's policies, including the leader cult. The argument holds that apathy, unconcern, and ignorance did not simply emerge spontaneously as a response to repression or economic hardships but were also engendered by unqualified and unmotivated propagandists or Party functionaries who failed to execute the Party's directives. The intimate connection between incompetence and indifference implies that the latter could—to

---

[2] Ibid., xxii. Here he reflected on his oft-cited argument that "the road to Auschwitz was built by hate, but paved with indifference." Ian Kershaw, *Hitler, the Germans, and the Final Solution* (New Haven, CT: Yale University Press, 2008), 186.

[3] Paul Corner, "Fascist Italy in the 1930s: Popular Opinion in the Provinces," in Corner, *Popular Opinion in Totalitarian Regimes*, 122–46.

[4] The term "muddling through" is used by a number of historians to describe popular attitudes to dictatorial regimes. See, for example, Mary Fulbrook, "Demography, Opportunity or Ideological Conversion? Reflections on the Role of the 'Second Hitler Youth Generation,' or '1929ers,' in the GDR," in Corner, *Popular Opinion in Totalitarian Regimes*, 199; János M. Rainer and György Péteri, *Muddling Through in the Long 1960s* (Budapest: 1956-os Intézet, 2005).

some extent—be considered one of the (many) unintended consequences of the regime's mobilization strategies. The fact that both incompetence and indifference feature prominently in the sources reflecting upon the efficiency of Communist propaganda and the general mood of the population provides a strong argument for a combined assessment of the two phenomena in the context of cult-building.

As was the case with positive and negative statements, opinions indicating indifference to and ignorance of the veneration of Rákosi were not abundant in the sources, and the reports that quoted them mostly focused on certain social groups—especially industrial workers—and not on the population as a whole. Indifference to politics and the regime's propaganda messages in general, however, was repeatedly observed in propagandists' reports during the Rákosi era. The phenomenon thus deserves some attention, as it could provide a broader framework for the interpretation of the reception of the cult. Historians' neglect of the study of political apathy in Hungarian society in the 1950s provides further arguments for an assessment of the phenomenon in the context of cult-building. Although scholars have occasionally commented on apathy and the depoliticization of popular attitudes, the widespread political resignation among social groups, and perceptions of the regime as an ephemeral entity, the subject has not been studied in detail.[5]

As Sarah Davies has observed, the inefficacy of propagandists in the Soviet Union was one reason why many Soviet citizens ignored or misinterpreted the Stalin cult.[6] Karen Petrone has also addressed the relationship between the incompetence of local Party cadres and the shortcomings of Communist propaganda in the 1930s.[7] Similarly, the popular perception of Rákosi's persona in Hungary was significantly influenced by the way in which the agents of Communist propaganda—Party functionaries, propagandists, "people's educators," and teachers—functioned as mediators of the cult. The dissemination of the cult was affected by their (lack of) bureaucratic skills and their degree of motivation, as well as the social and cultural milieu they came from. Insight into how the cult's

---

[5] Szabó, "Hétköznapi sztálinizmus"; Valuch, *Magyarország társadalomtörténete*, 248.
[6] Davies, *Popular Opinion*, 167.
[7] Petrone, *Life Has Become More Joyous, Comrades*.

agents felt about promoting it might shed some light on how effectively the cult propaganda functioned, and in what way cult intermediaries contributed to the shaping of popular perceptions of the cult. Such an analysis of the performance of Party functionaries in executing central directives might also enhance our general understanding of the functioning and the efficacy of propaganda in Soviet-type regimes.

The Cult's Audience

While one of the major pillars of the cult was the image of the enlightening effects of the leader's words, Rákosi's declarations were not always received with the enthusiasm that the Party expected. The stylistic turgidity of the leader's speeches and their heavy reliance on Marxist vocabulary sometimes caused listeners to misinterpret his words or fail to grasp their essence. Rákosi's January 1949 article in *Szabad Nép*, for example, which famously declared the people's democracy of Hungary to be a special type of proletarian dictatorship (without the adoption of the Soviet form), was met by a total lack of understanding among certain social groups.[8] An Agitprop Department report complained that "workers who are not members of the Party do not understand the article; they are not even concerned with it, and the same holds true for the village as well." The document lamented that aside from Somogy County, none of the regional Party committees had prepared reports on the issue.[9] A remarkable number of similar grievances, criticizing workers' lack of interest in studying the "sacred" words of the leader, were submitted to the Agitprop Department in the same year. One report of the letters department of *Szabad Nép*, for example, noted the passivity and lack of enthusiasm among workers in the Kőbánya tobacco factory, and at the national railway company (MÁV), following Rákosi's speech on April 19, 1949, the first of the election campaign.[10] Although the leader's failure to arouse waves of enthusiasm was only reported in these two companies, many

---

[8] Mátyás Rákosi, "A népi demokrácia néhány problémájáról," *Szabad Nép*, January 16, 1949.
[9] The report from Somogy referred to the peasants' alleged joy when Rákosi announced the dictatorship of the proletariat MOL, 276. fond 108/7.
[10] MOL, 276. fond 108/17.

other accounts observed widespread indifference and political passivity among industrial workers at the time of the 1949 general elections. Most frequently, people questioned the utility and function of voting in a one-party system. They wondered why general elections were organized in a country where proposing alternatives to Communist Party policies could be punished.[11] Some sections of Hungarian society almost certainly shared the cynical opinion of a reader's letter to *Szabad Nép*: "What is this clowning all about? These won't be democratic elections; they will elect those whom Rákosi wants anyway."[12]

According to the reports on the mood of the population, indifference to propaganda, including the MDP secretary's speeches, remained a lasting phenomenon in the Rákosi era. One account from the Drasche Brick Factory in early September 1949 complained about the lack of enthusiasm that met Rákosi's announcement at the meeting of the Budapest Party Committee about the working morale in factories.[13] As the document testifies, the local Party functionaries did not pay much attention to promoting the speech, and when asked by those writing the report, none of the people's educators in the factory could recall the actual topic of Rákosi's talk.[14] A report of *Szabad Nép*'s letters section later that month described a similar degree of indifference in several industrial units following the leader's speech at the Budapest Party *aktíva*, where he denounced the "Rajk gang" and announced the introduction of "peace loans."[15] An account of the visits of journalists to a few selected factories complained that Rákosi's speech had had no effect on the workers whatsoever. The gatherings for the public radio broadcast of the talk were poorly organized, and most of the people had no idea of the major themes it covered.[16] The Department report remarked with disappointment that the leader's words had generally failed to leave a lasting impact on most workers. In the MÁVAG factory Rákosi's speech "had no resonance at all"; in Ganz Electric most of the people had neither heard nor read it; and in EMAG there was no

---

[11] MOL, 276. fond 108/11.
[12] MOL, 276. fond 108/17.
[13] "Nagyobb munkafegyelemmel…," *Szabad Nép*, September 2, 1949.
[14] MOL, 276. fond 108/18.
[15] Mátyás Rákosi, "A Rajk-bandáról," *Szabad Nép*, October 1, 1949.
[16] MOL, 276. fond 108/18.

discussion of the talk.[17] Apart from reporting on the manifestations of neglect of Rákosi's speech in industrial units, many popular mood reports complained about the general indifference of workers and intellectuals to the Rajk trial. One account of the Agitprop Department in mid-September noted that the intelligentsia reacted to the publication of the accusations against Rajk with unconcern and passivity.[18] A similar report submitted by *Szabad Nép* informed the Party authorities disappointedly that workers from the MÁVAG factory had failed to understand the significance of the Rajk case, and that one of them even stated that "he couldn't care less about what Rajk did."[19]

The degree of indifference to the leader's announcements that was observed during the Rajk trial continued to feature in mood reports throughout the period. Rákosi's report on Hungary's internal and foreign affairs in the Parliament on December 15, 1952, for example, seems to have failed to inspire the workers in several industrial units.[20] Propagandists complained that people had skipped through the text and read it only superficially, "although every single word of Comrade Rákosi is of high significance and a guideline for the future."[21]

While reports on the popular mood seldom recorded incidents of ignorance specifically regarding the cult, the reports frequently mentioned an overall lack of concern with politics and propaganda. The regime, which desperately tried to inspire political activism and expected its citizens to continually express loyalty, grew disappointed as the population sank into apathy as a result of Party policies.[22] *Szabad Nép* journalists and Party propagandists who traveled to factories in Budapest and the provinces delivering presentations on various propaganda issues related to internal or foreign policy repeatedly complained that they were met with an acute lack of interest. These reports often noted passivity, unconcern, and

---

[17] Ibid.
[18] MOL, 276. fond 108/7.
[19] MOL, 276. fond 108/18.
[20] Mátyás Rákosi, "A kül- és belpolitikai helyzet és feladataink. Beszámoló az országgyűlés 1952. december 15-i ülésén," *Szabad Nép*, December 16, 1952.
[21] MOL, 276. fond 89/614.
[22] Valuch, *Magyarország társadalomtörténete*, 231, 259; Gyarmati, "A társadalom közérzete a fordulat évében"; Szabó, "Hétköznapi sztálinizmus," 160–67.

ignorance among factory workers. The accounts regularly informed the Party center of a "general bad mood" and a lack of interest in daily politics and propaganda matters.[23] Remarks such as "the workers are not really concerned with political questions at all" were common, and factories with a particularly low level of political activism were often singled out for condemnation. One report observed that at the Salgótarján Engine Works, at the time of the 1949 general elections, 96 percent of the workers were not concerned with political matters.[24] The reports of propagandists and journalists regularly remarked, sometimes with resignation, that many of the workers never read newspapers, and even if they did, they skipped the political articles.[25] Frequently a propaganda lecture, or the "Party day" designed to provide the framework for such a talk, had to be canceled or postponed because few people, or no one at all, showed up. If a presentation actually took place, the speakers frequently complained about the low turnout, people falling asleep or leaving the room during the presentation, and the lack of questions or comments after the talk.[26] According to propagandists' reports, sometimes even local Party secretaries gave up, claiming that the workers could not be talked out of their utter indifference.[27]

The scale of indifference among the subjects of such reports (mostly industrial workers) could be explained in part by their increasing economic hardships.[28] Stalinist industrialization caused large-scale social uprooting and rapid changes in personal circumstances, which reoriented

---

[23] Ernő Szücs, deputy head of the ÁVH, was once reported to have removed a paragraph from a report about the bad mood in a factory. He claimed that there was no need to send such reports to the Party, since this bad mood was a general phenomenon. Müller, "A politikai rendőrség tájékoztató szolgálata," 117.

[24] MOL, 276. fond 108/17.

[25] "She doesn't really deal with *Szabad Nép*, especially not with the sections on politics. Politics is above her, and she never reads those parts of the newspapers that deal with politics." MOL, 276. fond 89/612.

[26] The majority of reports are from the period 1949 to 1952. MOL, 276. fond 89/612; MOL, 276. fond 108/17; MOL, 276. fond 65/72.

[27] MOL, 276. fond 89/612.

[28] On the working and living conditions of Hungarian industrial workers, see Gyula Belényi, "A nagyipari munkásság élet- és munkakörülményei az 1950-es években," in *Politika, gazdaság és társadalom a XX. századi magyar történelemben II.*, ed. Levente Püski, Lajos Tímár, and Tibor Valuch (Debrecen: KLTE Történelmi Intézet, 2000), 229–37.

the individual's thinking toward mundane, material problems.[29] Workers were more preoccupied with contracts, norms, wages, working hours, holidays, and the prices of goods than with the constitution or Party leaders' speeches. Comments like "the workers do not care much about politics, they complain more about hard work" were regularly forwarded to the Party center by propagandists and Party activists.[30] Besides difficult working conditions at the factory, the hardships facing the family, the spread of state repression, and the use of coercion to combat workplace absenteeism also contributed to Hungarian society's deepening unconcern with politics. Since dissent could easily trigger punishment, people often hid their actual political stances and critical opinions behind a mask of indifference and neglect, and they pretended not to have been adequately informed about the current state of affairs. The proportion of actual and feigned political unconcern toward the regime's policies in the 1950s, however, remains difficult to establish and warrants further historical research. Despite the regime's and the local authorities' efforts to enhance political activity, factory workers seem to have remained indifferent to politics and propaganda.[31] The degree of unconcern and ennui, combined with the element of threat, was well illustrated by a worker at the Electric Works who, in 1952, expressed only resignation when December 26 was turned into a working day: "I don't say anything anymore, and I think this is a common phenomenon among the rest of the workers too. One becomes so numb that he automatically does what he is told. One cannot really have a private opinion here."[32]

---

[29] On the effect of Stalinist industrialization on the workers, see Gyula Belényi and Lajos Sz. Varga, eds., *Munkások Magyarországon 1958–1956* (Budapest: Napvilág, 2000); Gyula Belényi, *A sztálini iparosítás emberi ára 1948–1956* (Szeged: JATEPress, 1993); Gyula Belényi, "Fordulat a munkaerőpiacon az 1940-es évek végén és a nagyipari munkásság helyzete az 1950-es években," in Feitl et al., *Fordulat a világban*, 161–81.

[30] MOL, 276. fond 108/17.

[31] As the numerous complaint letters submitted to *Szabad Nép* show, the abuse of power by the often incompetent factory directors and by local Party functionaries was common. Besides the authors of readers' letters, propagandists also constantly protested against the various strategies that local authorities applied to ensure participation in political meetings and propaganda lectures. At times, managers and Party secretaries suspended public transport in the neighborhood of the factory until the end of the meeting or lecture. Workers were also often punished for not showing up at meetings.

[32] MOL, 276. fond 89/614.

The Cult's Agents

Party functionaries

Grave indifference toward Communist propaganda was not restricted to the audience of the cult alone. Local Party functionaries, propagandists, and people's educators, who were supposed to participate in the leader cult wholeheartedly and act as its chief mediators, were frequently criticized for their lack of enthusiasm in studying and popularizing propaganda, including Rákosi's speeches and articles. The journalists of *Szabad Nép* and employees of the MDP's Agitprop Department frequently complained in their reports to the Party headquarters about the generally low performance of Party functionaries or their utter failure to popularize a particular Party decree or keynote announcement of the leader. Propaganda officials and Party secretaries in industrial units were repeatedly criticized for not being up-to-date on political proceedings. According to the reports, they rarely read books or *Szabad Nép* or other newspapers and hardly ever consulted the decisions of the Party. Zoltán Bíró, Rákosi's brother, warned the MDP secretary of the phenomenon in a letter as early as 1948.[33] The ignorance of local functionaries, however, remained a recurrent theme of propagandist reports for the entire period, and complaints about the superficial treatment of Central Committee or Politburo decisions by regional Party committees continued to trouble the Party center.[34] Those functionaries who were criticized for not fulfilling their tasks usually defended themselves by citing their other—sometimes related—duties and obligations.[35] Since local Party secretaries and propagandists were not always able to comprehend the symbolic significance of signals from the Party center, they sometimes failed to understand the implication of Party decisions and *Szabad Nép* articles and therefore could not explain them to the workers.

---

[33] MOL, 276. fond 65/77.

[34] Including the one that accused the district Party committees of Budapest and the Agitprop Department of Miskolc of ignoring the decrees of the Politburo and the Central Committee, both circulated in May 1950. MOL, 276. fond 65/61.

[35] "In the Screw Factory, propagandist Ferenc Szoszna said that he had attended a training course for factory managers and that he was also preparing a report for a meeting. Why is it required of him to read *Szabad Nép* on top of all these duties? Not even 20 percent of the leadership reads *Szabad Nép*." MOL, 276. fond 108/17.

The reports sent to the Party center usually complained that local Party committees were not devoting enough attention to popularizing Rákosi's announcements. The letters department of *Szabad Nép*, which regularly sent out observers to factories, often described indifference and ignorance among Party functionaries concerning a particular speech or article by Rákosi. Reports on local Party secretaries and propagandists who showed no interest in consulting and discussing such texts were common. For example, Rákosi's article in *Szabad Nép* in January 1949 declaring the dictatorship of the proletariat was received with little enthusiasm in the industrial units visited by the newspaper's journalists, because members of local Party committees had simply never read the article.[36] Sometimes even the workers were better informed about the content of a Rákosi speech than members of the local Party committee, as in the case of the Party leader's report to the Central Committee on October 31, 1953. Even though the APO described the "great fascination" with which workers responded to the address and the decree of the Central Committee, it bitterly remarked that out of six local Party secretaries checked at random, none had actually read the circulated texts.[37]

In order to avoid condemnation or criticism for not promoting the words of Rákosi, local Party functionaries developed various strategies. Most frequently, they cited the many obligations they were supposed to carry out as functionaries. Some—like the Party secretary of the Taktaharkány machine station—occasionally drafted fictitious minutes of meetings that never took place, which they then submitted to the Party center as proof of their commitment.[38] The local Party committees' frequent failure to popularize and propagate the leader's words provoked harsh censure from the Party center. For example, the lack of attention Rákosi's article on "Yugoslav Trotskyism"—published in *Szabad Nép* in June 1949—received from local Party secretaries triggered a critical outburst from the letters department.[39]

---

[36] Ibid. The article was Rákosi, "A népi demokrácia néhány problémájáról."
[37] MOL, 276. fond 89/267; *Az MDP Politikai Bizottságának beszámolója a Központi Vezetőség 1953. június 28-i határozatainak végrehajtásáról. Rákosi Mátyás előadói beszéde és a Központi Vezetőség 1953. október 31-i határozata* (Budapest, 1953). The Central Committee meeting was only briefly reported by the official newspaper: *Szabad Nép*, November 1, 1953.
[38] MOL, 276. fond 108/8.
[39] Mátyás Rákosi, "A jugoszláv trockisták az imperializmus rohamcsapata," *Szabad Nép*, June 8, 1949.

This is not the first case in which we have pointed out that a Rákosi article was not discussed immediately, or was not discussed at all. Last week two articles by Rákosi were published in *Szabad Nép*, and neither of them was dealt with properly.[40] The most important and immediate task of our functionaries and our most qualified cadres is to read Rákosi articles, and they should not be given additional warnings to do so. Comrade Rákosi writes rarely. No special theoretical education is needed to realize that Comrade Rákosi always has something special and important to say. It seems that the articles of Comrade Rákosi are treated equally with other *Szabad Nép* articles. In our opinion, someone who does not pay attention to the words of the Party leadership is not a good Party member and not a good Communist.[41]

Besides the lack of commitment Party functionaries showed toward consulting Rákosi's speeches, Party decrees, and *Szabad Nép*, there were also problems with their enthusiasm in executing organizational duties. They were often reported to have ignored their obligation to organize propaganda talks, seminars, or Party gatherings on current political issues. Propagandists sent dozens of notifications to the Party Center about lectures that had to be canceled because local Party officials failed to advertise the event properly. They were often blamed for failing to recruit larger audiences—sometimes even coercion did not help—and their neglect of decorating rooms for special occasions prompted further criticisms. The failure to raise workers' interest in propaganda issues was caused by the frequent lack of communication between the Party committees and factory employees. There were places where the workers did not even know the members of the local Party committee, because Party officials never visited the industrial units for which they were responsible. Local Party sections were also frequently reprimanded for abandoning the task of organizing and monitoring the activity of people's educators. In many places there were no regular meetings convened for them, and in some cases the list of educators submitted to the Party Center included

---

[40] The report most likely referred to the publication of Rákosi's speech and his concluding remarks at the Central Committee's meeting in April 1949. "Pártunk vezeti az egész dolgozó népet. Rákosi elvtárs beszéde a Központi Vezetőség ülésén," *Szabad Nép*, June 1, 1949; "Rákosi Mátyás elvtárs zárszava a Központi Vezetőség ülésén," *Szabad Nép*, June 5, 1949.

[41] MOL, 276. fond 108/17.

fictitious names, or the names of people appointed to the post without even being informed. Apart from the fact that people's educators were frequently left without guidelines and instructions regarding their actual tasks, the network of such agitators often contained uneducated and politically untrained cadres. There were also some who became agitators only on paper, in the hope of material rewards or privileges. These people's commitment to popularizing the Party's ideology and its policies could certainly be doubted.[42] The frequency of complaints sent to the Central Committee and the Rákosi Secretariat by the Agitprop Department seems to indicate that the system of people's educators rarely managed to meet Party leaders' expectations. Although attempts were made by the Party center—particularly Márton Horváth—to improve the efficacy of agitators, the network of people's educators remained defective during the whole period. One desperate report of the Agitprop Department from 1952 described the general situation in the following way: "It happens that they [i.e., local Party committees] can show that there are people's educators on paper, but the comrades don't know if they are actually people's educators. Meetings for people's educators are rare events at our core Party organizations. Consequently, the decisions of the Party and the government usually get as far as the meetings of the local Party leadership; they hardly ever reach the masses. As a result, our workers are uninformed and uninterested."[43]

The weak performance of propagandists, people's educators, and Party cadres in general in executing the directives of the Party center could be explained in a number of ways. The low educational level of newly elected functionaries, their inexperience in bureaucratic practices, the Party's inability to upgrade its cadres in quick training courses, and the frequent rotation of personnel within the Party administration —which was a key part of the regime's cadre policy—all contributed to the defects of propagandists and local Party secretaries in promoting the

---

[42] The following fonds contain regular complaints about the agitation work of Party functionaries and people's educators: MOL, 276. fond 65/61–62; MOL, 276. fond 108/17–19; MOL, 276. fond 89/612–13.
[43] MOL, 276. fond 89/612.

Party's ideology, and consequently, in publicizing the leader cult.[44] Since social background and political loyalty were more important factors in the selection of cadres than professional skills or experience, Party functionaries often lacked the necessary qualifications and were usually not acquainted with the tasks and responsibilities of their position.[45] They often required instructions from the Party center, and their activity had to be regularly monitored.[46] These people rarely came up with individual initiatives, and unless they received detailed directives on how to organize certain activities and events, they remained mostly passive. The lack of education and administrative skills coincided with an inadequate knowledge of Marxist ideology at the lower levels of the Party hierarchy. The coalition years witnessed a sudden influx of people into the ranks of the Communist Party, and the membership of the MKP became permeated with people of worker or peasant origin, most of whom were uneducated and therefore were not always familiar with the Party's ideological predisposition and its political aims.

The Communist Party's dire need for politically reliable cadres elevated a large number of uneducated, inexperienced, and ideologically untrained people into functionary positions. To combat this problem, the MKP invested remarkable efforts into educating and training politically committed cadres, preferably of worker and peasant background. Nevertheless, the special cadre-training courses such as the *szakérettségi*, or those organized by Party schools, do not seem to have significantly improved Party functionaries' educational level.[47] These courses mostly covered political and ideological topics—an equally important subject was Hungarian spelling—but without the necessary background, the students could not understand the highly abstract concepts of Marxism-Leninism.

---

[44] On the cadre system in the Rákosi era: Mária M. Kovács and Antal Örkény, *Káderek* (Budapest, 1991); Mária M. Kovács and Antal Örkény, "Promoted Cadres and Professionals in Post-War Hungary," in *Economy and Society in Hungary*, ed. Rudolf Andorka and László Bertalan (Budapest: Karl Marx University of Economic Sciences, 1986), 139–52; György Gyarmati, "A káderrendszer és a rendszer kádere az 50-es években," *Valóság* 34, no. 2 (1991): 51–63; György Gyarmati, "Káderpolitika a Rákosi-korszak tanácsrendszerében, 1950–1953," *Magyar Tudomány*, no. 10 (1998): 1183–94.

[45] Valuch, "A magyar művelődés," 494.

[46] Gyarmati et al., *Magyar hétköznapok*, 241.

[47] Mária M. Kovács and Antal Örkény, "Szakérettségisek," *Mozgó Világ* 7, no. 5 (1981): 102–10.

Students' yen for learning was further decreased by the low quality of tutors in such courses and seminars, the bad conditions in classrooms and dormitories, and the high dropout rate. Neither coercion in selecting students nor the grant they received at the *szakérettségi* courses motivated them to study.[48] Due to a combination of these factors, Party functionaries remained uninterested in educating themselves, and even if they were motivated, short-term courses alone could not fill the knowledge gap.

The lack of education and interest of students enrolled in special training courses was a recurrent topic of reports sent to Party and government officials. Party schools often complained about students' low intellectual level and ideological ignorance, and the serious defects in their knowledge about politics as well as in their general educational background. Those taking such courses did not read the recommended readings and newspaper articles, and their obliviousness to political and ideological matters often shocked the Party center.[49] When confronted with the situation in 1952, a bewildered István Kovács—one of the secretaries of the Central Committee and member of the Politburo—wrote to Rákosi: "Are you aware of the fact that at the Party Academy, the students rarely read the classics [of Marxism], and that the students of the two-year-long course haven't read a single work by Lenin or Stalin?"[50] The survey carried out at the main Party school of the MDP, the Party Academy, in the summer of 1952 on the students' acquaintance with political, economic, geographical, and cultural affairs was probably the source of Kovács's astonishment. The results shocked the directors of the institutions as well as the MDP leadership. According to the summary report, 94.3 percent of the students could not list the members of the Politburo (someone even left out Rákosi), and they had difficulties identifying prominent international Communists. The answers to the questions that were supposed to measure general education further astonished the leaders of the Party school. Leonardo da Vinci was identified as a French philosopher by one student; others believed he was an Italian progressive singer, a French peace activist, or a member of the International Peace Council. There were also problems with the students' familiarity with Hungarian literature. Someone thought that Shakespeare

---

[48] Kovács and Örkény, "Szakérettségisek," 107.
[49] MOL, 276. fond 65/78.
[50] Ibid.

wrote the famous nineteenth-century Hungarian drama *Bánk bán* (by József Katona), and some of them even got the author of the national anthem wrong (crediting Mihály Vörösmarty instead of Ferenc Kölcsey). The Party Academy summary concluded that those with the worst results on the test had never completed primary education.[51]

The number of uneducated cadres in all levels of Party administration was extremely high. The nationwide statistics prepared by the Ministry of Internal Affairs in 1954 revealed that 79 percent of the staff working in council administration had no primary education, and only 10 percent of them had actually finished their primary-school studies.[52] A much-lower-scale research project carried out in 1955 revealed that out of 730 propagandist officials investigated, one-third had only finished the eight-grade primary school, and another one-third lacked even elementary-school education.[53] Based on these figures, it could be tentatively argued that at least 60–70 percent of the Party's propagandists, agitators, and people's educators had only a primary-school education or no education at all. Because the Party administration teemed with uneducated, incompetent, and often barely literate functionaries, the directives of the Party center could not be executed at the local level as effectively as the Party leaders had originally planned.[54] Local Party committees often failed to understand the Party center's instructions, not to mention the complexities of the Party's ideology, Marxism-Leninism, which they usually perceived in terms of slogans and catchphrases.[55]

Incompetence and the failure to decipher the Party's instructions were coupled with a common indifference among Party functionaries that was caused by the regular reshuffling of cadres at all levels of the Party hierarchy. The rotation of Party officials was a deliberate policy in the early 1950s. It was implemented so that Party staff would not develop emotional attachments to their environment, so that they could execute the Party's

---

[51] Ibid.
[52] Gyarmati, "Káderpolitika a Rákosi-korszak tanácsrendszerében," 1190.
[53] Sixty-three percent of these people were labeled "workers" and 23 percent peasants. MOL, 276. fond 65/62.
[54] Gyarmati, "Káderpolitika a Rákosi-korszak tanácsrendszerében," 1187; Valuch, *Magyarország társadalomtörténete*, 155.
[55] As indicated by the summary report about the activity of Party schools in 1949/1950. MOL, 276. fond 89/4.

directives more effectively and without hesitation.⁵⁶ Nevertheless, it seems that instead of strengthening one's commitment to the cause, the frequent replacement of cadres triggered immense uncertainty among these people, especially in the countryside. Moreover, the constant reshuffling of Party administrators made it difficult to plan ahead on a local level and, consequently, to maintain an even level of performance in propaganda affairs. The regular change of cadres and the problems it caused became the subject of complaints sent from local Party committees to the Party Center. As the cadre department of the Budapest Party Committee reported to the Rákosi Secretariat in the first half of 1949, out of 257 functionaries who worked at district and the city Party committees, only fifty-five had spent more than a year in their position, and forty-nine had been working in a particular position for only three months.⁵⁷

The incompetence and lack of motivation among cadres at the lower echelons of the Party hierarchy could often impede the flow of the leader cult within the maze of the Party bureaucracy. The indifference of local functionaries, caused by their pressing material concerns, usually manifested itself in neglect of the promotion of the Party leader's words. Ineptitude and lack of education could result in the failure to understand the meaning and the function of the cult, or the particular directives from the Party Center that prescribed how to popularize Rákosi and other leaders. Besides the indifference and ineffectiveness of cadres, one might also wonder how prewar socialization experiences, traditional perceptions of politics, and religious views shaped the attitude of Party functionaries toward the deification of the Party secretary.⁵⁸ Did Party cadres with a religious upbringing see Rákosi as a god-like figure, a second messiah, or did they see the cult as blasphemous? How did these people reconcile the leader cult with their traditional religious beliefs? Did they try to reconcile the two at all, or did the conflict between the leader worship and Christian faith remain largely unacknowledged?

The question of religious influence on the mentality of Party cadres is highly relevant. Almost 90 percent of the population was found to be

---

⁵⁶ Gyarmati, "Káderpolitika a Rákosi-korszak tanácsrendszerében," 1187.
⁵⁷ MOL, 276. fond 65/71.
⁵⁸ On the survival of traditional rural mentalities in the urban environment of Sztálinváros in Hungary, see Sándor Horváth, "A parasztság életmódváltozása Sztálinvárosban," *Mozgó Világ* 26, no. 6 (2000): 30–40.

religious in the 1949 census—around two-thirds actually practiced their faith. Furthermore, many with religious convictions joined the Communist Party in 1945, when it claimed to support freedom of religion.[59] Due to the acute cadre shortage during this period, some Party members who retained their religious worldview were appointed as Party functionaries and were sent to the usual upgrading courses. Although the actual number of Party members who practiced their religion at the time is unknown, the reports that reached the Party center following the radical shift in the MDP's policy toward the Church in 1948 suggest that the number was high. According to one ÁVO report to Rákosi in 1948, 50–60 percent of the members of rural congregation councils were also members of the MDP and continued to practice their religion after joining the Party.[60] As it directed the onslaught on organized religion, the Party leadership apparently had reason to be concerned with the way individual Party functionaries in the traditionally more religious countryside carried out its instructions.[61] The Ministry of Internal Affairs reported to Rákosi that an MDP secretary had participated in a confirmation performed by the bishop of Veszprém in September 1949, and more reports of this kind reached Rákosi's office in subsequent years.[62] In 1950 the Orgburo—at Rákosi's request—prepared a summary on Party functionaries who were "under the influence of the Church" and submitted it to the Party leader in early May. The summary reported on local Party secretaries who participated in religious processions (some carried candles), signed up their children or family for religious classes, and regularly attended religious sermons. Some were members of the presbytery (in Hejőpapi, for example).[63] Despite the fact that the responsible county Party committees were ordered to rebuke the unruly individuals within two days of the report's

---

[59] Valuch, "A magyar művelődés," 506; Gyarmati, "A társadalom közérzete a fordulat évében," 97.
[60] Gyarmati, "A társadalom közérzete a fordulat évében," 98.
[61] On the relationship of state and church in Hungary: Jenő Gergely, *A katolikus egyház Magyarországon 1944–1971* (Budapest: Kossuth, 1985); Jenő Gergely, *Az 1950-es egyezmény. A szerzetesrendek feloszlatása Magyarországon* (Budapest: Vigilia, 1990); Jenő Gergely, "1948 és az egyházak Magyarországon," in Feitl et al., *Fordulat a világban*, 138–51; Jenő Gergely, "A szétválás konfliktusai. A magyar állam és a katolikus egyház viszonya 1945 és 1951 között," *Társadalmi Szemle* 44, no. 6 (1989): 32–47.
[62] MOL, 276. fond 65/359.
[63] Ibid.

submission, many other examples of Party members paradoxically retaining religious convictions were found. The Party leadership of Pély in Heves County, for example, received a reprimand in May 1950, because instead of trying to prevent the Catholic procession at Pentecost, they waited for the procession in front of the church and attended the sermon along with the participants.[64] In a village in Szolnok County, to decorate the walls of the Party office for Stalin's seventieth birthday, local MDP leaders hung a cross decorated with red ribbons. In the same village the people's educators were reported to have propagandized the inhabitants while holding Bibles in their hands.[65] In the village of Zsámbok, the Party secretary regularly participated in processions, made confessions, and took communion in the local church. If someone greeted him or other local Party leaders in their office with "Freedom!" they would reply, "*Isten hozta!*" ("God brought you here!").[66] Another functionary went even further and claimed during the 1949 elections—in a speech promoting the Communist Party—that "only he who sits in the first row in church could be a real Communist!"[67] Reports of Party functionaries enrolling their children in religion classes also remained a constant source of concern for the leadership in later years. The Ministry of Education, for example, discussed a series of such incidents in September 1952.[68] Not only Party secretaries continued to practice their religion: ordinary Party members did the same. Some of them did so openly, but many chose to conceal their beliefs and keep their religious participation secret, such as the woman who hid under the sheets during a Bible class in a house but was accidentally noticed by someone who sat on the bed (and her).[69]

Besides gathering information on religious Party members, the MDP was also keen to observe clergymen—aside from the officially promoted "peace priests"—who showed sympathy with the regime's goals. During the 1949 elections, for example, the Agitprop Department filed regular reports on Protestant and Catholic priests who participated in, or even

---

[64] MOL, 276. fond 108/8.
[65] MOL, 276. fond 108/19.
[66] Ibid.
[67] MOL, 276. fond 65/61.
[68] Kardos, *Iskola a politika sodrásában*, 51–52.
[69] Pünkösti, *Rákosi a csúcson*, 259.

spoke at, election meetings. There were some who came from giving Mass and brought along the people from the church.[70] One priest in Zala County went so far as to announce at Easter that everything that happened to the workers' benefit should be credited to Rákosi alone.[71] In one exceptional letter from 1951, a priest asked the Ministry of Heavy Industry for permission to build "the first Worker-Christ Church." In his argument he emphasized the spiritual closeness of the working-class movement and the egalitarian tendencies of Christianity and claimed that "this church would profess that socialism and Christianity are full brothers!"[72] Despite the emphasis on Christ's social background ("Christ was a worker too"), such a proposal could never have gained the regime's approval. (The priest's previous links with the fascist Arrow Cross movement meant that such permission was unlikely anyway.)

It seems that Party functionaries with a religious upbringing had trouble leaving their faith behind. For the most part, they were reluctant to carry out the MDP's instructions during the campaign against the Church. Although it would also be interesting to examine how the religious predisposition of such functionaries influenced their individual perception of the Rákosi cult, the lack of primary and secondary sources in this respect prevents the formulation of any tentative conclusions. While it seems clear that coming from a religious background could influence the cadres' attitude toward the execution of the Party's policies, it remains uncertain to what extent Christian beliefs shaped one's attitude to the cult and whether religious influence actually fostered acceptance of the phenomenon or instead strengthened the aversion and disgust among the agents of the cult. It is also difficult to interpret the behavior of those priests who displayed sympathies with the Communist Party. There were certainly some who found that egalitarianism was the common denominator between Communism and Christianity and rejected the material wealth accumulated by higher church officials. Nonetheless, many more people were coerced to support the Party than did so willingly.

---

[70] MOL, 276. fond 65/61.
[71] MOL, 276. fond 108/11.
[72] MOL, 276. fond 65/70.

Teachers

The neglect of the promotion of the leader's persona by Party functionaries, propagandists, and people's educators significantly set back the development of the cult. The spread of the Rákosi cult, however, was also hindered by the lack of motivation of other intermediaries to actively participate in cultic practices. The failure of teachers as cult mediators, for example, demonstrates that in some areas of the public sphere, the cult was not operating as smoothly as planned.[73]

As the waves of nationalization reached the field of education, the institutional structure, as well as the social composition of teachers and pupils alike, drastically changed. Nevertheless, due to the abrupt nature of the reforms and the lack of competent cadres to carry them out, many problems were left unresolved. The sudden increase in the number of students (especially of worker and peasant origin) enrolled in schools coincided with a shortage of teaching personnel and classrooms. The extensive layoff of "politically unreliable" teachers, mostly in schools previously owned by the Church, made the situation worse. The Party leadership was aware of staffing problems and endorsed the mass training of teachers in short courses that, in the long run, resulted in the employment of poorly trained teaching staff. The exponential rise in the number of students in educational institutions, coupled with the scarcity of teachers, triggered a rapid decrease in the quality of education. A growing number of unqualified and underpaid teachers, who were supposed to maintain commitment to the cause even in the most desperate circumstances, gradually lost motivation and became less enthusiastic about the regime's aims. At the same time, teachers who represented a more traditional—usually religious— way of thinking further impeded the Party's efforts to enhance political indoctrination.[74]

---

[73] The function of teachers as transmitters of Communist propaganda in the Soviet context is analyzed by Brandenberger, *National Bolshevism*. On the situation of teachers and the educational system in the 1950s in Hungary: Attila Horváth, "Orvosok-pedagógusok. Értelmiségi pályák presztízse 1950–1983," *Valóság* 29, no. 4 (1986): 59–67; Mihály Kornidesz, "Az MKP és az MDP közoktatási politikájához (1945–1954)," *Párttörténeti Közlemények* 34, no. 4 (1988): 112–48; Mária M. Kovács, "Közalkalmazottak 1938–1949," *Valóság* 25, no. 9 (1982): 41–54; Romsics, *Magyarország története*, 318–31 and 357–74; Valuch, *Magyarország társadalomtörténete*, 149–70; Kardos, *Iskola a politika sodrásában*; József Kardos and Mihály Kornidesz, eds., *Dokumentumok a magyar oktatáspolitika történetéből 1945–1972*, 2 vols., (Budapest: Tankönyvkiadó, 1990).

[74] The different attitudes of teachers (with different socialization experiences) toward the Rákosi regime is exemplified by Márkus Keller, "Utak és emlékezetek. Két tanári pálya a XX. századi

As early as 1949, the Rákosi Secretariat received alarming reports about financially strapped teachers who had to sell their belongings and who borrowed textbooks from the students because they could not afford to purchase them.[75] The severe problems of the educational sector remained on the Party leadership's radar in subsequent years. The Central Committee devoted an entire meeting in March 1950 to the dreadful state of the country's schools, and Révai continued to express his concerns about the situation of teachers in later years.[76] Nevertheless, the living conditions of teachers did not improve—which is partly explained by the suspicion with which the Communist regime viewed teachers in general—and reports submitted to the Ministry of Education or the Party Center in the 1950s continued to emphasize teachers' low salary and heavy workload.[77] Many were forced to take part-time jobs in addition to teaching, or decided to leave the field of education entirely.[78] A survey by the Ministry of Education found that in September 1951 alone, 25–30 percent of all the newly appointed teachers in the country refused to accept their assigned positions.[79] At the same time, the number of older and more experienced teachers continued to decrease; indeed, several schools could not begin the term in September due to the lack of personnel.[80] Despite the worrying signs, no significant measures were taken to improve the situation, and in 1953 the wages of teachers were still among the lowest of all intellectual professions.[81] The enduring hardships and existential uncertainties provoked discontent among members of the teaching profession. One mood report from May 1954 remarked on village teachers' constant complaints

---

Magyarországon," in Évkönyv 2003, XI: Magyarország a jelenkorban, ed. János M. Rainer and Éva Standeisky (Budapest: 1956-os Intézet, 2003), 164–80.

[75] MOL, 276. fond 65/71.
[76] Kardos, Iskola a politika sodrásában, 61–66.
[77] Horváth, "Orvosok-pedagógusok," 63.
[78] MOL, 276. fond 65/343.
[79] Twenty-five percent of newly appointed teachers in primary schools and 35–37 percent in secondary schools failed to take up their positions at the beginning of the academic year. The worst results came from Somogy County, where 35–40 percent of the newly appointed primary-school teachers, and 40 percent of the newly appointed secondary-school teachers, failed to show up at their workplaces in September. The survey was based on data collected from sixteen counties (thirteen in the case of secondary schools). MOL, 276. fond 65/341.
[80] There were twelve schools with such problems in Bács-Kiskun County alone. Ibid.
[81] Ibid.

about their low salary and their tendency to compare their income to the wages of others (such as manual workers), especially of those in jobs that required few or no qualifications.[82] In one school someone bitterly exclaimed that "a swine-herd is a more respected member of the democracy than they [i.e., the teachers] are."[83] References to Lenin, who declared that the "educators of the people" should be respected, were common, as were comparisons with the Hungarian Republic of Soviets of 1919, which had significantly increased the salary of teachers.[84] Although the government under the premiership of Imre Nagy implemented a general pay raise for teachers in July 1954, their financial problems remained unresolved.[85] An exhaustive account prepared by the Party Executive Committee of Pest County reported to Nagy in January 1955 that the inadequate number of teachers in the county, coupled with stiff curricular demands, had resulted in the severe overburdening of the teachers' workload.[86] In Pest County it was not uncommon for a teacher to work thirty to forty hours a week, not including after-school activities, such as organizing study circles, Pioneer and sports events, or choirs. Although teachers often had to stay at school for ten to twelve hours a day, they were not compensated accordingly. According to the Pest report (which also crossed Rákosi's desk), a young village teacher starting his/her career earned around 700 forints a month, of which he/she had to spend at least 500–600 forints on accommodation, provided he/she could actually find some.[87] Due to the dire financial situation, it became common practice for teachers—especially those with a family—to look for a second job after school. Some teachers of a school in Ráckeve, for example, plowed for the local collective farm during the summer holidays, while others

---

[82] Ibid.

[83] Ibid.

[84] Ibid.

[85] Imre Knausz, "'Új szakasz' az oktatáspolitikában, 1953–1954," *Magyar Pedagógia* 89, nos. 3–4 (1989): 268–84.

[86] MOL, 276. fond 65/341.

[87] The (monthly) starting salary of a primary-school teacher in 1951 was 786 forints; for secondary-school teachers the amount was 1,004 forints. Teachers with twelve to fifteen years of experience earned 858 forints in primary schools and 1,076 forints in secondary schools in 1953. There was no increase in the starting salary until 1956. Kovács, "Az értelmiségi keresetek változása (1920–1975)," 254–55.

loaded coal at the railway station in nightshifts. Woodcutting seems to have been a frequent "extracurricular activity," reported in many places (including Nagymaros, Visegrád, Dunabogdány, Albertirsa, and Szokonya), but dire economic conditions forced the educators to take any job available, including cleaning in factories, knitting, giving tetanus injections, and working as waiters. Due to the pressure of having two jobs, the teachers had less time and energy to prepare for the lessons or to keep up-to-date with the relevant academic literature in their field. As a consequence of the withering away of enthusiasm, teachers paid less attention to their students' problems and stopped consulting regularly with the parents. Furthermore, because of acute financial problems, very few of them could afford to buy new books, subscribe to newspapers and journals, or purchase a radio. Hence, they had scant access to news and were often uninformed about the current political line of the Communist Party. Although the document reporting the desperate situation of teachers focused on Pest County only (excluding the capital), schoolteachers in other regions of Hungary (except Budapest) faced similar financial difficulties. As Andics informed Rákosi, the report reflected the generally neglected state of the entire educational system.[88]

In addition to the indifference of many teachers in propaganda matters, the failure of the Communist regime to replace prewar teaching staff with well-trained and committed Party cadres further contributed to the shortcomings of political socialization.[89] Although the Communist Party organized crash courses in Party schools for teachers concerning the regime's ideological aspirations, these courses most often had no apparent impact on the participants. Due to the chronic shortage of teaching personnel in general, the tutors of such seminars were also untrained and lived in the same conditions as their colleagues sitting behind the desks. In several cases, the lecturers were not even members of the Communist Party. Not surprisingly, neither the lecturers nor the audience were particularly interested in the topics under discussion—such as the history of the Soviet Communist Party. As one 1955 overview on the state of such special

---

[88] MOL, 276. fond 65/341.
[89] In 1949, 66 percent of Hungarian public sector employees (including teachers and civil servants) were appointed before 1945. Kovács, "Közalkalmazottak," 50–51.

courses organized for teachers remarked, these courses "did not work at all." The participants remained uninterested in the themes the lessons covered, and they occasionally became cynical about, or even hostile to, the topics discussed during the classes.[90]

The forlorn state of the Hungarian educational system in the mid-1950s seems to indicate that the Communist Party's obsession with education did not lead to schools becoming the most important institutions of political indoctrination. Although the curricula and textbooks were rapidly Sovietized after the Communist takeover and much of the old teaching staff was replaced, the failure to recruit a well-qualified and highly committed army of teachers, or to provide educators with a system of incentives, largely influenced the way the ideological tenets of the regime were transmitted and perceived. Undoubtedly, the Communist Party possessed the means to discipline teachers, but such a wide-scale lack of motivation was unlikely to be fully overcome with pure coercion. The general preoccupation with financial problems among teachers and students alike led to the rapid decrease in the quality of instruction and to taking up physical work at the expense of learning. As education was rarely rewarded with wide-scale career opportunities or a significant increase in salary, studying was generally regarded as futile. Labor migration, existential hardships, and coercion resulted in an overall lack of interest in education among the population. Learning was usually regarded as pointless, lacking any guarantee of material benefit. In fact, those workers who were selected from factories and joined various courses saw their standard of living worsen; thus many of them tried to escape back to production. Although many more students with worker or peasant background enrolled in educational institutions in the postwar period, a great number of them did not complete their studies. Reports submitted to Party or government institutions on uneducated and incompetent people in the Party bureaucracy, in schools, or among the workers of factories and kolkhozes continued to lament the overall low level of qualification and general lack of interest in education.[91]

---

[90] MOL, 276. fond 65/62.
[91] One report submitted in March 1955 and based on research carried out at eighteen different workplaces—factories and collective farms alike—observed that less than 50 percent of the employees between the age of seventeen and twenty-four had finished their elementary studies

The generally distressing situation in Hungarian education in the 1950s might well raise doubts about the efficiency of teachers in transmitting Communist propaganda, including the promotion of the leader cult. Although the life and achievements of Stalin, Lenin, and Rákosi dominated in textbooks, the biographies of the leaders were taught in Party schools, the portraits of the Hungarian Party secretary decorated classrooms, and his sixtieth birthday was commemorated all over the country, the apathy of teachers discouraged students from responding positively to the cult. Of course, further research is needed before we can draw a comprehensive picture of the social and intellectual position of the agents of Communist propaganda. However, there is good reason to argue that the attitude of cult intermediaries to the dissemination of the regime's ideas and values contributed to the growing indifference toward the cult in Hungarian society in general.

The Rákosi Cult: Circulation and Responses

Was the campaign to construct a cultic persona for Rákosi ultimately successful? To be sure, the general tone of propagandist reports regarding the promotion of the key pillars of the cult—Rákosi's biography and his image as an omnipresent national hero—remained shamelessly triumphant. Such documents clearly demonstrate the extraordinary effort the Party invested in the construction of the cult and in the monitoring of its reception. The tons of mood reports that flooded the archives of the Party Center, however, revealed significant cracks in the system. Thus the documents of the Propaganda Department tell a story of both success and failure. Failure, however, was rarely—if ever—acknowledged openly; the symptoms of an ineffective cult were barely visible in official documents. Reports on the reception of the biographical narrative, for

---

(35.8 percent of the workers and 21.4 percent of the peasants). The number of those with a secondary-school certificate was significantly less, demonstrating more embarrassing results for the Party center. Of the young industrial workers, only 3.3 percent had completed secondary school, whereas only 1.5 percent of the young peasants finished secondary school. The report also referred to the low-level qualifications of those in higher positions, such as brigade leaders or members of the factory management. MOL, 276. fond 65/341.

example, generally emphasized the lack of manifestations of hostility. As one document put it: "In this field the enemy has no foothold."[92] However, since positive responses to Rákosi's life story in the archives were resonant with similar reactions published in the Communist press at the time, the value of such accounts is doubtful.

Reports of the Agitprop Department on the promotion of national Communist themes also demonstrate the continuing enthusiasm of propagandists. After the 1949 elections, for example, an evaluation of the Party's propaganda work in the countryside proudly reported to the Party center that the popularity of the Party and Rákosi had increased substantially as a result of the systematic exploitation of national traditions and the cult of Kossuth in particular.[93] However, regardless of the efforts of Communist propaganda to emphasize the Party's national features through verbal, visual, and ritualistic means, in the minds of the population, the country's subordination to the Soviets seems to have overshadowed the national visage of the MDP and its leaders. A substantial part of Hungarian society apparently regarded the national façade of the Communist Party as a cynical propaganda strategy or as an outright abuse of national traditions. Despite Révai's claim at the congress of the Hungarian-Soviet Society in 1953 that loyalty to the Soviet Union necessarily entailed loyalty to the Hungarian nation, the Communist Party was generally perceived as the advocate of foreign interests, and the cult of Rákosi was usually regarded as an essentially Soviet phenomenon.[94]

The lack of success of the leader's biographies and the attempt to turn him into a national hero was replicated in the campaign to promote images of his omnipresence. Although the spatial extension of the cult was centrally coordinated, the flooding of public spaces with the leader's name and his pictures reduced the symbolic value of both. The monotony and grayness of leader images and the drill-like mass processions further contributed to the inflation of the Rákosi cult in Hungary. It thus seems tempting to claim that the spatial arrangement of the cult (i.e., its ubiquitousness) proved counterproductive, and instead of sparking devotion

---

[92] MOL, 276. fond 89/10.
[93] MOL, 276. fond 108/11.
[94] "He who stands behind the Soviet Union stands behind the Hungarian people, the Hungarian nation, the Hungarian homeland." *Szabad Nép*, February 15, 1953.

and admiration for the leader, it caused disapproval, irritation, and hostility in Hungarian society. Not surprisingly, then, the dismantling of the cult started with the removal of Rákosi's name from institutions that bore it, and the gradual withdrawal of Rákosi's portraits from the public sphere, culminating in the iconoclastic acts of the 1956 revolution.

The main factor that thwarted the regime's attempts to popularize its leaders was ignorance. Additionally, the sources frequently mention popular indifference, which raises doubts as to the credibility of reports boasting of popular enthusiasm. While both of these factors were recorded meticulously by Party functionaries, their correlation remains difficult to establish on the basis of available archival material. Summary reports that reached the Party center normally included references to the most noteworthy examples but contained limited information about broader trends, or patterns in a certain region or industrial unit, and revealed very little about the representativeness of such attitudes among specific social groups. Nonetheless, whereas reports about popular support seem ritualistic, the Party's anxiety about the spread of popular indifference appears to have been genuine. Existential security was the primary concern among the agents and audiences of the cult in the 1950s, and thus there was a general indifference toward the spiritual medicine the Rákosi cult was meant to provide. Unmotivated cult mediators—though often unintentionally—contributed to the spread of political indifference in Hungarian society. By skipping their reading assignments or ignoring the directions of their superiors, Party functionaries caused ruptures in the transmission of the Party's ideological message to the workers. Therefore, they often failed to operate as proper intermediaries between state and society. The totalitarian ambitions of the state were also thwarted by local officials who willingly cooperated with the peasants for pragmatic reasons or simply because their ties to the local community were stronger than their loyalty to the Party.[95] The unconcern and incompetence of Communist cadres was coupled with their inability to come to terms with the conceptual difficulty of the ideological system that they were meant to be popularizing. Since most Party cadres lacked the necessary educational background to appreciate the philosophical complexities of Marxism, they remained

---

[95] Rév, "Az atomizáció előnyei," 144–45; Viola, "Introduction," 11–13.

largely incapable of promoting its tenets to a society that was generally unfamiliar with Marxist tradition. As Rákosi's speeches and articles were loaded with Marxist terminology, many uneducated propagandists had difficulty understanding them and thus could not adequately explain the leader's words to the target audience, even if they were motivated to do so. The passive, neglectful attitude of Party functionaries toward the cult could—to some extent—also be explained by the clash of traditional mentalities with the way of thinking the Communist Party represented. Some of the swiftly recruited cadres struggled to reconcile Marxist ideology with their own religious worldview and remained hesitant to carry out Party directives on the deification of leaders.

Rákosi's popularity in the coalition period, combined with a political culture accustomed to the cult of authority figures, could potentially have paved the way for the acceptance of yet another form of leader worship. After the Communist takeover, however, the emerging cult triggered more ambivalent feelings in Hungarian society. Although the population rarely reflected upon the cult in public, it seems that, notwithstanding voices of affirmation, people found many of its manifestations repugnant. However, the Party remained more preoccupied with the popular indifference that informants and propagandists experienced every day. The lack of commitment of some of the cult's agents to promoting the leader's persona and the recurrent shortcomings of communist propaganda both influenced the way the Rákosi cult was spread and perceived, and thus further emphasize the importance of ignorance regarding the cult's reception. The complexity of meanings and functions assigned to the cult by its designers was reduced and simplified by the incompetence, neglect, and indifference of intermediaries. Sometimes the message was completely lost in the web of cult promotion. As a consequence, certain segments of Hungarian society were not exposed to propaganda as intensely as the regime intended, and thus they misunderstood, failed to grasp the essence of, or ignored the leader cult. Even if popular indifference cannot be accurately measured on the basis of archival material, it does seem that large sections of Hungarian society had trouble deciphering the codes of the cult or lacked the motivation to internalize them. Popular indifference, combined with the prevalence of Christian beliefs, seems to have prevented the attempt of Communist propaganda in the Rákosi era to successfully install a Soviet-type cult structured around the leader's persona. Compared with the Soviet experience, where the Lenin and Stalin cults were in some ways resonant with the population's expectations and convictions, the Rákosi cult, despite the rich cultic traditions in Hungarian history and the leader's early popularity, found little fertile ground. Nonetheless, the cult did function at the time, and it assumed monumental proportions, due to the Party's control over the public sphere and the sophisticated institutional background of cult construction. The functioning of the cult, however, could also be related to political apathy and unconcern. While indifference prevented affirmative sentiments from emerging in relation to the Rákosi myth, it also allowed the cult to function: people who largely ignored the phenomenon also participated in the rituals of the cult—willingly or under pressure—and therefore helped sustain it to a certain degree.

The scarcity of reports on popular responses to the Rákosi myth shows that the cult's reception was supervised less systematically than its planning and construction. Nonetheless, the mood reports indicate that the population had internalized the vocabulary and rhetoric of the official propaganda discourse and could "speak Bolshevik." People usually knew what was acceptable to say in the context of the controlled public sphere.[96] Responses to the cult, although few, assumed a ritual character. The language of the cult, when used as a mode of communication between the authorities and its citizens, became repetitive, and, like the overall cult propaganda, it was superficial, monotonous, and dull. Given that the cult was only rarely referred to in the mood reports, we cannot be sure that such documents provide a representative overview of how Hungarian society viewed the leader cult. What these reports provide is mostly a ritualized presentation of reactions—invented or real—to the cult, seen through the prism of the Party bureaucracy.

---

[96] Szabó recalls that saying things in accordance with the general line was a kind of an intellectual game at the time. Szabó, "Hétköznapi Sztálinizmus," 161.

PART III

THE DISMANTLING OF THE CULT

Chapter 9
The "New Course" and the Decay of the Rákosi Cult, 1953–1956

The period following the death of Stalin in March 1953 witnessed a series of political and economic changes in the Soviet Union, as well as in Central and Eastern Europe. Stalin's heirs, in the midst of political struggles for positions of power, initiated a set of "correction" policies in order to reinforce the standing of the new collective leadership.[1] One of the first issues that the new leaders addressed was the ominous "cult of personality." Only a day after Stalin was buried, Malenkov highlighted the problem at a Presidium meeting, emphasizing the need to end "the policy of the cult of personality."[2] However, eliminating the system of myths and rituals that had dominated the spectacle of Communism for about two decades was not an easy task, and the Soviet leaders were not yet prepared to do a thorough sweep. Although the Stalin cult suddenly contracted after the mourning period, its decline had more to do with the general unwillingness to build upon it further than with a consistent policy to remove it from the public sphere entirely.[3] While the textual aspects of the cult

---

[1] On correction policies in the Soviet Union and the Eastern bloc: Stephen F. Cohen, "The Stalin Question since Stalin," in Stephen F. Cohen, ed., *An End to Silence: Uncensored Opinion in the Soviet Union* (New York: Norton, 1982), 30–50; François Fejtő, *A History of the People's Democracies: Eastern Europe since Stalin* (New York: Praeger, 1971), 17–30; Donald Filtzer, *The Khrushchev Era: De-Stalinisation and the Limits of Reform in the USSR, 1953–1964* (Basingstoke: Palgrave, 1993); Albert P. van Goudoever, *The Limits of De-Stalinization in the Soviet Union: Political Rehabilitation in the Soviet Union since Stalin* (London: Croom Helm, 1986); Vladimir V. Kusin, "An Overview of East European Reformism," *Soviet Studies* 28, no. 3 (1976): 338–61; Yoram Gorlizki, "Party Revivalism and the Death of Stalin," *Slavic Review* 54, no. 1 (1995): 1–22; Károly Lipkovics, "A Szovjetunió Kommunista Pártjának politikájáról, 1953–1957," *Múltunk* 36, no. 1 (1991): 3–34.

[2] Aleksandr V. Pyzhikov, "The Cult of Personality during the Khrushchev Thaw," *Russian Studies in History* 50, no. 3 (Winter 2011–2012): 12.

[3] On the erosion of the Stalin cult in the Soviet Union after the Party secretary's death: Brooks, *Thank You, Comrade Stalin!*, 233–47; Jones, "Strategies of De-Mythologisation," 43–50; and

started to disappear from Communist propaganda—there was less praise in the press, and a new Party history was written—Stalin's name continued to feature in the speeches of Party and government leaders, his pictures dominated Soviet symbolic space, and his birthday—particularly his seventy-fifth—was celebrated after his death.[4] The ambivalent attitude of Stalin's successors to the cult was demonstrated by the fact that the critique of the "cult of personality" was never linked to Stalin in the period before the "secret speech." The attempt to safeguard his name from criticism and eliminate the cult at the same time triggered confusion among ordinary Party members as well as Communist leaders in the Eastern bloc.[5] While the apparent decline of the Stalin cult in the Soviet Union must have alerted the leaders of the satellite parties to Moscow's changing attitudes, the lack of a negative evaluation of the deceased dictator convinced them to adhere to the Stalinist practice of representing the leadership in cultic terms. This resulted in a situation that would have been unimaginable before: while the cult of the "Father of Peoples" was eroding in the Soviet Union, the cults of his "best disciples" continued to thrive—at least until June 1953.

The issue of the "cult of personality" was raised in the countries of the bloc in connection with the proclamation of the "New Course" in the summer of 1953. The introduction of the new political line was followed by the tempering of the cults of Party secretaries in the region. In Bulgaria, the cult of the "Little Stalin," Vŭlko Chervenkov, was toned down significantly, and he also had to resign his position as general secretary in March 1954.[6] In the GDR, the celebration of Ulbricht's sixtieth birthday—scheduled for June 30, 1953—was canceled, and the construction of his cult was halted

---

Polly Jones, "From Stalinism to Post-Stalinism: De-Mythologising Stalin, 1953–56," in *Redefining Stalinism*, ed. Harold Shukman (London and Portland, 2003), 127–48.

[4] On the decay of the Stalin cult in the period between the leader's death and Khrushchev's "secret speech," see Jones, "Strategies of De-Mythologisation," 43–50. On the survival of cultic representations of Stalin, see Pyzhikov, "The Cult of Personality."

[5] Pyzhikov remarked, "This was the distinguishing feature of domestic politics in 1953–55, when, officially and ostensibly, the concept of the cult of personality and the name of Stalin had nothing in common. This created some strange situations, such as when Communists at Party meetings asked who precisely the personalities in question were and how exactly propaganda for the cult of personality had manifested itself." Pyzhikov, "The Cult of Personality," 14.

[6] Wien, "Georgi Dimitrov," 202.

until 1958.[7] Bierut's birthday received only modest press coverage in 1954, and in 1955 Polish newspapers did not mention it at all. At the same time, other Communist leaders' portraits started to appear alongside Bierut's, indicating the significance the Party attributed to the notion of collective leadership.[8] Only Czechoslovakia resisted de-Stalinization and continued to nurture cultic images of the Party's leaders. Although Gottwald died a few days after Stalin, his body was embalmed and displayed in a mausoleum that was completed in December 1953. The unveiling in Prague of the largest Stalin statue in the Eastern bloc on May Day 1955 further indicated the Czechoslovak leadership's commitment to the symbols and myths of the Stalinist era.[9] Despite the general decay of leader cults in the Soviet bloc after June 1953 (with the exception of Czechoslovakia), the "deconstruction" of the phenomenon remained ambivalent and unfinished. This was related mostly to the fact that Stalin remained beyond criticism until 1956—Beria assumed the role of the villain instead—but also to the fact that debates about the "cult of personality" took place within the close confines of the Party leadership and excluded the public.

Between 1953 and 1956, the Rákosi cult followed a similar trajectory to other Communist leader cults in the bloc. It was toned down significantly after June 1953: its textual components were weakened, and images of the Party secretary started to disappear from public spaces. However, despite the many similarities, the "deconstruction" of the cult in Hungary had several unique features. Following Moscow's attack on the Rákosi line in June 1953, the Party leader became more exposed to intra-Party criticisms—and thus suffered a more drastic decline in his symbolic standing—than any of his colleagues in the Soviet bloc. However, the cult was not removed completely from the public sphere, and it even underwent a certain revival in 1955. This chapter will focus on the development of the Hungarian Party leader's cult between 1953 and 1956 and will discuss strategies of cult-dismantling in this period.

---

[7] Behrends, "Nach dem Führerkult," 62–63.
[8] Main, "President of Poland," 185.
[9] Many thanks to Luděk Vacín for sharing his thoughts and images on the Gottwald Mausoleum with me. For more details see the special issue of *Acta Musei Nationalis Pragae* 68, no. 1–2 (2014). The issue was edited by Luděk Vacín. For the history of the Stalin statue in Prague, see Hana Pichova, "The Lineup for Meat: The Stalin Statue in Prague," *Publications of the Modern Language Association of America* 123, no. 3 (May 2008): 614–30.

The Death of Stalin and the Rákosi Cult

The orchestrated enthusiasm in the Hungarian Party secretary's cult in 1952 diminished significantly during the mourning period following the death of Stalin in March 1953. The last monumental manifestation of the worship of the Soviet leader in the Soviet bloc temporarily diverted attention from Rákosi and the satellite leaders and gave way to the grief that the entire Soviet bloc was supposed to demonstrate after the demise of the "teacher of humanity." The news of the Soviet dictator's death reached the Hungarian public on March 6. That day, *Szabad Nép* published a large picture of Stalin on the front page, placed in a thick black frame. The newspaper published countless telegrams and letters of condolence from international Communist leaders, including from Rákosi, and assured the Soviet Union of the fraternal solidarity of the Hungarian people in such difficult times. Although the heart of the Soviet leader had stopped beating, Rákosi reassured Moscow, "our heart beats together with the hearts of the Soviet people."[10] The major theme of the subsequent issues of *Szabad Nép*—all decorated with a large black frame on the front page until the funeral day—remained the mourning of the Soviet Party leader. The newspaper published detailed reports on the funeral preparations in Moscow, the floods of telegrams sent to the CPSU, the position of Rákosi and Dobi as guards of honor beside Stalin's body as it lay in state, the crowds of people paying their respects at the Soviet embassy in Budapest, and popular reactions—invented or real—to the news of the Soviet leader's death. Along with the press, Party and government institutions were also quick to pay homage to the memory of Stalin. The special session of Parliament on March 8 codified the historical merits of the generalissimo, while the Budapest City Council renamed Felvonulási Square—the location of the Stalin statue—"Stalin Square."[11] On the day of the funeral, a mass meeting was organized in Budapest in front of the monumental Stalin statue, and at the time of Stalin's burial, salutes were fired from various points of the capital, at Farkas's order. At the moment Stalin was laid to rest, life stopped in Hungary, and sirens, car horns, factory horns,

---

[10] *Szabad Nép*, March 6, 1953.
[11] *Szabad Nép*, March 9, 1953.

and locomotive whistles were sounded all around the country for about five minutes.[12] Although the black frame disappeared from the front page of *Szabad Nép* on March 11, the newspaper continued to publish lengthy homages to Stalin, as well as descriptions and photos of the funeral, even after he was laid to rest next to Lenin, the founder of the Soviet state. Telegrams of condolence sent by Hungarian workers, for example, featured in the columns of the daily until mid-April, irrespective of the celebrations of April 4 and the approach of the general elections in May. Meanwhile, when Czechoslovak Party leader Klement Gottwald died, he received only a half-page frame from *Szabad Nép*'s editors on March 15. Although Rákosi himself praised Gottwald in an obituary, and Ganz Electrics was renamed for Gottwald a month later,[13] mourning over Stalin's death remained the key theme in Communist propaganda in the spring of 1953.

During the weeks of official mourning, the Rákosi cult kept a low profile. Since the issues of the official Communist newspaper on March 9 and 10 were almost exclusively dedicated to Stalin's funeral, the sixty-first birthday of the MDP secretary received no attention from the press. Moreover—unlike the year before—no commemorations were organized to celebrate the anniversary of the Hungarian Party leader's birth. Nevertheless, the cult of Rákosi was kept alive during the mourning period, and the death of Stalin even contributed to some extent to the exaltation of the Hungarian Party leader. As was the case at the time of the Rajk trial, or the rift with Yugoslavia, the emotional shock of Stalin's demise was meant to prompt loyalty and devotion toward Rákosi. A sharp increase in expressions of support and affection at times of hardships, insecurity, or threat was seen in the development of Communist leader cults in general. The death of Stalin, which brought about immense uncertainty and evoked a wide range of ambiguous feelings, was no exception. The waves of sorrow, instigated in part by Communist propaganda, reactivated or intensified the—largely paternalistic—"defender" image of the mini-Stalins in the countries of the Soviet bloc. With the exception of Czechoslovakia, where Gottwald died before his cult could exploit the symbolic value of the Soviet Party leader's death (he received a mausoleum instead), in

---

[12] *Szabad Nép*, March 10, 1953.
[13] *Szabad Nép*, April 15, 1953.

Central and Eastern Europe the manifestations of grief felt over the loss of the "Father of Peoples" bolstered expressions of support and love toward local Party leaders. In Hungary, the joint announcement of the Central Committee of the MDP, the Council of Ministers, and the Presidential Council on March 7 already called for the strengthening of support for the regime, as well as the reinforcement of emotional bonds between the people and Rákosi, the Party, and the government.

> To the Hungarian people!
> Our people mourn the friend, the teacher, and the leader. Let us tighten our lines, let us cluster more closely around our great Party, the government of our people's republic, and the true apprentice of Comrade Stalin: Comrade Rákosi.[14]

A similar call was made by Imre Nagy in his mourning speech for Stalin in the Parliament on March 8. Gerő, at the mass meeting on the day of Stalin's funeral, also requested that the population "cluster in unity around the best Hungarian apprentice of Comrade Stalin, the leader of our Party and our people: Comrade Rákosi."[15] The calls of Party leaders were not left unanswered: factories, brigades, and individuals responded by making pledges and swearing oaths to the Hungarian Party leader, as well as intensifying work efforts.

Despite the closing of ranks around Rákosi, the currents of adulation remained modest in the period following Stalin's death. As soon as the weeks of mourning elapsed, however, the panegyrics started to re-emerge, and the cult of Rákosi regained its previous magnitude. The resurgence of the cult was closely tied to the coming of the 1953 general elections. *Szabad Nép* announced that the labor competition organized for the occasion of April 4 would continue until the elections as a demonstration of the Hungarian people's loyalty "to the director of our victories: the Party, and our deeply beloved leader, Comrade Rákosi."[16] Nevertheless, the actual agitation campaign only started on April 11, when the Csepel constituency nominated Rákosi as their prime candidate.

---

[14] *Szabad Nép*, March 7, 1953.
[15] *Szabad Nép*, March 9, 1953, and *Szabad Nép*, March 10, 1953.
[16] *Szabad Nép*, April 3, 1953.

We give thanks for our new life, our happiness, and the disappearance of the cursed poverty of the past to the Soviet Union that liberated us; to the immortal Comrade Stalin, who will live in our hearts forever; to our glorious Party that was educated by the example of the Communist Party of the Soviet Union; and personally to our dear and deeply loved Comrade Rákosi. As a sign of our never-ending gratitude and our deep affection, we nominate Comrade Mátyás Rákosi to be the first candidate of the Mátyás Rákosi Works in our people's Parliament.[17]

Similar requests from various constituencies were published daily in *Szabad Nép* until late April, and in the end Rákosi was nominated as the prime candidate in all electoral districts. The nomination ceremonies displayed a standardized format. At the district meetings, the main speaker usually praised the Hungarian Party leader's role in the construction of socialism, expressed the gratitude of the people for all achievements, and requested that Rákosi stand as the first candidate in the respective constituency. Nomination proposals were often interrupted by rhythmic applause and the lengthy chanting of the names of the Party and its leader.

In the month before the elections, Rákosi appeared frequently in public. As in previous years, he was depicted as the symbolic center during the April 4 and May 1 demonstrations, which took place—for the first time—on Stalin Square, in front of the bronze likeness of the deceased Soviet leader. Although the April 4 celebrations were relatively modest due to the proximity to the mourning period—there was no civilian demonstration, for example—the spectacle of May 1 was dominated by the symbols of the Communist leader cult. The demonstrators carried large portraits of Rákosi and Stalin and marched past the monumental Stalin statue and the tribune, which was decorated with photos of Stalin, Lenin, and Rákosi. *Szabad Nép* reported enthusiastically on participants' ecstatic reactions to catching a glimpse of the leader, as well as on the touching scene when two Pioneer children presented him with a bouquet.[18]

Arguably, Rákosi's most impressive public appearance in this period was the electoral mass meeting on May 10, 1953, on Kossuth Square, in front of the Parliament. The meeting illustrates the proportions that the

---

[17] *Szabad Nép*, April 11, 1953.
[18] *Szabad Nép*, May 2, 1953.

cult of the Hungarian Party secretary assumed after the death of Stalin. *Szabad Nép* described the event in detail, using the well-established patterns of representing the leader's persona. The enthusiastic anticipation of the event, the massed crowds at the spot, the frantic outburst of joy when Rákosi appeared, and the speech interrupted by frequent applause and cheering rituals were all highlighted by the journalists of *Szabad Nép*. When describing the setting and the audience, for example, the newspaper noted that "the hundreds of thousands of people could not even fit in the square," and "the flow of people filled the neighboring streets up to Szabadság Square."[19] The MDP secretary, or "the prime candidate of the Hungarian people," was welcomed with "endless cheering, storms of applause, and repeatedly erupting enthusiasm," and the moment he walked to the microphone, "a storm of applause swept over the entirety of Kossuth Square and the neighboring streets," which only died away when Rákosi started speaking. The report on the speech and its effects, besides involving ritual references to Rákosi's image as the greatest hero of the national pantheon, was dominated by the trope depicting the Party leader as a paternal figure maintaining a close relationship with the Hungarian people. The descriptions of the event reiterated the image of what Katerina Clark labeled the "Stalinist myth of the great family" and postulated the gathering as an intimate meeting of the Father of the Nation and his children:[20] "The crowd gives the impression of one great family, and this family is now looking forward to meeting its father."[21] Although promoting a primal sense of social allegiance had been an essential aspect of the leader cult discourse, the prevalence of the family theme regarding the election meeting was still remarkable at the time of the stagnation of the Stalin cult. The image of the great family, with Rákosi as its father, nevertheless remained the main subject of evaluations and appraisals following *Szabad Nép*'s report on Rákosi's appearance. Tibor Méray's assessment of the speech, for example, emphasized the familiarity and the intimacy of the meeting, but the flood of similar appraisals in the press in the days

---

[19] The report was published in *Szabad Nép*, May 11, 1953.
[20] Clark, *The Soviet Novel*, 114–15.
[21] *Szabad Nép*, May 11, 1953.

to come all contributed to the effort of buttressing the image of society as one family, and the image of Rákosi as its father.[22]

Although the Stalin cult in the Soviet Union experienced an apparent setback after March 1953, the cult of Rákosi continued to flourish in the period after Stalin's death (with the exception of the weeks of mourning), and the public veneration of the Hungarian leader might even have seemed more ostentatious with the disappearance of the primary restrictive factor. Although during the mourning period, the exaltation of Rákosi was tempered somewhat, Rákosi's political and symbolic position remained unquestionable during the spring of 1953.[23] Understandably, then, Rákosi's replacement by Imre Nagy as prime minister, barely a month after the election meeting in May, astonished and shocked Hungarian society.

Cult Criticism in 1953–1956

In June 1953 the Presidium of the Central Committee of the CPSU asked a delegation of Hungarian Party and state leaders to travel to Moscow for "consultations."[24] The fact that two of the most influential members of the pre-1953 leadership, Farkas and Révai, were excluded from the list of those invited, while the previously neglected Nagy was invited, produced a somewhat ominous atmosphere in the upper echelons of the MDP before the group left for the Soviet Union. At the meetings with the Presidium on June 13–16, the Hungarian delegation, headed by Rákosi, received an unexpectedly harsh critique.[25] The Soviet leaders criticized

---

[22] Méray claimed that "this was a great speech that evaluated the past and illuminated the future. Yet this was not just a simple speech delivered on a crowded square, it was more than that: it was a conversation, a conversation between the people and their leader." Ibid.

[23] On the rise of uncertainty following Stalin's death, see Wolfgang Leonhard, *The Kremlin Since Stalin* (London: Praeger, 1962), 49–68.

[24] The meeting and its effect is discussed in detail by János M. Rainer, *Nagy Imre: Politikai életrajz*, vol. 1 (1896–1953) (Budapest: 1956-os Intézet, 1996), 509–30. See also Pünkösti, *Rákosi bukása*, 19–36.

[25] The notes taken by Béla Szalai at the meeting were published in György T. Varga, "Jegyzőkönyv a szovjet és a magyar párt és állami vezetők tárgyalásairól," *Múltunk* 37, nos. 2–3 (1992): 234–69. Rudolf Földvári's notes were published by Mária Palasik, "Látlelet a magyar függetlenségről," *Kapu* 2, no. 5 (1989): 4–10, For Rákosi's perception of the events: Rákosi, *Visszaemlékezések 1940–1956*, vol. 2, 911–26.

their Hungarian colleagues for the lack of collective decision-making, for the grave economic problems triggered by forced industrialization, and for the violations of law, including show trials and the establishment of internment camps. Even the dogmatism of the cultural scene was addressed at the meetings. The Soviet leaders—of whom Beria was the most active—chose Rákosi as their scapegoat and suggested replacing Stalin's former "best apprentice" with Nagy as prime minister. Apart from evaluating the political "mistakes" of Rákosi, the Presidium also condemned him for promoting the cultic veneration of his own persona. Although the expression "cult of personality" did not appear in the notes taken at the meeting, Rákosi was repeatedly accused of "leaderism" by the Soviet leaders, and he was also blamed for pretending to be infallible.[26] Beria criticized Rákosi for behaving as if he could never err; Molotov described Rákosi as someone who thought he "knows everything, sees everything, and is always competent"; Anastas Mikoian claimed that Rákosi had become overweening; and Khrushchev blamed the MDP secretary for not being able to work in a collective way.[27]

The Presidium came up with a series of suggestions concerning the correction measures to be implemented. According to these guidelines, the Hungarian delegation worked out the principles of the new Party line while still in Moscow—a Party line that was discussed and eventually approved by the Soviet Party leadership on June 16. The draft became the basis of the policies that were instituted after June 1953, in the period commonly labeled the "New Course."

As soon as the delegation returned to Hungary, the Secretariat summoned the Politburo and the Central Committee in order to authorize the introduction of the new policies. On June 20, at the meeting of the Politburo, Rákosi presented his report—prepared for the Central Committee—on the Moscow consultations, seeking the approval of the Party Department. The discussion of the draft provided a forum for the first

---

[26] Despite the fact that the notes taken at the meeting do not mention the actual phrase "personality cult," it is quite likely that the Soviet leaders used the phrase to criticize Rákosi. Rákosi's subsequent reports before the Politburo and the Central Committee strictly followed the guidelines given by the Presidium, and it is quite unlikely that he would have used the term without being sure of its applicability.

[27] T. Varga, "Jegyzőkönyv," 240–44.

intra-Party criticism of the Rákosi cult.[28] Rákosi's self-criticism was followed by the self-criticism of those Politburo members who had also been condemned in Moscow. Farkas and Révai, for example, both joined the Party secretary in condemning the practice of "leaderism" *(vezérkedés)* and unrestrained self-aggrandizement. They both confessed to having accepted and promoted their own cults. Farkas denounced the exaggerated veneration of his persona in the army, whereas Révai acknowledged his quasi-dictatorial position in the cultural sphere that triggered the spreading of "excessive bootlicking" *(túlnyalás)* among artists and intellectuals. In his confession, Révai referred to the thunderous applause in celebration of his personality and to descriptions of his announcements as "revelations" by the cultural intelligentsia.

A balance of criticism and self-criticism was also deployed by less prominent Politburo members, all of whom had read the notes that were taken at the consultations in the Kremlin. András Hegedüs asked that Rákosi develop his self-criticism further. István Dénes recalled an incident when Rákosi privately complained about the overextension of the cult but refused to rein it in. Both Hegedüs and Dénes admitted their own responsibility in the emergence of the "cult of personality," like Károly Kiss, who pled guilty to not speaking out against the cult, and Márton Horváth, who voiced his embarrassment for having tolerated the adulation of the MDP secretary in the press. Gerő, in his concluding remarks, admitted that signs of undeserved veneration also appeared concerning his personality and had reached proportions similar to the cults of Farkas and Rákosi. He even identified the Soviet Union as the place where the cult had originated but avoided criticizing Stalin. On the contrary, he continued to use cultic epithets when referring to the deceased Soviet leader.

> Comrades! We were told—this is no consolation for us, however—that this cult of personality originates in the Soviet Union. Our mistake was that the phenomenon emerged in connection with three people: Gerő, Rákosi, and Farkas, who are not particularly great, whereas in the Soviet Union there was a giant, Comrade Stalin. This is our fault and we are responsible.[29]

---

[28] All further references to the meeting are taken from MOL, 276. fond 53/122.
[29] Ibid.

Besides providing a criticism of the Rákosi cult, accompanied by ritual acts of self-criticism, the meeting of the Politburo failed to come up with concrete suggestions to eliminate or temper the veneration of the leader. Although Révai proposed ending the teaching of Party history in Party schools, he remained unsure as to the correct interpretation of Rákosi's role in the history of the working-class movement. Rákosi supported Révai's idea about the re-evaluation of Party history ("Everything should be taken out that is connected with the personality cult") but did not specify what areas of the subject needed to be reconsidered.

"It Was Like a Phonograph Record": The Meeting of the Central Committee on June 27–28

The critique of the cult continued during the session of the Central Committee on June 27–28.[30] The portrait of Rákosi was taken off the wall in the conference room—leaving an ominous mark behind—which foreshadowed the agenda of the meeting of the highest Party organ.[31] At the meeting, Rákosi—according to the expectations of Moscow—performed his ritual self-criticism again, this time in front of an audience that was larger than the Politburo and was less familiar with the new winds blowing from Moscow. Rákosi's report, which had been approved by the Politburo in advance, gave a thorough critique of the policies of the Party before 1953 and denounced the leadership's incorrect methods after 1949.[32] Rákosi's self-criticism, based on Moscow's instructions, emphasized that all errors originated from the lack of collective leadership after 1949 and the emergence of a one-man leadership (his own) that was accompanied by the "cult of personality." Rákosi admitted that he overplayed his role as a leader ("leaderism") and became conceited and overweening while ignoring the principle of Communist modesty. The report underlined the responsibility of the press in the glorification of the leader's persona, and in the promotion of grand epithets attached to Rákosi's name. The Party leader also criticized the routine of calling his announcements revelations:

---

[30] All references to the meeting—if not indicated otherwise—are from MOL, 276. fond 52/24.
[31] Pünkösti, *Rákosi bukása*, 46.
[32] Rákosi's report was published in György T. Varga, "Rákosi Mátyás referátuma az MDP Központi Vezetőségének 1953. júniusi ülésén," *Múltunk* 35, no. 1 (1990): 141–62.

My name was always accompanied by accolades in the press and in our Party organizations. I became the wise leader of the Hungarian people, the best Hungarian apprentice of Lenin and Stalin. If I gave a short speech on some current matters, then they said that I had illuminated the path of the Party.[33]

Rákosi acknowledged that he had endorsed the proliferation of his own cult, which in turn overshadowed the significance of other leaders. He also confessed to concentrating positions in his own hands and admitted that he had exercised personal control over the ÁVH. Because the principle of collective leadership was ignored, Party democracy was suppressed and criticism and self-criticism were neglected. This provoked abuses of power and resulted in a general disdain of cadres, the extensive use of "administrative methods" (i.e., coercion and terror) and the loosening of links with the masses.

Rákosi's self-castigating report was followed by similar contributions, resulting in a collective criticism/self-criticism ritual within the confines of the Central Committee. Although such contributions mostly focused on the political and economic aspects of the wrongdoings of the "Rákosi clique," many speakers addressed the leader cult in one way or another. The first to speak was Imre Nagy, who gave an extensive critique of the "cult of personality." As he was well aware of the limits of Bolshevik criticism rituals, he did not deviate substantially from Rákosi's argument. He thus used the phrase "cult of personality" in the same meta-conceptual framework as the embattled Party secretary had (lack of collective leadership, emergence of a clique leadership, the concentration of positions in the hands of Rákosi, the suppression of Party democracy, criticism and self-criticism, loosening of ties with the masses, lack of Communist modesty, and so on).[34] Nagy's example was followed by subsequent speakers, especially those who had witnessed Rákosi's humiliation in Moscow. These functionaries reiterated the same charges that the Hungarian Party leader raised in his report—which was, in turn, written according to the guidelines received from the Kremlin. However, some members of

---

[33] Ibid., 144.
[34] All subsequent quotations from the meeting are from MOL, 276. fond 52/24.

the Central Committee—particularly regional Party bosses—were less familiar with the Presidium's critique and were thus shocked by the sharpness of Rákosi's self-criticism. They joined the ritual verbal castigation of the leader nonetheless, by mechanically enlisting the concepts that Rákosi used with regard to the cult, but they also added their own personal experiences to the general picture he described (overuse of portraits and quotations, applause, etc.).

The most extensive and most vigorous cult critique at the meeting was that of the leader of the KEB, Károly Kiss. He called the veneration of the leader a monotonous, largely routinized phenomenon, pointing out the rhythmic applause and never-ending cheering at gatherings every time Rákosi's name was mentioned. According to Kiss, the cult "was built to one pattern; it was [like] a phonograph record that was constantly played, but has not been playing clear notes for a long time." Kiss also highlighted the centralized, manufactured nature of the cult, claiming that it had originated in the Party center and was not the product of popular affection toward the Hungarian Party leader. Such an effort to create an "artificial aura" around Rákosi was described as harmful by Kiss, who also criticized Révai and Gerő for tolerating it and failing to voice their disapproval. The ritual nature of the cult, manifested in the lengthy celebration of the leader during festivities in the Opera or at mass meetings, was also addressed by Rudolf Földvári, who admitted—like Kiss—that such expressions of "disgusting sycophancy" were, for the most part, "organized by us." He blamed the Party bureaucracy for making Rákosi believe that he was infallible and for regarding his words as everlasting guidelines. Földvári also criticized the spread of "leaderism" in the lower levels of the Party hierarchy and the emergence of "mini-Rákosis" in regional Party committees. While he referred to the proliferation of sub-cults in the Hungarian context, Révai, in his lengthy contribution, addressed the burgeoning of the cult in the countries of the Soviet bloc. He regarded the development of cultic practices as a common phenomenon in Central and Eastern Europe, but he considered the Hungarian version to be the most inflated and distorted. As an example of distasteful flattery, he recalled an incident when, during a field exercise, the soldiers, echoing the Red Army's famous wartime battle-cry ("For Stalin! For the Motherland!"), shouted "For Rákosi! For the Motherland!"

Even if the criticism of the cults of regional Party bosses was left unelaborated, the bizarre veneration of lesser Party leaders remained a charged issue at the Central Committee meeting. Farkas, Gerő, and Révai were all blamed for accepting the systematic exaltation of their personae and for not trying to restrain its excesses. Farkas received a particularly harsh critique for promoting his cult in the army, and he was also forced to repent in front of the Party leadership. The one to launch the attack on the general was Sándor Nógrádi, who was one of Farkas's closest associates in military affairs. Nógrádi claimed that Farkas craved admiration and played a major part in promoting his own cult: "Comrade Farkas was only happy when his name appeared in the newspaper *Néphadsereg* in connection with some quote, or when he was referred to in the editorial, or when some photo was published of him . . . " Farkas, responding to the accusations, admitted his guilt for "leaderism," self-aggrandizement, and encouraging sycophancy in the army, as well as for ignoring the principle of Communist modesty.

The unusually critical tone of Rákosi's report, and the even stronger criticisms by members of the Party elite, surprised and confused some in the Central Committee, especially regional Party secretaries, who were less familiar with the outcome of the Moscow meeting or were less acquainted with Stalinist criticism/self-criticism rituals. Since the sudden blow to Rákosi's reputation was difficult to digest, some of these people continued to use the cult language in their contributions, trying to diminish the significance of the consequences of the cult. Ferenc Keleti, Gyula Egri, and Ferenc Dávid, for example, all stood up for the MDP secretary and attempted to resuscitate his prestige. The Szolnok County secretary, Dávid, for example, refused to condemn Rákosi for his mistakes, claiming that his "burning love" for the leader had been cemented well before the Communist takeover, and it had not been weakened by the troika's abuses of power. Keleti supported Dávid and argued that popular respect and love for the Party's leaders remained unchanged despite their mistakes. Despite the frail efforts to save Rákosi's prestige, however, the overall atmosphere of the meeting continued to be critical of him. Dávid's contribution, for example, infuriated the Borsod secretary, István Kovács, who blamed Dávid and those like him for promoting sycophantic practices in the Party. Kovács recalled a 1952 letter in which Dávid exercised self-criticism in a disgustingly ingratiating tone and "swore allegiance to Comrade Rákosi in the manner of a lackey and not of a Party member." In spite of the damning criticism, Dávid, in his reply to Kovács, assured the Central Committee of his solid affection for the MDP secretary: "I maintain everything that I wrote in that letter, because I still love Comrade Rákosi, and this is a deep-rooted relationship."

Those who were censured also attempted to temper the wave of criticism. Rákosi and Gerő, for example, when addressing the issue of the cult, talked in generalities and remained somewhat vague with regard to the question of responsibility. Révai recalled incidents when he had actually tried to rein in the excesses of the cult. The writer and fellow-traveler József Darvas also warned the audience not to take criticism too far. He believed that making too much of the errors could backfire, resulting in the loss of popular support for the Party.

> We should be careful not to throw out the baby with the bath water. What do I mean? It is true that an exaggerated personality cult emerged around Comrades Rákosi, Gerő and Révai, but it would be incorrect to claim that there was only that. Truly, there was a deep respect toward these people that is still there, and that will remain. Therefore, we should pay attention to maintaining the right proportions during the execution of the Party decree, in order not to let the power of that affection suddenly pass out of our hands.

Despite efforts to save the remnants of the leaders' prestige, the meeting of the Central Committee became the forum for the most elaborate intra-Party cult criticism in the Rákosi period. Besides the general condemnation of the policies of Rákosi and his clique—cultural dogmatism, economic mismanagement, the abuses of legality—the participants contributed to the formulation of a detailed critique of the leader cult phenomenon. The speakers addressed the cult's rituals (applause and chanting), its manufactured and centrally orchestrated nature, the spreading of the cult and the emergence of mini-Rákosis, and the collective responsibility of the Party bureaucracy for the promotion of the leader's exaltation. Besides that, members of the Central Committee often referred to the cult's most excessive manifestations, such as the overuse of portraits and quotations in public spaces and the tendency to interpret the leaders' utterances as revelations. Even the Soviet origins and the international dimensions of leader reverence in the Soviet bloc were referred to—although Stalin was never criticized. Nevertheless, the decree that was eventually accepted by the Central Committee failed to present an in-depth analysis of the phenomenon. It was more in line with the general—and rather vague—interpretation presented by Rákosi and Gerő.[35] The resolution—like Rákosi's report—identified the lack of collective leadership as the source of all problems. It claimed that one-man leadership had prevented the "healthy development" of cadres, impeded the normal functioning of Party organizations, and poisoned the Party's relationship with the masses. According to the document, the emergence of a one-man leadership was accompanied by the development of the "cult of personality" and "leaderism" that overshadowed the principle of Communist modesty. Although the cult itself was defined by the resolution as a by-product of dictatorial leadership, Rákosi and Farkas were nevertheless stigmatized as those most responsible for its promotion. However, the decree of the Central Committee kept the discussion of the cult at a basic level, ignoring the predominance of the phenomenon in Communist propaganda before June 1953. The document also failed to outline the exact measures to be taken to eliminate the cult and its remnants from the MDP. Although the resolution ordered the revision of teaching material on Party history for Party schools, the decree indicates that the Party elite was convinced that the replacement of clique leadership with collective leadership would—as if by magic—make the cultic veneration of leaders disappear.

The first major attempt to bid farewell to Stalinist political rituals was expressed in traditional Stalinist terms. The meeting of the MDP's Central Committee respected the rules and conventions of criticism/self-criticism rituals that characterized similar assemblies of the Party elite in the period of High Stalinism.[36] During the session on June 27–28, Rákosi performed an apology ritual according to the accepted norms, while the membership of the Central Committee joined the rite through the mechanic repetition of accusations and charges raised by the Party secretary. The denunciation of scapegoats, combined with the assumption of collective responsibility for the errors, was meant to demonstrate unity and cohesion in times of confusion and disarray.

---

[35] "A Központi Vezetőség határozata a párt politikai irányvonalában elkövetett hibákról, s az ezek kijavításával kapcsolatos feladatokról," in Izsák, *A Magyar Dolgozók Pártja határozatai*, 188–206. See also MOL, 276. fond 52/24.

[36] On criticism rituals in the Central Committee of the CPSU, see Getty, "*Samokritika* Rituals in the Stalinist Central Committee."

"We Spit in Our Own Face If We Discredit Our Leaders": Cult-Dismantling Efforts during the "New Course" (June 1953–March 1955)

The resolution of the Central Committee signaled the beginning of de-Stalinization in Hungary. As was the case with Stalinization, the process of de-Stalinization was initiated by Moscow, and as the examples of the GDR and Hungary showed, the Soviet leadership was ready to intervene in local politics if it sensed hesitation and doubt in executing the required measures. Rákosi, for example, had already been invited to Moscow in late May 1953, when the Presidium informed him of the need to modify MDP policy, but due to the Party secretary's hesitant attitude in carrying out the necessary reforms, the Soviet leaders chose a harsher way to discipline the unwilling Hungarian leader, which eventually took place during the consultations in mid-June.[37] In Hungary the new political line was ratified by the meeting of the Central Committee on June 27–28, and Imre Nagy, the new prime minister, inaugurated the "New Course" in his speech in Parliament on July 4.[38] The new government, which did not include Rákosi, introduced a series of measures to improve the popular mood. As in the Soviet Union, the pace of industrialization was slowed down, and more attention was paid to agricultural problems and the production of consumer goods. The modifications in economic policy and the effort to improve the population's standard of living were followed by the disbanding of some internment camps and the gradual release of political prisoners. Changes in politics were combined with the restructuring of Party and government institutions. According to the directives of Moscow, the positions of the Party's general secretary and the

---

[37] On the meeting in late May: Rákosi, *Visszaemlékezések 1940–1956*, vol. 2, 909–11.

[38] On the "New Course" in Hungary: Bálint Szabó, *Az "ötvenes évek"* (Budapest: Kossuth, 1986), 65–226; János M. Rainer, *Nagy Imre. Politikai életrajz, 1953–1958*, vol. 2 (Budapest: 1956-os Intézet, 1999), 9–140; Pünkösti, *Rákosi bukása*, 5–280. See also Sándor Balogh, "Politikai reformpróbálkozások és kudarcaik 1953 és 1956 között," *Társadalmi Szemle* 44, nos. 8–9 (1989): 19–35; Magdolna Baráth, "Az MDP vezetése és a rehabilitáció (1953–1956)," *Múltunk* 44, no. 4 (1999): 40–97; Károly Urbán, "Nagy Imre első miniszterelnöksége," *Társadalmi Szemle* 47, no. 6 (1992): 72–81; Miklós Vásárhelyi, "Az első meghiúsított reformkísérlet. Az 1953-as kormányprogram," in Miklós Vásárhelyi, *Ellenzékben* (Budapest: Szabad Tér Kiadó 1989), 238–313. A comparative analysis of the Soviet and Hungarian "New Course" projects is provided by Károly Urbán, "Nagy Imre és G. M. Malenkov. Két miniszterelnök Sztálin után," *Múltunk* 41, no. 1 (1996): 129–80. See also Valerij Muszatov, "Szovjet-magyar kapcsolatok, 1953–1956," in *Évkönyv V: 1996/1997*, ed. János Bak (Budapest: 1956-os Intézet, 1997), 43–48.

prime minister were separated—with the latter gaining more power—and the number of ministries was reduced. The authority of the ÁVH was substantially restricted, and the secret police was incorporated into the Ministry of Internal Affairs.

Despite the departure from Stalinist political practices, the "New Course" in the Soviet bloc remained limited in scope and featured half-hearted measures and contradictory policies. This was largely because only a few changes took place at the apex of the Party after the death of Stalin. Despite the fierce power struggles in the leadership—marked by Beria's elimination in the Soviet Union—Stalin's heirs in the bloc redistributed the most important positions among themselves. Thus the top leadership of the Communist parties of Central and Eastern Europe remained more or less intact.[39] Although Gottwald died soon after Stalin, his cult lingered on, while Gheorghiu-Dej in Romania and Bierut in Poland both kept their positions. Ulbricht in the GDR also remained in power, despite the June 1953 uprising in East Berlin.[40] Only Chervenkov lost his position as general secretary, although he remained prime minister of Bulgaria until 1956.

The Hungarian "New Course" was also ambiguous. Uncertainty among the MDP's leaders was caused partly by Moscow's unpredictability; its stance constantly shifted according to the changes in power relations within the Soviet leadership (such as the Beria affair, or Khrushchev's ascendance). Although Rákosi's self-abasement at the Central Committee meeting was proposed by the Presidium, due to yet another intervention of the CPSU—urged by the June uprising in East Germany—the decision was not made public (until the 1980s), and the Party membership only received information about the decree in a condensed form.[41] At Nagy, Gerő, and Rákosi's July 8 meeting with the Presidium in Moscow, where the Hungarian leaders—along with their Romanian and Bulgarian

---

[39] Robert Service, "The Road to the Twentieth Congress," *Soviet Studies* 33, no. 2 (1981): 232–45. Beria's life was assessed in Amy Knight, *Beria, Stalin's First Lieutenant* (Princeton: Princeton University Press, 1993).

[40] On the Berlin uprising, see Christian Ostermann, ed., *Uprising in East Germany 1953: The Cold War, the German Question, and the First Major Upheaval behind the Iron Curtain* (Budapest-New York: CEU Press, 2001).

[41] Pünkösti, *Rákosi bukása*, 55–59.

comrades—were informed of Beria's arrest, the Soviet leadership again warned them not to take self-criticism too far.[42] Although at the same meeting, the Soviet leaders reassured Nagy of their support, Rákosi perceived the warning as a call to restrain the scope of criticism, and at the Budapest Party *aktíva* on July 11, he delivered a speech that was composed according to pre-June rhetorical standards and differed greatly in style from Nagy's speech in Parliament, which announced the beginning of the "New Course." While Nagy's proclamation was welcomed by the overall population, Rákosi's talk convinced Party functionaries of the continuity of the "old line." The two speeches gave the impression of the existence of a dual leadership, which contributed considerably to the ambiguous and incoherent coloring of "New Course" policies. Despite Nagy's commitment to the "June Path," his efforts were constantly impeded by the Party bureaucracy, which remained dependent on and loyal to Rákosi. Rákosi, who remained first secretary of the Party, attempted to block Nagy's feeble reform attempts and tried to regain the trust of the Soviet leadership. The power struggle between Rákosi and Nagy shaped the whole period of the "New Course" and ended with the reinforcement of Rákosi's political positions and the denunciation and removal of Nagy in March 1955.

Ambivalence and half-hearted measures also marked the dismantling of the Rákosi cult. Since Moscow's proclamations in this respect at times seemed volatile, the Hungarian leadership remained uncertain as to the limits of possible cult criticism and the extent to which the glorification of leaders could and should be reduced. The Party leadership apparently wanted to curb the excesses of the "cult of personality" quietly, in order to prevent the criticism from spreading to the population at large. Keeping in mind the Presidium's suggestion that "the errors should be corrected in a way that does not damage Rákosi's prestige, because that is also the prestige of the Party," the Hungarian Party leaders excluded the public from the dismantling of the cult and tried to save what was left of the leadership's credibility.[43] Decisions condemning the veneration of leaders

---

[42] Rákosi, *Visszaemlékezések 1940–1956*, vol. 2, 937–39.

[43] This was suggested by the Presidium at the meeting with the Hungarian Party delegation in Moscow on May 5, 1954. The notes of the meeting were published by János M. Rainer and Károly Urbán, eds., "Konzultációk. Dokumentumok a magyar és a szovjet pártvezetők két moszkvai találkozójáról 1954–1955-ben," *Múltunk* 37, no. 3 (1992): 124–49.

were rarely issued by the central Party organs in the period, and even if they were, they were never published, as happened to the Central Committee's decree. Furthermore, the Party center did not always give clear instructions on how to abolish cultic practices, leaving the regional Party committees unsure what the new leadership expected. This resulted in considerable confusion at the local level and created grounds for extremism. Some regional Party sections interpreted the incoherent signs from the center in a radical way, which led to the banning of applause and the sudden removal of Rákosi's portraits in some places. In some regions, however, where the prestige of the local Party boss was dependent on Rákosi's halo, the purging of the cult proceeded much more slowly and with less resolve. The inconsistent attitude of Party authorities to the adoration of its leaders, and the inadequate explanation of the changes in cult policies, triggered bewilderment among the MDP membership. As mood reports from the summer of 1953 show, rank-and-file Party members reacted to the new Party line with a wide variety of sentiments. There was disappointment, rage, and devotion, but most of all, there was confusion. Respondents from Zala County, for example, did not understand the lack of applause after Rákosi's speech to the Budapest Party *aktíva*; in Ózd a disappointed worker tore a Rákosi portrait off the wall; and rumors spread around the country that Rákosi and Farkas had been arrested, or had fled to Moscow.[44] In Szeged, Party members expressed their great disillusionment in Rákosi, whom they had thought of as the Hungarian Stalin, whereas one villager felt reassured about the continuity of the "old line" after Rákosi's announcement on July 11.[45]

Rákosi's reluctance to commit himself to the "New Course" and his ambiguous attitude to the elimination of the cult contributed significantly to the controversial and half-hearted nature of anti-cult measures. Although it was he who suggested the removal of his portraits in 1954, and although he also apparently supported Révai's argument about the need to rewrite Party history, he still had trouble digesting the criticism targeted at him and the diminishing of his authority. Rákosi remained convinced that Moscow's critique had been a mistake, and he identified Beria as the

---

[44] Pünkösti, *Rákosi bukása*, 71–80.
[45] Ibid., 66, 80.

culprit responsible for what he saw as the rude and erroneous reprimand he received in June 1953. Despite the fact that the Presidium reassured the Hungarian delegation during the May 1954 consultations of its support for the Nagy government, the Soviet leaders' inconsistent pronouncements about the need to maintain Rákosi's prestige, and their occasional warnings to temper criticism in general, reassured Rákosi of the correctness of his beliefs. For example, when Rákosi was advised by the Kremlin to moderate the tone of the Central Committee's decision in June 1953, he did not hesitate to suggest withholding the Party decree altogether.[46] In a similar way, when Rákosi was informed of Beria's arrest, he became convinced that the signal to restore the "old line" had finally arrived, as was reflected in the tone of his speech to the Party *aktíva* on July 11.[47] Rákosi's contemporaries immediately recognized his unwillingness to support the new Party line. Nagy, for example, repeatedly complained to the Soviet ambassador, Fiodor D. Kiseliov, about the difficulties of "re-educating" the MDP secretary. Nagy regretted that Rákosi could not accept the curtailment of his authority and the new patterns of political decision-making. At the meeting with Kiseliov on January 12, 1954, the Hungarian prime minister expressed disappointment that Rákosi was more preoccupied with his reputation than with everyday political matters.[48]

The Party leader's lack of commitment toward the "New Course" and his ambiguous attitude toward the withdrawal of the cult had a major effect on the way the Party bureaucracy perceived the disruption of the cult. Since Rákosi gave no clear signals in public as to the proper attitude toward the veneration of leaders, Party functionaries who were dependent on the Party secretary—as well as rank-and-file Party members—remained uncertain of the necessary actions to be taken with regard to the cult. Moreover, Rákosi's announcements, such as the one on July 11 that emphasized continuity with pre-June policies, gave the impression that

---

[46] Magdolna Baráth, *Szovjet nagyköveti iratok Magyarországról 1953–1956. Kiszlejov és Andropov titkos jelentései* (Budapest: Napvilág, 2002), 104.

[47] Rákosi's memoirs indicate that he never stopped believing that Beria was responsible for the unfavorable political changes in June 1953.

[48] According to Nagy, Rákosi made a great fuss about the way Politburo and government members were seated in the Parliament, but he never read the report on the peasants who quit the kolkhozes. Baráth, *Szovjet nagyköveti iratok*, 119.

although things had changed somewhat, he was still the man in charge. Party functionaries thus showed a mixture of bewilderment and hesitation about carrying out the orders of the Party center on the dismantling of the cult. The overall uncertainty and confusion, and the occasional resistance of Party functionaries to devote themselves to anti-cult policies, was criticized by the Central Committee at its meeting on October 31, 1953.[49] The Department admitted that the dismantling of the cult proceeded slowly and was impeded by Party functionaries who became frustrated by the tide of criticism and lost the motivation to correct their previous mistakes. Although the Central Committee's resolution warned the Party membership not to perceive the "New Course" as a short detour from the regular Party line, Party functionaries showed doubt and vacillation over the task of eradicating the cult throughout the entire period.[50] The attempt to tone down the cult while simultaneously maintaining some of its aspects can be recognized in the statements of those regional Party secretaries, Party functionaries, and members of the pre-1953 leadership who owed their allegiance to the MDP leader (Egri, Dénes, Dávid, Farkas, Horváth, Földvári, and Lajos Ács). But even those who were purged or removed from the Party leadership before the "New Course," such as Kovács, Kádár, and István Szatmári, viewed the process of cult deconstruction in a similar way.

The reluctance of Party functionaries to face the task of eradicating the cult's remnants became apparent soon after the Politburo accepted the proposal to remove Rákosi's portraits and busts from public spaces on March 31, 1954.[51] The suggestion, put forward by Rákosi himself, ordered the removal of Rákosi's likenesses from government and Party premises and the offices of other Party- or state-affiliated authorities. The same resolution instructed the leaders of regional Party committees to remove the pictures of all other members of the Politburo as well. Doubts about the effective execution of the decree, however, were already raised at the meeting. The incident that stimulated a discussion about the appropriate methods of dismantling the cult was the letter from the Borsod County

---

[49] MOL, 276. fond 52/25.
[50] "A Központi Vezetőség határozata az 1953. júniusi ülésén hozott határozatok végrehajtásáról," in Izsák, *A Magyar Dolgozók Pártja határozatai*, 216–25.
[51] MOL, 276. fond 53/168.

secretary István Kovács which caused a minor storm within the Politburo.[52] Kovács, who had been a prominent member of the leadership until he was almost purged in early 1953, perceived the "New Course" as an opportunity to regain his previous position in the Party hierarchy. His political maneuvers, which involved regular visits to the Soviet ambassador and subtle intrigue against both Nagy and the former Rákosi clique, began with a letter in which he criticized the division in the leadership—i.e., the Nagy-Rákosi "duel"—as confusing to Party functionaries and threatening to the Party's authority. Writing about the "cult of personality," Kovács welcomed its dismantling but expressed dissatisfaction with the radical way the issue was handled. The letter claimed that due to the Party's failure to clarify the proper use of portraits and busts, and to establish the right proportions of applause, the dismantling process led to extremes and had undesirable effects. Kovács referred to the commemoration of the thirtieth anniversary of Lenin's death; at the Opera, after Dobi's speech welcoming foreign guests and delegations, including the Soviet ambassador, no one in the audience applauded. The same cold reception marked the visits of prominent Party members to the countryside. Kovács suggested that although there was no need for meetings with people applauding every minute, the issue of paying respect to the Party's leaders in order to re-establish their "necessary prestige" should be raised in a careful way.[53] Despite the fact that the discussion of the letter was postponed, Földvári was quick enough to back Kovács, declaring that "every leader should be given the respect they deserve."[54]

Kovács's letter was not the only sign that indicated the discomfort of the Party bureaucracy with the cult's withdrawal. During the week that followed the Politburo's resolution on March 31, the Rákosi Secretariat received several complaints about the inappropriate explanation of the decree to the Party membership. Szatmári reported to Rákosi on April 5 that those at the Party meeting in the Kistext factory were largely unhappy with the removal of Rákosi's portraits and warned the leaders that if it continued, it would provoke opposition among the workers. Szatmári also

---

[52] On the Kovács letter, see Rainer, *Nagy Imre*, vol. 2, 55–57. For Rákosi's version of the story: Rákosi, *Visszaemlékezések 1940–1956*, vol. 2, 953–54.
[53] MOL, 276. fond 65/41.
[54] MOL, 276. fond 53/168.

spoke of the confusion among Central Committee members triggered by the Politburo's resolution. Since most of them had not been informed of the decision beforehand, they remained unsure of its applicability, and some local Party sections even declared the document to be the work of the enemy. On April 7, Zoltán Fodor wrote to the MDP's Secretariat to complain about the way the Politburo's decree was executed. Fodor criticized the excesses of cult dismantling and envisaged a situation in which the Rákosi Works would be renamed the "Politburo Works." In his opinion, Rákosi should have declared in public the needlessness of portraits, and then Rákosi's likenesses could have been gradually withdrawn from Party and government offices. In a note to Rákosi about Fodor's letter on April 9, Farkas also asserted that "the way we are orchestrating the removal of Rákosi portraits is not correct."[55]

Due to the negative feedback from Party organizations concerning the removal of pictures and busts, the Politburo decided to re-evaluate its previous decision and eventually modified the decree on April 14.[56] At the meeting, where both the Budapest Party meeting and the Kovács letter were discussed, the problem of establishing the limits of cult criticism was a recurring theme. Farkas expressed his disappointment with the lack of applause and the "ice-cold reception of Politburo members" at the Party meeting, and Gerő called the same meeting gray and monotonous, acknowledging Party members' general puzzlement concerning the right attitude toward the Party's leaders. The debate on what was perceived as excessive in the dismantling of the cult continued when the Politburo moved on to discuss the Kovács letter. Farkas criticized the hasty removal of Rákosi's pictures and the withholding of applause when Rákosi or members of the Politburo appeared in public. Although he admitted that it was wrong to create an "artificial cult," he added that it was equally wrong to "artificially undermine" the leaders' prestige. The radical—or, as Farkas put it, "anarchist"—approach to the dissolution of the cult threatened to undermine the reputation of the leadership. Farkas claimed that "we spit in our own face [if] we discredit our leaders." At the end of the discussion, even Rákosi warned the Politburo—in his usual

---

[55] MOL, 276. fond 65/41.
[56] MOL, 276. fond 53/170.

paternalistic style—not to overdo criticism and the tempering of the leader cult. "Be careful, comrades, not to strike the Party's reputation to death during the elimination of the personality cult."

As a result of the resistance of both the Party bureaucracy and the dogmatist section of the Party leadership to dismantling the cult, the Politburo resolution was modified, and the emphasis shifted toward promoting the idea of collective leadership.[57] Although the original proposal to remove Rákosi's pictures and statues from government and Party offices remained valid, the decision suggested the installation of the portraits of Politburo members on the premises of Party and mass organizations, and in government buildings. Despite the rephrasing of the decree and the overall attempt to promote the Politburo as a collective body instead of only Rákosi, the implementation of the resolution provoked further disdain and confusion among rank-and-file Party members and Party functionaries. Complaints were submitted from the main Party school about the rapid removal of pictures, and mood reports criticized the practice of removing the portraits in food stores in full view of the customers. However, cases where a local Party committee refused to get rid of the portraits of the leaders, or re-installed them after some time, were also reported to the Party center. The degree of uncertainty among the population, who were accustomed to the omnipresence of cultic imagery, manifested itself in requests to take the portraits home, and inquiries about the fate of institutions named after Rákosi.[58] One member of the Central Committee, József Köböl, at the meeting of the department on October 1–3, 1954, recalled that he first perceived the order to remove Rákosi's portraits from offices as an enemy provocation.[59] The improper execution of the decree and the bewilderment it caused was also criticized by Kádár (who was released from prison in the autumn of 1954) in a November 1954 letter to Rákosi in which he condemned the inappropriate application of the Politburo's instructions and emphasized the need to increase Rákosi's visibility.[60]

---

[57] "A Politikai Bizottság határozata a személyi kultusz maradványainak felszámolására," in Izsák, *A Magyar Dolgozók Pártja Határozatai*, 258.
[58] Pünkösti, *Rákosi bukása*, 164.
[59] MOL, 276. fond 52/27.
[60] MOL, 276. fond 65/44.

Although the Party bureaucracy's hesitation to curb the cult posed obstacles to eliminating it, the gradual disillusionment of cult mediators led to a halt in the spread of the phenomenon during the "New Course." The problems of cult promotion that had been observed before June 1953 persisted after the proclamation of the "June Path," and the loosening of the Party center's grip further contributed to the slow erosion of the Rákosi myth. Under these new circumstances Communist propaganda became less pervasive; central directives were issued less often, and their execution was monitored less thoroughly than it had been before June. Although the commitment of agitators, people's educators, and teachers to transmit propaganda messages had been frequently questioned before June 1953, their motivation was weakened further due to the waning of control during the "New Course."[61]

Besides the deterioration in the efficacy of agitators and pedagogues in promoting the MDP's ideology, the gradual disillusionment of the young, Party-affiliated intelligentsia after 1953 also contributed significantly to the disintegration of the leader cult. Most sycophantic literary praises, and many of the eulogizing articles in *Szabad Nép*, were composed by these people. Therefore, their disenchantment with their idol during the "New Course" dealt a severe blow to the cult's construction. The most important experiences that influenced their political views in 1953–1955 included personal visits to the countryside and to factories, encounters with former political prisoners (such as Géza Losonczy, Ferenc Donáth, Sándor Haraszti, and Kádár), and the generally more liberal tone of the press, which permitted the publication of concealed or moderate criticism (such as *Irodalmi Újság, Művelt Nép*, and *Új Hang*).

The beginning of unrest among the young literary intelligentsia is usually connected to the publication of Péter Kuczka's poem, *Nyírségi Napló* (Nyírség Diary), in *Irodalmi Újság* on November 7, 1953, which caused a rift in the ranks of Communist writers.[62] Kuczka's poem, inspired by the

---

[61] Reports about the weakening of the motivation of agitators after June 1953 can be found at MOL, 276. fond 65/62. Reports about the circumstances of teachers MOL, 276. fond 65/341.

[62] The emergence of intellectual resistance during the "New Course" has a rich literature. See especially Aczél and Méray, *The Revolt of the Mind*, 184–231; János M. Rainer, *Az író helye. Viták a magyar irodalmi sajtóban 1953–1956* (Budapest: Magvető, 1990); Éva Standeisky, "Hit-viták. Az írók és az 1953-as 'új szakasz,'" *Mozgó Világ* 29, no. 8 (2003): 27–43.

author's confrontation with rural poverty in the Nyírség region, was not, however, an isolated outcry of frustration. An explicit cult critique was conveyed by Ernő Urbán's drama *Uborkafa* (The Cucumber Tree), which was staged with great success in the National Theater in late 1953. In the drama, a biting satire on the "mini-Rákosis" and their abuses of power on a local level, the protagonist—a factory director—who decorates his office with his own portraits is driven away by the locals.[63]

The enlightenment of Communist writers was followed by the disillusionment of the young journalists of *Szabad Nép* in late 1954. During a heated meeting of the newspaper's editorial board on October 22–25, where Tibor Méray called for a "cleansing storm," the disappointed journalists (János Kornai, Péter Kende, Tibor Tardos, Lajos Szilvási, Endre Kövesi, et al.) fervently criticized the falsification of local election results, the forging of letters of gratitude to the leader and the Party, and the practice of embellishing the situation of industrial workers.[64]

With the gradual sobering of young Communist intellectuals, one of the most important screws fell out of the machinery of cult production. The disillusioned journalists and writers turned to Nagy for political guidance and became the core of the intra-Party opposition group that was to solidify in early 1956. Although in 1955, the Party leadership still possessed the means to discipline them, the retreat of the most effective and most committed agents of the Rákosi cult from the field of propaganda created a vacancy that remained unoccupied for the rest of the Rákosi era.

Despite the hesitation to "deconstruct" the leader's persona, the cult suffered a remarkable decline from July 1953 onwards. This largely had to do with the decrease in the intensity of leader-centered propaganda, and with the general reorientation of the APO's focus. The leader cult was no longer the dominant propaganda campaign, and the language of the cult became less pervasive. The popularization of Rákosi was limited to the press, as it had been in the coalition years. References to Rákosi's persona

---

[63] Aczél and Méray, *The Revolt of the Mind*, 211–12. Urbán was put under political pressure, however, and eventually had to rewrite the play.

[64] On the meeting of *Szabad Nép*'s journalists: Péter Kende, "A Szabad Nép szerkesztőségében," in *Tanulmányok a magyar forradalomról*, ed. Gyula Borbándi and József Molnár (Munich: Aurora könyvek, 1996), 119–32; László Szalay, "Előhang 1954-ből: A Szabad Nép taggyűlése," *Világosság* 35, no. 10 (1994): 48–56.

became less frequent, and the eulogizing style of the articles focusing on the Party leader was significantly tempered. Applause and cheering featured less often at the public appearances of the Party secretary, and there were fewer insertions in newspapers indicating the alleged enthusiasm of the audience—although the tone of such articles never became critical or pejorative. The relative modesty of applauding rituals is exemplified by audience reactions to Rákosi's six-hour report at the Third Congress of the MDP in May 1954. As Árpád Pünkösti has observed, out of the ninety-one-minute fragment of Rákosi's speech in which the elimination of the cult was listed as an achievement, only 6 percent was occupied by applause. Cheering and the rhythmic chanting of the Party leader's name were also abandoned—even the mention of Lenin did not receive any outcry—and the Party was hailed only once.[65] In addition, the literary glorifications of Rákosi's character disappeared during the "New Course," and the leader's image became less omnipresent. The number of portraits carried at demonstrations and the number of portraits appearing in the press were reduced, and a remarkable number of busts and pictures were quietly removed. The decline of Rákosi's symbolic stature also had an impact on state protocol procedures. During the period of the "New Course," Rákosi stopped receiving and sending official invitations for national holidays and festivities, and on one protocol list at least—a 1955 ceremony at the Opera—he was relegated to the eighth position.[66]

The tempering of the cult was also manifested in attempts to rewrite Party history. At the meeting of the Politburo on June 20, 1953, Révai already emphasized the urgency of the issue, and Rákosi supported him. In the interest of the reinterpretation of Party history, the APO submitted a proposal on July 20 that transferred authority in that field. Besides admitting that "the cult of personality prevailed in teaching material," the document restored the authority of the Hungarian Academy of Sciences to coordinate the functioning of working groups in history. By doing so, it weakened the status of the Institute for the History of the Working-Class Movement as the main arbiter in the field of the history of the Communist

---

[65] Pünkösti, *Rákosi bukása*, 179–80.
[66] MOL, 276. fond 89/163.

movement.⁶⁷ The teaching material in Party schools was quickly revised, and Rákosi proudly reported to the Central Committee on October 31 that the most excessive manifestations of the "cult of personality" had been erased from the curriculum.⁶⁸ Apart from the sudden removal of cultic references from the material of history courses in Party-affiliated educational institutions, there was an attempt to formulate a more thorough reinterpretation of Party history. One of the first results of "New Course historiography" was reviewed by the Politburo on March 31, 1954, when the Party leaders discussed a draft—submitted by a committee including Erzsébet Andics, Dezső Nemes, Zoltán Bíró, and Zoltán Szántó—on the history of the Hungarian Communist Party between 1929 and 1939.⁶⁹ Although the manuscript emphasized Rákosi's leading role in the course of events, and it was decorated with quotations from Stalin, the document significantly differed from pre-1953 textbooks. Rákosi was still portrayed as the unquestionable leader of the Hungarian working-class movement; nevertheless, the biographical prism through which Party history had previously been viewed was abandoned, and the life story of the MDP secretary was separated from the narrative of the history of the Communist Party. During the discussion of the material, which was meant to be used in Party schools, even the role of Béla Kun was raised. Although the Politburo's decision did not remove the label "deviationist" from the leader of the 1919 Hungarian Republic of Soviets, it declared that Kun was not always wrong and that a "politically correct characterization" of his personality was needed.⁷⁰

The decay of the Rákosi cult triggered the decline of the cultic veneration of lesser leaders at the lower levels of the Party hierarchy. The Party center acknowledged with embarrassment that the phenomenon had flourished in local Party committees and that regional Party bosses had often promoted the sycophantic veneration of their personae in their own

---

⁶⁷ MOL, 276. fond 65/62.
⁶⁸ MOL, 276. fond 52/25.
⁶⁹ MOL, 276. fond 53/168.
⁷⁰ Although Rákosi was labeled the leader of the Soviet Republic of 1919, he was not in favor of deleting Kun from Party history. During the meeting of the committee responsible for writing the history of the Party, on November 3, 1951, Rákosi declared that "Kun can't be left out" from the narrative of the Hungarian Republic of Soviets. MOL, 276. fond 65/80.

backyard. The Szolnok regional Party secretary, for example, was received in a village with a triumphal arch decorated with flowers. Another local Party secretary in Pest County was accompanied to a meeting by a motorcycle escort. A third one, in Kőszeg, made a lesser functionary stand in the corner for an hour because he dared to approach him for advice.[71] Similar incidents of "leaderism" and abuses of power were reported from many places. Local Party secretaries were often reported to have suppressed those who criticized them and even used the ÁVH for personal aims, such as the arrest of their political rivals. There were attempts to curtail the proliferation of mini-tyrants and the spreading of sub-cults before 1953, but the anti-cult milieu of the "New Course" created new grounds to do away with them.

Due to the new political atmosphere, the cult of Rákosi was not supplemented after June 1953. However, the myth surrounding him persisted, through the maintenance of tropes that had been part of his myth even before the Communist takeover (the myth of Salgótarján, the Rákosi trials, and the rebuilding myth). Nevertheless, the "June Path" disrupted the rising trajectory of the Rákosi cult and narrowed its range significantly. The efforts to dismantle the cult in 1953–1954, however, remained rather limited and controversial. Although some of Rákosi's pictures were taken down, they were soon reinstated alongside the portraits of the entire Politburo. Also, apart from the tempering of the cult's excessive visual manifestations and the slight modification of "cultic" Party history, other aspects of the cult received little or no attention from the central Party organs. School textbooks, for example, continued to teem with quotations from Rákosi, and his life remained the subject of history books in both primary and secondary schools. As the first secretary of the MDP, Rákosi also received notable attention from the press. Rákosi's public appearances were reported less often than in previous years, and there were no greetings to him for his birthday. Nevertheless, if an account of a visit or a speech by him was published, it received considerable attention. For example, on May 25, 1954, *Magyar Nemzet* published Rákosi's speech at the Third Party Congress on six full pages. Even the incidental remarks indicating audience reaction to the leader's words resurfaced every now

---

[71] Pünkösti, *Rákosi bukása*, 81.

and then.[72] Another sign that the cult critique was restricted in 1953–1954 was the fact that the luminaries at the summit of the Communist pantheon remained untouchable. The Politburo's decision to remove Rákosi's pictures in April 1954, for example, forbade the removal of the portraits of Marx, Engels, Lenin, and Stalin.[73] Although the waves of criticism did not reach the highest echelons of the cult hierarchy, the manifestations of "leaderism" in the lower levels of the Party structure were quickly squelched. However, even there it is difficult to discern a consistent strategy applied by the central authorities to overcome the traces of the "cult of personality." It appears as if the first attempts at the cult's deconstruction were spontaneous, ad hoc measures. In addition, the goal emerged, albeit inconsistently, to replace the "cult of personality" with a "cult of collective leadership." The problems in cult-dismantling were rooted in the attitude of the Party bureaucracy, which mostly remained hesitant—or even resistant—to take the necessary measures. Nevertheless, the disillusionment of the young intelligentsia and the fading of the commitment of lesser cult agents—such as agitators, people's educators, and teachers—severely damaged the cult's constitution.

The Cult's Renaissance in 1955

The meeting of the Central Committee in October 1954 saw the triumph of Nagy's political ideas over the Rákosi-Gerő line.[74] Nagy, however, did not have much time to enjoy the advantages of victory. By the beginning of December, the Rákosi group counter-attacked. Rákosi's offensive against his major political rival was backed by the Soviet leadership, which, after the fall of Malenkov, became more concerned with the worrying news about the strengthening of intellectual dissidence and about the "rightist tendencies" of Nagy's article, published after the meeting of the Central Committee.[75] After returning from a lengthy stay in Moscow, where he gained the Kremlin's consent to condemn the political views of Nagy,

---

[72] See, for example, the issue of *Népszava*, February 7, 1954: "Endless, stormy applause, cries of hurrah!"

[73] "A Politikai Bizottság határozata a személyi kultusz…," 258.

[74] The minutes of the meeting are in MOL, 276. fond 52/27. The significance of the meeting has been assessed by Rainer, *Nagy Imre*, vol. 2, 81–95.

[75] *Szabad Nép*, October 20, 1954.

Rákosi presented a devastating criticism of the political line represented by the prime minister.[76] At the meeting of the Politburo on December 1, 1954, Rákosi accused Nagy of rightist deviation and excessive self-criticism that had resulted in the decline of the Party's authority.[77] According to the norms of Stalinist criticism rituals, Nagy was also accused of promoting his own "cult of personality." The narrative of cult criticism that had been in use during the "New Course" mostly with regard to Rákosi was now turned against Nagy by Ács.

> We are fighting the cult of personality, but are we about to create another one at the same time? I have told the Secretariat that a new personality cult is emerging. No matter how we look at it, Comrade Nagy is perceived by many as the only man who sees politics correctly, who dares to speak his mind, and who says more than the Party does.

Nagy's humiliation continued at the next meeting of the Politburo, and during the consultations with the Soviet leadership in Moscow on January 8, 1955, where he received a reprimand almost as severe as the one that damaged Rákosi's prestige nearly a year and a half before.[78] The waves of criticism culminated at the March 2–4, 1955, meeting of the Central Committee that defined rightist deviation as the greatest threat and stigmatized Nagy as its personification.[79] The meeting, which discredited the concept of the "New Course" but also condemned Farkas as the scapegoat for "leftist" errors, was meant to demonstrate the Party leadership's unity in a ritual way. However, Nagy, who was subsequently removed from all his Party, government, and civilian positions, refused to participate in the standardized rite of criticism/self-criticism that was organized according to Stalinist norms.[80] The violation of the Party's ritual practices

---

[76] On Rákosi's political maneuvering, see his memoirs: Rákosi, *Visszaemlékezések 1940–1956*, vol. 2, 970. The counterattack of hard-liners was already foreshadowed by József Darvas's article, "A túllicitálók," published in *Szabad Nép* a few days before Rákosi's return: *Szabad Nép*, November 21, 1954.

[77] MOL, 276. fond 53/206.

[78] On the Moscow meeting in January, see Rainer and Urbán, "Konzultációk," 124–49. See also Rákosi, *Visszaemlékezések 1940–1956*, vol. 2, 974–75.

[79] MOL, 276. fond 52/28.

[80] Although the Central Committee denounced Nagy for his "errors" in March, it was only in April that the same body decided to remove him from all his Party positions.

triggered the inevitable exclusion of the ex-prime minister from the ranks of the MDP.

The stagnation and decline of the cult's development in the period of the "New Course" changed with Rákosi's re-ascendance to power, and the leader's cultic representations slowly started to re-emerge. As early as the Politburo meeting on December 1, 1954, József Mekis called for the re-establishment of Rákosi's prestige and emphasized the need for Rákosi to speak to the masses "in the old, well-known voice."[81] The issue of strengthening the Party's authority was also raised by the resolution of the Central Committee that followed its meeting in March 1955.[82] The signals of the center were welcomed by the Party bureaucracy (which had difficulties devoting itself to the dismantling efforts), resulting in the spread of eulogizing references to the Hungarian Party secretary. The press coverage of the resolution of the March meeting, involving the publication of letters of gratitude and loyalty to the Party and its leader, was already a clear sign of the cult's resurrection. Another symptom of the phenomenon's revival was the Central Committee's resolution on the historical significance of the first Rákosi trial (in 1925) on the thirtieth anniversary of the event (October 1955). The Department hailed the convicts: "The courage, heroism, and theoretical intransigence of our comrades before the court enriched the Party's armory enormously and will serve as an example and a resource to every Communist in the next stage of Party work."[83]

The jubilee was commemorated by *Szabad Nép*, but the newspaper also paid tribute to the tenth anniversary of Rákosi's return to Hungary in 1945. Apart from the anniversaries, Rákosi appeared in public more frequently in 1955, and the number of press reports describing his visits and speeches increased. Such accounts were more extensive than during the "New Course," and their vocabulary became strikingly similar to the pre-1953 evaluations of Rákosi's public appearances. One report on Rákosi's speech in the Rákosi Works in August, for example, emphasized the outbursts of enthusiasm and the manifestations of devotion when he arrived.

---

[81] MOL, 276. fond 53/206.
[82] "A Központi Vezetőség határozata a politikai helyzetről és a part feladatairól," in *A Magyar Dolgozók Pártja határozatai*, 331–43.
[83] OSA, 300/40/3/264.

> The people of Csepel welcomed their candidate with expressions of warm love, applause lasting for minutes, and exclamations of "Long live the Party! Long live Rákosi!" And who knows how often applause and cheering were heard during the report.[84]

Love and devotion for the leader was also the main theme of the article in *Szabad Ifjúság* that described Rákosi's visit to a major Pioneer camp: "The little campers of the Csillebérc Pioneer camp surrounded their dear visitor, Comrade Rákosi, with warm love.... The little Pioneers were overjoyed."[85] Besides the intensification of press coverage, the number of letters Rákosi received also increased. Such letters usually asked for the leader's assistance with a problem or asked him to pay a visit to a factory. In one case, a letter asked him to write a foreword for a journal.[86]

Despite the obvious signs of its resurgence, the Rákosi cult could never reach the same proportions that it had before June 1953. The changes in domestic and foreign politics—especially the Soviet-Yugoslav rapprochement that caused the issue of responsibility for the Rajk trial to resurface—generally prevented the cult's full return. (Rákosi was even forced to acknowledge before the Central Committee in August that Rajk was innocent.) In addition, the spirit of the infamous "cult of personality" was all too vivid; therefore, the popularization of leaders was orchestrated in a very careful way in 1955. The Party leadership remained sensitive toward the phenomenon, and whenever the shadow of the "personality cult" was cast on some articles depicting Rákosi, the respective authorities acted swiftly to suppress these unwanted traits. When Oszkár Betlen, for example, complained from Bucharest about *Szabad Nép*'s overemphasis on the applause interrupting Rákosi's speech to the Budapest Party *aktíva* that followed the March resolution, Rákosi intervened personally with Márton Horváth to prevent similar incidents in the future.[87] However, despite all the efforts of the Party center to stop newspaper reports from

---

[84] *Szabad Nép*, August 9, 1955.
[85] *Szabad Ifjúság*, July 21, 1955.
[86] MOL, 276. fond 65/72, MOL, 276. fond 65/91.
[87] "... even if such cheering happens at meetings, *aktíva*s and so on, *Szabad Nép* should avoid reporting it, and, in general, *Szabad Nép* should be cautious to avoid any manifestations of the personality cult on its pages." MOL, 276. fond 65/91.

mentioning applause, such references continued to feature in articles in the press, although less frequently than before 1953. Reports on Rákosi's announcements were priority publications in Communist newspapers after the fall of Nagy, and even one spelling mistake in the Party secretary's speech could lead to a rebuke for the unwary editors.[88] Although the Party center was careful to avoid the recurrence of the infamous "personality cult," the control of the leader's representation seems to have retained a degree of spontaneity and inconsistency—as was the case before the "New Course"—and the borders between the "cult of personality" and the "necessary popularization of leaders" generally remained blurry.

Besides the self-restraint of Communist propaganda, the decimation of the army of cult intermediaries also helped curb the resurgence of the leader cult. As the cases of *Szabad Nép*'s journalists (such as Lajos Szilvási, Endre Kövesi, Péter Kende, and Tibor Méray) prove, the continuous desertion of the young Communist intelligentsia in 1955 could not be stopped. Although *Szabad Nép* dismissed the unrepentant journalists, *Irodalmi Újság* maintained a certain oppositionist attitude until its editor, Miklós Molnár, was fired. The same attitude also crept into the editorial offices of *Magyar Nemzet*, where Miklós Gimes raised the issue of Rajk's innocence after Khrushchev's meeting with Tito. The formation of a loose intra-Party opposition group was signaled by the November Memorandum of the Writers' Association—signed by several prominent Party-member intellectuals—that protested the dismissal of *Szabad Nép*'s journalists and the banning of theater plays because of their allegedly pessimistic approach.[89] The main consequence of the intellectual revolt sparked by the "New Course" was the waning of commitment and dedication to the Party's propaganda goals. As one report complained to the Rákosi Secretariat, journalism in general became monotonous and colorless after the March meeting of the Central Committee, and journalists' attitude to political matters became more restrained and moderate.[90]

---

[88] Horváth's letter on May 9, 1955 complained about a wrong prefix that changed the meaning of a sentence in the *Szabad Nép* report of a Rákosi speech. Instead of "repelling (*kivédeni*) the dreadful plans of the warmongers," the newspaper wrote "protecting (*megvédeni*) the dreadful plans of the warmongers." The editors received a reprimand from Horváth. Ibid.

[89] The "memorandum affair" is elaborated in Aczél and Méray, *The Revolt of the Mind*, 345–80. See also Rainer, *Az író helye*, 192–221.

[90] MOL, 276. fond 65/91.

Chapter 10
The Collapse of the Rákosi Cult

The Twentieth Congress and the "Secret Speech"

In November 1955, at around the same time that the meeting of the Central Committee was demonstrating its unity in confirming Rákosi's political line, Khrushchev set up a committee in the Soviet Union to investigate Stalin's abuses of power. The report of the Pospelov Committee supplied considerable evidence against the late dictator and provided the basis of what came to be known as the "secret speech."[1] The speech, together with the Twentieth Congress of the CPSU on February 14–25, 1956, contributed significantly to the erosion and eventual collapse of Stalinist-type leader cults in the Soviet Union, as well as in the Soviet bloc more generally.

It is generally acknowledged that Khrushchev's speech at the closed session of the congress sought, by denouncing Stalin, to legitimize the position of the new leader and, at the same time, to weaken the influence of the hard-line Stalinist group (Voroshilov, Molotov, and Kaganovich). The speech became one of the most famous texts of cult criticism and was largely responsible for both the solidification of the term "personality cult" in Soviet political language and the rapid spread of the concept in the countries of Central and Eastern Europe.[2] The way in which Khrushchev used the concept fundamentally determined the interpretation of the "cult of personality" in the satellite countries of the Soviet empire; it has also affected the perception of the phenomenon by Cold War historians on both sides of the Iron Curtain.

---
[1] Filtzer, *The Khrushchev Era*, 15–16.
[2] Khrushchev, *The "Secret" Speech*.

Although the speech indeed deserves credit for revealing some of the essential features of the Stalin cult, the text primarily focused on the purges, on the most extreme examples of Stalin's terror, and on the Soviet dictator's abuse of power. Khrushchev singled out Stalin's official biography and the *Short Course* as the typical manifestations of the deification of the leader. His attack was well-aimed: by discrediting the central component of the Stalin myth, which portrayed the Soviet dictator as the physical embodiment of the history of the Communist movement, Khrushchev severely damaged the cult. Besides questioning the credibility of the biographical narrative, Khrushchev attempted, by diminishing the role ascribed to Stalin in the "Great Patriotic War," to deal a blow to the war myth that functioned as the major pillar of the postwar Stalin cult and had also displayed remarkable resilience to the first de-Stalinization efforts.[3] The critique of the war myth and the official biography, however, was not followed by further analysis of the leader cult. Khrushchev failed to explain the reasons for the cult's emergence; nor did he elaborate on its ritual manifestations; nor did he comment on the spread of the cult to the peripheries of the Soviet empire. In his attempt at ritual de-sacralization, the Soviet Party secretary used the concept of "cult of personality" as an umbrella term for all the Stalin-era terror and abuses of power; the orchestrated veneration of Party leaders was classified as the consequence of one-man rule in the "era of the personality cult."

Khrushchev's speech provoked a wide range of responses in the Soviet Union and in the countries of Central and Eastern Europe.[4] Many felt reassured after learning of his denunciation of Stalin, while others refused to acknowledge the sins of the deceased dictator. However, the general attitude after the "secret speech" was mostly one of uncertainty, confusion, and insecurity.[5] The overall atmosphere of doubt was fueled by the fact that news of the speech first reached the public through informal channels. According to Rákosi's memoirs, several copies of the text—meant for

---

[3] On the endurance of the war myth, see Jones, "Strategies of De-Mythologisation," 125–53.

[4] On the Twentieth Congress and its effect in the Soviet bloc, see Ivan T. Berend, *Central and Eastern Europe, 1944–1993: Detour from the Periphery to the Periphery* (Cambridge: Cambridge University Press, 1996), 99–116; Brzezinski, *The Soviet Bloc*, 155–268; Fejtő, *A History of the People's Democracies*, 41–65; Geoffrey Swain and Nigel Swain, *Eastern Europe Since 1945* (Basingstoke: Palgrave, 2003), 85–113.

[5] On popular responses to the "secret speech" and its critique of the Stalin cult, see Jones, "Strategies of De-Mythologisation," 51–153; and Jones, "I've Held, and I Still Hold."

intra-Party distribution—got lost in Poland and were sold on the black market in Krakow, through which the speech was leaked to the West.⁶ Whatever the case, Western European radio stations quickly acquired the full text of the speech and broadcast it before local Communist parties could properly communicate its message to their respective populations. Party elites' tardiness in proceeding with the de-mythologization of Stalin could be explained by the confusion caused by the revelations at the closed session of the Twentieth Congress, and the subsequent hesitation of the previous mini-Stalins to devote themselves to a thorough self-criticism. Because of pressure from Moscow and from certain sectors of the population, however, the leaders of local parties were all compelled to assess the "cult of personality" during the spring of 1956 in various forums, most importantly at the meetings of central Party departments and at the gatherings of Party *aktívas*. The efforts of Eastern European Communist parties to face up to their Stalinist past nonetheless involved large-scale ambiguity and a general attempt to downplay the consequences of the cult, and the local leadership's responsibility in encouraging it. At the same time, debates about the "cult of personality" were closely linked—as in the Soviet Union—to power struggles in the leadership of local parties, which also impacted how the issue was tackled in the countries of the Soviet bloc.

The critique of the cult in Romania, for example, was combined with an attempt to overthrow Gheorghiu-Dej by Iosif Chișinevski and Miron Constantinescu. However, the Romanian Party leader maintained his authority in the Party: his rivals were expelled from the Politburo, and Ana Pauker became the scapegoat for the Stalinist excesses in Romania.⁷ Chervenkov in Bulgaria was much less fortunate: after having been accused of encouraging his cult and the "cult of brutality" in the country, he was forced to resign as prime minister in April 1956.⁸ The "secret speech" also contributed to the weakening of Ulbricht's position in the GDR. However, he managed to survive the de-Stalinization campaign by adjusting swiftly to the new line, as exemplified by his article in the *Neues Deutschland* on March 4 questioning Stalin's image as a Marxist theorist.⁹

---

⁶ Rákosi, *Visszaemlékezések 1940–1956*, vol. 2, 1001–1002.

⁷ Mocanescu, "Surviving 1956."

⁸ Wien, "Georgi Dimitrov," 202.

⁹ John C. Torpey, *Intellectuals, Socialism and Dissent: The East German Opposition and Its Legacy* (Minneapolis: University of Minnesota Press, 1995), 41.

The Polish Party leadership reacted to Khrushchev's denunciation of the "cult of personality" with a combination of confusion and power struggles. At the first Central Committee meeting after the Twentieth Congress, the Polish Communist leaders demonstrated their remarkable inability—or unwillingness—to define the cult in a consistent way. The fact that Poland's "domestic" cult figure, Bierut, died in Moscow during the Congress complicated the situation further.[10] In the spring of 1956, József Cyrankiewicz and Edward Ochab criticized the cult on a number of occasions, referring to its widespread nature, the Party bureaucracy's responsibility in promoting it, and the servility it triggered. Yet Jakub Berman admitted to a Party *aktíva* on March 7 that he simply could not explain the reasons for the cult's emergence.[11] Although Cyrankiewicz acknowledged in front of the Party leadership that the "cult of the individual" was rooted in "the system of governing over all spheres of life," it was not until October 1956 that a detailed criticism of the "personality cult" was articulated in Poland, by Gomułka. The rise of Gomułka—and the demise of Berman—also put an end to the post-Stalinist power struggles in the Polish leadership.

"We Were Surprised by the Twentieth Congress": The Effects of the "Secret Speech" on the Rákosi Cult

The immediate response of the MDP leadership to the Twentieth Congress and the "secret speech" was also inconsistent, and significant efforts were made to downplay the role of the leader cult in the Rákosi regime.[12] Nevertheless, the Party elite displayed less confusion than their comrades elsewhere in the Soviet bloc. Although the Politburo devoted three meetings in early March to drawing conclusions from the Congress, Rákosi and his entourage were not quite as shocked by the new political line as their colleagues in other countries. As the leadership had endured vehement criticism during the "New Course" and emerged triumphant,

---

[10] Zaremba, "The Second Step of a Ladder," 262–63.
[11] Tony Kemp-Welch, "Khrushchev's 'Secret Speech' and Polish Politics: The Spring of 1956," *Europe-Asia Studies* 48, no. 2 (1996): 183–85.
[12] The notes of the Hungarian delegation on the draft of Khrushchev's report is at MOL, 276. fond 65/115.

they perceived the "secret speech" as a mostly harmless, albeit important, criticism ritual that posed no threat to their political standing. From this point of view, Rákosi and the Party elite seem to have underestimated the political implications of the new political line signaled by Khrushchev's speech. Rákosi, for example, even asked the Soviet Party leader during the Congress—sometime before the speech—to reconsider the Presidium's critique of the Hungarian leadership that preceded the "New Course." The request allegedly infuriated the Party secretary of the CPSU, and Rákosi decided not to raise the issue again.[13]

Rákosi's report to the Central Committee on March 12–13 exemplifies the attitude of the MDP leadership to the outcome of the Congress.[14] Rákosi praised the event as usual, claiming that the MDP's policies had already been in accordance with the new line, and generally behaving as if nothing unexpected had happened in Moscow.[15] The intensification of cult criticism, however, did leave its mark on Rákosi's speech. After years of controversial explanations of where the cult had originated, it finally became possible to name the main culprit: Stalin. In contrast to the events following the Moscow negotiations in June 1953, when Rákosi confessed his sins in promoting his cult but dared not mention the Soviet leader, at the March meeting of the Central Committee in 1956, the Hungarian Party secretary gave a thorough critique of Stalin while trying to avoid references to his own cult. Rákosi—like the Soviet leaders during the Congress—criticized Stalin's deification and the illusion of his infallibility, which had contributed to the violation of the principles of collective leadership.

The superficiality with which Rákosi treated the issue of his own cult was also evident in the contributions of other Central Committee members. Most of the speakers who addressed the issue (József Köböl, István Szabó, Tivadar Matusek, and Mihály Gábri, as well as Márton Horváth) generally emphasized that although significant steps had been taken to eliminate the remnants of the cult, such efforts were incapable of rooting out all cultic practices from Party life; thus it was essential to proceed with

---

[13] Rákosi, *Visszaemlékezések 1940–1956*, vol. 2, 999.
[14] The Politburo discussed the report on March 1. MOL, 276. fond 53/273.
[15] Rákosi's report to the Central Committee is available at MOL, 276. fond 65/24.

the dismantling of the cult.[16] The anti-cult rhetoric of the meeting, however, seems to have consisted solely of empty slogans. Moreover, as some of the contributions make clear, the level of criticism undertaken in this regard failed even to reach that commonly seen during the "New Course." Révai, Matusek, Betlen, and Szántó, for example, fervently advocated the use of leader portraits in public spaces, claiming that the expression of genuine devotion through the placement of pictures on walls did not mean the resurrection of the leader cult. Matusek and Horváth went so far as to blame the emergence of a certain Nagy cult for the lack of success in the struggle against the exaltation of Rákosi.[17]

The constantly shifting parameters of cult criticism, coupled with the Party elite's half-hearted efforts to do away with the remnants of the Rákosi cult, generated further confusion among the Party membership, not to mention the rest of the population. Kiss called the Central Committee's attention to the widespread public interest in cult criticism, whereas Mária Nagy, referring to the general bewilderment in society, emphasized the popular demand for a clear-cut definition of the cult phenomenon: "[A]t the moment it seems that we have a personality cult when we applaud, but there is no personality cult when we don't applaud."

Despite the lack of a swift response to the Twentieth Congress in terms of the cult's dismantling, the spirit of the meeting strongly affected the Hungarian Party elite's attitude toward the leadership. Although Rákosi's authority was not yet questioned, severe criticism was aimed at Farkas, and a committee was established to investigate the former defense minister's responsibility for violations of the law. (The head of the committee was Kovács.)[18]

---

[16] The minutes of the meeting: MOL, 276. fond 52/33.

[17] The ambivalent attitude of the Party leadership toward the liquidation of the cult was also exemplified by Gerő's statement during the session. When he was asked about the lack of dedication among the Party leadership toward eliminating the "cult of personality," he replied with a circular argument: "why didn't we do anything against the cult of personality and the overshadowing of collective leadership? . . . The reason is that, among these special historical circumstances, with the overshadowing of collective leadership, one-man leadership and the cult of personality gained ground." Ibid.

[18] Kádár, who had been interrogated by Farkas and his son Vladimir after his arrest, became the most ardent opponent of Farkas at the meeting. He ruled out any future relationship between himself and Rákosi's former right-hand man, claiming that "there are corpses between me and Mihály Farkas, corpses of innocent Communists who were murdered." Ibid.

Although Rákosi emerged from the Central Committee meeting relatively unharmed, the Twentieth Congress contributed to the long-term erosion of his cult. While the Hungarian delegation was still in Moscow, Rákosi was informed of *Pravda*'s intention to publish a laudatory article about Kun, written by Jenő Varga, as a sign of the historical rehabilitation of the real leader of the 1919 Hungarian Republic of Soviets. Since Rákosi's biographies gave all credit to him for the successes of 1919, the unexpected re-evaluation of Kun would have dealt a serious blow to Rákosi's reputation.[19] Although he seems to have favored the formulation of a positive representation of Kun's activity in 1919, he nevertheless disliked the way the Soviet leadership was proceeding with the matter. After a series of desperate pleas to the editors of *Pravda*, Rákosi eventually managed to gain agreement that a similar article about Kun could be published in Hungary, in *Szabad Nép,* on the same day as *Pravda*'s article.[20] It was probably the Kun incident that convinced Rákosi of the need to raise the issue of the re-evaluation of Party history at the meeting of the Central Committee. Following the resolution of the Committee, the Politburo on April 5 decreed the revision of school and university textbooks, as well as other material on Party history.[21]

Besides the partial disintegration of the biographical narrative, the Party leadership also had to follow the path of the CPSU in the public denunciation of the cult. The Politburo decided at its meeting on March 20 to draft a short outline of the official cult critique sent from Moscow and to distribute the summary among regional Party secretaries.[22] Party *aktíva*s and membership meetings were also to be held in order to inform the Party rank-and-file about the new policy guidelines laid down by the Twentieth Congress. Rákosi appeared at the *aktíva* meeting in the Thirteenth District of Budapest on March 24, where he first confessed his guilt in the promotion of the cult to ordinary Party members. Nevertheless,

---

[19] For more on the Kun affair, see MOL, 276. fond 53/272 and 275; Pünkösti, *Rákosi bukása,* 338; Rákosi, *Visszaemlékezések 1940–1956,* vol. 2, 994–95; Aleszandr Szergejevics Sztikalin, "A szovjet nagykövetség és az MDP-n belüli harc 1956 tavaszán-kora őszén," *Múltunk* 43, no. 2 (1998): 23–49.

[20] *Szabad Nép,* February 21, 1956.

[21] The tàsk was assigned to Szalai and Hegedüs. MOL, 276. fond 53/279.

[22] MOL, 276. fond 53/276.

the MDP secretary spoke about the cult in the past tense, claiming that its excesses had already been eliminated.

> In 1953 we realized the errors and troubles that the personality cult had caused in our country: we have sincerely unraveled it—I also unraveled it, among others—because I was not simply the admirer of the personality cult, but I was its object at the same time.... We have dissolved the personality cult that we adopted like others did. The applause that has been referred to has now gone out of fashion.[23]

Although Rákosi exercised self-criticism to a "closed public," he continued to downplay the consequences of errors and crimes committed between 1948 and 1953. By referring to the cult's hierarchical nature, Rákosi hoped to shift responsibility onto a wider social group for the construction and endorsement of the leader cult. He avoided naming those who shared the guilt of adopting the Soviet-type leader cult in Hungary, and he appealed to collective sin in his rhetoric in order to keep the analysis of the cult on a general level.

> A one-man cult has the potential to grow anywhere.... There could be a personality cult in a factory, within lower Party organizations, and also in a particular field of science, where one who fancies himself to be the pope has his own court of followers, he is courted and praised ... We also had a personality cult. And we will have a lot of work to do to eliminate its roots once and for all, because we have planted these roots ourselves, and now we are trying to pull them out.

Rákosi repeated his self-criticism in front of a wider audience at the Heves County *aktíva* meeting in Eger on March 27, where he delivered his official report on the Twentieth Congress and the "secret speech." At the meeting, where Rákosi first admitted that the Rajk trial was based on "provocation," he presented a conception of the cult that was very similar to the definition he came up with at the Party meeting in the Thirteenth District. He stated that the cult's emergence was "our fault" and repeated his idea that a number of local cults had emerged. He also spoke about the all-pervasiveness of the phenomenon, claiming that the cult had appeared

---

[23] Quoted in Nemes, *Rákosi Mátyás születésnapja*, 133.

in all spheres of Party life and the economy, where local leaders, whom he labeled "petty monarchs" or "infallible popes," ruled in a dictatorial manner and were surrounded by sycophants.[24]

The Party membership was informed of events at the Twentieth Congress during a series of membership meetings on city, district, and county levels. The official interpretation of the cult was also presented to the population on March 29, when *Szabad Nép* republished the article "Why Is the Cult of Personality Alien to the Spirit of Marxism-Leninism?" that had appeared in *Pravda* in the Soviet Union the day before.[25] The article, based mostly on Khrushchev's ideas of the cult, made a faltering attempt to identify the reasons for the emergence of the Stalin cult. Two main factors—"objective, historical circumstances" and subjective circumstances (the role of Stalin)—were highlighted in the rise of the cult. Apart from seeking the roots of the phenomenon, the article argued that the "cult of personality" had always been condemned by prominent political leaders and theoreticians. By referring to Marx, Engels, and Lenin, it tried to demonstrate that the concept and phenomenon was totally alien to the Marxist tradition. Although the *Pravda* editorial did not deny the role of great individuals in history, it claimed that the emergence of the cult violated the principle of collective leadership and the notion of Party democracy. It referred to certain manifestations of the Stalin cult, such as the embellishment of his biography and the history of the CPSU. Nevertheless, it failed to reflect on the cult's hierarchical nature and the ritualistic nature of the leader's veneration.

Despite the lack of an elaborate definition of the worship of leaders, the membership meetings and the publication of the *Pravda* article churned the still waters of popular opinion in Hungary. As summary reports from the *aktívas* in late March testify, ordinary Party members were generally shocked by the sudden denigration of Stalin and often expressed their confusion and bewilderment.[26] One Party secretary at the Rákosi Works, for example, at a meeting on April 3, complained about the difficulties of differentiating between the voice of the enemy and that of the workers and

---

[24] Ibid., 136.
[25] *Szabad Nép*, March 29, 1956.
[26] Pünkösti, *Rákosi bukása*, 349. One report prepared by the Ministry of Internal Affairs also observed the general confusion of Party members. "Most people don't know what to say or

referred to the "great ideological chaos in the Party."[27] The report on the Twentieth Congress also triggered heated debates and extreme emotional responses on both sides. Some were outraged by Kun's rehabilitation, and others asked about the Rajk trial or why Nagy had been expelled from the Party.[28] The radically new evaluation of Stalin also provoked mixed sentiments. Some workers at the Rákosi Works refused to believe the accusations, calling them lies, while some of their colleagues called for the removal of portraits of the former leader and the demolition of statues of him.[29] Rákosi was not spared either: people expressed their hope that he would eventually be removed, but there were others who were afraid of the changes anti-Rákosi sentiments might provoke.[30] Kovács, at the April 5 meeting of the Politburo, also recalled the immense bewilderment he found among the Party members at the meetings, caused by the shift in the interpretation of the Soviet dictator. He remembered functionaries whose faith in Stalin had been shaken by the "secret speech" and who became uncertain whom to trust. Kovács also cited examples of the other extreme, when people rejected the criticism of Stalin and declared their love and respect for the dead leader.[31] There were places in which the news of Stalin's sins immediately prompted requests to remove images of him from walls. This happened, for example, in a village called Nógrád, where local Party functionaries also welcomed the rehabilitation of Kun.[32] At several Party *aktíva*s, complaints were addressed to the leadership that criticized the Party's communication strategy around the Twentieth Congress and Khrushchev's speech. In Budapest, for example, the radio and *Szabad Nép* were blamed for being too slow to react to the events, and it was generally emphasized that Western European media had been quicker in reporting the Soviet reinterpretation of Stalin's character.[33]

Besides confusion and spontaneous emotional outbursts, there were some Party members who tried to articulate a more sophisticated inter-

---

what to do, because the official position has not been articulated yet." ÁBTL 3.1.2 M-20596/2.
[27] Nemes, *Rákosi Mátyás születésnapja*, 136.
[28] MOL, 276. fond 61/726.
[29] Nemes, *Rákosi Mátyás születésnapja*, 137.
[30] ÁBTL 3.1.2 M-20596/2.
[31] MOL, 276. fond 53/279.
[32] MOL, 276. fond 65/70.
[33] MOL, 276. fond 61/726.

pretation of the cult. The philosopher György Lukács, who fell from grace after 1949, was one of them.[34] Lukács believed that the Party apparatus had a crucial role in the promotion of the "personality cult." He described the bureaucracy as a social group full of "little Stalins" who behaved like dictators toward the population but who turned into sycophants when they communicated with the Party center. He also emphasized the lack of individual initiative in the decision-making process, the compilation of reports according to the center's expectations, and the widespread suppression of criticism.

The flood of criticism at the membership meetings in late March also reached the Hungarian Party secretary. Although Rákosi managed to keep the critical tone at a low level during the Central Committee meeting in mid-March, the meetings of Party *aktívas* that followed the session often raised the issue of his responsibility for crimes, most often in connection with the Rajk trial. There were reports of such incidents from János Hospital, but also from the Rákosi Works, where some workers questioned the need to carry leader portraits at the upcoming May 1 demonstrations.[35] At the Party *aktíva* meeting in the Thirteenth District of Budapest, one member of the audience, György Litván, even called for the ouster of Rákosi, who was present.[36] One report by Soviet diplomats from the city of Debrecen reflected on the same phenomenon, asserting that the Party meetings mostly attributed the errors to Rákosi.[37] Apart from the Party *aktívas*, the question of Rákosi's responsibility for the regime's misdeeds resurfaced at the meetings of various opposition and reformist forums (such as the Petőfi Circle, *Irodalmi Újság*, and *Művelt Nép*) from March onwards.[38]

---

[34] MOL, 276. fond 65/343.

[35] Pünkösti, *Rákosi bukása*, 362.

[36] Ibid., 351–54.

[37] Sztikalin, "A szovjet nagykövetség és az MDP-n belüli harc," 24.

[38] On reformist debates in literary journals during the spring of 1956, see Rainer, *Az író helye*, 222–99. The Party opposition that emerged after the fall of the "New Course" became active after the Twentieth Congress. Within the Petőfi Circle, which became the most popular and influential reformist forum in the spring of 1956, the intellectual debates—especially those on philosophy, literature, and journalism—attracted thousands of people and featured renowned intellectuals, such as Tardos, Lukács, and the writer Tibor Déry. For the minutes of the Petőfi Circle, see András B. Hegedüs et al., eds., *A Petőfi Kör vitái hiteles jegyzőkönyvek alapján*, 7 vols., (Budapest: 1956-os Intézet, 1989–1994).

The responses of Party members to the Twentieth Congress seem to have surprised the leadership, which was unsure as to how best to react to such an outburst of popular criticism. At the April 5 Politburo meeting, in a discussion of the results of the *aktívas*, Gerő admitted: "We were surprised by the Twentieth Congress, by the way the cult of personality was publicized."[39] Though it recognized the public demand for a clear explanation of events, the leadership remained hesitant over whether to go beyond the vague interpretation of the cult articulated by the CPSU.

The generally distracted state of the Hungarian Party leaders after membership meetings is indicated by the fact that, although the Politburo finally addressed the issue of Rákosi's responsibility, it still failed to come up with any concrete decisions as to the best means of eliminating his cult. Although Ács was well aware that the lack of determination in dismantling the cult would inevitably lead to the weakening of the Party's authority (this was also observed by Soviet diplomats[40]), his only initiative was to suggest that the MDP secretary perform another public self-criticism ritual. Likewise, Hegedüs, Antal Apró, and others hoped that if Rákosi led the struggle against the remnants of the "cult of personality," then the trust and loyalty of rank-and-file Party members could be regained. The attempt to save what was left of Rákosi's reputation while purging the cult from Party life was supported by Moscow as well. To demonstrate their trust in and support for the Hungarian Party leader, Khrushchev and Bulganin sent Rákosi and Hegedüs a telegram for Liberation Day (April 4) congratulating them and praising the first secretary.[41]

After the Politburo meeting, Rákosi decided to try to repel the waves of criticism in person. Four days after the heated membership meeting at the Rákosi Works, where his responsibility for the cult had been a central topic of debate, he visited the factory to meet the local Party functionaries. His hopes of calming them failed, however, and on April 7 he was forced to perform another self-criticism ritual regarding the cult. (He was even asked whether Khrushchev's telegram, mentioned above, was to be interpreted as a sign of the cult's rebirth.) Even then, he tried to convince the audience that the cult had actually occurred against his will.

---

[39] MOL, 276. fond 53/279.
[40] Sztikalin, "A szovjet nagykövetség és az MDP-n belüli harc," 24.
[41] *Szabad Nép*, April 6, 1956. For more on the "telegram affair," see Pünkösti, *Rákosi bukása*, 358–60.

The cult around me was wrong; I tried to temper this personality cult. For example, when they wanted to rename this factory after me, I did not want to accept it. Later, they offered to rename several bridges after me, but I did not approve. In spite of that, there was a superfluous personality cult around me, but it had already begun to recede in 1953.[42]

Rákosi's uncertain, inconsistent, and politically blind attitude toward the criticism was also evident at the April 9 meeting of the Secretariat, when the necessary tasks concerning the implementation of the new Party line after the Twentieth Congress were discussed (again).[43] Instead of tackling the problem of popular discontent provoked by the leadership's ambiguous announcements on the cult, Rákosi continued to emphasize the need to overcome the "rightist deviation" that he still considered to be the biggest threat to the stability of the Party's authority. In his report to the Secretariat on the critical atmosphere he experienced at the Rákosi Works, he complained about the fact that he had become the target of popular criticism. The "Litván affair" also seems to have left a mark on the leader, who even recounted the story to Andropov and remarked that people like Litván "were thrown out like snot" from the CPSU.[44] Rákosi's contribution at the meeting of the Secretariat gives the impression that he perceived the attacks against his person as attempts to weaken the Party's authority. He underlined several times that the "rightist opposition"—he meant the followers of Nagy—was exploiting the rhetoric of the Twentieth Congress in order to remove him from the leadership and thereby undermine the position of the Communist Party. He tended to interpret cult criticism as a conspiracy to remove him from power, as his discussions with Soviet ambassador Andropov in 1956 and his memoirs testify.

The waning of Rákosi's self-confidence inevitably led to the gradual weakening of his position in the Politburo. At a meeting on April 19, for example, Ács's proposal on the reconsideration of the Party line was accepted by the Politburo instead of the proposal supported by Rákosi.[45] A week later, the closed session of the Politburo decided to go further

---

[42] Nemes, *Rákosi Mátyás születésnapja*, 136.
[43] MOL, 276. fond 54/397.
[44] Baráth, *Szovjet nagyköveti iratok*, 272.
[45] MOL, 276. fond 53/277.

and finally clarify its stance on the "cult of personality."[46] The resolution stated that the "precondition of progress is the amplification of the fight against the remnants of the personality cult" and emphasized the need to strengthen collective leadership and to revitalize the practices of criticism and self-criticism.[47] Although such slogans had been resurfacing in Party decrees since 1953, this time Party rhetoric was backed with concrete suggestions. The Politburo expressed its will to rehabilitate those who had been imprisoned before 1953, and as a sign of its commitment, it decided to invite Kádár and Révai to join as members.[48] The document also compelled Rákosi to make a public announcement on the importance of the Twentieth Congress and on his responsibility for the regime's misdeeds, generally referred to as the "cult of personality."

The nomination of Kádár and Révai as Politburo members, the threat that the investigations in the Farkas case would reveal the Party secretary's responsibility for the crimes of the regime, and the prospect of another public self-criticism in front of the Party membership all added to Rákosi's growing insecurity and the withering of the Rákosi myth within the Party leadership. In search of reassurance before the Budapest Party *aktíva*, where he was supposed to deliver his report on the regime's violations of law, Rákosi visited Andropov and summarized his speech. He was probably hoping for a last-minute Soviet intervention that would save him from having to face the crowd of curious Party functionaries. Rákosi informed Andropov that instead of talking in generalities, he would refer to concrete incidents and would take all responsibility for the Rajk case and for the promotion of the cult.[49] The Soviet diplomat, however, mostly agreed with the proposed speech, as had the Politburo, which had discussed the document the day after Rákosi's visit to the embassy on May 11.[50] Nevertheless, some Politburo members found some of the claims in the report too self-critical. Gerő, for example, questioned Rákosi's emphasis on the need to rewrite Party history, arguing that it would be enough to erase the

---

[46] MOL, 276. fond 53/283.

[47] "A Politikai Bizottság 1956. április 26-i zárt ülésének határozata," in Izsák, *A Magyar Dolgozók Pártja határozatai*, 404–8.

[48] Kádár and Révai were eventually co-opted at the meeting of the Central Committee on July 18–21, 1956.

[49] Baráth, *Szovjet nagyköveti iratok*, 292–94.

[50] MOL, 276. fond 53/286.

remnants of the "cult of personality." Kovács also found Rákosi's self-criticism exaggerated concerning the cult and suggested that he give more attention to the all-pervasive and hierarchical nature of the phenomenon. In addition, Hegedüs proposed that the leader detail the measures taken since 1953 to purge the cult from the Party.

The Budapest Party *aktíva* meeting on May 18, where the speech was eventually presented, became the setting for Rákosi's last public appearance.[51] After outlining Stalin's sins to the audience, the Party secretary admitted his personal responsibility for the errors committed and discussed the consequences and the characteristics of the "personality cult." He emphasized that attributing omnipotence to the leaders undermined the historical role of the Party and the masses. He insisted that the "cult of personality" contributed to the emergence of dogmatism and the spreading of "administrative methods." The principle of collective leadership had been ignored, and in general, the "Leninist norms" of Party life had been neglected.

Despite the symbolic significance of Rákosi's confession in front of the Party membership, his interpretation of the term "personality cult" was far from original, and he continued to use the meta-conceptual framework that had been ascribed to the term as early as 1953. Nevertheless, there was a major difference between Rákosi's speech at the Party *aktíva* and his previous announcements on the topic. Namely, the leader finally took the blame for promoting the exaltation of his persona:

> We have mostly talked in general terms about the cult of personality that became dominant here. This is not enough. It has to be said to our working people overtly and honestly that this personality cult was connected to me; I pursued and supported this personality cult. Until we say this explicitly, a lot of honest comrades may get the impression that we are just beating around the bush.

At the same time, he emphasized the negative consequences of the spread of the cult phenomenon and the proliferation of careerists, sycophants, "despots," "petty monarchs," and "yes-men" who outshone the older, respectable comrades. Rákosi pointed out that the Twentieth

---

[51] The speech was published by *Szabad Nép* on May 19, 1956.

Congress had brought about a crucial change and that significant steps had been taken to eradicate the "cult of personality" from Party life.

The incentive behind Rákosi's self-criticism was the Politburo's hope that the speech would help to re-establish the shattered authority of both Rákosi and the Party leadership. Nevertheless, the Party *aktíva* could not stop the withering of Rákosi's (ascribed) charisma; nor could it prevent the decline in the Party's status. In fact, the condemnation of the ritualized veneration of leaders by the leader himself reaffirmed the rumors of Rákosi's responsibility and inevitably weakened loyalty to, and confidence in, the MDP secretary among the Party membership. Rákosi's standing also continued to weaken within the Politburo. On June 4, Gerő warned Andropov that Rákosi was becoming isolated. A day later, Kovács complained to the Soviet ambassador about Rákosi's resistance to the principles of collective leadership.[52] Even the Soviet leaders noticed the Party leader's unstable position and sent Suslov to Budapest to investigate the situation.[53]

In this unfavorable situation, Rákosi received an unexpected show of support from Moscow. After a meeting of the leaders of the Eastern bloc in the Soviet capital on June 22–23, the Hungarian Party secretary returned to Budapest with the endorsement of the CPSU.[54] The temporary strengthening of hard-line politics in the Soviet Union, which was triggered by the uprising in Poznań, was also manifested in a tempering of cult criticism. As a result of the unforeseen effects of Khrushchev's revelation, the consequences of the events in Poland, and the resurgence of Stalin's former entourage, the Central Committee of the CPSU passed a resolution that represented a retreat from the tone of the "secret speech" and the *Pravda* article in late March.[55] The decree, entitled "On Overcoming the Cult of Personality and its Consequences," blunted the sharp edges of the critique, claimed that the "cult of personality" was not inherent in the system, and shifted the responsibility for its emergence exclusively onto Stalin.[56]

---

[52] Baráth, *Szovjet nagyköveti iratok*, 299–310.

[53] Sztikalin, "A szovjet nagykövetség és az MDP-n belüli harc," 32.

[54] Károly Urbán and István Vida, "Az MDP Politikai Bizottsága 1956. június 28-i ülésének jegyzőkönyve. Az 1956. júniusi kommunista csúcstalálkozó és Magyarország," *Társadalmi Szemle* 48, no. 2 (1993): 83–94. See also Rákosi, *Visszaemlékezések 1940–1956*, vol. 2, 1013–14.

[55] *Szabad Nép*, July 2, 1956.

[56] The attempt to gloss over responsibility in the promotion of the cult becomes apparent when the document tries to explain the lack of cult criticism during Stalin's lifetime. It simply claims

Soviet support for Rákosi, however, came too late to prevent his downfall. Although the Petőfi Circle was temporarily silenced, critical voices among the Party membership were heard more frequently in the last two weeks of June. Party sections in factories, at the Academy of Sciences, and even at the Party Academy expressed their solidarity with the Petőfi Circle and their growing impatience with Rákosi and the MDP leadership.[57] Rákosi, before leaving Moscow, complained to Voroshilov on June 26 about some "less educated Party members" demanding his dismissal and expressed his worries that the Farkas case might worsen his reputation.[58] Rákosi's fears became reality when the previous ÁVH chief, Gábor Péter, sent Kovács a letter on July 10 blaming Rákosi for personally directing the secret police at the time of the Rajk trial and the purges.[59] Seeking to assist Rákosi and reprimand Kovács, the Soviet leadership sent Anastas Mikoian to Budapest. The Soviet emissary arrived on July 13, but after consulting members of the Hungarian Party elite, he realized how precarious Rákosi's position was and instead suggested his removal.[60]

"It Hurts to See Comrade Rákosi Leave Like This": Rákosi's Abdication and the Uprising of 1956

Rákosi's letter of resignation to the Central Committee stated that he was stepping down mainly because of worsening health.[61] In addition, he admitted that the obstacles to the rehabilitation process and to the dismantling of the "personality cult" were mostly his fault. Rákosi argued that, as he had downplayed the significance of the errors, his resignation from the Central Committee and the Politburo was essential in order to reconstruct the unity of the Party leadership.

---

that "nothing could have been done in the given circumstances."
[57] Baráth, *Szovjet nagyköveti iratok*, 313–14.
[58] Éva Gál et al., eds., *A "Jelcin-dosszié." Szovjet dokumentumok 1956-ról* (Budapest: Századvég, 1993), 24–26.
[59] Gábor Koltay and Péter Bródy, eds., *El nem égetett dokumentumok* (Budapest: Szabad Tér Kiadó, 1990), 13–29.
[60] Sztikalin, "A szovjet nagykövetség és az MDP-n belüli harc," 38.
[61] MOL, 276. fond 65/28.

The Central Committee discussed Rákosi's letter on the first day of its four-day session, which lasted from July 18 to 21.[62] Mikoian, who was also present at the meeting, declared that the official line of the CPSU was anti-cult and consented to Rákosi's resignation.[63] Elements of the cult were not completely absent from the meeting, however. József Harustyák, for example, refused to accept the proposal, stating: "Comrade Rákosi is a name; Comrade Rákosi is a leader who fought, struggled, and sacrificed his life for the liberation of the Hungarian workers, for the rights of the Hungarian people, for the establishment of Hungarian socialism." Andics suggested retaining at least Rákosi's Politburo membership, as the workers and peasants "deeply loved" him, and they would not understand his resignation. She declared that "the authority of Comrade Rákosi is the authority of the Party" and that the Party was not strong enough to jettison its most valuable asset. István Friss also anticipated that the severing of the emotional bonds between the leader and the people would be painful: "It hurts to see Comrade Rákosi leave like this." Even Gerő, who replaced Rákosi as first secretary of the MDP, appealed to the language of the cult in his contribution:

> If I were to vote with my heart, I wouldn't accept the Politburo's proposal. I learned of the Communist Party mostly through Comrade Rákosi, and if something has changed me, it was largely his activity, his behavior, his relationship with the ordinary people.

Despite the notable presence of the cult discourse in the Central Committee session, Rákosi's resignation was ultimately accepted, largely due to the position of the Soviet representative. While the Committee continued its meeting and eventually expelled Farkas from the Party,[64] *Szabad Nép* informed the public of Rákosi's removal on July 19. Most of the population seems to have welcomed the changes,[65] but the news shocked certain

---

[62] MOL, 276. fond 52/35.
[63] He added that Farkas could be sacrificed too, if that served the Party's goals: "He could also be speared, if this was in the interest of the Party."
[64] "A Központi Vezetőség határozata: Pártegységgel a szocialista demokráciáért," in Izsák, *A Magyar Dolgozók Pártja határozatai*, 439–60. On the expulsion of Farkas from the ranks of the MDP: "A Központi Vezetőség határozata Farkas Mihály kizárásáról a Központi Vezetőségből és a part tagjainak sorából," in ibid., 461.
[65] ÁBTL 3.1.2 M-20596/2.

sections of the Party membership, despite the growing critical attitude toward the Party leadership during the spring of 1956. Some older Party members were reported to have cried at *aktíva* meetings, while others expressed their worries about Rákosi's health. The ex-leader even received gifts from some of the workers,[66] and there were rumors of a fistfight between the members of the Central Committee over his removal.[67] There was also a tendency in the Communist press to represent Rákosi's resignation as an act of political virtue. Reports and interviews in *Szabad Nép* and other newspapers cast his removal in a positive light in order to maintain what little was left of Rákosi's reputation. One worker, for example, was reported to have said: "I respect and admire Comrade Rákosi very much, because when he resigned, he referred not only to his illness but also to the mistakes that had been committed."[68]

Nevertheless, Rákosi's cult underwent a sudden decay after his resignation. He left Hungary for the Soviet Union on July 26—never to return—and, with the physical absence of the object of veneration, the manifestations of his "cult of personality" started to disappear. Rhythmic applause was stopped, the number of portraits carried at mass demonstrations was reduced, and his name appeared in political announcements less often.

The Party leadership also contributed to the collapse of the Rákosi myth. A significant step in dismantling the cult was the Politburo decree on August 9 that ordered the renaming of institutions named after Rákosi and forbade the naming of institutions and places after living Party leaders.[69] The major changes were quickly executed, and *Szabad Nép* reported these achievements in early September.[70] In the meantime, the revision of textbooks and educational material continued. The Party's Department of Science and Culture informed the leadership of the significant progress made in reviewing and correcting primary- and secondary-school history

---

[66] Pünkösti, *Rákosi bukása*, 424.
[67] ÁBTL 3.1.2 M-20596/2.
[68] *Szabad Magyarország*, July 20, 1956.
[69] MOL, 276. fond 53/298.
[70] *Szabad Nép*, September 2, 1956. Rákosi Works was renamed Csepel Steel and Metalworks, Rákosi University was turned into the Miskolc Technical University for Heavy Industry, and the Rákosi Study Contest changed its name to National Academic Competition for Secondary Schools.

books on June 25, while Rákosi was still the leader.[71] The report claimed that the revisions that had been implemented in the spirit of the struggle against the "personality cult" would also be extended to teaching material in higher education in the subsequent months.

The political environment in the autumn of 1956 was conducive to the dismantling of the cult. In October, Gomułka articulated one of the most accurate cult criticisms in the Soviet bloc up to that point. At the meeting of the Central Committee of the Polish United Worker's Party, he defined the cult as a system that originated in the Soviet Union from Stalin and was later exported to the countries of Eastern Europe.[72] He highlighted the hierarchical nature of the phenomenon and compared the structure of cults to a ladder, with the Stalin cult on the top and the cults of national Party leaders at its lower rungs.[73] The Hungarian Party leadership was less critical than the Poles, and it seems to have considered the fight against the cult concluded with the purging of Rákosi's name from the public sphere. Hungarian society was not forgetful, however, as was demonstrated at the founding assembly of the Hungarian Association of University and College Unions (MEFESZ) on October 16 in Szeged, where some participants even demanded that Rákosi be hanged for his involvement in the ÁVH's crimes.[74]

The 1956 revolution rapidly swept away what was left of the cult of Rákosi; there was no longer any place for sophisticated dismantling strategies. Popular discontent turned against the emblematic figure of Hungarian Stalinism and against the most pervasive feature of the regime: the leader cult. The revolutionary atmosphere also amplified the most common resistance strategies to the cult; therefore, outrage and discontent often took the form of iconoclasm. The destruction of Stalinist icons started with the eight-meter-tall Stalin statue in Budapest on October 23.[75] The fall of the master was followed by the fall of his "best Hungarian apprentice." Both in Budapest and in the provinces, Rákosi statuettes were frequently smashed by angry crowds. In a Varsád machine station, for example, a bust of Rákosi was crushed in the smithy, while in

---

[71] MOL, 276. fond 65/343.
[72] Zaremba, "The Second Step of a Ladder," 262.
[73] Brzezinski, *The Soviet Bloc*, 65, 273.
[74] Baráth, *Szovjet nagyköveti iratok*, 362.
[75] Pótó, *Az emlékeztetés helyei*, 226–32.

Kiskundorozsma, gypsum busts of Stalin and Rákosi were destroyed by the demonstrators, and statues made of porcelain were broken into pieces in the famous Herend China Factory.[76] Portraits of the leaders were not spared either. In most places, the revolutionary crowd took the pictures of Stalin and Rákosi off the walls of Party offices and other public buildings and ripped them up or burned them.[77] Photographs taken on the streets of Budapest of people burning portraits of Rákosi also bear witness to the frequency of iconoclastic actions during the 1956 uprising. There were also other ways of getting rid of traces of the leader cult in public spaces. In the village of Demjén, for example, an enthusiastic local revolutionary not only destroyed all the pictures of the leader but also covered all the street signs on the street bearing Rákosi's name.[78]

"We Should Not Let Even the Illusion of the Personality Cult Appear": Denouncing the Cult in the Kádár Era

Despite the cleansing effects of the Uprising, vestiges of the Rákosi cult endured, and the problem of dealing with the consequences of institutionalized leader worship resurfaced after the re-establishment of Communist rule in Hungary. The Kádár government paid significant attention to the wrongdoings of the Rákosi regime as early as November 1956, when the Hungarian Socialist Workers' Party (MSZMP) started to formulate its new ideological base. The new leadership tried to detach itself from the Rákosi era and emphasized that there was a break between the policies of the Party before and after 1956. There were indeed discontinuities with the past, mostly because almost the entire MDP leadership had fled to Moscow during the uprising, which meant the disappearance of a potential leftist-dogmatist opposition.[79] The vanishing of the pre-1956 elite, the individual motives of the new leaders, and the general political

---

[76] ÁBTL 3.1.9. V-153 308; ÁBTL 3.1.5. O-14975/142; Pünkösti, *Rákosi bukása*, 440.

[77] ÁBTL 3.1.5. O-14975/181.

[78] ÁBTL 3.1.5. O-11737/1.

[79] Two previous general or first secretaries (Rákosi and Gerő), two prime ministers (Rákosi and Hegedüs), several ministers, Politburo members, and secretaries of the Central Committee (Révai), etc. Those who stayed in Hungary in October and participated in the new Party leadership were mostly second-rank leaders who had also spent some time in prison at the time of the purges (Gyula Kállai, Lajos Fehér, György Aczél, György Marosán, and Kádár himself).

atmosphere in Hungary in 1956 all favored the formulation of an official anti-Rákosi critique. The demand to draw a line between the Rákosi era and the ideology of the new leadership was raised at one of the earliest sessions of the MSZMP's Provisional Executive Committee, and it frequently resurfaced in the subsequent meetings. It was usually Kádár who advocated the idea, but he enjoyed the support of the majority in this regard.[80] Yet the formulation of a new interpretation of the past provoked agitated debates in the leadership. Some Central Committee members went so far as to claim that the errors committed in the Rákosi era were inherent in the political system and that the MDP was not a Marxist-Leninist Party at all.[81] Kádár normally played a mediating role during these disputes, and his contributions generally determined their outcome. It was Kádár, for example, who declared that the political misdeeds of the pre-1956 period originated in Rákosi's leadership methods and were not inherent in the political structure of the people's democracy. Kádár's role in shaping the interpretation of the 1950s was also crucial. He was the one who formulated the (in)famous "four causes" that had led to the outbreak of the 1956 "events." The first of these reasons was the "anti-Leninist, bureaucratic leadership methods of the Rákosi-Gerő clique."[82] The four-reason framework was the central theme of the renowned Party resolution in December 1956 that laid down the ideological foundations of the post-1956 political system and became the general guideline for subsequent historical interpretations.[83]

The issue of the "cult of personality," and Rákosi's responsibility for its promotion, was repeatedly raised during the meetings of the provisional Party organs, especially in early 1957. There was a debate, for example, at the meeting of the Provisional Executive Committee (IIB) on March 26 about the use of portraits of the leaders. Although several IIB members suggested that the use of pictures at demonstrations could lead to the revival of

---

[80] To indicate the frequency of this issue: Sándor Balogh et al., eds., *A Magyar Szocialista Munkáspárt ideiglenes vezető testületeinek jegyzőkönyvei*, vol. 1 (Budapest: Gondolat, 1993), 38, 62, 113, 149, 155, 187, 202, 232–33, 284.

[81] On the formation of ideology in the early Kádár era, see Melinda Kalmár, *Ennivaló és hozomány: A kora kádárizmus ideológiája* (Budapest: Magvető, 1998).

[82] Balogh et al., *A Magyar Szocialista Munkáspárt*, vol. 1, 139, 141, 210, 214–15.

[83] "Az MSZMP Ideiglenes Központi Bizottságának határozata a forradalom okairól, a kialakult helyzetről és a part feladatairól," ibid., 238–46.

the "personality cult,"[84] Deputy Prime Minister Ferenc Münnich emphasized the significance of leader portraits in the representation of power:

> The question of pictures is not a question of modesty, it is a political question. We are a political party, and our leaders must be known by the people. *We are a Communist Party, and in our Party, respect, based on the leaders' popularity, has a crucial role. We need this.*[85]

Marosán took the middle road and argued for the limited use of portraits, proposing the equal use of pictures of all the important leaders. He argued that carrying only the portrait of the first secretary might suggest the rebirth of the cult: "We should not let even the illusion of the personality cult appear. If we put out only one man's portrait, that would definitely mean a personality cult."[86]

Kádár himself retained a strong anti-cult stance during this time. On April 5, 1957, he called for an end to ritualized applause ("we don't want the rebirth of the cult of personality. Stop thunderous applause, it is not correct").[87] On June 17 he categorically rejected the leader cult altogether: "Is there any need for the cult of personality? No, there isn't."[88] Apart from the critique of portraits and mechanical applause, manifestations of the cult were not discussed by the new leadership in the immediate post-1956 period.

The term "personality cult" nonetheless recurred at the meetings of the IIB in late 1956 and early 1957, and it was generally used in the same conceptual context as before the revolution. The draft resolution of the MSZMP on April 9, 1956, for example, claimed that the concentration of power in the hands of the Rákosi clique was coupled with the spreading of "bureaucratic methods" and violations of the law.[89] Party democracy and the Leninist norms of Party life were desecrated, and criticism and self-criticism were suppressed, which gave rise to the "cult of personality" and led to a loosening of the ties between the workers and the Party.

---

[84] For example, Mrs. Ferenc Cservenka, Dezső Nemes, and Sándor Orbán.
[85] Emphasis added. Balogh et al., *A Magyar Szocialista Munkáspárt*, vol. 2, 331.
[86] Ibid., 331–32.
[87] Balogh et al., *A Magyar Szocialista Munkáspárt*, vol. 3, 42.
[88] Balogh et al., *A Magyar Szocialista Munkáspárt*, vol. 4, 203–4.
[89] Balogh et al., *A Magyar Szocialista Munkáspárt*, vol. 3, 73.

With the proclamation of the MSZMP's December Decree in 1956, the Kádár system considered the legacy of the Rákosi era settled, and the problematic issues of the pre-1956 years were shelved for some time. However, Rákosi's growing impatience in the Soviet Union, and his obvious intention to return to Hungary, manifested in petitions to the Soviet as well as to the Hungarian Party leadership, made Kádár increasingly uncomfortable and kept the issue of the cult on the agenda. The MSZMP leaders tried to keep the ex-leader away from Hungary for as long as possible, and the Politburo eventually turned down his request to return to the country in January 1958.[90] The Central Committee subsequently informed the Party leadership of the decision in a letter, claiming that Rákosi had "gradually sunk deeper into the swamp of the cult of personality" after 1949, which became the source of critical errors. The letter also declared that the return of the MDP's ex-leader to Hungary would not be desirable, as it could trigger bewilderment among the Party rank-and-file.[91]

At the MSZMP congress in late November 1959, the stigmatization of Rákosi continued. Kádár, in his contribution, attempted to exempt the Party from blame in the promotion of the cult and held Rákosi solely responsible for the development of an exaggerated leader-worship.

> For the cult of personality and for the grave errors it caused ... the Hungarian Communists, the Party, and the people who followed Rákosi before cannot be blamed. We can blame only those who invoked these [phenomena]: Mátyás Rákosi himself.[92]

Rákosi was very unhappy with the way the MSZMP treated him, and he grew more impatient and menacing in his petitions to return to Hungary.[93] In desperation he left Krasnodar, where he had settled, and secretly traveled to Moscow (in June 1960) to plead his case with the respective Soviet and Hungarian authorities, including the Hungarian ambassador.

---

[90] Rákosi was the only one of the group of exiles in the Soviet Union (i.e., the pre-1956 leadership) whose request was rejected.
[91] Pünkösti, *Rákosi bukása*, 466–68.
[92] Ibid., 484.
[93] For Rákosi's efforts to come home, see István Feitl, *A bukott Rákosi (Rákosi Mátyás 1956–1971 között)* (Budapest: Politikatörténeti Alapítvány, 1993); Pünkösti, *Rákosi bukása*, 425–563. For

Although Rákosi's mission was unsuccessful, the MSZMP commissioned Sándor Nógrádi and György Aczél to investigate the affair and Rákosi's attitude to the new Party line. During the seven-hour-long interview with the two delegates in August 1960, Rákosi showed no signs of self-criticism or remorse. He refused to admit his responsibility for the errors, and, staying true to his own mythical persona, he continued to claim all credit for the Party's successes before 1956.[94]

The Twenty-Second Congress of the CPSU in 1961, and the new wave of de-Stalinization campaigns it ushered in, highlighted the issue of the cult once again. Khrushchev's speech at the Congress undermining the linking of Stalin's persona to the war myth condemned the ex-dictator much more openly than the "secret speech" had done. Stalin's body was subsequently removed from the Lenin Mausoleum and was buried under concrete beside the Kremlin wall.[95] Unlike in 1956, Stalin's second symbolic dethronement in the Soviet Union was not followed by general confusion or heightened power struggles in the countries of the Eastern bloc. There were no significant changes in the upper echelons of the satellite parties, except in Bulgaria, where Todor Zhivkov used the opportunity to get rid of his main rival, Prime Minister Anton Yugov. The only country that implemented conspicuous anti-cult policies after the Twenty-Second Congress was the one that had not done so in 1956: Czechoslovakia. The demolition of the Stalin statue in Prague in November 1962—which took a month—symbolizes the ultimate demise of the Soviet leader's cult in the Eastern bloc.[96] The cult of Gottwald also started to disintegrate in 1956, although his embalmed body was only removed from his mausoleum in 1962.

The revival of anti-cult policies in the Soviet Union contributed to another reassessment of the legacy of the Rákosi years in Hungary. In 1962,

---

Rákosi's petitioning activity in the period following the revolution, see István Feitl, "A moszkvai emigráció és az MSZMP (Rákosi Mátyás 1956–1958 között)," *Múltunk* 36, no. 4 (1991): 3–30. See also Magdolna Baráth, "A Moszkvába menekült magyar pártvezetők 1956. október végi-november eleji tevékenységéről," *Múltunk* 50, no. 1 (2005): 272–96.

[94] Pünkösti, *Rákosi bukása*, 486–88.

[95] Filtzer, 21–22. On the effect of the 22nd Congress on the Stalin cult, see Jones, "Strategies of De-Mythologization," 191–243.

[96] On the demolition of the statue, see Pichova, "The Lineup for Meat," 622–27.

the Central Committee of the MSZMP set up a three-member committee to investigate the violations of the law during "the era of the personality cult." The members of the committee were Béla Biszku, Antal Apró, and Nógrádi, who assigned Aczél and Nógrádi to interrogate Rákosi again concerning his responsibility for the abuses of power. However, Rákosi remained unwilling to show penitence in front of the delegates. Thus the final report of the committee, submitted in August 1962, took a virulent anti-Rákosist attitude.[97]

Although the document failed to provide a detailed analysis of the cult—it focused on the intra-Party purges instead—it offered a limited overview of the nature and the extent of the misdeeds, and it officially denounced and stigmatized Rákosi and his "clique" for the errors committed. The document provided a rather narrow definition of the "personality cult"; in fact, it was more limited than similar assessments from before 1956. The resolution defined the cult as "the deification of one person and the underestimation of the historical role of the masses,"[98] and it generally demonstrated the new leadership's attempt to blame Rákosi alone for it. The document made no reference to the hierarchical nature of the cult; it did not name any other leaders who had been responsible for its promotion; it did not explain how the cult emerged; and it failed to provide insights into the mechanisms and the functioning of the cult. By giving such a restricted explanation of the cult and shifting all responsibility for its emergence to Rákosi, the Kádár regime whitewashed its leaders, especially those who had been deeply involved in the wrongdoings of the Rákosi era, including Nógrádi, as well as Kádár himself.[99] Even so, the August 1962 decision of the Central Committee that was based on the report meant a symbolic break with the past and relegated the Rákosi cult to the dustbin of history.[100]

---

[97] Levente Sipos, "Hiányos leltár (I.) MSZMP-dokumentumok a 'személyi kultusz idején elkövetett törvénysértésekről,'" *Társadalmi Szemle* 49, no. 11 (1994): 72–94.

[98] Levente Sipos, "Hiányos leltár (I.)," 78.

[99] Kádár, as a minister of internal affairs, played a crucial role in the Rajk trial at the time.

[100] The minutes of the meeting of the Central Committee on August 12–14, 1962, and the decision are located at MOL, 288. fond. 4/50–55.

From Politics to History

After the MSZMP Congress in 1962 that expelled Rákosi from the Party, the issue of the "cult of personality" had been gradually transferred from the sphere of politics to the domain of history. Nevertheless, the transmission was not smooth. The first major synthesis that incorporated the 1950s into the narrative of Party history only appeared in the late 1970s. The reason for this silence in Hungarian historiography is generally rooted in the ideology of the Kádár system and its view on the 1956 revolution and the Rákosi years. The official interpretation of the period—crystallized in the December Resolution in 1956—hindered the formation of critical academic interpretations and determined the approach of historical studies that were written after 1956. In essence, academic assessments of the topic rearticulated the official interpretation of the period; thus the critical tone of the works published in the 1970s and 1980s never exceeded the limits of criticism set by the regime. Using the Party resolution as a guideline, historians elaborated a theoretical framework to interpret Party history in the 1950s, usually referred to as the "distortion theory."[101] According to the argument of one of the most significant works discussing the period of the people's democracy, all errors began in September 1947 with the formulation of the Cominform's principle of the leading role of the Soviet Union, which led to the mechanical copying of the Soviet model and resulted in grave economic and political distortions.[102] The distortions involved the concentration of power in the hands of the "Rákosi clique" (including Rákosi, Gerő, and Farkas), which walked the path of adventurism, conspiracy, and careerism. Collective leadership, criticism, and Party democracy were overshadowed by dictatorial leadership, which led to sectarianism, dogmatism, and violations of the law.

Although the first narrative of Party history that discussed the Rákosi era was soon followed by the publication of other syntheses, such books

---

[101] The very word "distortion" had already been used in 1953 to indicate the "Rákosi clique's deviation" from the "Party line."

[102] Sándor Balogh et al., *A magyar népi demokrácia története, 1944–1962* (Budapest: Kossuth, 1978), 210–39. For the "distortion theory" in English, see György Borsányi and János Kende, *The History of the Working Class Movement in Hungary* (Budapest: Corvina, 1988).

also adopted the same interpretational framework.[103] Rákosi was usually interpreted negatively in the works of Party historians, or his name was simply omitted from the history books.[104] Regardless of the positions he had held and of his undeniable influence on Hungarian politics in the coalition period,[105] he virtually disappeared from the history of the pre-takeover years. The lack of reference to him partly reflects the tendency of post-1956 socialist historiography to place historical scholarship on a more genuine Marxist footing by associating progress, development, and success with collective efforts (the people and the Party) and by identifying errors, deviation, and reactionary activity with individuals. For this reason, Rákosi's responsibility for the abuses of power was strongly emphasized, while his contribution to the establishment of the Communist system was not acknowledged.

Historians addressed the 1950s mostly in general Party histories, and thus there was no elaborate analysis of the leader cult in academic works published during the Kádár era. However, comments and remarks on the cult appeared in such texts. Some authors mentioned the flood of greetings, especially from athletes, and the fusion of the Party and Rákosi's persona in Communist propaganda. The elections of 1953, when Rákosi, Gerő, and Farkas were nominated in all electoral districts in the country as the primary candidates, were also referred to as the "orgy of the personality cult."[106] Irrespective of their generally broad focus, historical works about the 1950s all condemned the extreme worship of Rákosi and the exaggerated reverence of his persona.

In the historical narrative of the Kádár era, the phrase "cult of personality" occurs within the meta-conceptual framework of the distortion theory, alongside expressions such as the "lack of Party democracy," "lack of collective leadership," "lack of criticism," "dictatorial and bureaucratic leadership," "violations of legality," "concentration of positions," and so on. The term also recurs when the June (1953) decision of the MDP or the

---

[103] Sándor Balogh et al., *Magyaroszág a XX. században* (Budapest: Kossuth, 1986); Szabó, *Az "ötvenes évek"*; Korom, "A személyi kultusz néhány kérdése"; Sándor Orbán, "A szocializmus építésének első fél évtizede (1948–1953)," *Századok* 119, no. 2 (1985): 462–98.

[104] For example, in the book *A magyar népi demokrácia története*, Rákosi's name is only mentioned three times in about 140 pages.

[105] It is enough to mention the phrase "salami tactics," coined by Rákosi.

[106] Gyarmati et al., *Magyar hétköznapok*, 249.

CPSU's Twentieth Congress is discussed. Nevertheless, the term is most commonly used as part of the set phrase "the period of the personality cult."[107] Due to the Kádár regime's rigid ideological stance on Rákosi, and due to the nature of historical works published at the time, the concept of the "cult of personality" remained vague and general. The lack of a detailed analysis of the notion and its use in a general sense implies that in the Kádár era, the expression was regarded as a blanket term for the Stalinist era in Hungary. Reflecting upon the general nature of the concept, one Party historian observed: "With the aim of describing the hardest few years [of distortion] from a uniform ideological point of view, they [i.e., historians] willingly used the flourishing label 'cult of personality.'"[108]

The "Withering Away" of the Rákosi Cult

The spatial-visual, as well as the textual, manifestations of the Rákosi cult vanished in 1956, and the continuing de-Stalinization campaign after the revolution led to the Kádár regime's official condemnation of the "cult of personality" on several occasions. Furthermore, the traumatic experience of 1956 prevented the restoration of the Rákosi myth in later years. Memories of the terror and the revolution remained all too vivid to allow for a revival of Rákosi's adoration. Despite the fact that the Soviet Union and most countries in the Soviet bloc witnessed either the persistence or a certain revival of the cultic representation of leaders, the Hungarian leadership remained dedicated to erasing the memory of the times when Communist politicians were treated as divine. Although elements of the Stalin cult were recycled during the Brezhnev era, Kádár's government did not follow this return to pre-Twentieth Congress political rituals.[109] After the

---

[107] Normally in a context where historians claim that these two events meant the beginning of suppressing the "cult of personality."

[108] Orbán, "A szocializmus építésének…," 488.

[109] On the renaissance of the Stalin cult in the Brezhnev period, see Victor Zaslavsky, "The Rebirth of the Stalin Cult in the USSR," in Victor Zaslavsky, *The Neo-Stalinist State: Class, Ethnicity and Consensus in Soviet Society* (New York, 1994), 3–21. For an analysis of ambivalent representations of Stalin in the Brezhnev era, see Polly Jones, *Myth, Memory, Trauma: Rethinking the Stalinist Past in the Soviet Union, 1953–70* (New Haven, CT: Yale University Press, 2013), 212–57.

temporary setback caused by Khrushchev's de-Stalinization campaigns, cultic representations of leaders persisted in the countries of Central and Eastern Europe, with the exception of Hungary. This partly had to do with the fact that the language of the cult never really disappeared from Soviet political discourse, despite the general abandonment of Stalinist rituals and political practices after 1953. Khrushchev himself was also described occasionally in ways reminiscent of Stalin—"close friend to all the country's peoples," "cosmic father," "steward of truth, progress, life and happiness," and so on—especially after the June 1957 plenum of the Central Committee.[110]

The cult also crept back into the countries of the Soviet bloc. The Communist Party in Poland, for example, resumed representing its leaders in cultic terms after the fall of Gomułka, manifested in the glorification of Edward Gierek and Wojciech Jaruzelski.[111] Cultic representations were used to depict Erich Honecker in the GDR and Todor Zhivkov ("Uncle Tosho") in Bulgaria. In Czechoslovakia, while living leaders were not venerated under Gustáv Husák, the country witnessed a certain revival of the Gottwald cult in the 1970s.[112] One of the most remarkable signs of the return of Communist idols to Eastern Europe was the birth in Romania of the Ceaușescu cult (after a brief renaissance of the cult around Gheorghiu-Dej). Besides using the Stalinist model, the Ceaușescu cult absorbed Chinese and North Korean Communist patterns of leader veneration.[113] The myths of Tito and Enver Hoxha were largely unaffected by the overall decay of the cult during the de-Stalinization campaigns and continued to flourish throughout the period. They were even supplemented after

---

[110] Pyzhikov, "The Cult of Personality," 23. On the emergence of the Khrushchev cult, see James George Boylan, "The Development of the Khrushchev 'Cult of Personality': A Survey and Interpretation of *Pravda* and *Izvestia*" (MA thesis, University of Washington, 1961).

[111] Zaremba, "The Second Step of a Ladder." For a comparison of the representation of leaders in Poland and the GDR after the death of Stalin, see Behrends, "Nach dem Führerkult."

[112] I am indebted to Luděk Vacín for this observation.

[113] Alice Mocanescu, "The Cult of Ceaușescu in Painting: The Soviet Pattern Meets the Romanian Tradition," paper presented at the workshop *Stalin and the Lesser Gods: The Leader Cult in Communist Dictatorships in Comparative Perspective, 1928–1961*, European University Institute, Florence, May 15–16, 2003; Ádám Tolnay, "Ceaușescu's Journey to the East," unpublished paper (special thanks to the author for sending the paper). On the cult of Gheorghiu-Dej, see Mocanescu, "Surviving 1956."

1964.[114] While the cultic images of Communist leaders after 1956 undoubtedly had their roots in Stalinism, the public personae of the leaders were crafted with respect to the changing political environment and took social expectations into account (to some extent at least). The imagery of Party secretaries was significantly "modernized": national interests, consumption, and welfare became important themes in the cultic discourse, and Communist propaganda made a notable shift toward emphasizing the leaders' managerial skills and not their mystical, divine powers. In addition to the tempering of irrational elements in representations of authority, there was also a tendency in the late socialist era to distribute symbolic capital in a more balanced way and to strengthen the symbolic appeal of impersonal institutions (the Party) and offices (the president).

Several factors explain the general aversion to creating new "divinities" in Hungarian politics during the Kádár era. Kádár's faithfulness to the Khrushchev line even after the fall of the Soviet leader, the anti-Rákosi stance of the new elite, and the artificiality and weakness of the Rákosi myth all contributed to the fact that there were no significant manifestations of the Communist leader cult in Hungary after 1956. The symbols of Rákosi's exaltation were mostly destroyed in 1956, and memories of the once-deified leader gradually faded in the decades that followed the Uprising. At the same time, an unusual consensus emerged in society on the historical interpretation of Rákosi. As one of the most loathed figures in Hungarian history, he never became the target of nostalgic feelings, and there was no attempt to commercialize his image after the collapse of Communism in Hungary either. (Unlike what happened in the Soviet Union after 1991 with regard to Lenin.)[115] Rákosi's marginal—and indisputably negative—position in contemporary Hungarian historical consciousness is demonstrated by the fact that a recent book about popular perceptions of twentieth-century Hungarian history devoted only three pages to the

---

[114] Sretenovic and Puto, "Leader Cults in the Western Balkans."

[115] On the erosion of the Lenin cult, see Trevor J. Smith, "Lenin for Sale: The Rise and Fall of the Personality Cult of V. I. Lenin in Soviet Russia" (MA thesis, Carleton University, 1995); Trevor J. Smith, "The Collapse of the Lenin Personality Cult in Soviet Russia, 1985–1995," *Historian* 60, no. 2 (1998): 325–43. With the exception of the Rákosi candles sold in the museum/memorial called the House of Terror in Budapest, there have been no significant attempts to create a commercial item out of the ex-leader of the MDP.

Rákosi era.[116] The fact that few longed for the return of Rákosi after 1956 does not mean that the cult of "Stalin's best Hungarian disciple" disappeared without a trace. Although it would be difficult to assess the attitude of the Party bureaucracy toward the Rákosi myth after 1956, the dogmatist, leftist political line embodied by Rákosi evidently retained some support among Party functionaries. Stalinist practices, attitudes, and mentalities survived 1956 and resurfaced during the retribution after the Uprising. The revival of the legal practices of the "era of the cult" is demonstrated by the occasional inclusion of iconoclastic acts—involving pictures or busts of Stalin and Rákosi—in the list of charges against individuals persecuted for their involvement in the revolutionary events.[117] Despite the official condemnation of Stalin and his "best Hungarian apprentice," it seems that some courts—and some police departments—continued to consider the defiling of the fallen leaders' images to be expressions of hostility toward the regime, and they acted accordingly.[118] There was even one police agent in Bács-Kiskun County who felt it necessary (in 1959!) to inform on a retired village notary who, while in prison, had written an anti-Rákosi poem titled "The Death of Rákosi."[119]

There were several reasons for the endurance of fragments of pro-Rákosi sentiments, but one of them was certainly the dominance of anti-Kádár sentiments in the first few years after the suppression of the 1956 revolution. Popular antagonism toward the Kádár regime was so strong that even rumors of a leftist—and by implication pro-Rákosist—coup d'état led by László Piros, former minister of internal affairs, excited certain sections of society.[120] However, the new leadership's firm stance against Rákosi and the "cult of personality" prevented the articulation of pro-Rákosi comments or opinions in public. Indications of enduring support

---

[116] Mária Vásárhelyi, *Csalóka emlékezet. A 20. század történelme a magyar közgondolkodásban* (Bratislava: Kalligram, 2007), 126–28.

[117] See the examples above. The archival references to such cases are ÁBTL 3.1.9. V-153 308, ÁBTL 3.1.5. O-14975/142, ÁBTL 3.1.5. O-11737/1, ÁBTL 3.1.9 V-155806.

[118] It should be noted that all the cases I have come across were discussed by county courts. I have not found similar examples from Budapest.

[119] ÁBTL 3.1.2. M-15907.

[120] ÁBTL 3.1.2 M-20596/3. Kádár was not very popular among dogmatist left-wing members of the Party either, mostly because of his attempts to marginalize the pre-1956 leadership *en masse*.

for the fallen Party leader are extremely rare and are far from representative. The example of a man who, in January 1957, placed a portrait of Rákosi in the hallway of a toilet in the local house of culture in Somogyvár with the inscription "Long live Rákosi, our leader; down with the Kádár government" and then urinated in one of the rooms cannot be interpreted as a typical manifestation of love for the dismissed Party secretary.[121] The 1994 book by Eugénia Bíró (Rákosi's sister-in-law) that portrays the Party leader in a positive light cannot be used for similar purposes either, due to its obvious emotional bias.[122] Evidence of the cult's endurance could also be found beyond the borders of Hungary. Jenő Fock, for example, known for his strongly anti-Rákosist stance after 1956, recalled a 1958 visit to a Communist district mayor in Paris whose office still displayed Rákosi's portrait. To explain his abiding respect for Rákosi, the mayor exclaimed: "He gave us Thorez!"[123]

Probably the last person to demonstrate faith in the extraordinary qualities of the MDP leader was Rákosi himself. In a private letter in 1956, he claimed that "the construction of Hungarian socialism hasn't got a single brick or stone up to the present day that doesn't bear the marks of my hand in a positive or a negative way."[124] Besides appealing to the image of the leader as the embodiment of socialist construction, Rákosi also tended to equate himself with the Party, even after his dismissal, as Aczél and Nógrádi reported in July 1962.[125] His memoirs also attempt to justify his deeds in the working-class movement and thereby demonstrate his own exceptional nature. As the editors of the memoirs suggest, this attempt is, in fact, one of the major tropes in the book.[126] The author's frequent emphasis on the importance of his insignificant relationship with Lenin testifies to this point. Thus besides being probably the first to use the phrase "Rákosi cult," he was also the last to demonstrate a sincere attachment to the imagery of his cult.

---

[121] ÁBTL 3.1.9. V-144922.
[122] Eugénia Bíró, *Száműzetésben* (Budapest: Littoria, 1994).
[123] Pünkösti, *Rákosi bukása*, 451.
[124] Ibid., 528.
[125] Ibid., 500.
[126] Feitl and Sipos, "Előszó," vii–ix.

After the "secret speech," the phrase "personality cult" was used more frequently in Hungary, as in the entire Soviet bloc, and the phrase became prominent in political vocabulary. The definition of the phenomenon, however, remained somewhat narrow, despite regular references to the typical manifestations of leader worship. Nevertheless, Khrushchev's criticism of the cult led to an increase in public discontent within the bloc that eventually caused local leader cults to be significantly scaled back. The launching of the de-Stalinization campaign also influenced the Hungarian version of the cult; indeed, in the long run, it put an end to its short renaissance. The dismantling process, however, was not without obstacles. The MDP leadership, just like the Party elites in other parts of Central and Eastern Europe, remained uncertain after the Twentieth Congress as to how to proceed with de-Stalinization policies. Moreover, Rákosi's illusions concerning the correctness of his political line prevented the Party from fully confronting its troubled legacy, including the infamous "personality cult." Although during the "New Course" Gerő and Nagy had already dropped hints about Rákosi's responsibility in a closed circle, and Kovács used the Farkas case in 1956 to put the Party secretary under pressure, for a long time Rákosi remained reluctant to admit his role in the promotion of the cult. (He maintained this disposition in exile, as his memoirs prove.) The Party leader's erratic and unconvincing attempts to salvage himself necessarily failed in the heated oppositionist atmosphere of 1956, despite the fact that Communist propaganda never turned against Rákosi until the Kádár era. The erosion of the Rákosi cult was unstoppable; the last remnants were wiped out by the uprising in October.

Rákosi never witnessed firsthand the collapse of his cult, since he resigned in July and shortly afterwards flew to the Soviet Union, where, in the early 1960s, his medical treatment gradually turned into an exile. The ex-dictator, or "Lenin's last living colleague," as he often described himself in his memoirs, saw all of his efforts to return to Budapest blocked by the new political elite. He died in the Soviet Union on February 5, 1971.

The history of the dismantling of the Rákosi cult is largely the history of a problem of conceptualization. The fact that the Soviet leadership refused, or failed, to provide a clear-cut definition of the cult left the Party leaders of the Soviet bloc in a state of uncertainty regarding the applicability of the concept. Moreover, the lack of directives from Moscow and the constantly changing parameters of cult criticism triggered confusion as to which measures to take in order to de-sacralize the "lesser gods." The difficulty of coming to terms with the "cult of personality" had already left an imprint on anti-cult policies during the "New Course"; however, the dilemma became much more acute after the "secret speech." When the denunciation of Stalin became public, the MDP leadership faced popular demands for a credible explanation, at a time when Moscow was providing less and less assistance. The decreasing frequency with which guidelines were issued from the Presidium, and the endurance of the Rákosi myth within the Party bureaucracy, combined with a growing pressure from below, resulted in the initiation of half-hearted and often contradictory anti-cult measures. It seems that neither the MDP nor the MSZMP leaders were absolutely sure of the actual limits of the cult. Setting up the cult's parameters and drawing the line between the excessive exaltation of leaders and the necessary popularization of them thus remained a difficult task for both regimes.

Besides its revelations regarding the Great Terror, Khrushchev's "secret speech" provided an unsystematic and somewhat vague approach to the ritualized exaltation of Communist leaders. As Jan Plamper observed, Khrushchev used "cult of personality" as a blanket term that included the abandonment of collective decision-making practices and wide-scale purges, as well as the personification of the narrative of Party history.[127] The interpretation of the term "cult of personality" in official documents also remained remarkably vague in Hungary, despite the fact that several members of the MDP leadership seem to have had a reasonably complex perception of the roots, the functions, and the major characteristics of the phenomenon. Although the announcements of the MDP regarding the cult were limited and vague, a narrowing of the cult's semantic field followed the 1956 revolution. Kádár and the new Party leadership exploited the negative symbolic value of the concept in order to delegitimize Rákosi's rule and to lend legitimacy to their own regime. Strictly defining the cult as Rákosi's alone was, in fact, an essential part of the MSZMP's legitimation strategy. In this way it hoped to whitewash other leaders who had also been involved in the crimes—euphemistically referred to as

---

[127] Plamper, "Introduction," 13–42.

"errors"—of the "Rákosi clique." The gradual reduction of the scope of the cult's definition culminated in 1962, by which time there was no mention of its ritual nature in Party documents, the discursive influence of the phenomenon was ignored, and no one talked about the emergence and the hierarchical structure of leader veneration anymore. The resolution of the MSZMP Congress in 1962 used the concept "cult of personality" as an umbrella term that offered an essentialized view of the Rákosi regime. The term came to be identified with the show trials, mass deportations, and purges of the early 1950s.

Conclusion

The leader cult in Central and Eastern Europe was a propaganda campaign deployed to advance the ultimate goal of Communism: the transformation of collective identities. The construction of the leader's charismatic persona was assisted by the promotion of Stalinist notions of patriotism in a complex ideological offensive that aimed to reconfigure traditional perceptions of the self and the community.[1] The fusion of Soviet mythology with ideas of nationhood was reflected in the emergence of hybrid narratives about the nation's past. The biographies of Communist Party secretaries did not merely offer a personification of the history of the movement; they also incorporated the leader into the history of the nation. His ascension to leadership was usually described as a decisive moment in the people's struggle for freedom that opened up the path toward a glorious future. The struggles of the past, the hopes of the present, and confidence in the future converged in the persona of the Party secretary, who came to embody the whole community in his link to its fate. By advancing the image of the leader as the epitome of the new socialist nation, the cult contributed to the Soviet-type nation-building project and to the erosion of traditional perceptions of belonging. Nevertheless, while Stalinism—both in Soviet Russia and the Soviet bloc—produced new collective identities, the ideal-typical "New Man," the shining example of class consciousness, who possessed a certain vaguely defined supra-national identity, never materialized.

---

[1] On the duality of Stalinist mobilization, see Brandenberger, *National Bolshevism*. For parallels between nation-building and attempts to create a Soviet community, see Joshua Sanborn, "Family, Fraternity, and Nation-Building in Russia, 1905–1925," in *A State of Nations: Empire and Nation-Making in the Age of Lenin and Stalin*, ed. Terry Martin and Ronald Grigor Suny (New York and Oxford: Oxford University Press, 2001), 93–110.

The cult of Stalin in Central and Eastern Europe was a direct consequence of Sovietization after World War II. In fact, the cult was a critical component in the expansion of Soviet domination after the war. Through the continuous ritual endorsement of Moscow's control over the satellite states, it contributed to the consolidation of Stalinist regimes and the transformation of identities in the countries of the bloc. The cult was also a way to link the center and the peripheries by emotional means: the peoples of Central and Eastern Europe were supposed to feel love and gratitude toward Stalin and the Soviet Union, and they were expected to nurture bonds of friendship with the other satellite states. The worship of Stalin prompted the emergence of a transnational system of leader cults intended to reinforce the illusion of an affective relationship between Moscow and the countries of the Soviet bloc. The orchestrated veneration of Mátyás Rákosi in Hungary assumed prominence in this particular historical context. His exaltation did not develop in isolation; it was entangled with processes of Sovietization and was embedded in a hierarchical system of cults. His "cult of personality" was not merely the excessive self-adulation of a Communist dictator; it was an integral part of a transnational system of cultic representations that characterized Stalinist political culture.

The influence of Soviet directives on the construction of mythical figures remains unclear, but it seems likely that the choreographed veneration in the satellite parties was advanced mostly by the national Party elites. The varying scale of the public adulation of mini-Stalins, and the role of national traditions in the shaping of godlike representations of Party secretaries, also indicate that the phenomenon emerged primarily as the result of self-Sovietization rather than explicit Soviet orders. The Rákosi cult certainly seems to provide an example of such self-Sovietization. The diligence with which the Hungarian leader adopted the Soviet model after World War II indicates that no external pressure was needed to encourage him to implement the Soviet-type veneration of leaders. His regular involvement in propaganda affairs and his control over the secret police enabled him to oversee and monitor the shaping of his mythical persona. He was not as a meticulous an editor of cult material as Stalin, but he did play a role in the manufacture of certain cult products. His position at the top of the institutional hierarchy also allowed him to define the dimensions of leader worship in Hungary. While he objected to some of the absurdly irrational aspects of his constructed persona, he was certainly responsible for the fact that his cult became one of the most pervasive in the Soviet bloc. Rákosi's attachment to his own myth was clearly demonstrated by his hesitation in tempering cultic practices after 1953.

Although Moscow's direct influence in the creation of Communist divinities in Hungary remains unclear, Soviet strategies of cult-building were applied extensively to advance the apotheosis of the Communist Party secretary. Discursive strategies to portray him as an omnipresent leader, a wise teacher, a benevolent father, and the epitome of the nation's history were clearly inspired by the Soviet model. These images were endorsed by a set of rituals and visual techniques similar to those in the Soviet Union. The cult's demolition, unlike its construction, was the result of a direct order from Moscow. In the Soviet bloc, the cults of local Party secretaries were gradually restrained after Stalin's death, and in the case of Hungary (and the GDR), de-Stalinization also included criticism—and reprimands—of the leader. The reluctance and inconsistency the Party elite showed in revisiting the problematic aspects of the regime's symbolic foundations were related to the Kremlin's shifting stance in this regard. Moscow's attitude to the de-mythologization of leaders changed according to the power struggle among Stalin's heirs, and as a result, the Hungarian leadership's commitment to the tempering of the Rákosi myth was also constantly changing.

While the main impetus to transform ordinary Party functionaries into extraordinary personalities originated in the Soviet Union, the actual vocabulary used to depict such figures did not: it was rooted in national cultic traditions. The endurance of cult language is demonstrated by the persistence of imaginary leader representations in state and nation-building strategies in modern Hungary. The pervasiveness of such images indicates the continuing vitality of a cultic political culture in Hungarian society, which certainly casts doubt on Weber's argument linking the rise of charismatic personalities and extraordinary events. As Jan Plamper has also observed, cults tend to develop more intensely in periods of consolidation, and not necessarily during times of social upheaval.[2] The Stalin

---

[2] For Plamper's view of the notion of "charisma" and for critical reflections on his approach, see the blog debate on his monograph at http://russianhistoryblog.org/2012/04/the-stalin-cult-once-more-on-weber-reception/#fn-2499-1 (accessed December 22, 2014).

cult began to grow after the first Five-Year Plan, which was in line with the Soviet leader's attempt to consolidate the achievements of his "revolution from above." Similarly, the ritualization of satellite leader cults took place not during the turbulent postwar period but after the consolidation of Communist rule in the respective countries—with the possible exception of Yugoslavia. In other words, there was no real "charismatic moment" that provoked the ascension of Party secretaries in Central and Eastern Europe. Communist politicians generally elicited little "charismatic response" from the population; they were *made* charismatic. The campaign to fabricate a persona for the leader and generate an aura of exceptionality around him was a complex one: it included Party and government institutions and prominent members of the new elite, including intellectuals and propagandists. The serpentine institutional framework of cult-building and the national roots of the Rákosi myth suggest that the glorification of the leader in Hungary was not merely the self-aggrandizement of an over-diligent Stalinist puppet. Nonetheless, Rákosi's dependence on the Kremlin, and the evident resemblance of his imagery to representations of Stalin, leave no doubt as to the prime source of inspiration for his cult.

The imagined persona fabricated for the purposes of the cult was largely figurative.[3] The leader was generally portrayed as an abstract symbol and the personification of the cause; his actual personality was buried under the makeshift façade of cultic propaganda. The manufactured persona of the Party secretary assumed a collective personality that suppressed the individual behind the mythical mask. This was not a chance occurrence. The de-individualization of cultic figures was part of a conscious strategy to separate the real person from the invented persona. As Sarah Davies has suggested, Stalin objected to the intimacy of the cult and was inclined to eradicate the personal element from it.[4] His occasional attempts to rein in the excesses of cultic veneration indicate that he was very much aware

---

[3] The impersonal features of the cult have been recognized and commented upon by a number of historians. On Stalin's "cult of impersonality," see Robert Service, *Stalin: A Biography* (Basingstoke: Palgrave, 2010), 357–66. Juliane Fürst has also argued that Stalin's mythical figure was distant and intangible, like a movie hero. Fürst, *Stalin's Last Generation*, 125. On the impersonality of the Rákosi cult, see Pünkösti, *Rákosi a hatalomért*, 45. On the impersonalization of the official biography of Thorez and the "primacy of collective identity over ego," see Pennetier and Pudal, "Stalinism," 26–27.

[4] Davies, "Stalin and the Making of the Leader Cult," 29–46.

of the mobilizing potential of his fictitious and impersonal persona, which symbolized the abstract ideals and principles of Bolshevik ideology. Stalin's decision to prevent the publication of a book on his childhood and his active involvement in the revision of his official biography support this argument. It seems that Lenin had a similar view of his cult. He was generally dismissive of the glorification of his character, but he acknowledged the advantages of representing politics in personalized terms. He often criticized expressions of public adulation, yet he tended to appreciate embellished representations of his figure that portrayed him as the embodiment of the Party and the history of the working-class movement. When he reviewed a short biography written by his wife in 1919, Lenin removed all personal details and deliberately portrayed himself as the personification of the Party and its revolutionary past.[5] The result was an impersonal life story that lacked private details and was totally dedicated to the cause. It seems that both Lenin and Stalin valued the benefits of a depersonalized cult in galvanizing popular support. Soviet propaganda eventually turned both leaders into impersonal idols that epitomized the values and the utopian aspirations of the Communist movement and functioned as major rallying points in the regime's mobilization campaigns. Stalin, in fact, emerged as the embodiment of the Soviet Union and the symbol of Soviet power in the world.

The attempt to construct an impersonal leader image stemmed from the ideological foundations of the regime. Marxism generally dismissed the "cult of the individual" and postulated the masses as the force that pushed the wheel of history forward. The role of individuals was appreciated only to the extent that they personified the goals and aspirations of wider social forces. In this sense, Stalin's understanding of the "cult of the individual" was in accord with the main trends of Russian Marxist thought.[6] Therefore, the tendency to portray political leaders as representatives of abstract ideals and mobilizing symbols was harmonious with the regime's ideological foundations. It seems that under the surface of sycophantic eulogy and excessive flattery, the cult retained a degree of consistency with Marxist tradition.

---

[5] Tumarkin, *Lenin Lives!*, 76–77.
[6] For Stalin's ideological convictions and his view of the cult, see van Ree, *The Political Thought of Joseph Stalin*, 155–68.

The determination to depersonalize the public images of leaders could also be attributed to the militant, conspiratorial, and messianic character of the Communist movement. The Bolsheviks advocated the subordination of the individual to the cause and expected total commitment from their followers. Many of the first-generation communist leaders devoted themselves completely to the revolution, suppressing their individual needs and ambitions—although not to the extent suggested in their biographies. Rákosi could also be considered a representative of the committed Bolshevik revolutionary. Although he was ambitious and driven, he scarcely had any personal life outside the Communist Party after he joined its ranks. As one of his brothers remarked, the scope of his private life was narrow, and he hardly had any real friends.[7] Whenever he was invited to recount his life, he would only talk about his role in the movement—which he tended to exaggerate—and rarely mentioned his personal life. He retained a patronizing and paternal attitude toward people, and despite his obvious social skills, he remained lonely and austere.[8] Even his memoirs—written in exile—are dedicated exclusively to politics. Apart from the first few chapters, in which the fallen leader shared stories of his childhood, the autobiography lacks private details.

This depersonalization remained a key trope of Stalinist discourse, and it was one of the distinguishing features of Stalinist leader cults, including the cult of Rákosi.[9] As opposed to the celebration of modern celebrities, or cults based on aesthetic attachment (Princess Diana or Princess Elisabeth of Austria), for example, the institutionalized worship of Communist Party secretaries rarely exploited the personal character or magnetism of the individual leader. Prominent Bolsheviks were all portrayed as approachable people, but details about their personalities or their private lives were banished from officially approved narratives. The image of the accessible Party secretary rarely went hand-in-hand with a strong emphasis on that leader's individual traits. The aim of promoting the image of

---

[7] Pünkösti, *Rákosi a hatalomért*, 154–55.

[8] Ibid, 43.

[9] As Katerina Clark has observed, privacy was rarely depicted in Socialist Realist literature: heroes and heroines appear mainly in public (often at their workplace), and they are hardly ever portrayed in their domestic environment. The private sphere is either absent from such stories, or it is subordinated to the realm of the political. Clark, *The Soviet Novel*.

the "friend of the people" in an impersonal discursive framework proved counter-productive. The impersonal charisma of the Party secretary, in fact, rendered his figure remote and somewhat obscure. While the image of a distant, divine figure was counter-balanced with representations of an approachable, down-to-earth man, it mostly amplified the impersonal aspects of the cult.

However, the vagueness of the leader's constructed persona also had its advantages. Like representations of deities in traditional religions, the image of the Party secretary was elusive, indefinite, and impersonal, which added an element of majesty to the depictions of such individuals. Because little was known of the leader's actual personality, the grounds upon which he could be criticized were also narrow. The absence of any mention of Rákosi's Jewish background, for example, was related to the attempt to render the image of the leader invulnerable. Despite all efforts, however, the Rákosi myth remained weak and fragile. He was often disparaged for his Jewish origins—even by the Soviet Presidium—and though the cult invoked national traditions, he was primarily viewed as Moscow's puppet. The rigid, monotonous, and repetitive nature of cultic practices contributed further to the erosion of Rákosi's symbolic authority.

The "cult of personality," then, was a misnomer, since it was not a cult of *personality*. This is partly because it had very little to do with the actual personality of the leader, and partly because the worship of individual politicians emerged as part of a hierarchical system of myths and rituals. But this system was not the "cults of personalities" either. Since it was the depersonalized, public persona of the leader that was glorified instead of the actual person, the phenomenon should instead be defined as the "cult of persona" (or "cults of personae" to indicate the hierarchical dimensions of leader worship). It was the abstract symbol—the leader as the personification of the Party, the nation, and the working class—that was exalted in Communist propaganda, and not the personal qualities of individual Party secretaries. The charismatic features—whatever they were—of the given leader mattered little: he was glorified as the embodiment of a depersonalized, collective charisma that was constructed for the entire regime.

Paradoxically, the cult of Rákosi was both a success and a failure at the same time. It could be considered successful in the sense that it existed and functioned. It occupied center stage in the Party's mobilization campaigns;

the regime was able to ensure participation in its most significant rituals; and certain cult projects were realized. Moreover, involvement in the veneration of the Party secretary was not necessarily the result of compulsion. While coercion certainly played its part, some people used the cult to further their own ends, while others joined the ritual celebrations of the leader simply because their friends did the same. At the same time, the cult generally failed to accomplish what it set out to achieve: the consolidation of Soviet power in Hungary through ritual means. The reasons for this were numerous. The cult remained a somewhat chaotically managed campaign, and its development was further impeded by popular indifference as well as the incompetence endemic to the Communist propaganda institutions. Its trajectory, therefore, was generally conditioned by the structural defects that the Hungarian Stalinist regime had gradually accumulated along the way. Flaws in the system imposed excessive strain on the resources of the Party-state and posed an ever-deepening threat to its stability. Rákosi's Hungary, in fact, was a failing state with a malfunctioning propaganda machine, encumbered by inefficiency, incompetence, and ignorance.[10] In addition to systemic deficiencies, the cult was burdened by a certain potential for self-destruction implicit in its development. The continual expansion of the worship of Rákosi, therefore, inevitably led to the devaluation of his imagined persona. Inefficient propaganda, however, was only one of the reasons why Hungarian society failed to respond affirmatively to the leader's godlike imagery. The brevity of the cult's existence, the evident disparity between myth and reality, and the lack of a credible rationale for exalting uninspiring individuals were all responsible for the widespread lack of commitment in society to the veneration of Communist notables.

Although Rákosi was one of the most popular political figures during the coalition period, his reputation declined as his cult became ritualized. The Communist leader's popularity stemmed from the achievements of the postwar rebuilding process, while the gradual atrophying of his symbolic authority had to do with the rapid deterioration of living standards and the intensification of state violence after 1949. The regime was not

---

[10] György Gyarmati has argued that the general incompetence of the Party's cadres almost incapacitated the Hungarian state in the early 1950s. Gyarmati, *A Rákosi-korszak*, 215–19.

entirely aware of the gradual devaluation of Rákosi's persona: the loss of the means to accurately monitor shifts in popular opinion resulted in false perceptions and misinterpretations of the general mood in Hungarian society.

In general, the Rákosi myth failed to recruit a lasting social base for the Communist regime. Nevertheless, the cult had its supporters. Party functionaries, whose careers were linked to the leader's authority, recognized him as the safeguard of their privileges and the guarantor of the Party's unity and power. The majority of Hungarians, however, seem to have remained indifferent to, and even hostile toward, the choreographed veneration of Communist politicians. The propaganda campaign to create a role model for the population, therefore, remained mostly unsuccessful. While the image of Rákosi as a role model generally failed to inspire ordinary citizens to follow in his footsteps, the cult functioned as a model for some. The spread of "leaderism" indicates that some local notables drew inspiration from the Rákosi cult to exercise power in their locality. Unsanctioned cultic practices and abuses of authority, however, were sometimes deemed undesirable by the regime and were quelled. Besides influencing representations of power at the lower ends of the Party hierarchy, the cult also had a remarkable impact on popular communication strategies. Believers and non-believers alike tended to exploit the vocabulary of the Rákosi myth for pragmatic purposes, which ultimately turned the language of the cult into one of the communication codes of the Stalinist era in Hungary.

Despite the cult's failure to extend the social base of the regime, the Rákosi myth remained the central theme of Communist mobilization offensives until the introduction of the "New Course" in 1953. The regime's insistence on promoting a remarkably fragile persona for the leader contributed, ultimately, to an ever-increasing legitimacy deficit after 1949. The cult's weakness essentially derived from the undeniable link between the Party secretary and the Sovietization of Hungary—a connection that not even the appeal to national traditions could eclipse. As if sustaining a malfunctioning propaganda campaign was not enough, the dismantling and eventual collapse of the cult caused the Party elite further headaches. With the discrediting of the "cult of personality" after the death of Stalin, the regime had to start looking for alternative strategies of legitimation.

The vain attempt of the cult to boost social support for the Communist system was one of the reasons why Kádár crafted an anti-Rákosist façade for the post-1956 establishment. The Kádár regime, in fact, managed to gain broader social acceptance with its anti-cult rhetoric than the Rákosi cult could ever achieve. The shining halo of the leader gradually dimmed and was ultimately replaced by soft background lights.

After 1956, the Stalinist cultic system in Eastern Europe was dissolved. The role of Moscow as the sacred center of the Soviet symbolic universe faded somewhat, as the Kremlin made little effort to initiate and coordinate monumental ritual projects on an international scale. While cultic representations of leaders continued to feature in mobilization campaigns in the countries of the Soviet bloc, the closely integrated, hierarchical system of myths and rituals of the late Stalinist era fell apart. Leader cults after Stalin became increasingly localized; the imagery of individual Party secretaries became more diverse, and the construction of myths was more intimately tied to national (Communist) aspirations—as in the case of Gomułka or Ceaușescu—than to Soviet expansionism. The fabricated personae of prominent politicians lost their divine aura and became more down-to-earth and technocratic in appearance. Their connection to the Bolshevik master narrative was undeniable, of course, but this bond was loose, and it gradually eroded until Communist leader cults were buried in 1989 under the ruins of the Soviet project.

Bibliography

Abel, Ulf. "Icons and Soviet Art." In Arvidsson and Blomqvist, *Symbols of Power*, 141–62.
Aczél, Tamás. "Sztálin szobra – a béke jelképe" [Stalin's statue: The symbol of peace]. *Szovjet Kultúra* 4, no. 1 (1952): 6.
Aczél, Tamás, and Tibor Méray. *The Revolt of the Mind: A Case History of Intellectual Resistance behind the Iron Curtain*. Westport, Conn.: Greenwood Press, 1974.
Åman, Anders. "Symbols and Rituals in the People's Democracies during the Cold War." In Arvidsson and Blomqvist, *Symbols of Power*, 43–60.
Apor, Balázs. "Kommunikáció és rítusnyelv: 'személyi kultusz' és kommunista nyelvhasználat" [Communication and ritual Language: The 'cult of personality' and communist language use]. *Korunk* 3, no. 3 (2010): 69–75.
Apor, Balázs, Jan C. Behrends, Polly Jones, and E. A. Rees, eds. *The Leader Cult in Communist Dictatorships: Stalin and the Eastern Bloc*. Basingstoke: Palgrave, 2004.
Apor, Péter. "The Eternal Body: The Birth of the Pantheon of the Labor Movement in Budapest." *East Central Europe/L'Europe du Centre Est* 31 (2004): 23–42.
———. *Fabricating Authenticity in Soviet Hungary: The Afterlife of the First Hungarian Soviet Republic in the Age of State Socialism*. London: Anthem Press, 2014.
Arvidsson, Claes, and Lars Erik Blomqvist, eds. *Symbols of Power: The Esthetics of Political Legitimation in the Soviet Union and Eastern Europe*. Stockholm: Almqvist & Wiksell International, 1987.
Aulich, James and Marta Sylvestrová. *Political Posters in Central and Eastern Europe 1945–95*. Manchester: Manchester University Press, 2000.
Ausch, Sándor. *Az 1945–1946. évi infláció és stabilizáció* [Inflation and consolidation in 1945–1946]. Budapest: Kossuth, 1958.
Bakhtin, Mikhail. *Rabelais and His World*. Cambridge, MA: MIT Press, 1968.
Bakos, Katalin. "Folyamatosság és törés a plakátművészetben" [Continuity and break in poster art]. In Standeisky et al., *A fordulat évei*, 239–64.
Balogh, Margit. "Kommunizmus és egyházi ellenállás Magyarországon" [Communism and religious resistance in Hungary]. In *Mérlegen a XX. századi magyar*

történelem – értelmezések és értékelések [The balance sheet of Hungarian history in the twentieth century—interpretations, evaluations], edited by Levente Püski and Tibor Valuch, 271–85. Budapest: Debreceni Egyetem Törénelmi Intézete és az 1956-os Intézet, 2002.

Balogh, Sándor, ed. *Nehéz esztendők krónikája 1949–1953. Dokumentumok* [The chronicle of hard years, 1949–1953: Documents]. Budapest: Gondolat, 1986.

———. "Politikai reformpróbálkozások és kudarcaik 1953 és 1956 között" [Political reform attempts and their failure between 1953 and 1956]. *Társadalmi Szemle* 44, nos. 8–9 (1989): 19–35.

Balogh, Sándor, István Birta, Lajos Izsák, Sándor Jakab, Mihály Korom, and Péter Simon. *A magyar népi demokrácia története, 1944–1962* [The history of the Hungarian people's democracy, 1944–1962]. Budapest: Kossuth, 1978.

Balogh, Sándor, Jenő Gergely, Lajos Izsák, Sándor Jakab, Pál Pritz, and Ignác Romsics. *Magyaroszág a XX. században* [Hungary in the twentieth century]. Budapest: Kossuth, 1986.

Balogh, Sándor et al., eds. *A Magyar Szocialista Munkáspárt ideiglenes vezető testületeinek jegyzőkönyvei* [The minutes of the meetings of the provisional leading bodies of the Hungarian Socialist Workers' Party]. 4 vols. Budapest: Intera Rt, 1993–1998.

Baráth, Magdolna. "A Moszkvába menekült magyar pártvezetők 1956. október végi-november eleji tevékenységéről" [About the activity in late October–early November 1956 of Hungarian party leaders who fled to Moscow]. *Múltunk* 50, no. 1 (2005): 272–96.

———. "Az állambiztonsági iratok selejtezése, megsemmisítése" [The scrapping and destruction of the documents of the security police]. In *Trezor 3. Az átmenet évkönyve* [The year-book of transition], edited by György Gyarmati, 255–80. Budapest: Állambiztonsági Szolgálatok Történeti Levéltára, 2004.

———. "Az MDP vezetése és a rehabilitáció (1953–1956)" [The MDP leadership and rehabilitation, 1953–1956]. *Múltunk* 44, no. 4 (1999): 40–97.

———. *Szovjet nagyköveti iratok Magyarországról 1953–1956. Kiszlejov és Andropov titkos jelentései* [The documents of Soviet ambassadors to Hungary, 1953–1956: The secret reports of Kiseliov and Andropov]. Budapest: Napvilág, 2002.

Barber, John. "Stalin's Letter to the Editors of Proletarskaya Revolyutsiya." *Soviet Studies* 28, no. 1 (1976): 21–41.

Barbusse, Henri. *Stalin*. New York: The Macmillan company, 1935.

Bauer, Raymond A., and David B. Gleicher. "Word-of-Mouth Communication in the Soviet Union." *Public Opinion Quarterly* 17, no. 3 (1953): 297–310.

Becher, Johannes R. *Walter Ulbricht: Ein deutscher Arbeitersohn*. Berlin, 1958.

Behrends, Jan C. *Die erfundene Freundschaft: Propaganda für die Sowjetunion in Polen und in der DDR (1944–1957)*. Cologne: Böhlau, 2006.

———. "Exporting the Leader: The Stalin Cult in Poland and East Germany (1944/45–56)." In Apor et al., *The Leader Cult in Communist Dictatorships*, 161–78.

———. "Nach dem Führerkult. Repräsentationen des Generalsekretärs in Polen under DDR." In *Medien und Imagepolitik im 20. Jahrhundert. Deutschland, Europa, USA*, edited by Daniela Münkel, and Lu Seegers, 57–83. Frankfurt am Main: Campus, 2008.

———. "Rokossowski Coming Home. The Making and Breaking of an (inter-)national Hero in Stalinist Poland, 1949–1956." *Hungarian Historical Review* 5, no. 4 (2016): 767–89.

———. "Stage-managed Charisma. The Leader Cult in Nazism and Communism." In *German Zeitgeschichte: Konturen eines Forschungsfeldes*, edited by Thomas Lindenberger, and Martin Sabrow, 80–108. Göttingen: Wallstein Verlag, 2016.

Békés, Csaba, Malcolm Byrne, and János M. Rainer, eds. *The 1956 Hungarian Revolution: A History in Documents*. Budapest-New York: CEU Press, 2002.

Belényi, Gyula. "A nagyipari munkásság élet- és munkakörülményei az 1950-es években" [The living and working conditions of industrial workers in the 1950s]. In *Politika, gazdaság és társadalom a XX. századi magyar történelemben II.* [Politics, economy and society in twentieth-century Hungarian history], edited by Levente Püski, Lajos Tímár, and Tibor Valuch, 229–37. Debrecen: KLTE Történelmi Intézet, 2000.

Belényi, Gyula. *A sztálini iparosítás emberi ára 1948–1956* [The human costs of Stalinist industrialization 1948–1956]. Szeged: JATEPress, 1993.

———. "Fordulat a munkaerőpiacon az 1940-es évek végén és a nagyipari munkásság helyzete az 1950-es években" [Changes on the labour market at the end of the 1940s and the situation of industrial workers in the 1950s]. In Feitl et al., *Fordulat a világban*, 161–81.

Belényi, Gyula, and Lajos Sz. Varga, eds. *Munkások Magyarországon 1948–1956* [Workers in Hungary 1948-1956]. Budapest: Napvilág, 2000.

Belting, Hans. *Bild und Kult*. Munich: Beck'sche Verlag, 1990.

Bényei, József. *A személyi kultusz humora* [The humor of the age of personality cult]. Debrecen: Csokonai, 1989.

Berend T., Ivan. *Central and Eastern Europe, 1944–1993: Detour from the Periphery to the Periphery*. Cambridge: Cambridge University Press, 1996.

Béres, Katalin. "Születésnapok anatómiája. Zala, 1949, 1952. Sztálin és Rákosi születésnapja" [The anatomy of birthdays, Zala county, 1949, 1952: The birthdays of Stalin and Rákosi]. *História* 9, nos. 5–6 (1987): 27–29.

Bíró, Eugénia. *Száműzetésben* [In exile]. Budapest: Littoria, 1994.

Blagoeva, Stella Dimitrova. *Dimitrov: A Biography*. New York: International Publishers, 1934.

Blieseman de Guevara, Berit, and Tatjana Reiber, eds. *Charisma und Herrschaft: Führung und Verführung in der Politik*. Frankfurt am Main: Campus Verlag, 2011.

Blomqvist, Lars Erik. "Introduction." In Arvidsson and Blomqvist, *Symbols of Power*, 7–19.

Blumstock, Robert. "Public Opinion in Hungary." In Connor and Gitelman, *Public Opinion in European Socialist Systems*, 132–66.

Bokor, Miklós, ed. *Népünk szeretete. Népművészeink ajándékai Rákosi Mátyás 60 éves születésnapjára* [The love of our people: The gifts by our folk artists for Mátyás Rákosi's 60th birthday]. Budapest: Képzőművészeti Alap, 1952.

Bonnell, Victoria E. *Iconography of Power. Soviet Political Posters under Lenin and Stalin.* Berkeley: University of California Press, 1997.

Borhi, László. "Stalinist Terror in Hungary, 1945–1956." In *Stalinist Terror in Eastern Europe: Elite Purges and Mass Repression*, edited by Kevin McDermott and Matthew Stibbe, Manchester: Manchester University Press, 2010.

Börrnert, René. *Wie Ernst Thälmann treu und kühn! Das Thälmann-Bild der SED in Erziehungsalltag der DDR.* Bad Heilbrunn: J. Klinkhardt, 2004.

Borsányi, György, and János Kende. *The History of the Working Class Movement in Hungary.* Budapest: Corvina, 1988.

Böszörményi, Géza, ed. *Recsk.* Budapest: Széphalom Könyvműhely, 2006.

Botos, János. *Politikai humor, 1945–1948* [Political humor, 1945–1948]. Budapest: Reflektor Kiadó, 1989.

Boylan, James George. "The Development of the Khrushchev "Cult of Personality": A Survey and Interpretation of Pravda and Izvestia." M.A. Thesis, University of Washington, 1961.

Brandenberger, David. *National Bolshevism: Stalinist Mass Culture and the Formation of Modern Russian National Identity, 1931–1956.* Cambridge, MA, and London: Harvard University press, 2002.

———, ed. *Political Humor under Stalin: An Anthology of Unofficial Jokes and Anecdotes.* Bloomington: Slavica, 2009.

———. *Propaganda State in Crisis: Soviet Ideology, Indoctrination, and Terror under Stalin, 1927–1941.* New Haven, CT: Yale University Press, 2011.

———. "Stalin as Symbol: A Case Study of the Personality Cult and its Construction." In Davies and Harris, *Stalin: A New History*, 249–70.

Brooks, Jeffrey. *Thank You, Comrade Stalin! Soviet Public Culture from Revolution to Cold War.* Princeton: Princeton University Press, 2000.

Brown, Archie. *The Myth of the Strong Leader. Political Leaderhip in the Modern Age.* London: Vintage books, 2014.

Brown, Archie, and Jack Gray, eds. *Political Culture and Political Change in Communist States.* New York: Holmes & Meier Publishers, 1979.

Brown, Karl. "Regulating Bodies: Everyday Crime and Popular Resistance in Communist Hungary, 1948–1956." Dphil dissertation, The University of Texas at Austin, 2007.

Brown, Peter. *The Cult of Saints: Its Rise and Function in Latin Christianity.* Chicago: University of Chicago Press, 1981.

Brzezinski, Zbigniew. *The Soviet Bloc: Unity and Conflict*. Cambridge, MA: Harvard University Press, 1967.

Buda, Attila, and László L. Simon, eds. *Munkás, paraszt, értelmiség munkaverseny lázában ég!* [Worker, peasant, intellectual, all fired with enthusiasm for the labour competition!]. Budapest: Korona Kiadó, 2002.

Burant, Stephen R. "The Influence of Russian Tradition on the Political Style of the Soviet Elite." *Political Science Quarterly* 102, no. 2 (1987): 273–93.

Burrin, Philippe. "Political Religion: The Relevance of a Concept." *History and Memory* 9, nos. 1–2 (1997): 321–49.

Cavalli, Luciano. *Charisma, Dictatorship and Plebiscitary Democracy*. Florence: Università degli studi di Firenze, 1984.

"Charisma and the Cult of Personality in Modern Italy." Special Issue, *Modern Italy* 3, no. 2 (1998).

Chase, William J. *Enemies within the Gates? The Comintern and the Stalinist Repression, 1934–1939*. New Haven, CT: Yale University Press, 2001.

Cherniavsky, Michael. *Tsar and people: Studies in Russian Myths*. New Haven, CT: Yale University Press, 1961.

Clark, Katerina. *Moscow, the Fourth Rome: Stalinism, Cosmopolitanism, and the Evolution of Soviet Culture, 1931–1941*. Cambridge, MA: Harvard University Press, 2011.

———. "Socialist Realism and the Sacralizing of Space." In Dobrenko and Naiman, *The Landscape of Stalinism*, 8–19.

———. *The Soviet Novel: History as Ritual*. Bloomington: University of Indiana Press, 2000.

Cohen, Stephen F. "The Stalin Question since Stalin." In *An End to Silence: Uncensored Opinion in the Soviet Union*, edited by Stephen F. Cohen, 30–50. New York: Norton, 1982.

Cohen, Yves. "The Cult of Number One in an Age of Leaders." *Kritika: Explorations in Russian and Eurasian History* 8, no. 3 (2007): 597–634.

"Communism and the Leader Cult." Special Issue, *Twentieth Century Communism* 1, no. 1 (2009).

Congdon, Lee. *Seeing Red: Hungarian Intellectuals in Exile and the Challenge of Communism*. DeKalb: Northern Illinois University Press, 2001.

Connery, Brian A., and Kirk Combe. *Theorizing Satire: Essays in Literary Criticism*. Basingstoke: Macmillan, 1995.

Connor, Walker. *The National Question in Marxist-Leninist Theory and Strategy*. Princeton: Princeton University Press, 1984.

Connor, Walter D., and Zvi Y. Gitelman, eds. *Public Opinion in European Socialist Systems*. New York and London: Praeger, 1977.

Corner, Paul. "Fascist Italy in the 1930s: Popular Opinion in the Provinces." In Corner, *Popular Opinion in Totalitarian Regimes*, 122–46.

———, ed. *Popular Opinion in Totalitarian Regimes: Fascism, Nazism, Communism.* Oxford: Oxford University Press, 2009.

Cullerne Bown, Matthew. *Art under Stalin.* Oxford: Phaidon, 1991.

Cullerne Bown, Matthew. *Socialist Realist Painting.* New Haven, CT: Yale University Press, 1998.

Czigány, Lóránt. "'Neved ki diccsel ejtené…' Személyi kultusz Ferenc József és Rákosi Mátyás korában" ["He, who would praise thy name…": Cult of personality in the age of Franz Joseph and Mátyás Rákosi]. In *Nézz vissza haraggal! Államosított irodalom Magyarországon* [Look back in anger: Nationalised literature in Hungary], edited by Lóránt Czigány, 70–98. Budapest: Gondolat, 1990.

Davies, R. W., E. A. Rees, O. V. Khlevnyuk, L. P. Kosheleva, and L. A. Rogovaya, eds. *The Stalin-Kaganovich Correspondence, 1931–1936.* New Haven, CT: Yale University Press, 2003.

Davies, Sarah. "The 'Cult' of the *Vozhd*': Representations in Letters, 1934–1941." *Russian History/Histoire Russe* 24, nos. 1–2 (1997): 131–47.

———. *Popular Opinion in Stalin's Russia: Terror, Propaganda and Dissent, 1939–1941.* Cambridge: Cambridge University Press, 1997.

———. "Stalin and the Making of the Leader Cult in the 1930s." In Apor et al., *The Leader Cult in Communist Dictatorships*, 29–46.

Davies, Sarah, and James Harris, eds. *Stalin: A New History.* Cambridge: Cambridge University Press, 2006.

Deák, István. *The Lawful Revolution: Louis Kossuth and the Hungarians, 1848–1849.* London: Phoenix, 2001.

Dedijer, Vladimir. *Josip Broz Tito: prilozi za biografiju.* Zagreb, 1953.

Devlin, Judith. "Beria and the Development of the Stalin Cult." In "Stalin – His Times and Ours." Special issue, *Irish Slavonic Studies* 22, (2005): 25–46.

Dobrenko, Evgeny, and Eric Naiman, eds. *The Landscape of Stalinism: The Art and Ideology of Soviet Space.* Seattle and New York: University of Washington Press, 2003.

Dömötörfi, Tibor. "A Horthy-kultusz elemei" [The components of the Horthy cult]. *História* 12, no. 12 (1990): 23–26.

Egy nagy harcos életéből. Rádióbeszélgetés Rákosi Mátyással 1945. október 4-én [Episodes from the life of a great warrior: Radio conversation with Mátyás Rákosi on October 4, 1945]. Budapest: Szikra, 1945.

Emlékkönyv Kossuth Lajos születésének 150. Évfordulójára [Memorial book on the occasion of Lajos Kossuth's 150th birthday]. 2 vols. Budapest: Akadémiai kiadó, 1952.

Ennker, Benno. *Die Anfänge des Leninkults in der Sowjetunion.* Cologne: Böhlau, 1997.

———. "Leninkult und mythisches Denken in der sowjetischen Öffentlichkeit 1924." *Jahrbücher für Geschichte Osteuropas* 44, no. 3 (1996): 431–55.

———. "The Origins and Intentions of the Lenin Cult." In *Regime and Society in Twentieth Century Russia*, edited by Ian D. Thatcher, 118–28. Basingstoke: Macmillan, London 1999.

———. "Politische Herrschaft und Stalinkult 1929–1939." In *Stalinismus: neue Forschungen und Konzepte*, edited by Stefan Plaggenborg, 151–84. Berlin: Berlin Verlag Arno Spitz, 1998.

———. "The Stalin Cult, Bolshevik Rule and Kremlin Interaction in the 1930s." In Apor et al., *The Leader Cult in Communist Dictatorships*, 83–101.

Ennker, Benno, and Heidi Hein-Kircher. *Der Führer im Europa des 20. Jahrhunderts*. Marburg: Herder Institut, 2010.

Erényi, Tibor. "A nemzeti ünnep és a pártok (1848-ról 1948-ban)" [The national holiday and the political parties: About 1848 in 1948]. *Századok* 132, no. 2 (1998): 477–88.

Erich Honecker: Skizze eines politische Lebens. Berlin: Institut für Marxismus-Leninismus, 1977.

Erpenbeck, Fritz. *Wilhelm Pieck: Ein Lebensbild*. Berlin: Dietz, 1951.

Faber, Richard, ed. *Politische Religion – religiöse Politik*. Würzburg: Königshausen & Neumann, 1997.

Falasca-Zamponi, Simonetta. *Fascist Spectacle: The Aesthetics of Power in Mussolini's Italy*. Berkeley: University of California Press, 1997.

Faludy, György. *My Happy Days in Hell*. London: Penguin, 2010.

Feitl, István. *A bukott Rákosi (Rákosi Mátyás 1956–1971 között)* [The fallen Rákosi: Mátyás Rákosi Between 1956 and 1971]. Budapest: Politikatörténeti Alapítvány, 1993.

———. "A moszkvai emigráció és az MSZMP (Rákosi Mátyás 1956–1958 között)" [The Moscow emigration and the MSZMP: Mátyás Rákosi between 1956 and 1958]. *Múltunk* 36, no. 4 (1991): 3–30.

———. "Az első népfrontválasztás" [The first popular front elections]. *Társadalmi Szemle* 49, no. 5 (1994): 73–85.

Feitl, István, and Levente Sipos. "Előszó" [Preface]. In Rákosi, *Visszaemlékezések, 1892–1925*, vol. 1, vii–lxiii. Budapest: Napvilág, 2002.

Feitl, István, Lajos Izsák, and Gábor Székely, eds. *Fordulat a világban és Magyarországon 1944–1949* [Change in the world and in Hungary, 1944–1949]. Budapest: Napvilág, 2000.

Fejérdy, András. "Rákosi Mátyás és az olasz munkásmozgalom (1920–1923)" [Mátyás Rákosi and the Italian working class movement, 1920–1923]. MA thesis, Eötvös Loránd Tudományegyetem, Budapest, 2001.

Fejtő, François. *A History of the People's Democracies: Eastern Europe since Stalin*. New York: Praeger, 1971.

Ferkai, András. "A sztálinizmus építészetéről" [About the art of Stalinism]. In György and Turai, *A művészet katonái*, 24–33.

Fiatal írók antológiája [An anthology of young writers]. Budapest: Szépirodalmi kiadó, 1951.

Figes, Orlando, and Boris Kolonitskii. *Interpreting the Russian Revolution. The Language and Symbols of 1917*. New Haven, CT: Yale University Press, 1999.

Filtzer, Donald. *The Khrushchev Era. De-Stalinisation and the Limits of Reform in the USSR. 1953–1964*. Basingstoke: Palgrave, 1993.

Fitzpatrick, Sheila. *Everyday Stalinism. Ordinary Life in Extraordinary Times: Soviet Russia in the 1930s*. Oxford: Oxford University Press, 1999.

———. "Patronage and the Intelligentsia in Stalin's Russia." In *Challenging Traditional Views of Russian History*, edited by Stephen G. Wheatcroft, 92–111. Basingstoke: Palgrave, 2002.

———. "Readers' Letters to Krest'ianskaia Gazeta, 1938." *Russian History/Histoire Russe* 24, nos. 1–2 (1997): 149–70.

———. "Signals from Below: 'Soviet Letters of Denunciation of the 1930s.'" In "Practices of Denunciation in Modern European History, 1789–1989." Special issue, *The Journal of Modern History* 68, no. 4 (1996): 831–66.

———. "Supplicants and Citizens: Public Letter-Writing in Soviet Russia in the 1930s." *Slavic Review* 55, no. 1 (1996): 78–105.

Foucault, Michel. *The History of Sexuality*, vol. 1, *An Introduction*. New York: Pantheon books, 1978.

Fowkes, Reuben. "The Role of Monumental Sculpture in the Construction of Socialist Space in Stalinist Hungary." In *Socialist Space: Sites of Everyday Life in the Eastern Bloc*, edited by David Crowley, and Susan E. Reid, 65–84. Oxford: Berg, 2002.

Freud, Sigmund. *Der Witz und Seine Beziehung zum Unbewussten*. Vienna: Deuticke, 1905.

Fulbrook, Mary. "Demography, Opportunity or Ideological Conversion? Reflections on the Role of the 'Second Hitler Youth Generation,' or '1929ers,' in the GDR." In Corner, *Popular Opinion in Totalitarian Regimes*, 184–207.

Fürst, Juliane. "Prisoners of the Soviet Self? Political Youth Opposition in Late Stalinism." *Europe-Asia Studies* 54, no. 3 (2002): 353–75.

———. *Stalin's Last Generation. Soviet Post-War Youth and the Emergence of Mature Socialism*. Oxford: Oxford University Press, 2010.

G. Merva, Mária, ed. *'48 kultusza. Tanulmányok* [The cult of 1848: Essays]. Gödöllő: Gödöllői Városi Múzeum, 1999.

Gáborjáni Szabó, Botond, "A Kossuth 'magyarok Mózese' toposz történeti háttere" [The historical background of the topos, Kossuth "the Moses of the Hungarians"]. *Debreceni Szemle* 6, no. 3 (1998): 340–46.

Gál, Éva et al., eds. *A "Jelcin-dosszié." Szovjet dokumentumok 1956-ról* [The "Yeltsin dossier": Soviet documents about 1956]. Budapest: Századvég, 1993.

Gardner, Jane F., ed. *Leadership and the Cult of Personality*. London: Edgar Kent, 1974.

Geertz, Clifford. "Centers, Kings, and Charisma: Reflections on the Symbolics of Power." In *Rites of Power: Symbolism, Ritual, and Politics since the Middle Ages*, edited by Sean Wilentz, 13–38. Philadelphia: University of Pennsylvania Press, 1985.

Geldern, James von. *Bolshevik Festivals, 1917–1920*. Berkeley: University of California Press, 1993.

Geldern, James von and Richard Stites, eds. *Mass Culture in Soviet Russia. Tales, Poems, Songs, Movies, Plays and Folklore, 1917–1953*. Bloomington: Indiana University Press, 1995.

Gentile, Emilio. *Politics as Religion*. Princeton: Princeton University Press, 2006.

Gergely, Jenő. "1948 és az egyházak Magyarországon" [1948 and the churches in Hungary]. In Feitl et al., *Fordulat a világban*, 138–51.

———. *A katolikus egyház Magyarországon 1944–1971* [The Catholic Church in Hungary, 1944–1971]. Budapest: Kossuth, 1985.

———. "A szétválás konfliktusai. A magyar állam és a katolikus egyház viszonya 1945 és 1951 között" [The conflicts of separation: The relationship of the Hungarian state and the Catholic Church between 1945 and 1951]. *Társadalmi Szemle* 44, no. 6 (1989): 32–47.

———. *Az 1950-es egyezmény. A szerzetesrendek feloszlatása Magyarországon* [The accord of 1950: The abolition of religious orders in Hungary]. Budapest: Viglia, 1990.

———. *Gömbös Gyula. Politikai pályakép* [Gyula Gömbös: A political biography]. Budapest: Vince, 2001.

Gerő, András. *Az államosított forradalom. 1848 centenáriuma* [Nationalized revolution: The centenary of 1848]. Budapest: Új Mandátum, 1998.

———. *Emperor Francis Joseph, King of the Hungarians*. Boulder: Social Science Monographs; Wayne, NJ: Center for Hungarian Studies and Publications, 2001.

———. *Képzelt történelem. Fejezetek a magyar szimbolikus politika XIX-XX. századi történetéből* [Imagined history: Chapters from nineteenth- and twentieth-century Hungarian symbolic politics]. Budapest: Eötvös Kiadó, PolgART, 2004.

———. *Modern Hungarian Society in the Making: The Unfinished Experience*. Budapest-New York: CEU Press, 1995.

Getty, J. Arch. *Practicing Stalinism: Bolsheviks, Boyars and the Persistence of Tradition*. New Haven, CT: Yale University Press, 2013.

———. "*Samokritika* Rituals in the Stalinist Central Committee, 1933–38." *The Russian Review* 58, no. 1 (1999): 49–70.

Gh. Gheorghiu-Dej. Bucharest: Román Munkáspárt, 1951.

Gill, Graeme. "Personal Dominance and the Collective Principle: Individual Legitimacy in Marxist-Leninist Systems." In *Political Legitimation in Communist States*, edited by T. H. Rigby and Ferenc Fehér, 94–110. London: Macmillan, 1982.

———. "Personality Cult, Political Culture and Party Structure." *Studies in Comparative Communism* 17, no. 2 (1984): 111–21.

———. "Political Myth and Stalin's Quest for Authority in the Party." In *Authority, power and policy in the USSR. Essays dedicated to Leonard Schapiro*, edited by T. H. Rigby, Archie Brown and Peter Reddaway, 98–117. London: Macmillan, 1983.

———. "The Soviet Leader Cult: Reflections on the Structure of Leadership in the Soviet Union." *British Journal of Political Science* 10, no. 2 (1980): 167–86.

———. *Symbols and Legitimacy in Soviet Politics*. Cambridge: Cambridge University Press, 2011.

Golomstock, Igor. *Totalitarian Art in the Soviet Union, the Third Reich, Fascist Italy and the People's Republic of China*. New York: IconEditions, 1990.

Gorlizki, Yoram. "Party Revivalism and the Death of Stalin." *Slavic Review* 54, no. 1 (1995): 1–22.

Goscillo, Helena. *Putin as Celebrity and Cultural Icon*. London and New York: Routledge, 2013.

Gotovitch, José. "Construction and deconstruction of a cult: Edgar Lalmand and the Communist Party of Belgium." In "Communism and the Leader Cult." Special issue, *Twentieth Century Communism* 1, no. 1 (2009): 128–52.

Goudoever, Albert P. van. *The Limits of De-Stalinization in the Soviet Union: Political Rehabilitation in the Soviet Union since Stalin*. London: Croom Helm, 1986.

Gradel, Ittai. *Emperor Worship and Roman Religion*. Oxford: Clarendon Press, 2002.

Groys, Boris. *The Total Art of Stalinism. Avant-garde, Aesthetic Dictatorship and Beyond*. Princeton: Princeton University Press, 1992.

Günther, Hans, ed. *The Culture of the Stalin Period*. London: Macmillan, 1990.

———. "The Heroic Myth in Socialist Realism." In *Dream Factory Communism. The Visual Culture of the Stalin Era / Traumfabrik Kommunismus. Die visuelle Kultur der Stalinzeit*, edited by Boris Groys and Max Hollein, 106–24. Ostfildern: Hatje Cantz, 2003.

Gyarmati, György. "A káderrendszer és a rendszer kádere az 50-es években" [The cadre system and the cadre of the system in the 1950s]. *Valóság* 34, no. 2 (1991): 51–63.

———. *A Rákosi-korszak: Rendszerváltó fordulatok évtizede Magyarországon, 1945–1956* [The Rákosi era: The decade of system changes in Hungary, 1945–1956]. Budapest: ÁBTL-Rubicon, 2011.

———. "A társadalom közérzete a fordulat évében. Közvéleménykutatások és ÁVO hangulatjelentések 1948-ban" [Social mood in the year of the turn: Public opinion polls and ÁVO mood reports in 1948]. *Mozgó Világ* 24, no. 10 (1998): 95–111.

———. "Káderpolitika a Rákosi-korszak tanácsrendszerében, 1950–1953" [Cadre policy in the council system of the Rákosi era, 1950–1953]. *Magyar Tudomány* 10 (1998): 1183–94.

———. *Március hatalma – a hatalom márciusa: fejezetek március 15. ünneplésének történetéből* [The power of March—the power's March: Chapters from the history of celebrating March 15]. Budapest: Paginarium, 1998.

Gyarmati, György, János Botos, Tibor Zinner, and Mihály Korom, *Magyar hétköznapok Rákosi Mátyás két emigrációja között 1945–1956* [Daily life in Hungary between Mátyás Rákosi's two emigrations, 1945–1956]. Budapest: Minerva, 1988.

Győrffy, Sándor, ed. *A Rákosi-per* [The Rákosi trial]. Budapest: Szikra, 1950.

Győri Szabó, Róbert. *A kommunizmus és a zsidóság az 1945 utáni Magyarországon* [Communism and the Jews in Hungary after 1945]. Budapest: Gondolat, 2009.

György, Péter. "A mindennapok tükre, avagy a korstílus akarása" [The mirror of daily life or the yearning for the style of the age]. In György and Turai, *A művészet katonái*, 12–23.

György, Péter, and Hedvig Turai, eds. *A művészet katonái: Sztálinizmus és kultúra* [Soldiers of art: Stalinism and culture]. Budapest: Corvina, 1992.

Hajdu, Tibor. "Kérdőjelek Rákosi Mátyás hiányzó portréjához" [Question marks in Mátyás Rákosi's non-existent biography]. In *Vélemények/Viták A felszabadulás utáni történetünkről* [Opinions/debates about our history after liberation], edited by Sándor Balogh, 1:312–18. Budapest: Kossuth, 1987.

Halmesvirta, Anssi, ed. *Cultic Revelations: Studies in Modern Historical Cult Personalities and Phenomena*. Spectrum Hungarologicum 4. Jyväskylä-Pécs: University of Jyväskylä, 2010.

———. "A Foreign Benefactor and a Domestic Liberator: the cults of Lenin and Mannerheim in Finland." *Scandinavian Journal of History* 34, no. 9 (2009): 414–32.

Hammer, Ferenc. *Diktatúra és vezérkultusz: A magyarországi kommunista diktatúra létrejöttének tudásszociológiai előzményei* [Dictatorship and leader cult: The antecendents of the establishment of the Hungarian communist dictatorship from a sociology of knowledge perspective]. Budapest: Oktatáskutató Intézet, 1992.

Hanebrink, Paul A. *In Defense of Christian Hungary: Religion, Nationalism and Antisemitism, 1890–1944*. Ithaca and London: Cornell University Press, 2006.

Hazareesingh, Sudhir. *The Legend of Napoleon*. London: Granta Books, 2004.

———. *The Shadow of the General: Modern France and the Myth of de Gaulle*. Oxford: Oxford University Press, 2012.

Hegedüs B., András et al., eds. *A Petőfi Kör vitái hiteles jegyzőkönyvek alapján* [The debates of the Petőfi Circle on the basis of authentic minutes]. 7 vols. Budapest: 1956-os Intézet, 1989–1994.

Hein-Kircher, Heidi. *Der Piłsudski-Kult und seine Bedeutung für den polnischen Staat 1926–1939*. Marburg: Herder Institut, 2002.

Heizer, James L. "The cult of Stalin, 1929–1939." Ph.D. dissertation, University of Kentucky, 1977.

Held, Joseph, ed. *The Cult of Power: Dictators in the Twentieth Century*. Boulder: East European Monographs, 1983.

Hellbeck, Jochen. "Liberation form Autonomy: Mapping Self-Understandings in Stalin's Time." In Corner, *Popular Opinion in Totalitarian Regimes*, 49–63.

Hellebust, Rolf. "Reflections of an Absence: Novelistic Portraits of Stalin before 1953." In *Socialist Realism Revisited: Selected Papers from the McMaster Conference*, edited by Nina Kolesnikoff and Walter Smyrniw, 111–20. Hamilton, Ont.: McMaster University, 1994.

Heller, Klaus, and Jan Plamper, eds. *Personality Cults in Stalinism – Personenkulte im Stalinismus*. Göttingen: V & R Unipress, 2004.

Hermann, Róbert. "A Kossuth-kultusz" [The Kossuth cult]. In *"…leborulok a nemzet nagysága előtt": A Kossuth-hagyaték* ["…I bow before the greatness of the nation": The legacy of Kossuth], edited by Katalin Körmöczi, 155–59, Budapest: Magyar Nemzeti Múzeum, 1995.

———. *Kossuth Lajos élete és kora* [The life and times of Lajos Kossuth]. Budapest: Pannonica, 2002.

Hét évszázad magyar versei [Seven centuries of Hungarian poems]. Budapest: Szépirodalmi kiadó, 1951.

Hirsch, Francine. *Empire of Nations: Ethnographic Knowledge and the Making of the Soviet Union*. Ithaca, NY: Cornell University Press, 2005.

History of the Communist Party of the Soviet Union (Bolsheviks): Short Course. New York: International Publishers, 1939.

Hobsbawm, Eric. "Introduction: Inventing Traditions." In *The Invention of Tradition*, edited by Eric Hobsbawm and Terence Ranger, 1–14. Cambridge: Cambridge University Press, 1983.

Hoffmann, David L. *Stalinist Values. The Cultural Norms of Soviet Modernity, 1917–1941*. Ithaca: Cornell University Press, 2003.

Holquist, Peter. "'Information Is the Alpha and Omega of Our Work': Bolshevik Surveillance in Its Pan-European Context." *Journal of Modern History* 69, no. 3 (1997): 415–50.

Horváth, Attila. "Orvosok-pedagógusok. Értelmiségi pályák presztízse 1950–1983" [Doctors-teachers: The prestige of intellectual professions, 1950–1983]. *Valóság* 29, no. 4 (1986): 59–67.

Horváth, Márton. *Lobogónk, Petőfi* [Petőfi, our banner]. Budapest: Szikra, 1951.

Horváth, Sándor. "A parasztság életmódváltozása Sztálinvárosban" [The transformation of the peasantry's lifestyle in Sztálinváros]. *Mozgó Világ* 26, no. 6 (2000): 30–40.

———. "Munkás, paraszt, értelmiség munkaverseny lázában ég" [Worker, peasant, intellectual, all fired with enthusiasm for the labour competition]. In *Mérlegen a XX. századi magyar történelem – értelmezések és értékelések* [The balance sheet of Hungarian history in the twentieth century—interpretations and evaluations], edited by Levente Püski and Tibor Valuch, 345–57. Budapest: Debreceni Egyetem Törénelmi Intézete és az 1956-os Intézet, 2002.

Horváth, Zsolt. "Tá-tá tá-ti-tá, tá-ti-ti-tá!" *História* 9, nos. 5–6 (1987): 13–15.

Howe, Antony. "'Our only ornament': Tom Mann and British communist 'hagiography'." In "Communism and the Leader Cult." Special issue, *Twentieth Century Communism* 1, no. 1 (2009): 91–109.

Illés, Béla. *Népünk szabadságáért* [For our people's freedom]. Budapest: Szikra, 1952.

Izsák, Lajos. *A koalíció évei Magyarországon 1944–1948* [The coalition years in Hungary, 1944–1948]. Budapest: Kozmosz könyvek, 1986.

———, ed. *A Magyar Dolgozók Pártja Határozatai 1948–1956* [The decrees of the Hungarian Workers' Party, 1948–1956]. Budapest: Napvilág, 1998.

———. "A parlamentarizus vesztett csatája – 1947" [The lost battle of parliamentarianism]. In *Parlamenti választások Magyarországon, 1920–1998* [Parliamentary elections in Hungary, 1920–1998], edited by György Földes and László Hubai, 235–58. Budapest: Napvilág, 1999.

———. "A Rákosi-rendszer (1948 ősze–1956 nyara)" [The Rákosi regime, autumn 1948–summer 1956]. *Történelmi Szemle* 21, no. 1 (1995): 55–68.

J. V. Sztálin. Rövid életrajz [Stalin: A short biography]. Budapest: Szikra, 1949.

Jones, Polly. "From Stalinism to Post-Stalinism: De-Mythologising Stalin, 1953–56." In *Redefining Stalinism*, edited by Harold Shukman, 130–52. London: Frank Cass, 2003.

———. "'I've Held, and I Still Hold, Stalin the Highest Esteem': Discourses and Strategies of Resistance to De-Stalinisation in the USSR, 1953–62." In Apor et al., *The Leader Cult in Communist Dictatorships*, 227–45.

———. *Myth, Memory, Trauma: Rethinking the Stalinist Past in the Soviet Union, 1953–70*. New Haven, CT: Yale University Press, 2013.

———. "Strategies of De-Mythologisation in Post-Stalinism and Post-Communism: A Comparison of De-Stalinisation and De-Leninisation." PhD dissertation, University of Oxford, 2002.

Kalla, Zsuzsa, ed. *Az irodalom ünnepei. Kultusztörténei tanulmányok* [Festivals of literature: Essays on the history of cults]. Budapest: Agroinform, 2000.

Kallis, Aristotle A. "Fascism, 'Charisma', and 'Charismatisation': Weber's Model of 'Charismatic Domination' and Interwar European Fascism." *Totalitarian Movements and Political Religions* 7, no. 1 (2006): 25–43.

Kalmár, Melinda. *Ennivaló és hozomány: A kora kádárizmus ideológiája* [Food and dowry: The ideology of early Kádárism] Budapest: Magvető, 1998.

Kantorowicz, Ernst. *The King's Two Bodies: A Study in Mediaeval Political Theology*. Princeton: Princeton University Press, 1957.

Kardos, József. "Fordulat a közoktatásban" [Change in the education system]. In Feitl et al., *Fordulat a világban*, 152–60.

———. *Iskola a politika sodrásában, 1945–1993* [Schools in the drift of politics, 1945–1993]. Budapest: Gondolat, 2007.

Kardos, József, and Mihály Kornidesz, eds. *Dokumentumok a magyar oktatáspolitika történetéből 1945–1972* [Documents about the history of Hungarian education policy 1945–1972]. 2 vols. Budapest: Tankönyvkiadó, 1990.

Kardos, László. "Rákosi Mátyás alakja a magyar költészetben" [The figure of Mátyás Rákosi in Hungarian poetry]. *Irodalomtörténet* 34, no. 2 (1952): 129–44.

Katona, Imre, ed. *Viccek Sztálinról, Rákosiról és Ceauşescuról* [Jokes about Stalin, Rákosi, and Ceauşescu]. Budapest: Új Aurora Könyvek, 1989.

Keller, Márkus. "Utak és emlékezetek. Két tanári pálya a XX. századi Magyarországon" [Paths and memories: Two teacher careers in twentieth-century Hungary]. In *Évkönyv 2003 XI: Magyarország a jelenkorban* [Year-book 2003, no. 9: Hungary in modern times], edited by János M. Rainer and Éva Standeisky, 164–80. Budapest, 1956-os Intézet, 2003.

Kelly, Catriona. *Comrade Pavlik: The Rise and Fall of a Soviet Boy Hero*. London: Granta, 2004.

——. "Grandpa Lenin and Uncle Stalin: Soviet Leader Cults for Little Children." In Apor et al., *The Leader Cult in Communist Dictatorships*, 102–22.

Kemp, Walter A, *Nationalism and Communism in Eastern Europe: A Basic Contradiction?* Basingstoke: Palgrave, 1999.

Kemp-Welch, Tony. "Khrushchev's 'Secret Speech' and Polish Politics: The Spring of 1956." *Europa-Asia Studies* 48, no. 2 (1996): 181–206.

——. *Stalin and the Literary Intelligentsia 1928–39*. Houndmills: Macmillan, 1991.

Kende, Péter. "A Szabad Nép szerkesztőségében" [In the editorial department of Szabad Nép]. In *Tanulmányok a magyar forradalomról* [Studies on the Hungarian revolution], edited by Gyula Borbándi and József Molnár, 119–32. Munich: Aurora könyvek, 1996.

Kenez, Peter. *The Birth of the Propaganda State: Soviet Methods of Mass Mobilization, 1917–1929*. Cambridge: Cambridge University Press, 1985.

Kershaw, Ian. *The "Hitler Myth": Image and Reality in the Third Reich*. Oxford: Oxford University Press, 2001.

——. *Hitler, the Germans, and the Final Solution*. New Haven, CT: Yale University Press, 2008.

——. *Popular Opinion and Political Dissent in Third Reich, Bavaria, 1933–1945*. Oxford: Clarendon Press, 1983.

——. "'Working Towards the Führer.' Reflections on the Nature of the Hitler Dictatorship." *Contemporary European History* 2, no. 2 (1993): 103–18.

Khlevniuk, Oleg V. "Stalin as Dictator: The Personalization of Power." In Davies and Harris, *Stalin: A New History*, 108–20

Khrushchev, Nikita Sergeevich. *The "Secret" Speech: Delivered to the Closed Session of the Twentieth Congress of the Communist Party of the Soviet Union*. Nottingham: Spokesman Books, 1976.

Khrushchev, Sergei N., ed. *Memoirs of Nikita Khrushchev. Volume 2: Reformer (1945–1964)*. University Park: Pennsylvania State University, 2006.

———. *Nikita Khrushchev and the Creation of a Superpower*. University Park: Pennsylvania State University, 2000.

Kincses, Katalin Mária. *Kultusz és hagyomány. Tanulmányok a Rákóczi-szabadságharc 300. Évfordulójára* [Cult and tradition: Essays on the occasion of the 300th anniversary of the Rákóczi War of Independence]. Budapest: Argumentum, 2003.

King, David. *The Commissar Vanishes: The Falsification of Photograph and Art in Stalin's Russia*. New York: Metropolitan books, 1997.

Kiteme, B. C. "The Cult of Stalin: National Power and the Soviet Party State." PhD dissertation, Columbia University, 1989.

Klaniczay, Gábor. *Holy Rulers and Blessed Princesses: Dynastic Cults in Medieval Central Europe*. translated by Éva Pálmai, Cambridge: Cambridge University Press, 2002.

Klaniczay, Tibor, and József Jankovics. *Matthias Corvinus and the Humanism in Central Europe*. Budapest: Balassi, 1994.

Klimo, Árpád von. *Nation, Konfession, Geschichte: zur nationalen Geschichtskultur Ungarns im europäischen Kontext (1860–1948)*. Munich: Oldenbourg, 2003.

———. "'A very modest man': Béla Illés or how to make a career through the leader cult." In Apor et al., *The Leader Cult in Communist Dictatorships*, 47–62.

Kline, George Louis. "The 'God-Builders': Gorky and Lunacharsky." in *Religious and Anti-Religious Thought in Russia*, edited by George Louis Kline, 103–26. Chicago: University of Chicago Press, 1968.

Knausz, Imre. "'Új szakasz' az oktatáspolitikában, 1953–1954" [The 'New Course' in education policy, 1953–1954]. *Magyar Pedagógia* 89, nos. 3–4 (1989): 268–84.

Knight, Amy. "Beria and the Cult of Stalin: Rewriting Transcaucasian Party History." *Soviet Studies* 43, no. 4 (1991): 749–63.

———. *Beria, Stalin's First Lieutenant*. Princeton: Princeton University Press, 1993.

Kő, András, and Lambert Nagy J., eds. *Levelek Rákosihoz* [Letters to Rákosi]. Budapest: Maecenas, 2002.

Kocsis, Piroska. "Rákosi Mátyás hatvanadik születésnapjának megünneplése" [The celebration of Mátyás Rákosi's 60th birthday]. *Archivnet* 6, no. 2 (2006). Accessed January 14, 2017. http://www.archivnet.hu/politika/rakosi_matyas_hatvanadik_szuletesnapjanak_megunneplese.html

———. "'Sztálinhoz száll a hálaének, ki a jövőnk apja lett...' Sztálin 70. születésnapja Magyarországon" ["The song praises Stalin, who became the father of our future...": Stalin's 70th birthday in Hungary]. *Archivnet* 7, no. 6 (2007). Accessed January 14, 2017. http://www.archivnet.hu/politika/sztalin_70._szuletesnapja_magyarorszagon.html

Koenen, Gerd, *Die großen Gesänge. Lenin, Stalin, Mao Tse Tung. Führerkulte und Heldenmythen des 20. Jahrhunderts*. Frankfurt am Main: Eichborn, 1991.

Kojevnikov, Alexei. "Rituals of Stalinist Culture at Work: Science and the Games of Intraparty Democracy circa 1948." *Russian Review* 57, no. 1 (1998): 25–52.

Koltay, Gábor and Péter Bródy, eds. *El nem égetett dokumentumok* [Unburnt Documents]. Budapest: Szabad Tér Kiadó, 1990.

Kornidesz, Mihály. "Az MKP és az MDP közoktatási politikájához (1945–1954)" [About the education policies of the MKP and MDP, 1945–1954]. *Párttörténeti Közlemények* 34, no. 4 (1988): 112–48.

Korom, Mihály. "A személyi kultusz néhány kérdése és az európai népi demokráciák" [The question of the cult of personality and the European people's democracies]. Manuscript, Budapest: MSZMP Politikai Főiskola, 1987.

Korsch, Boris. *The Brezhnev Personality Cult – Continuity: The Librarian's Point of View*. Jerusalem: Hebrew University of Jerusalem, 1987.

Kotkin, Stephen. *Magnetic Mountain: Stalinism as a Civilization*. Berkeley: University of California Press, 1995.

Kovács, András Bálint. "Adalékok az ötvenes évek magyar filmhíradóinak ikonográfiájához" [Contributions on the iconography of Hungarian newsreels in the 1950s]. In György and Turai, *A művészet katonái*, 91–98.

Kovács M., Mária. "Közalkalmazottak 1938–1949" [Public servants 1938–1949]. *Valóság* 25, no. 9 (1982): 41–54.

Kovács M., Mária, and Antal Örkény. *Káderek* [Cadres]. Budapest: ELTE Szociológiai és Szociálpolitikai Intézet és Továbbképző Központ, 1991.

———. "Promoted Cadres and Professionals in Post-War Hungary." In *Economy and Society in Hungary*, edited by Rudolf Andorka and László Bertalan, 139–52. Budapest: Karl Marx University of Economic Sciences, 1986.

———. "Szakérettségisek" [The vocational leaving certificate]. *Mozgó Világ* 7, no. 5 (1981): 102–10.

Kövér, György. *Losonczy Géza, 1917–1957*. Budapest: 1956-os Intézet, 1998.

Kovrig, Bennett. *Communism in Hungary: From Kun to Kádár*. Stanford: Hoover Institution Press, 1979.

Kowalczyk, Józef. *Bolesław Bierut: Życie i działalność*. Warsaw, 1952.

Kula, Marcin. "Communism as Religion." *Totalitarian Movements and Political Religions* 6, no. 3 (2005): 371–81.

———. "Poland: The Silence of Those Deprived of Voice." In Corner, *Popular Opinion in Totalitarian Regimes*, 149–67.

Kun, Miklós. "Hőskultusz és deheroizáció a szovjet rendszerben" [Hero cult and de-heroization in the Soviet system]. *Café Babel,* no. 3 (1994): 87–90.

Kusin, Vladimir V. "An Overview of East European Reformism." *Soviet Studies* 28, no. 3 (1976): 338–61.

Lackó, Miklós. "A magyar kommunista mozgalom és a nemzeti kérdés 1918–1936" [The Hungarian Communist movement and the national question, 1918–1936]. In *Gazdaság, társadalom, történetírás* [Economy, society, historiography], edited by Ferenc Glatz, 255–72, Budapest: MTA Történettudományi Intézet, 1989.

Lane, Christel. *The Rites of Rulers. Ritual in Industrial Society – the Soviet Case*. Cambridge: Cambridge University Press, 1981.

Lányi, Gusztáv. "Rákosi Mátyás politikai antiszemitizmusa. Pszichohistóriai és történelmi szociálpszichológiai elemzés" [The political anti-Semitism of Mátyás Rákosi: An analysis in psycho-history and historical sociology]. *Világosság* 35, no. 10 (1994): 21–47.

LaPorte, Norman, and Kevin Morgan. "'Kings among their subjects'? Ernst Thälmann, Harry Pollitt and the Leadership Cult as Stalinization." In *Bolshevism, Stalinism and the Comintern: Perspectives on Stalinization, 1917–53*, edited by Norman LaPorte, Kevin Morgan, and Matthew Worley, 124–45. Basingstoke: Palgrave, 2008.

Leese, Daniel. "The Cult of Personality and Symbolic Politics." In *The Oxford Handbook of the History of Communism*, edited by Stephen A. Smith, 339–54. Oxford: Oxford University Press, 2014.

———. *Mao Cult. Rhetoric and Ritual in China's Cultural Revolution*. Cambridge: Cambridge University Press, 2011.

Lemmons, Russel. *Hitler's rival. Ernst Thälmann in myth and memory*. Lexington: University Press of Kentucky, 2013.

Lénárt, András. "'Nevet nem szabad kérdezni!' Közvélemény-kutatás Magyarországon 1945 és 1949 között" ["Don't ask names!": Public opinion polls in Hungary between 1945 and 1949]. In *A demokrácia reménye – Magyarország 1945* [The Hope of Democracy: Hungary 1945], edited by János Rainer M., and Éva Standeisky, 146–75. Budapest: 1956-os Intézet, 2005.

Leo, Anette. "'Deutschlands unsterblicher Sohn…' Der Held des Widerstands Ernst Thälmann." In *Sozialistische Helden. Eine Kulturgeschichte von Propagandafiguren in Osteuropa und der DDR*, edited by Silke Satjukow and Rainer Gries, 101–14. Berlin: Links, 2002.

Leonhard, Wolfgang. *The Kremlin Since Stalin*. London: Praeger, 1962.

Levendel, Ádám. "A Magyar Közvéleménykutató Intézet (1945–1949)" [The Hungarian Public Opinion Research Institute, 1945–1949]. *Jel-Kép* 4, no. 3 (1983): 134–39.

Lewin, Moshe. "Introduction: Social Crises and Political Structures in the USSR." In *The Making of the Soviet System: Essays in the Social History of Interwar Russia*, 3–47. London: Pantheon Books, 1985.

Lindenberger, Thomas. "Tacit Minimal Consensus: The Always Precarious East German Dictatorship." In Corner, *Popular Opinion in Totalitarian Regimes*, 208–22.

Lipkovics, Károly. "A Szovjetunió Kommunista Pártjának politikájáról, 1953–1957" [On the policies of the Communist Party of the Soviet Union]. *Múltunk* 36, no. 1 (1991): 3–34.

Löhmann, Reinhard. *Der Stalinmythos. Studien zur Sozialgeschichte des Personenkultes in der Sowjetunion (1929–1935)*. Münster: Lit, 1990.

Loiperdinger, Martin, ed. *Führerbilder: Hitler, Mussolini, Roosevelt, Stalin in Fotografie und Film*. Munich: Piper, 1995.

Magyar, Zoltán. *Rákóczi a néphagyományban* [Rákóczi in folk traditions]. Budapest: Osiris, 2000.

Maier, Hans, ed. *"Totalitarismus" und "Politische Religionen": Konzepte des Diktaturvergleichs*. Paderborn: Schöningh, 1996.

Main, Izabella. "President of Poland or "Stalin's most faithful pupil"? The Cult of Bolesław Bierut in Stalinist Poland." In Apor et al., *The Leader Cult in Communist Dictatorships*, 179–93.

———. "The Weeping Virgin Mary and the Smiling Comrade Stalin: Polish Catholics and Communists in 1949." In *Sphären von Öffentlichkeit in Gesellschaften sowjetischen Typs/ Public Spheres in Soviet-Type Societies*, edited by Gábor T. Rittersporn, Malte Rolf and Jan C. Behrends, 255–78. Frankfurt am Main: Peter Lang, 2003.

Major, Ákos. *Népbíráskodás – forradalmi törvényesség. Egy népbíró visszaemlékezései* [People's Tribunals—revolutionary justice: Memoirs of a people's judge]. Budapest: Minerva, 1988.

Majtényi, György. *Vezércsel. Kádár János mindennapjai* [Queens' gambit: The daily life of János Kádár]. Budapest: Libri, 2012.

Margócsy, István. "A Petőfi-kultusz határtalanságáról" [About the boundlessness of the Petőfi cult]. In *Petőfi Sándor*, edited by István Margócsy, 11–47. Budapest: Korona, 1999.

Marsh, Rosalind. *Images of Dictatorship: Portraits of Stalin in Literature*. London: Routledge, 1989.

Martin, Terry. *The Affirmative Action Empire: Nations and Nationalism in the Soviet Union, 1923–1939*. Ithaca, NY: Cornell University Press, 2001.

Masing-Delic, Irene. "Purges and Patronage: Gor'kii's Promotion of Socialist Culture." In Heller and Plamper, *Personality Cults in Stalinism*, 443–68.

Mátyás Rákosi: On the occasion of his sixtieth birthday. London: Hungarian News and Information Service, 1952.

Mead, Margaret. *Soviet Attitudes towards Authority: An Interdisciplinary Approach to Soviet Character*. London: Tavisctock Publications, 1955.

Medvedev, Roy. *Let History Judge: The Origins and Consequences of Stalinism*. Oxford: Oxford University Press, 1988.

Melograni, Piero. "The Cult of the Duce in Mussolini's Italy." In "Theories of Fascism." Special issue, *Journal of Contemporary History* 11, no. 4 (1976): 221–37.

Mevius, Martin. *Agents of Moscow: The Hungarian Communist Party and the Origins of Socialist Patriotism 1941–1953*. Oxford: Oxford University Press, 2005.

———. "Reappraising Communism and Nationalism." *Nationalities Papers* 37, no. 4 (2009): 377–400.

Miller, Frank J. *Folklore for Stalin: Russian Folklore and Pseudofolklore of the Stalin Era*. Armonk: M.E. Sharpe, 1990.

Mocanescu, Alice. "Surviving 1956: Gheorghe Gheorghiu-Dej and the 'Cult of Personality' in Romania." In Apor et al., *The Leader Cult in Communist Dictatorships*, 246–60.

Molnár, Mátyás. "A Rákóczi-hagyomány 1945 után" [The Rákóczi tradition after 1945]. In *Rákóczi-tanulmányok* [Essays on Rákóczi], edited by Béla Köpeczi, Lajos Hopp, and Ágnes R. Várkonyi, 223–38. Budapest: Akadémiai Kiadó, 1980.

Molnár, Tibor. "A Rákosi-család kapcsolata Bácskával" [The Rákosi-family's links to the Bácska region]. *Archivnet* 14, no. 3 (2014). Accessed April 4, 2016. http://www.archivnet.hu/hetkoznapok/a_rakosicsalad_kapcsolata_bacskaval.html?oldal=1

Murasko, Gavlina Pavlovna. "Néhány ecsetvonás Rákosi Mátyás politikai portréjához" [Some contributions to Mátyás Rákosi's political biography]. *Múltunk* 44, no. 2 (1999): 160–69.

Müller, Rolf. "A politikai rendőrség tájékoztató szolgálata 1945–1962" [The information department of the political police 1945–1962]. In *Trezor 2. A Történeti Hivatal évkönyve, 2000–2001* [The year-book of the Office of History, 2000–2001], edited by György Gyarmati, 111–35. Budapest: Történeti Hivatal, 2002.

Muszatov, Valerij. "Szovjet-magyar kapcsolatok, 1953–1956" [Soviet-Hungarian relations, 1953–1956]. In *Évkönyv V: 1996/1997.* [Year-book 5: 1996/1997], edited by János Bak, 43–48. Budapest: 1956-os Intézet, 1997.

Nečásek, František. *Klement Gottwald: Communist Premier of Czechoslovakia: A Biography*. London, 1946.

———. *Klement Gottwald. Rövid életrajz* [Klement Gottwald. A short biography]. Bratislava: Polit. Kiadó, 1955.

Nemes, Dezső. "A néptömegek történelmi szerepe és a személyi kultusz kérdése" [The historical role of the masses and the question of the cult of personality]. *Századok* 86, no. 3 (1956): 441–51.

Nemes, János. *Rákosi Mátyás születésnapja* [The birthday of Mátyás Rákosi]. Budapest: Láng, 1988.

Nothnagle, Alan L. *Building the East German Myth: Historical Mythology and Youth Propaganda in the German Democratic Republic, 1945–1989*. Ann Arbor: University of Michigan Press, 1999.

Orbán, Sándor. "A szocializmus építésének első fél évtizede (1948–1953)" [The first half decade of the building of socialism, 1948–1953]. *Századok* 119, no. 2 (1985): 462–98.

Ortutay, Gyula. *A nép művészete* [The art of the people]. Budapest: Gondolat, 1981.

Ostermann, Christian, ed. *Uprising in East Germany 1953: The Cold War, the German Question, and the First Major Upheaval behind the Iron Curtain.* (Budapest-New York: CEU Press, 2001).

Oushakine, Serguei. "Laughter under Socialism: Exposing the Ocular in Soviet Jocularity." *Slavic Review* 7, no. 2 (2011): 247–55.

Pakulski, Jan. "Legitimacy and Mass Compliance: Reflections on Max Weber and Soviet-Type Societies." *British Journal of Political Science* 16, no. 1 (1986): 35–56.

Palasik, Mária. "A jogállam csapdái Magyarországon 1947 első felében. (A Magyar Közösség pere mint eszköz a kisgazdapárt hatalomból történő kiszorításához)" [The shortcomings of the rule of law in Hungary in early 1947: The trial of the "Hungarian Community" as a means to force the Smallholders out of power]. *Századok* 125, no. 6 (1995): 1305–35.

———. "A szólásszabadság deklarálása és korlátainak kezdete Magyarországon (1946–1949)" [The declaration of freedom of speech and the beginning of its limitations in Hungary, 1946–1949]. *Századok* 132, no. 3 (1998): 585–606.

———. *Chess Game for Democracy: Hungary between East and West, 1944–1947.* Montréal: McGill-Queen's University Press, 2011.

———. "Látlelet a magyar függetlenségről" [A snapshot of Hungarian independence]. *Kapu* 2, no. 5 (1989): 4–10.

Paltiel, Jeremy T. "The Cult of Personality: Some Comparative Reflections on Political Culture in Leninist Regimes." *Studies in Comparative Communism* 16, nos. 1–2 (1983): 49–64.

Paperno, Irina. "Intimacy with Power: Soviet Memoirists Remember Stalin." In Heller and Plamper, *Personality Cults in Stalinism*, 331–61.

Passerini, Luisa. *Mussolini immaginario. Storia di una biografia, 1915–1939.* Bari: Laterza, 1991.

Payne, Stanley G. "On the Heuristic Value of the Concept of Political Religion and its Application." *Totalitarian Movements and Political Religions* 6, no. 2 (2005): 163–74.

Pennetier, Claude, and Bernard Pudal, "Stalinism: Workers' Cult and Cult of Leaders." In "Communism and the Leader Cult." Special issue, *Twentieth Century Communism* 1, no. 1 (2009): 20–29.

Perrie, Maureen. *The Cult of Ivan the Terrible in Stalin's Russia.* Basingstone: Palgrave, 2001.

Peternák, Miklós. "Az államosított látás. Kísérlet az allegorikus dokumentarizmus megteremtésére" [Nationalised gaze: An attempt at creating allegorical documentarism]. In György and Turai, *A művészet katonái*, 80–90.

———. "Lenin mauzóleuma" [The Lenin mausoleum]. In *Mauzóleum. Halálirodalom* [Mausoleum: Death literature], edited by Lajos Adamik, István Jelenczki, and Miklós Sükösd, 338–54. Budapest: ELTE BTK, 1987.

Petrák, Katalin. *Magyarok a Szovjetunióban 1922–1945* [Hungarians in the Soviet Union, 1922–1945]. Budapest: Napvilág, 2000.

Petrone, Karen. *Life Has Become More Joyous, Comrades: Celebrations in the Time of Stalin*. Bloomington: University of Indiana Press, 2000.

Pichova, Hana. "The Lineup for Meat: The Stalin Statue in Prague." *Publications of the Modern Language Association of America* 123, no. 3 (2008): 614–30.

Plamper, Jan. "Beyond Binaries: Popular Opinion in Stalinism." In Corner, *Popular Opinion in Totalitarian Regimes*, 64–80.

———. "Georgian Koba or Soviet 'Father of Peoples'? The Stalin Cult and Ethnicity." In Apor et al., *The Leader Cult in Communist Dictatorships*, 123–40.

———. "Introduction: Modern Personality Cults." In Heller and Plamper, *Personality Cults in Stalinism*, 13–42.

———. "'The Hitlers Come and Go…' the Führer Stays: Stalin's Cult in East Germany." In Heller and Plamper, *Personality Cults in Stalinism*, 301–29.

———. *The Stalin Cult: A Study in the Alchemy of Power*. New Haven, CT: Yale University Press, 2012.

———. "The Spatial Poetics of the Personality Cult: Circles around Stalin." In Dobrenko and Naiman, *The Landscape of Stalinism*, 20–45.

Pogány Ö., Gábor. "Rákosi Mátyás és a művészet" [Mátyás Rákosi and the arts]. *Szabad Művészet* 6, no. 3 (1952): 97–103.

Pollock, Ethan. "Stalin as the coryphaeus of science: Ideology and knowledge in the post-war years." In Davies and Harris, *Stalin: A New History*, 271–88.

Postoutenko, Kirill, ed. *Totalitarian Communication: Hierarchies, Codes and Messages*. Bielefeld: Transcript, 2010.

Pótó, János. *Az emlékeztetés helyei. Emlékművek és politika* [Mnemonic sites: Memorials and politics]. Budapest: Osiris, 2003.

Potts, John. *A History of Charisma*. Basingstoke: Palgrave, 2009.

Prokhorov, Geb. *Art under Socialist Realism: Soviet Painting, 1930–1950*. East Roseville: Craftsman House, 1995.

Pünkösti, Árpád. "Névtelen leveleket forgatva" [Browsing through anonymous letters]. *Jel-Kép* 4, no. 3 (1983): 74–86.

Pünkösti, Árpád. *Rákosi a csúcson 1948–1953* [Rákosi at the peak of his career, 1948–1953]. Budapest: Európa, 1996.

———. *Rákosi a hatalomért 1945–1948* [Rákosi vying for power, 1945–1948]. Budapest: Európa, 1992

———. *Rákosi bukása, száműzetése és halála, 1953–1971* [Rákosi's fall, exile and death, 1953–1971]. Budapest: Európa, 2001.

Pyzhikov, Aleksandr V. "The Cult of Personality during the Khrushchev Thaw." *Russian Studies in History* 50, no. 3 (2011–12): 11–27.

Rainer M., János. *Az író helye. Viták a magyar irodalmi sajtóban 1953–1956* [The place of the writer: Debates in the Hungarian literary press, 1953–1956]. Budapest: Magvető, 1990.

Rainer M., János. "Kádár János: A kultusz nélküli ember" [János Kádár: The man without a cult]. *Rubicon* 18, no. 9 (2007): 42–49.

———. *Nagy Imre: Politikai életrajz*, vol. 1 *(1896–1953)* [Imre Nagy: A political biography, 1896–1953]. Budapest: 1956-os Intézet, 1996.

———. *Nagy Imre: Politikai életrajz*, vol. 2 *(1953–1958)* [Imre Nagy: A political biography, 1953–1958]. Budapest: 1956-os Intézet, 1999.

———. "Sztálin és Rákosi, Sztálin és Magyarország 1949–1953" [Stalin and Rákosi, Stalin and Hungary, 1949–1953]. In *Évkönyv VI: 1998* [Year-book 6: 1998], edited by György Litván, 91–100. Budapest: 1956-os Intézet, 1998.

———. "Távirat 'Filippov' elvtársnak. Rákosi Mátyás üzentei Sztálin titkárságának 1949–1952" [Telegrams for Comrade "Filippov": Mátyás Rákosi's message for Stalin's secretariat, 1949–1952]. In *Évkönyv VI: 1998* [Year-book 6: 1998], edited by György Litván, 103–18, Budapest: 1956-os Intézet, 1998.

Rainer M., János, and György Péteri, *Muddling Through in the Long 1960s*. Budapest: 1956-os Intézet, 2005.

Rainer M., János, and Károly Urbán, eds. "Konzultációk. Dokumentumok a magyar és a szovjet pártvezetők két moszkvai találkozójáról 1954–1955-ben" [Consultations: Documents of the two meetings between Hungarian and Soviet party leaders in Moscow in 1954–1955]. *Múltunk* 37, no. 3 (1992): 124–49.

Rákosi elvtárs élete. Szakszervezeti Ismeretterjesztő előadások [The life of comrade Rákosi: General lectures for trade unions]. Budapest, 1952.

"Rákosi Mátyás elvtárs 60. születésnapja: az új magyar népi díszítőművészet fejlődésének hatalmas forrása" [Mátyás Rákosi's 60th birthday: The monumental source of the development of new Hungarian decorative folk arts]. *Ethnographia* 53, nos. 1–2 (1952): 1–9.

Rákosi elvtárs harca [Comrade Rákosi's struggle]. 3 vols. Sztálinváros, 1952.

Rákosi Mátyás élete képekben [The life of Mátyás Rákosi in pictures]. Budapest: Szikra, 1952.

Rákosi Mátyás és a magyar történettudomány [Mátyás Rákosi and Hungarian historiography]. Budapest: Akadémiai kiadó, 1952.

Rákosi, Mátyás. "A dolgozó parasztság a szövetkezés útján" [The working peasantry on the road to collectivization]. In *Építjük a nép országát* [We are building the country of the people], 281–315, Budapest: Szikra, 1949.

———. *A fordulat éve* [The year of the turn]. Budapest: Szikra, 1948.

———. *Visszaemlékezések 1892–1925* [Memoirs, 1892–1925]. 2 vols. Budapest: Napvilág, 2002.

———. *Visszaemlékezések 1940–1956* [Memoirs, 1940–1956]. 2 vols. Budapest: Napvilág, 1997.

Ree, Erik van. *The Political Thought of Joseph Stalin: A Study in twentieth-century Revolutionary Patriotism*. London, New York: RoutledgeCurzon, 2002.

Rees, E. A. "Leader Cults: Varieties, Preconditions and Functions." In Apor et al., *The Leader Cult in Communist Dictatorships*, 3–28.

———, ed. *The Nature of Stalin's Dictatorship: The Politburo, 1924–1953*. Basingstoke: Palgrave, 2004.

Rehák, László. "Tito életrajzának első kötete" [The first volume of Tito's biography]. *Létünk*, May 20, 1981, 987–91.

Rév, István. "Az atomizáció előnyei" [The advantages of atomization]. *Replika*, nos. 23–24 (1996): 141–57.

———. "Paraszti ellenállás a klasszikus szocializmusban" [Peasant resistance in classical socialism]. In *Múltunk Jövője. Szabadelvűek a népi kultúráról*, 75–84. Budapest: T-Twins, 1993.

Révai, József. *48 útján* [On the path of 1848]. Budapest: Szikra, 1948.

Réz, Pál, and István Vas, eds. *Magyar Írók Rákosi Mátyásról* [Hungarian writers about Mátyás Rákosi]. Budapest: Szépirodalmi kiadó, 1952.

Riall, Lucy. *Garibaldi: Invention of a Hero*. New Haven, CT: Yale University Press, 2008.

Rigby, T.H., and Ferenc Fehér, eds. *Political Legitimation in Communist States*. Oxford: Macmillan, 1982.

Ripp, Zoltán. "A sztálinizmus rendszerének és restaurációjának elvi kérdéseiről" [On the theoretical questions of the restoration of the Stalinist system]. *Múltunk* 35, no. 1 (1990): 129–40.

———. "Példaképből ellenség: A magyar kommunisták viszonya Jugoszláviához, 1947–1948" [From icon into enemy: The Hungarian communists' attitudes toward Yugoslavia, 1947–1948]. In Standeisky et al., *A fordulat évei*, 45–62.

Roberts, David R. "'Political Religion' and the Totalitarian Departures of Inter-war Europe: On the Uses and Disadvantages of an Analytical Category." *Contemporary European History* 18, no. 4 (2009): 381–414.

Rolf, Malte. "A Hall of Mirrors: Sovietizing Culture." *Slavic Review* 68, no. 3 (2009): 601–30.

———. "The Leader's Many Bodies: Leader Cults and Mass Festivals in Voronezh, Novosibirsk, and Kemerovo in the 1930s." In Heller and Plamper, *Personality Cults in Stalinism*, 197–206.

———. *Soviet Mass Festivals, 1917–1991*. Pittsburgh: University of Pittsburgh Press, 2013.

———. "Working Towards the Centre: Leader Cults and Spatial Politics in Pre-war Stalinism." In Apor et al., *The Leader Cult in Communist Dictatorships*, 141–57.

Romsics, Ignác. *Magyarország története a XX. Században* [The history of Hungary in the twentieth century]. Budapest: Osiris, 2000.

Saarela, Tauno. "Dead Martyrs and Living Leaders: The Cult of the Individual within Finnish Communism." In "Communism and the Leader Cult." Special issue, *Twentieth Century Communism* 1, no. 1 (2009): 30–49.

Sabrow, Martin. "Consent in the Communist GDR or How to Interpret Lion Feuchtwanger's Blindness in Moscow 1937." In Corner, *Popular Opinion in Totalitarian Regimes*, 168–83.

Samueli, Georg. *Rakoshi, Matias*. Moscow: Molodaia gvardiia, 1935.

Sanborn, Joshua. "Family, Fraternity, and Nation-Building in Russia, 1905–1925." In *A State of Nations: Empire and Nation-Making in the Age of Lenin and Stalin*, edited by Terry Martin and Ronald Grigor Suny, 93–110. New York and Oxford: Oxford University Press, 2001.

Santana, Marco Aurélio. "Re-Imagining the Cavalier of Hope: The Brazilian Communist Party and the Images of Luis Carlos Prestes." In "Communism and the Leader Cult." Special issue, *Twentieth Century Communism* 1, no. 1 (2009): 110–28.

Sárközi, Mátyás. *A Rákosi-korszak irodalompolitikája* [The literary politics of the Rákosi era]. London: Fehér Holló, 1980.

Satjukow, Silke, and Rainer Gries, eds. *Sozialistische Helden: Eine Kulturgeschichte von Propagandafiguren in Osteuropa und der DDR*. Berlin: Links, 2002.

Scott, James C. *Domination and the Arts of Resistance: Hidden Transcripts*. New Haven, CT: Yale University Press, 1990.

Scott, John. *Behind the Urals: An American Worker in Russia's City of Steel*. Enlarged edition prepared by Stephen Kotkin. Bloomington: Indiana University Press, 1989.

Service, Robert. "The Road to the Twentieth Congress." *Soviet Studies* 33, no. 2 (1981): 232–45.

———. *Stalin: A Biography*. Basingstoke: Palgrave, 2010.

Shukman, Harold, ed. *Redefining Stalinism*. London, Portland: Frank Cass, 2003.

Sinkó, Katalin. "A politika rítusai: emlékműállítás, szobordöntés" [The rituals of politics: Building monuments, tearing down statues]. In György and Turai, *A művészet katonái*, 67–79.

Sipos, Levente. "Hiányos leltár (I.): MSZMP-dokumentumok a 'személyi kultusz idején elkövetett törvénysértésekről'" [Incomplete inventory (1.): MSZMP documents about 'the violations of legality during the time of the cult of personality']. *Társadalmi Szemle* 49, no. 11 (1994): 72–94.

Sipos, Péter. *Legális és illegális munkásmozgalom Magyarországon 1919–1944* [Legal and illegal working class movement in Hungary, 1919–1944]. Budapest: Gondolat, 1988.

Slezkine, Yuri. "The USSR as a Communal Apartment, Or How a Socialist State Promoted Ethnic Particularism." *Slavic Review* 53, no. 2 (1994): 414–52.

Smith, Trevor J. "The Collapse of the Lenin Personality Cult in Soviet Russia, 1985–1995." *The Historian* 60, no. 2 (1998): 325–43.

———. "Lenin for Sale: The Rise and Fall of the Personality Cult of V.I. Lenin in Soviet Russia." MA Thesis, Carleton University, 1995.

Spira, György, *Kossuth Lajos a szabadságharc vezére: Útmutató városi és falusi előadók számára* [Lajos Kossuth, the leader of the war of independence: Guidelines for speakers in the cities and the villages]. Budapest: Művelt Nép, 1952.

Sretenovic, Stanislav, and Artan Puto. "Leader Cults in the Western Balkans (1945–1990): Josip Broz Tito and Enver Hoxha." In Apor et al., *The Leader Cult in Communist Dictatorships*, 208–25.

Ssorin-Chaikov, Nikolai, and Olga Sosnina. "The Faculty of Useless Things: Gifts to Soviet Leaders." In Heller and Plamper, *Personality Cults in Stalinism*, 277–300.

Standeisky, Éva. "A kígyó bőre. Ideológia és politika" [The snake's skin: Ideology and politics]. In Standeisky et al., *A fordulat évei*, 151–71.

———. *A Magyar Kommunista Párt irodalompolitikája 1944–48* [The literary politics of the Hungarian Communist Party, 1944–48]. Budapest: Kossuth, 1987.

———. "Hit-viták: Az írók és az 1953-as 'új szakasz.'" [Polemics on faith: Writers and the New Course of 1953] *Mozgó Világ* 29, no. 8 (2003): 27–43.

———. "Lánc-reakció: A magyar irodalmi élet szovjetizálása 1949 és 1951 között" [Chain reaction: The Sovietization of Hungarian literary life between 1949 and 1951]. *Múltunk* 49, no. 1 (2004): 48–81.

Standeisky, Éva, Gyula Kozák, Gábor Pataki, and János Rainer M., eds. *A fordulat évei: Politika - Képzőművészet - Építészet, 1947–1949* [The years of the turn: Politics–arts–architecture, 1947–1949], Budapest: 1956-os Intézet, 1998.

Stephenson, Jill. "Popular Opinion in Nazi Germany: Mobilization, Experience, Perceptions: The View from the Württemberg Countryside." In Corner, *Popular Opinion in Totalitarian Regimes*, 107–21.

Stites, Richard. "The Origins of Soviet Ritual Style: Symbol and Festival in the Russian Revolution." In Arvidsson and Blomqvist, *Symbols of Power*, 43–60.

———. "Utopian or Antiutopian? An Indirect Look at the Cult of Personality." In *The Cult of Power: Dictators in the Twentieth Century*, edited by Joseph Held, 77–94. Boulder: East European Monographs, 1983.

Stölting, Erhard. "Charismatische Aspekte des politischen Führertums: Das Beispiel Stalins." In *Politische Religion - religiöse Politik*, edited by Richard Faber, 45–74. Würzburg: Königshausen & Neumann, 1997.

Strong, Carol, and Matt Killingsworth. "Stalin the Charismatic Leader?: Explaining the 'Cult of Personality' as a Legitimation Technique." *Politics, Religion and Ideology* 12, no. 4 (2011): 391–411.

Swain, Geoffrey, and Nigel Swain. *Eastern Europe Since 1945*. Basingstoke: Palgrave, 2003.

Szabó, Bálint. *Az "ötvenes évek"* [The Fifties]. Budapest: Kossuth, 1986.

Szabó, Ildikó. *A pártállam gyermekei. Tanulmányok a magyar politikai szocializációról* [The children of the party state: Essays about political socialization in Hungary]. Budapest: Új Mandátum, 2000.

Szabó, Márton. "Munkaszervezet és munkáskép az ötvenes évekből" [Labor organization and the image of the worker in the 1950s]. *Ipar-Gazdaság*, no. 3 (1987): 29–34.

———. "A rendi szocializmus eszméje: Adalékok az 50-es évek ideológiatörténetéhez" [The idea of estate socialism: Contributions to the history of ideology in the 1950s]. *Mozgó Világ* 14, no. 2 (1988): 3–11.

Szabó, Miklós. "Hétköznapi sztálinizmus Magyarországon" [Everyday Stalinism in Hungary]. *Századvég*, nos. 6–7 (1988): 160–67.

———. *Politikai kultúra Magyarországon 1896–1986* [Political culture in Hungary, 1896–1986]. Budapest: Medvetánc, 1989.

Szabó, Róbert. "Politikai propaganda – történelmi ünnepek 1945–1956" [Political propaganda—historical anniversaries, 1945–1956]. PhD dissertation, Eötvös Loránd Tudományegyetem, Budapest, 1988.

———. "Politikai propaganda és történelmi ünnep: Adalékok az 1948. márciusi centenáriumi ünnepségek történetéhez" [Political propaganda and historical holidays: Contributions to the history of the centenary celebrations of March 1948]. *Történelmi Szemle* 40, nos. 3–4 (1998): 215–27.

Szakadát, István, and Gábor Kelemen. "Karriertípusok és mobilitási csatornák a Magyar Kommunista Párton belül (1945–1989)" [Career types and mobility channels in the Hungarian Communist Party, 1945–1989]. In *Magyar társadalomtörténeti olvasókönyv 1944-től napjainkig* [A reader in Hungarian social history from 1944 to the present], edited by Tibor Valuch, 664–77. Budapest: Argumentum, 2004.

Szalay, László. "Előhang 1954-ből: A Szabad Nép taggyűlése" [A prelude from 1954: The membership meeting of Szabad Nép]. *Világosság* 35, no. 10 (1994): 48–56.

Székely, András. "Az 'ötvenes évek' művészetéhez" [On the art of the 1950s]. *Mozgó Világ* 10, no. 3 (1984): 23–28.

Szekeres, József. "Egy dokumentum története: Rákosi Mátyás 1925. évi rendőrségi és ügyészségi vallomásainak jegyzőkönyve" [The history of a document: The minutes of Mátyás Rákosi's testimony at the police and the public prosecutor's office in 1925]. *Történelmi Szemle* 33, nos. 1–2 (1991): 89–106.

Szerencsés, Károly. *A kékcédulás hadművelet (Választások Magyarországon 1947)* [Operation blue sheet: Elections in Hungary in 1947]. Budapest: IKVA, 1992.

Szetelszky, Zsuzsanna. "A pletyka pszichológiája" [The psychology of rumor]. PhD dissertation, Pécsi Tudományegyetem, Pécs, 2010.

Szilágyi, Ákos. "Istenek, cárok, főtitkárok: A Sztálin-vallás eredete" [Gods, Tsars, Party general secretaries: The origins of the Stalin religion]. *Rubicon* 3, no. 7 (1992): 23–26.

Szporluk, Roman. *Communism and Nationalism: Karl Marx versus Friedrich List*. Oxford: Oxford University Press, 1988.

Sztikalin, Aleszandr Szergejevics. "A szovjet nagykövetség és az MDP-n belüli harc 1956 tavaszán–kora őszén" [The Soviet embassy and struggles in the Party in the Spring–early Autumn of 1956]. *Múltunk* 43, no. 2 (1998): 23–49.

Szücs, György. "A képfelség elve" [The principle of the supremacy of image]. In György and Turai, *A művészet katonái*, 44–57.

———. "Rákosi Mátyás Művek. (A szocialista vezető képi megjelenítésének kérdéséhez.)" [Mátyás Rákosi Works: On the question of the socialist leader's visual representation]. In *Az ostromtól a forradalomig: Adalékok Budapest múltjához 1945–1956* [From siege to revolution: Contributions to Budapest's past, 1945–1956], edited by Zsuzsanna Bencsik, and Gábor Kresalek, 63–90. Budapest: Budapest Főváros Levéltára, 1990.

Tallár, Ferenc. "Sztálinizmus és reszakralizáció" [Stalinism and re-sacralization]. *Valóság* 32, no. 2 (1989): 32–51.

Taylor, Lily Ross. *The Divinity of the Roman Emperor*. Middletown, Conn.: American Philological Association, 1931.

Taylor, Richard. *The Aesthetic Arsenal: Socialist Realism under Stalin*. New York: Institute for Contemporary Art, 1993.

Téglás, E. *Mátyás Rákosi*. Moscow, 1937.

Thompson, Robert J. "Reassessing Personality Cults: The Case of Stalin and Mao." *Studies in Comparative Communism* 21, no. 1 (1988): 99–128.

Thurston, Robert. "Social Dimensions of Stalinist Rule: Humor and Terror in the USSR, 1935–1941." *Journal of Social History* 24, no. 3 (1991): 541–62.

Tikhomirov, Alexey. "The Stalin Cult between Center and Periphery: The Structures of the Cult Community in the Empire of Socialism, 1949–1956—The Case of GDR." In *Der Führer im Europa des 20. Jahrhunders*, edited by Benno Ennker, and Heidi Hein-Kircher, 297–321. Marburg: Herder Institut, 2010.

Torpey, John C. *Intellectuals, Socialism and Dissent: The East German Opposition and Its Legacy*. Minneapolis: University of Minnesota Press, 1995.

Tóth, Ágnes. *Telepítések Magyarországon 1945–1948 között. A németek kitelepítése, a belső népmozgások és a szlovák-magyar lakosságcsere összefüggései* [Population movements in Hungary between 1945 and 1948: The German expulsion, internal migration and the Slovak-Hungarian population exchange]. Kecskemét: Bács-Kiskun Megyei Önkormányzat Levéltára, 1993.

Tóth, Szergej. "A szovjet birodalmi nyelv, avagy a totalitarizmus grammatikája" [Soviet imperial language or the grammar of totalitarianism]. *Aetas* 6, no. 1 (1991): 5–39.

———. "Nyelvhasználat egy totalitárius rendszerben (Nyelvszociológiai megközelítés)" [Language use in a totalitarian system: A sociolinguistic approach]. PhD dissertation, Eötvös Loránd Tudományegyetem, Budapest, 1999.

Tucker, Robert C. "The Politics of Soviet De-Stalinization." *World Politics* 9, no. 4 (1957): 550–78.

———. "The Rise of Stalin's Personality Cult." *The American Historical Review* 84, no. 2 (1979): 347–66.

———. *Stalin in Power: The Revolution from Above, 1928–1941*. New York: Norton, 1990.

———. "The Theory of Charismatic Leadership." In "Philosophers and Kings: Studies in Leadership." Special issue, *Daedalus* 97, no. 3 (1968): 731–56.
Tumarkin, Nina. *Lenin lives! The Lenin Cult in Soviet Russia*. Cambridge, MA: Harvard University Press, 1997.
———. "Religion, Bolshevism and the Origins of the Lenin Cult." *Russian Review* 40, no. 1 (1981): 35–46.
Turbucz, Dávid. "A Horthy-kultusz" [The Horthy cult]. In *A magyar jobboldali hagyomány* [The Hungarian right-wing tradition], edited by Ignác Romsics, 138–66. Budapest: Osiris, 2009.
———. *A Horthy-kultusz* [The Horthy cult]. Budapest: MTA Bölcsészettudományi Kutatóközpont, 2016.
———. "A Horthy-kultusz kezdetei" [The origins of the Horthy cult]. *Múltunk* 54, no. 4 (2009): 156–99.
———. "Az 'országépítő' kormányzó képének megjelenése az 1920-as évek második felében" [The emergence of the image of the Regent as the builder of the country]. *Kommentár*, no. 3 (2011): 32–44.
T. Varga, György. "Jegyzőkönyv a szovjet és a magyar párt és állami vezetők tárgyalásairól" [Minutes of the meetings of Soviet and Hungarian Party and government leaders]. *Múltunk* 37, nos. 2–3 (1992): 234–69.
———. "Rákosi Mátyás referátuma az MDP Központi Vezetőségének 1953. júniusi ülésén" [Mátyás Rákosi's report to the Central Committee of the MDP in June 1956]. *Múltunk* 35, no. 1 (1990): 141–62.
Urbán, Károly. "Nagy Imre első miniszterelnöksége" [Imre Nagy's first premiership]. *Társadalmi Szemle* 47, no. 6 (1992): 72–81.
———. "Nagy Imre és G.M. Malenkov: Két miniszterelnök Sztálin után" [Imre Nagy and G. Malenkov: Two prime ministers after Stalin]. *Múltunk* 41, no. 1 (1996): 129–80.
Urbán, Károly, and István Vida. "Az MDP Politikai Bizottsága 1956. június 28-i ülésének jegyzőkönyve: Az 1956. júniusi kommunista csúcstalálkozó és Magyarország" [The minutes of the meeting of the MDP's Politburo on 28 January 1956: The Communist summit of June 1956 and Hungary]. *Társadalmi Szemle* 48, no. 2 (1993): 83–94.
Úttörőmozgalom. Iskolai ünnepély Rákosi Mátyás 60. születésnapja tiszteletére [Pioneer movement: The celebration of Mátyás Rákosi's birthday in schools]. Budapest, 1952.
Vacín, Luděk. *Studie a materiály k mauzoleu Klementa Gottwalda / Studies and Materials on the Mausoleum of Klement Gottward*. Special issue, *Sborník Národního Muzea v Praze / Acta Musei Nationalis Pragae* 68, nos. 1–2 (2014).
Valuch, Tibor. "A magyar művelődés 1948 után" [Hungarian culture after 1948]. In *Magyar művelődéstörténet* [Hungarian cultural history], edited by László Kósa, 460–547. Budapest: Osiris, 2000.
———. *Magyarország társadalomtörténete a XX. század második felében* [The social history of Hungary in the second half of the 20th century]. Budapest: Osiris, 2001.

Vas, Zoltán. *Tizenhat év fegyházban* [Sixteen years in prison]. Budapest: Szikra, 1951.
Vásárhelyi, Miklós. "Az első meghiúsított reformkísérlet: Az 1953-as kormányprogram." [The first failed reform attempt: The government program of 1953]. In *Ellenzékben* [In opposition], edited by Miklós Vásárhelyi, 238–313. Budapest: Szabad Tér Kiadó, 1989.
Vásárhelyi, Mária. *Csalóka emlékezet. A 20. század történelme a magyar közgondolkodásban* [Deceptive memory: Twentieth-century history in Hungarian public thinking]. Bratislava: Kalligram, 2007.
Velikanova, Olga. "The Function of Lenin's Image in the Soviet Mass Consciousness." In *Soviet Civilization between Past and Present*, edited by Mette Bryld and Erik Kulavig, 13–38. Odense: Odense University Press, 1998.
———. *Making of an Idol: On Uses of Lenin*. Göttingen: Muster-Schmidt, 1996.
———. *The Public Perception of the Cult of Lenin Based on Archival Materials*. Lewiston: Edwin Mellen Press, 2001.
Verdery, Katherine. *What Was Socialism and What Comes Next?* Princeton: Princeton University Press, 1996.
Vida, István. "A Magyar Közösség és a Kisgazdapárt" [The 'Hungarian Community' and the Smallholders' Party]. *Történelmi Szemle* 12, no. 1 (1970): 111–24.
———. *Koalíció és pártharcok 1945–1948* [Coalition and party struggles in 1945–1948]. Budapest: Magvető, 1986.
Viola, Lynne. "Introduction." In *Contending with Stalinism*, edited by Lynn Viola, 1–16. Ithaca and London: Cornell University Press, 2002.
———. "Popular Resistance in the Stalinist 1930s: Soliloquy of a Devil's Advocate." In *Contending with Stalinism*, edited by Lynn Viola, 17–43. Ithaca and London: Cornell University Press, 2002.
Voigt, Vilmos. "Éljen és virágozzék... (A budapesti május elsejékről)" [Long live and let it blossom...: About May 1 celebrations in Budapest]. In "Kultuszok és kultuszhelyek" [Cults and sites of cults]. Special issue, *Budapesti Negyed* 2, no. 1 (1994): 166–86.
Vonyó, József. "Diktatúra – olasz mintára: A Gömbös-csoport az államról a harmincas évek első felében" [Dictatorship following the Italian model: The Gömbös group about the state in the first half of the 1930s]. In *Gömbös Gyula és a jobboldali radikalizmus: Tanulmányok* [Gyula Gömbös and right-wing radicalism: Essays], edited by József Vonyó, 52–65. Budapest: Pannónia, 2001.
Voronytsin, Sergei. "The Lenin Cult and Soviet Youth." *Studies on the Soviet Union* 9, no. 1 (1969): 31–36.
Vörös, Boldizsár. "1848–49 történelmi személyiségei – 1918–19-ben" [The historical figures of 1848–49 in 1918–19]. In *Emlékezet, kultusz, történelem. Tanulmányok az 1848–49-es forradalom és szabadságharc 150. évfordulója alkalmából* [Memory, cult, history: Essays on the occasion of the 150th anniversary of the revolution and war of independence of 1848–49], edited by József Hudi, and Péter Tóth G., 45–50. Veszprém: Laczkó Dezső Múzeum, 1999.

———. *"A múltat végképp eltörölni"? Történelmi személyiségek a magyarországi szociáldemokrata és kommunista propagandában 1890–1919* ["Of the past let us make a clean slate"? Historical personalities in the propaganda of Social Democrats and Communists in Hungary in 1890–1919]. Budapest: MTA Történettudományi Intézet, 2004.

———. "Mitikus hős és példakép: Lenin-kép a hazai átalános iskolákban az 1940-es évek végétől 1953-ig." [Mythical hero and role modell: The image of Lenin in Hungarian primary schools from the late 1940s until 1953]. *Mozgó Világ* 18, no. 2 (1992): 14–27.

———. "Szamuelli repülőgépen Oroszországba szökött.' Álhírek Budapesten a Magyarországi Tanácsköztársaság idején" ['Szamuelli fled to Russia on an aeroplane' Fake news in Budapest during the Hungarian Soviet Republic]. *Budapesti Negyed* 13, nos. 1–2 (2005): 31–62.

———. "Történelmi hősök, új rendszerek: Emlékszobrok Szovjet-Oroszországban és a magyarországi Tanácsköztársaságban 1917–1919." [Historical heroes, new systems: Monuments in Soviet Russia and the Hungarian Soviet Republic in 1917–1919]. *Mozgó Világ* 24, no. 5 (1998): 85–105.

Vorsteher, Dieter, ed. *Parteiauftrag: Ein neues Deutschland. Bilder, Rituale und Symbole der frühen DDR*. Munich, Berlin: Koehler & Amelang, 1997.

Walker, Barbara. "Iosif Stalin, 'Our Teacher Dear': Mentorship, Social Transformation, and the Russian Intelligentsia Personality Cult." In Heller and Plamper, *Personality Cults in Stalinism*, 45–59.

Weber, Max. *Economy and Society: An Outline of Interpretive Sociology*. 2 vols. Berkeley: University of California Press, 1978.

White, Stephen. *The Bolshevik Poster*. New Haven, CT: Yale University Press, 1988.

———. *Political Culture and Soviet Politics*. Basingstoke: Macmillan, 1979.

Wien, Markus. "Georgi Dimitrov: Three Manifestations of his Cult." In Apor et al., *The Leader Cult in Communist Dictatorships*, 194–207.

Wilentz, Sean, ed. *Rites of Power: Symbolism, Ritual, and Politics since the Middle Ages*. Philadelphia: University of Pennsylvania Press, 1985.

Wortman, Richard S. *Scenarios of Power: Myth and Ceremony in Russian Monarchy: From Peter the Great to the Abdication of Nicholas II*. Princeton: Princeton University Press, 2006.

Zakar, Péter. "'Kossuth a magyarok Mózese' (Liberális egyháziak Kossuth-képe 1848/49-ben" [Kossuth, the "Moses of the Hungarians": The Kossuth image of the liberal clergy in 1848–49]. *Aetas* 18, nos. 3–4 (2003): 87–108.

Zaremba, Marcin. "The Second Step of a Ladder: The Cult of the First Secretaries in Poland." In Apor et al., *The Leader Cult in Communist Dictatorships*, 261–77.

Zaslavsky, Victor. "The Rebirth of the Stalin Cult in the USSR." In *The Neo-Stalinist State: Class, Ethnicity and Consensus in Soviet Society*, edited by Victor Zaslavsky, 3–21. Armonk: M. E. Sharpe, 1994.

Zeidler, Miklós. *A magyar irredenta kultusz a két világháború között* [The Hungarian irredentist cult between the two World Wars]. Budapest: Teleki László Alapítvány, 2002.

———. *A revíziós gondolat* [The revisionist thought]. Budapest: Osiris, 2001.

Zelnik, József. "Miskakancsó R. M. apánknak" ["Miska-jug" for our father, R.M.]. *Jel-Kép* 4, no. 3 (1983): 87–96.

Zwick, Peter. *National Communism*. Epping: Bowker, 1983.

Index

A

Ács, Lajos, 94, 285, 295, 310–11
Aczél, György, 319n, 323–24, 331
Aczél, Tamás, 84–85, 150, 156, 165
Adenauer, Konrad, 12
aktíva, 92, 197, 235, 282–84, 297, 301–2, 305–10, 312–14, 317
Albania, 16
Allied Control Commission, Hungary, 37
Andersen Nexö, Martin, 46
Andics, Erzsébet, 82, 173n, 253, 292, 316
Andropov, Yuri, 311–12, 314
Antikainen, Toivo, 49
"anti-republican conspiracy," 37, 55, 57
anti-Semitism,
applauding, applause (as a ritual), 6, 9, 44, 56–59, 66, 70, 83n, 84, 91, 160, 183, 187–91, 195, 198, 226, 229, 269–70, 273, 276, 278, 283, 286–87, 291, 294n, 297–98, 304, 306, 317, 321
Apró, Antal, 310, 324
artists, 84, 149, 157–59, 200, 273
Árpád, chieftain, 143
Aster Revolution of 1918, 34
ÁVO/ÁVH, 90, 178n, 181, 187, 203–4, 209, 211, 212n, 214–16, 223, 237n, 247, 275, 281, 293, 315, 318

B

Bánhegyi, Tibor, 158
Barbusse, Henri, 46, 101, 118, 147
Barta, Lajos, 106
Batthyány, Lajos, 40, 143
Béla IV, King, 136
Bem, József, 40
Benjámin, László, 84, 150
Beria, Lavrenti, 88n, 265, 272, 281–84
Berlin, 171, 281
Berman, Jakub, 302
Betlen, Oszkár, 297, 304
Bierut, Bolesław, 15, 19, 98, 134-35, 265, 281, 302
biographies (of leaders), 6, 9, 27, 95–125, 255, 335, 340;
  Bierut, 98;
  Dimitrov, 46n, 95, 98, 102, 116;
  Gheorghiu-Dej, 98, 117–20;
  Gottwald, 98, 116, 117–20, 134;
  Honecker, 98, 99n;
  Kirov, 97;
  Ordzhonikidze, 97;
  Lenin, 99, 104;
  Pieck, 98, 117–19;
  Rákosi, 25, 38, 46, 68, 73–74, 76, 82, 85, 91, 98–99, 101–17, 120–25, 142, 255–56, 292, 305;
  Tito, 98, 99n;

377

Stalin, 73, 86, 95, 97, 99–100, 104, 107–8, 116, 300, 307, 339;
Ulbricht, 98;
Voroshilov, 97
birthday celebrations (of leaders),
  Rákosi, 71–77, 85, 92–93, 98, 106, 108–10, 144, 150n, 165n, 169–70, 172, 203, 226, 255, 267, 293;
  Stalin, 14, 22, 68, 72–73, 90, 131, 217–18, 248, 264
Bíró, Eugénia, 331
Bíró, Zoltán, 45, 75, 80, 107, 239, 292
Biszku, Béla, 324
Brusilov, Aleksei, 97
Bucharest, 171, 297
Budapest, 26, 33–34, 43, 58–59, 66–67, 72, 101, 112, 114, 133, 149–50, 157, 165, 169, 170n, 172, 185, 189, 213, 215–16, 236, 253, 266, 308, 314–15, 318–19, 329n, 330n, 332;
  party organs in, 71n, 82, 92, 198, 235, 239n, 246, 282–83, 287, 297, 305, 309, 312–13,
Bukharin, Nikolai, 122
Bulganin, Nikolai, 310
Bulgaria, 73, 102, 171, 173, 200, 264, 281, 301, 323, 328

C

Ceaușescu, Nicolae, 8n, 220, 328, 344
Central Committee,
  of KMP, MKP, MDP, MSZMP, 123, 178n, 190n, 196–97, 239–42, 244, 251, 272, 274–81, 283–85, 287–88, 292, 294–99, 302–5, 309, 312n, 315–17, 319n, 320, 322, 324, 328;
  of CPSU, 268, 271, 314
charisma, 2–5, 11–12, 50n, 52, 68, 314, 335, 337–38, 341
chastushka, 183n, 223
Chervenkov, Vŭlko, 264, 281, 301
children (and the cult), 14, 59, 82–83, 92, 95, 104–5, 154, 166, 174, 203, 225, 226, 269, 270
Chișinevski, Iosif, 301
Churchill, Winston, 50, 227
clientelism, 10, 149, 202. *See also* patronage
Cold War, 21, 71, 132, 299
collective farms (kolkhoz, *termelőszövetkezet*), 19, 23, 29, 41, 74, 111, 148–49, 156, 167, 169–71, 173, 177, 194–97, 214, 252, 254, 284n
collective leadership, 263, 265, 272, 274–75, 279, 288, 294, 303, 304n, 307, 312–14, 325–26, 333
collectivization, 21, 38, 120, 183, 185, 214
Communist Information Bureau (Cominform), 227, 325
Communist International (Comintern), 34–35, 45–51, 94, 101–2, 112–13, 115–16, 118, 121–24, 128, 144n
Communist internationalism, 133–35
Communist takeover, Hungary, 38–39, 53, 65–69, 77, 130, 156, 168, 178n, 206, 219, 254, 258, 277, 293, 326
Constantinescu, Miron, 301
constitution,
  Stalin constitution (1936), 148, 182n, 192;
  Hungarian constitution (1949), 1, 38, 65, 68, 120, 182n, 191–95, 204–5, 238
"consultations" in Moscow,
  in June 1953, 117, 271–73, 280;
  in May 1954, 284;
  in January 1955, 295
CPSU, 144, 148, 266, 271, 279n, 281, 303, 305, 307, 310–11, 314, 316;
  Congresses of (Twentieth, Twenty-Second), 17, 28, 299–314, 323, 327, 332
criticism/self-criticism rituals, 7, 9, 29, 119, 197, 200–1, 273–79, 282, 295, 301, 303, 306, 310, 312, 314, 321

Csáki-Maronyák, József, 157
"cult of personality" (*also* "personality cult"), 3, 17, 26–30, 43, 71, 100, 125, 162n, 163, 263–65, 272–75, 278–79, 282, 286, 288, 291–92, 294, 295, 297–302, 304, 306–7, 309–15, 317–22, 324–27, 330, 332–34, 336, 341, 343. *See also* leader cult
Cyrankiewicz, József, 302
Czechoslovakia, 55, 59, 121–22, 128, 135, 173, 265, 267, 323, 328
Czeglédi, István, 158

D

Darázs, Endre, 141
Darvas, József, 84, 278, 295n
Dávid, Ferenc, 277–78, 285
death of leaders,
 Bierut, 302;
 Gottwald, 98, 134, 265, 267, 281;
 Rákosi, 224n, 229, 330, 332;
 Stalin, 26, 90, 98, 201, 263–64, 266–68, 270–71, 281, 337, 343
De Gaulle, Charles, 12
Democratic Alliance of Hungarian Women (MNDSZ), 187, 217
Dénes, István, 94, 273, 285
denunciation, 7, 28–29, 69, 197, 199–201, 203–4, 227, 279, 282, 300, 302, 305, 333
Déri, Tibor, 202
de-Stalinization, 64, 98, 105, 152, 265, 280, 300–1, 323, 327–28, 332, 337
Dimitrov, Georgi, 15, 34, 46n, 47, 49, 94–95, 98, 101–2, 106, 116, 118, 135, 170n
DISZ, 73, 83, 158
Dobi, István, 77, 266, 286
Donáth, Ferenc, 289
Dózsa, György, 105, 129, 142–43, 152, 163, 167, 172

E

East Germany (German Democratic Republic, GDR), 15, 72, 89, 98, 99n, 119, 131n, 132, 171, 182n, 188, 264, 280–81, 301, 328, 337
East German uprising (1953), 281
Eastern Europe, Central and, 2, 4–5, 11, 15–17, 20–22, 24, 81, 88, 98–99, 119, 127–28, 131–35, 149, 224, 263, 268, 276, 281, 299, 300–1, 318, 328, 332, 335–36, 338, 344
economic plans, 4, 21, 38, 65, 68, 130, 185, 193, 197, 338
education, 33, 53, 76, 81–82, 84, 95–96, 103, 110, 114, 118, 160, 167, 169, 171, 172, 173, 184, 214, 241–46, 250–55, 257, 292, 317–18. *See also* teachers; people's educators
Egri, Gyula, 94, 277, 285
Ék, Sándor, 158
elections in Hungary
 1935, 42;
 1945, 37, 91, 102, 161;
 1947, 61–64, 103, 161, 164;
 1949, 38, 64–68, 103, 164, 165n, 189–91, 214, 218, 235, 237, 248, 256;
 1953, 267–69, 326
Engels, Friedrich, 18, 162, 294, 307
Ennker, Benno, 88
Erdei, Ferenc, 84
exhibitions, 72, 74, 76, 106, 109, 157–58

F

family (as metaphor), 8, 13, 44–45, 53, 101, 124, 270–71
Farkas, Mihály, 18, 34–36, 63, 73n, 85, 92–93, 103, 107, 153, 200, 266, 271, 273, 277, 279, 283, 285, 287, 295, 304, 312, 315–16, 325–26, 332
fascism, 51, 94
father figure, the leader as, 8, 13–14, 40, 41, 45, 51–53, 60–61, 63, 75, 77, 83,

101–2, 115, 124–25, 131, 137, 143, 151, 155–57, 159, 160, 174, 199, 202–5, 225–26, 264, 268, 270, 271, 328, 337

"Father of peoples," Stalin as, 14, 131, 264, 268

Feitl, István, 122

festivities, *see* mass demonstrations

films/cinema/newreels (and the cult), 12, 21, 65, 73, 80, 81, 86, 95, 97, 106, 144-145, 155, 159-160, 226

Finland, 2, 49

FKgP (Smallholders' Party), 37, 55, 64

Fock, Jenő, 331

Fodor, Zoltán, 287

Földvári, Rudolf, 94, 271n, 276, 285, 286

folklore, 76, 136, 139, 140

France, 23, 46n, 47, 50, 121

Franco, Francisco, 50

Franz Joseph I (Emperor of Austria), 41, 50n

friend figure, the leader as, 14–15, 63, 131–32, 134, 156, 160, 174, 268, 328, 341

friendship/fraternity, 76, 131, 160, 170, 336

Friss, István, 316

G

Gábor, Andor, 84

Gábri, Mihály, 303

Gerasimov, Aleksandr, 149

Gergely, Márta, 166

Gergely, Sándor, 84, 106, 202

Germany, 18, 35, 46n, 47, 50, 87, 121, 231–32. *See also* East Germany

Gerő, Ernő, 34–36, 48, 54–55, 77, 83n, 91–93, 107, 153, 181n, 200, 219n, 268, 273, 276–79, 281, 287, 294, 304n, 310, 312, 314, 316, 319n, 320, 325–26, 332

Gheorghiu-Dej, Gheorghe, 15, 19, 98, 117–19, 134, 170, 173, 281, 301, 328

Gierek, Edward, 328

Gimes, Miklós, 138n, 298

Gift, to leaders, 56, 59, 74, 76, 317; economy of, 14, 198, 203, 205

Göbbels, Joseph, 87

Gömbös, Gyula, 42–44, 48

Gomułka, Władysław, 18, 22, 302, 318, 328, 344

Gottwald, Klement, 15, 19, 98, 116–19, 134, 170, 265, 267, 281, 323, 328

gossip, 221, 223, 227, 229n. *See also* rumor

Gramsci, Antonio, 49

gratitude, expression of, 1, 6, 9, 14, 56, 57, 59–61, 65–66, 70, 76, 120, 169, 171, 188, 192–95, 197–98, 200, 203–5, 228, 269, 290, 296, 336

H

Haraszti, Sándor, 289

Harustyák, József, 316

Háy, Gyula, 84, 106

Házi, Árpád, 94

Hegedüs, András, 94, 273, 305n, 310, 313, 319n

heroes, cult of, 2, 6, 18, 20, 23, 25, 28n, 38–40, 45–46, 48–51, 53, 63, 65, 72, 77, 96–99, 101–2, 120, 125, 128–29, 133–36, 139–41, 143–44, 167–68, 255–56, 270, 340n

Heroes' Square, 143, 152–53

Hevesi, Gyula, 121

Hidas, Antal, 84

Hidas, István, 94

Hitler, Adolf, 2, 15, 23, 50, 86, 88, 132, 167, 186n, 219–20, 224, 232

holidays, 7, 143, 165, 291; April 4 (Liberation Day), 144, 152–53, 162, 190, 198, 216, 267–69, 310;

August 20 (Constitution Day), 66, 129, 136n, 152n, 193–94;
March 15, 40, 129, 144, 187, 267;
May 1, 54, 58–59, 129n, 144, 152, 154, 161–62, 269, 309;
November 7, 129n, 152n, 162
Honecker, Erich, 98, 328
Horthy, Miklós, 36, 38, 41–44, 48–50, 54, 59, 102, 113–14, 132, 142, 165, 204, 218
Horváth, Imre, 47
Horváth, Márton, 73, 80, 93, 107, 109, 242, 273, 285, 297, 298n, 303–4
Hoxha, Enver, 16, 21n, 328
Hungarian Communist Party (MKP), 35–37, 41, 45, 54–56, 58, 60–61, 63, 84, 92–93, 102, 105, 124–25, 129–31, 137, 143–44, 164, 167–68, 172, 186, 243, 292
Hungarian Party of Communists (KMP), 34–35, 47, 112, 121, 123
Hungarian Republic of Soviets (1919), 28n, 34–36, 47–48, 91, 94, 101n, 106, 112, 115, 120, 121n, 129, 139, 142, 227n, 252, 292, 305
Hungarian Revolution and War Independence of 1848–1849, 34, 39–40, 64, 129–31, 133, 138–39, 144;
centenary of, 64–65, 68, 130, 143–44
Hungarian Social Democratic Party (MSZDP), 33, 37, 111, 172n
Hungarian Socialist Workers' Party (MSZMP), 319–25, 333–34
Hungarian uprising of 1956, 116, 144, 152, 216, 257, 315, 318–20, 325, 329–30, 332–33
Hungarian Workers' Party (MDP), 38, 66, 68, 73, 103, 109, 159, 239, 244, 247–49, 256, 268, 273, 279–81, 283, 285, 287, 289, 291, 296, 302–3, 315–16, 319–20, 332–33
Husák, Gustáv, 328

I
Ibarruri, Dolores, 49
icons/iconography, 8, 9, 25, 161, 163, 166, 174, 318
iconoclasm, 155, 183, 215–17, 257, 318–19, 330
IIB, *see* Provisional Executive Committee
Illés, Béla, 33, 69n, 76, 84–85, 108–111, 113–16, 120, 202
Illyés, Gyula, 74, 145
incompetence (of propagandists), 232–33, 245–46, 254, 257–58, 342
indifference (towards the cult), 178, 185, 231–60, 342–43
industrialization, 11, 21, 28, 38, 120, 183, 185, 237, 238n, 272, 280
Institute of the Working-Class Movement, 76–77, 82
intelligentsia/intellectuals, 5, 14, 33, 36, 46, 81, 84–85, 106, 158, 183, 185, 187, 191, 200, 202, 236, 251, 273, 289–90, 294, 298, 338
irredentism/revisionism, 41, 42, 136, 162
Italy, 23, 50, 121
Ivan the Terrible, 96, 136

J
Jaruzelski, Wojciech, 328
jokes, 183, 209, 211, 219–29
journalists, 35, 57, 58, 64, 81, 84, 95, 153, 192, 235–37, 239–40, 270, 290, 298
Juhász, Ferenc, 84

K
Kádár, János, 24, 43, 63, 103, 116, 155, 285, 288–89, 304n, 312, 319–22, 324–27, 329–33, 344
Kaganovich, Lazar, 88n, 299
Kálmán, Sándor, 202
Karinthy, Ferenc, 106

Katona, József, 245
KEB, 276
Keleti, Ágnes, 70
Keleti, Ferenc, 277
Kende, Péter, 290, 298
Kennedy, John F., 12
Khrushchev, Nikita, 17, 28, 89–90, 100, 272, 281, 298–300, 302–3, 307–8, 310, 314, 323, 328–29, 332–33
Kirov, Sergei, 97
Kiseliov, Fiodor, 284
Kiss, Károly, 273, 276, 304
KMP, *see* Hungarian Party of Communists
Köböl, József, 288, 303
Kölcsey, Ferenc, 245
kolkhoz, *see* collective farms
Konecsni, György, 157, 159
Kornai, János, 290
Korondi, Margit, 70
Kossa, István, 190
Kossuth, Lajos, 40–41, 43, 50n, 75, 129–30, 133, 138–44, 163, 167, 256;
  Kossuth prize, 84, 105
  Kossuth Square, 143, 269–70
  Radio Kossuth, 35, 41
Kovács, István, 73n, 244, 277–78, 285–87, 304, 308, 313–15, 332
Kovai, Lőrinc, 106
Kövesi, Endre, 290, 298
Kremlin, 90, 273, 275, 284, 294, 323, 337–38, 344. *See also* Moscow
Kristóf, István, 73n, 94
Kuczka, Péter, 84, 289
kulaks, 183, 196
Kun, Béla, 34–35, 46, 48, 101, 111, 122–24, 292, 305, 308
Kutuzov, Mikhail, 96–97
Kuusinen, Otto, 49

L
Ladislaus I, Saint, 140
Lalmand, Edgar, 50
Landler, Jenő, 35, 122
land reform, 37, 55–56, 60, 91, 129, 135
leader cult
  and biographies, 6, 9, 25, 27, 38, 46, 68, 73–74, 76, 82, 85–86, 91, 95–125, 134, 142, 255, 335, 340;
  and children/youth, 14, 59, 82–83, 92, 95, 104–5, 154, 166, 174, 203, 225–26, 269, 270;
  dismantling of, 26, 257, 261–334, 343;
  ethnic aspects of, 14, 87, 127–45;
  hierarchical aspects of, 4, 17–18, 22–23, 24, 30, 69, 71, 93–94, 144, 150, 152–53, 163–64, 170, 292, 294, 306–7, 313, 318, 324, 334, 336, 341, 343–344;
  impersonal aspects of, 4–5, 87, 119, 125, 161, 174, 338n, 339–41;
  indifference towards, 178, 185, 231–59, 342–43;
  international dimensions of, 18–19, 22–23, 38, 46, 48–51, 63, 72, 94, 106, 113–14, 116, 118, 122, 124, 132–35, 156, 164, 170, 266, 278, 344;
  and language, 7, 17, 19, 28, 45, 69, 78, 93, 99, 173, 178, 181–82, 184, 188, 199, 202–6, 210, 213–15, 217, 225–26, 228, 259, 277, 290, 299, 316, 328, 337, 343;
  and nationalism, 127–45;
  popular attitudes to, 145, 175–259, 300;
  resistance to, 155, 179, 182, 185, 209–29;
  and religion, 8–9, 247–48, 341;
  and the retrieving of church bells, 57, 138, 203;
  spatial aspects of, 25, 40, 42, 147–74, 256, 264–65, 278, 285, 304, 319;
  support for, 1, 11, 16, 23, 90, 93, 124, 160, 178–79, 181–84, 189–207, 257, 267–68, 278, 330–31, 339, 343–44;
  and trees, 138;

visual aspects of, 9, 12, 16, 19, 21, 25, 27, 43, 56, 58, 65, 69, 73–76, 80–81, 86, 90, 92, 95, 97, 106, 109, 129, 139, 143–45, 147–74, 186, 211–19, 225–26, 229, 255–57, 265, 267, 269, 274, 276–78, 283, 285–88, 290–91, 293–94, 304, 308–09, 317, 319, 320–21, 327, 331, 337

leaderism, 18–19, 26, 272–74, 276–77, 279, 293–94, 343

legitimacy, 13, 29, 64–68, 99–100, 115, 127–28, 215, 218, 333, 343

Lenin, Valdimir Ilich, 5–6, 8n, 9, 11n, 17–18, 20–21, 28n, 34, 54, 58, 85, 92, 99–100, 103–4, 115–16, 118, 122, 136, 139n, 143, 153, 161–63, 165–67, 170, 174, 202, 217, 244, 252, 255, 259, 267, 269, 275, 286, 291, 294, 307, 323, 329, 331–32, 339

Leonardo da Vinci, 244

letters (of gratitude), greetings, petitions sent to leaders, 1, 6, 9, 45–47, 57, 61, 65–66, 69–70, 74, 84, 106, 111, 118, 137, 158, 168–69, 173, 183, 188, 192–95, 197, 199–208, 234–35, 240, 249, 266, 277–78, 290, 293, 296–97, 326

literature, 56, 65, 67, 69, 74, 80–81, 85, 91, 97, 139, 141, 150–51, 244, 289, 291; literary anthology, 69, 74–75, 150n; poems, 69, 74–75, 81, 92, 96, 139, 141, 150, 289, 330

Litván, György, 309, 311

London, 65, 112, 114, 115

Losonczy, Géza, 62–63, 289

Lukács, György, 309

M

Magyar Nemzet, 74, 293, 298

Malenkov, Georgi, 263, 294

Malinovskii, Rodion, 167

Mann, Tom, 49, 50

Mannerheim, Carl Gustaf von, 2

Mao Tse Tung, 95, 224

Marosán, György, 319n, 321

Marx, Karl, 18, 115–16, 162, 167, 294, 307

Marxism(-Leninism), 2, 5, 8, 13, 28n, 29n, 65, 86, 87n, 94, 97, 100, 112, 114, 116, 120, 128, 186, 234, 243–45, 257–58, 301, 307, 320, 326, 339

mass demonstrations (also festivities and rallies), 7, 9, 46, 54, 56, 58–59, 71, 77, 95, 111, 143, 149, 151–56, 161–63, 165–66, 190, 193, 198, 206, 226, 269, 276, 291, 309, 317, 320. *See also* holidays

Matolcsi, János, 94

Matthias Corvinus, 62, 136–37, 140, 202

Matusek, Tivadar, 303–4

mausoleum,
Batthyány, 143;
Gottwald, 265, 267, 323;
Kossuth, 143;
Lenin, 9, 323

MDP, *see* Hungarian Workers' Party

Mehring, Franz, 118

Mekis, József, 296

Méray, Tibor, 85, 142, 156, 165, 270, 271n, 290, 298

Mikoian Anastas, 272, 315–16

Mindszenty, József, 38, 50n, 219

mini-Stalins, 15, 19–21, 88, 99, 131, 170, 267, 301, 336

Ministry of Internal Affairs, 37, 156, 192, 245, 247, 281, 307n

Ministry of People's Education, 80, 93, 156

Ministry of Religion and Public Education, 162, 190n

MKP, *see* Hungarian Communist Party

MNDSZ, *see* Democratic Alliance of Hungarian Women

mobilization, 11, 13–14, 25, 37, 54, 65, 68–69, 79, 87, 93n, 96, 100, 103, 105, 183, 188, 194, 232–33, 335n, 339, 341, 343–44

modernity, 2, 7, 8n, 11–13
Molnár, Erik, 103
Molnár, Miklós, 298
Molotov, Vyacheslav, 167, 272, 299
mood reports, 177–84, 191, 194–95, 198, 204–6, 209, 214, 216, 223, 227, 235–37, 251, 255, 259, 283, 288
Moscow, 22, 34, 54, 89–90, 92, 101, 121–22, 148–49, 271–75, 277, 283, 294–95, 302–3, 305, 315, 319, 322, 341, 344;
    as a shorthand for Soviet leadership, 1, 26, 35, 46, 50, 72, 88, 147–48, 215, 264–66, 280–82, 301, 310, 314, 332–33, 336–37. *See also* Kremlin
MSZDP, *see* Hungarian Social Democratic Party
MSZMP, *see* Hungarian Socialist Workers' Party
Münnich, Ferenc, 321
Mussolini, Benito, 2, 42, 50, 86, 167, 232
myths, mythology (Bolshevik, Communist), 2, 5–6, 19, 27, 49, 96, 188, 222, 263, 265, 335, 344

N

Nagy, Imre, 55, 91, 135, 252, 268, 271–72, 275, 280–82, 284, 286, 290, 294–95, 298, 304, 308, 311, 332
Nagy, Mária, 304
Nagy, Sándor, 75, 139–40
naive monarchism, 10, 41
nationalism, 39, 44, 127, 217;
    and Communism, 25, 127, 128–31;
    and the cult, 127–45
National Peasant Party (Hungary), 55, 64, 218
National Socialism (Nazi), 9n, 18, 35, 49, 51, 87, 116, 132–33, 186n, 231–32
Nemes, Dezső, 292
Nevskii, Aleksandr, 97

New Course, 59, 64, 94, 105, 159n, 181n, 198, 263–64, 272, 280–86, 289, 291–93, 295–96, 298, 302–4, 309n, 332–33, 343
"New Man," 44–45, 125, 232, 335
NKVD, 35
Nógrádi, Sándor, 63, 80, 277, 323, 324, 331
North Korea, 171, 200, 328

O

Ochab, Edward, 302
omnipotence, of the leader, 8, 13, 56, 65, 75, 148, 150, 202, 228, 313
omnipresence, of the leader, 8, 9, 13, 25, 69, 79, 148–49, 155, 157, 160–61, 174, 183, 226, 229, 255–56, 288, 291, 337
Opera House, 72, 74, 77, 92, 152n, 276, 286, 291
Orbán, László, 80
Ordzhonikidze, Sergo, 97
Orgburo (MKP, MDP), 73–74, 80, 103, 109, 156, 161, 164, 168n, 172, 247
Örkény, István, 74, 75

P

paintings, 43, 65, 74, 139, 148–49, 155, 157, 158–61, 174, 217
Papp, László, 70
Paris, 331
partisans, 6, 63
Party Academy, 82, 173, 244, 245, 315
Party functionaries, 14, 21, 67, 79, 84, 153, 182, 184, 187, 223, 232–35, 239–50, 257–58, 275, 282, 284–86, 288, 293, 308, 310, 312, 330, 337, 343
Party history, 25, 86, 99–100, 119, 264, 274, 279, 283, 291–93, 305, 312, 325, 333
patronage, 10, 14, 25n, 115, 122, 200, 202. *See also* clientelism
Pátzay, Pál, 157
Pauker, Ana, 18, 301

peasants, 10, 56, 67, 77, 105, 111, 120, 129, 158–60, 174, 183, 190, 193–94, 196, 200–1, 213–14, 218, 243, 250, 254, 257, 316

people's educators, 81, 84, 233, 235, 239, 241–42, 245, 248, 250, 289, 294

Péter, Gábor, 315

Peter the Great, 96, 97, 136

Petőfi Circle, 309, 315

Petőfi, Sándor, 40, 129–30, 133, 141–44, 163, 167

photographs, 58, 65, 69, 75–76, 148–49, 155–61, 164–65, 174, 267, 269, 277, 319; photo anthology, 75, 92, 109

Pieck, Wilhelm, 98, 117-119, 135, 170

Piłsudski, József, 2, 50, 132

pioneers, 41, 77, 82–83, 155–56, 159, 166, 200, 252, 269, 297

Piros, László, 94, 330

pledges (in the economy), 6, 11, 70, 74, 83, 111, 166, 168–69, 193, 195, 197, 205, 214, 268

Plekhanov, Georgi, 5, 28n

Poland, 2, 15, 18, 50, 72, 128, 132–35, 281, 301–2, 314, 328

Politburo (MKP, MDP), 54, 73, 103, 152–53, 155, 190n, 239, 244, 272–74, 284n, 285–88, 291–96, 301–2, 305, 308, 310–12, 314–17, 319n, 322

political culture, 2, 7, 10–11, 22, 29, 50n, 87, 97–98, 100, 129n, 149, 187, 199n, 200, 204, 218, 220, 258, 336–37

Pollitt, Harry, 23, 50

popular opinion/public opinion, 177–259, 307, 343

Pór, Bertalan, 157

portraits of leaders, 9, 27, 58, 69, 74, 76, 90, 129, 143, 147–49, 153, 155–58, 161–66, 174, 211–19, 225–26, 229, 255, 257, 265, 269, 274, 276, 278, 283, 285–88, 290–91, 293–94, 304, 308–9, 317, 319, 320–21, 331. *See also* paintings; photographs; posters

posters, 56, 65, 148–49, 155, 158–61, 174

Poznań uprising (1956), 314

Prague, 134, 150, 265, 323

Pravda, 47, 224, 305, 307, 314

Prestes, Luis Carlos, 49–50

Propaganda Department, of the Communist Party (APO, OPO), 66–67, 73–74, 76, 80, 93, 104, 106–7, 109, 110, 156, 162–63, 169, 189, 193, 205, 240, 255, 290–91

Provisional Executive Committee (IIB), 320, 321

Pugachev, Emelian, 97

Putin, Vladimir, 11

R

Radek, Karl, 122

radio, 12, 35, 41, 66–67, 80, 102, 115, 188–89, 201, 203, 206–7, 226, 235, 253, 301, 308

Rajk, László, 50n, 65, 71, 167, 219, 227, 235, 297, 298; trial of, 68, 89, 117n, 194–95, 204, 212, 219, 236, 267, 297, 306, 308, 309, 312, 315, 324n

Rákóczi, Ferenc II, 39, 114, 129, 133, 137–38, 140–43

Ratkó, Anna, 201

rebuilding/reconstruction (after World War II), 37, 52, 54–55, 64, 91, 120, 130, 135, 138, 186, 293, 342

Red Army, 15, 36, 37, 133, 149, 170, 198, 276; Hungarian in 1919, 112, 121

Red Corners, 9, 69, 165–66

religion, 8–9, 33, 247–48, 341; Orthodoxy, 9, 97, 166; Catholicism, 15, 38, 217, 248

Reményi, Béla, 75
renaming (*toponomie*), 23, 42, 47, 74, 91, 147–48, 167–74, 317
resistance, to the cult, 155, 179, 182, 185, 209–29
Réti, László, 82, 91, 106–8
Révai, József, 34–36, 63, 73, 80–81, 92–93, 103, 106–7, 129–30, 133, 138, 145, 153, 158, 172, 200, 251, 256, 271, 273–74, 276–78, 283, 291, 304, 312, 319n
Rideg, Sándor, 106
Rokossovsky, Konstantin, 18
Rolland, Romain, 46
Romania, 8n, 18, 72, 171, 173, 281, 301, 328
Rudas, László, 82
rumor, 133, 139, 177, 183, 211, 213, 219, 221–23, 227, 229, 283, 314, 317, 330. *See also* gossip
Russia, 5, 10, 21, 34, 47, 85, 112, 133, 142, 200–1, 223–24, 335
Russian Civil War, 96–97, 112
Russian Revolution of 1917, 6, 20, 33, 96

S

saints, cult of, 2, 39, 97, 140, 148n, 166
Salgótarján, 75, 106n, 112, 121, 138, 159n, 237, 293
school textbooks, 57, 65, 81, 92, 104–5, 110, 203, 251, 254–55, 292–93, 305, 317
Secretariat (MKP, MDP), 72–73, 80, 83n, 106, 159n, 162, 107n, 173, 195, 199–201, 203, 216, 226, 242, 246, 251, 272, 286–87, 295, 298, 311
Secret Speech, 28, 100, 264, 299–303, 306, 308, 314, 323, 332–33
Shakespeare, William, 244
Short Course of the CPSU, 82, 86, 100, 300
Slánský, Rudolf, 89

slogans, 37, 68, 86, 130, 148, 155, 190, 194, 245, 304, 312
Socialist Realism, 76, 85, 97, 124–25, 157–60, 340n,
songs, 65, 77, 81, 96, 150, 155
Soviet bloc, 1, 11, 16, 19–20, 22–24, 82, 88, 117, 131–33, 135, 149, 170–71, 219, 264–67, 276–78, 281, 299, 301–2, 314, 318, 323, 327–28, 332, 335–37, 344
Sovietization, 1, 2, 14–17, 19–23, 26–27, 37–38, 69, 72, 78, 80–81, 84, 90, 92, 98, 131, 133, 148–49, 163, 173, 280, 336, 343
space, the use of, 25, 40, 42, 147–74, 256, 264–65, 278, 285, 304, 319
Spanish Civil War, 35, 47, 167
speeches, by party leaders, 11, 44, 51, 56, 58–60, 63–64, 66–67, 70, 77, 92, 94, 104, 123, 134, 137, 139, 142–43, 156, 159–60, 188–91, 195–98, 206, 214, 217, 226, 234–36, 238–41, 248, 258, 264, 268, 270, 275, 280, 282–84, 286, 291, 293, 296–98, 303, 312–14
sport, 70, 165-67, 252;
  Olympic games, 65, 66, 70-71, 203, 205
Stakhanovism/Stakhanovites, 6, 96
Stalin, Josif
  cult of, 3, 5–6, 8, 10, 14–15, 18, 20–23, 28, 54, 82, 88, 90, 92, 127, 131–34, 147–48, 173–74, 218, 233, 259, 263–64, 270–71, 300, 307, 318, 327, 336
  death of (and the cult), 26, 90, 98, 201, 263–64, 266–68, 270–71, 281, 337, 343
Stalin Square, 152, 161n, 266, 269
Stalinism, 8, 13n, 24, 26, 97, 279, 318, 329, 335
"Stalin's best disciple," 22, 88, 214, 225n, 330
statues (*also* busts), 21, 40, 43, 69, 72, 133, 143–44, 148–50, 152–53, 155–57, 161, 164–66, 174, 215, 265–66, 269, 285–88, 291, 308, 318–19, 323, 330

Stephen I, Saint, 39, 133, 136, 140, 172, 193
Suslov, Mikhail, 72, 89, 314
Suvorov, Aleksandr, 97, 100
Szabad Nép, 1, 52, 55–61, 63–65, 67, 71, 74, 82, 93, 103, 133, 142, 153–54, 166, 177n, 189, 192–95, 199, 201, 223–24, 234–36, 237n, 238n, 239–41, 266–70, 289–90, 296–98, 305, 307–8, 316–17
Szabó, István, 303
Szabó, Piroska, 201
Szalai, Béla, 94, 271n
Szálasi, Ferenc, 204, 219
Szántó, Zoltán, 292, 304
Szamueli, György, 101
Szatmári, István, 285–86
Szeged, 45, 72, 111, 114, 139, 140, 168n, 213, 283, 318
Szekeres, József, 123
Szilvási, Lajos, 290, 298
Szirmai, István, 201
Sztálinváros, 169, 198, 246n

T

Táncsics, Mihály, 130, 143, 163, 167
Tardos, Tibor, 290, 309n
teacher figure, the leader as, 8, 15, 52, 61, 75, 77, 81, 83, 114, 116, 151, 156, 160, 174, 204, 218, 266, 268, 337
teachers, 81–84, 110, 190, 225, 233, 250–55, 289, 294
terror (*also* coercion; state violence; purges), 21, 28, 181, 183, 185, 187, 206, 211, 214, 220, 238, 241, 244, 254, 275, 285–86, 300, 315, 324, 327, 333–34, 342; The Great Terror/Purges, 21, 34, 35, 38, 90n, 101–2, 122, 220, 333
television, 12
Thälmann, Ernst, 49
thanking rituals, 56, 57, 65, 169, 193, 194–95, 203–4, 269

Thorez, Maurice, 23, 50, 95, 125n, 331, 338n
Tildy, Zoltán, 64, 185
Tito, Josip Broz, 16, 21n, 50n, 98, 106, 219, 298, 328
totalitarianism, 2, 69n, 178–80, 184, 220, 231, 257
tradition, 2, 5, 7–13, 15, 20–22, 24–25, 36, 39–45, 51, 65, 68, 78, 96, 111, 124, 127–38, 140–44, 152, 193, 215, 222, 227, 229, 246, 250, 256, 258–59, 279, 307, 335–37, 339, 341
trials,
 Antikainen, 49;
 Dimitrov, 49, 101;
 Gheorghiu-Dej, 117–18;
 Prestes, 49;
 Rajk, *see* Rajk, László;
 Rákosi, 34, 46–49, 53, 64, 94, 101, 104, 106, 112–14, 116–18, 124, 134, 293, 296

U

Ulbricht, Walter, 98, 264, 281, 301
United States of America, 46, 47, 53
Urbán, Ernő, 290

V

Varga, Jenő, 305
Vas, Márton, 54
Vas, Zoltán, 53–54, 91–93, 107
Vég, Béla, 94
Veres, Péter, 64, 74, 84, 218
Vészi, Endre, 141
Vienna, 34–35, 123
visits of the leader (in factories and the countryside), 44, 59–60, 62, 64, 156, 159–160, 189–90, 286, 293, 296–97, 310
Voroshilov, Kliment, 37, 97, 149, 153, 167, 299, 315
Vörösmarty, Mihály, 245

W

Washington, George, 40

workers, 15, 35, 47–48, 60, 65, 67, 111, 113, 119–20, 159–60, 165–66, 168–69, 171, 174, 183, 185, 189–91, 193–97, 205, 213–14, 218, 232–43, 249–50, 252, 254, 257, 267, 283, 286, 290, 307–9, 316–18, 321

World War I, 5, 112, 114

World War II, 1, 6, 14–15, 21–22, 36, 41–43, 50, 53, 116, 124, 127–28, 131, 167, 201, 336;
  myth of (Great Patriotic War), 6, 23, 300, 323

writers, 64, 69, 74, 84–85, 97, 106, 108, 144, 200, 218, 278, 289–90, 298

Y

"Year of the turn," 37, 104–5

Yugoslavia, 16, 89, 227, 267, 338

Yugov, Anton, 323

Z

Zelk, Zoltán, 74

Zetkin, Klara, 46

Zhivkov, Todor, 323, 328

Zinoviev, Grigory, 122–23